From Stress to Growth:

Strengthening Asia's Financial Systems in a Post-Crisis World

Marcus Noland and Donghyun Park, editors

T0315148

A Copublication of
the Asian Development Bank and
Peterson Institute for International Economics

Washington, DC

October 2015

Peterson
Institute for
International
Economics

MIX
Paper from
responsible sources
FSC® C010236
FSC
www.fsc.org

Marcus Noland, executive vice president and director of studies, has been associated with the Peterson Institute for International Economics since 1985. From 2009 through 2012, he served as the Institute's deputy director. He is also senior fellow at the East-West Center. He was previously a senior economist at the Council of Economic Advisers in the Executive Office of the President of the United States. His numerous publications include Confronting the Curse: The Economics and Geopolitics of Natural Resource Governance (2014), Korea after Kim Jong-il (2004), and Avoiding the Apocalypse: The Future of the Two Koreas (2000), for which he won the 2000–01 Ohira Memorial Award.

Donghyun Park is principal economist at the Economic Research and Regional Cooperation Department (ERCD) of the Asian Development Bank (ADB), which he joined in April 2007. Prior to joining ADB, he was a tenured associate professor of economics at Nanyang Technological University in Singapore. His main research fields are international finance, international trade, and development economics. His research, which has been published extensively in journals and books, revolves around policy-oriented topics relevant for Asia's long-term development, including the middle-income trap, Asia's service sector development, and Asia's financial development. Park plays a leading role in the production of Asian Development Outlook, ADB's flagship annual economic publication.

ASIAN DEVELOPMENT BANK
6 ADB Avenue
Mandaluyong City
1550 Metro Manila, Philippines
Tel +63 2 632 4444   Fax + 63 2 636 2444
www.adb.org

PETERSON INSTITUTE FOR
INTERNATIONAL ECONOMICS
1750 Massachusetts Avenue, NW
Washington, DC 20036-1903
(202) 328-9000   FAX: (202) 659-3225
www.piie.com

Adam S. Posen, President
Steven R. Weisman, Vice President for Publications and Communications

Printed in the United States of America
17   16   15   5   4   3   2   1

Library of Congress Cataloging-in-Publication Data
From stress to growth : strengthening Asia's financial systems in a post-crisis world / Marcus Noland and Donghyun Park, editors.
    pages cm
    "June 2015."
    Includes bibliographical references.
    ISBN 978-0-88132-699-4
    1. Finance—Asia.   2. Financial crises—Asia.
3. Asia—Economic conditions—21st century.
I. Noland, Marcus, 1959- editor.   II. Park, Donghyun, editor.
    HG187.A2F76 2015
    332.095—dc23
                                    2015001799

Contents

Preface

Developing Asia is one of the most dynamic regions of the world economy, sometimes called "Factory Asia." The region, which encompasses a wide range of countries at different income levels, also varies widely in terms of financial sector development. Singapore and Hong Kong, China are international financial centers, many middle-income countries have a good mix of banks and capital markets, and in some low-income countries even banks, let alone capital markets, remain underdeveloped.

Although their financial development level varies, developing Asian countries as a whole have made significant strides in recent years. For example, the banking sectors of countries hit by the Asian financial crisis have become healthier due to extensive postcrisis reform. Another example comes from the People's Republic of China, which gave virtually every poor household a bank account ten years ago—to minimize the leakage from unconditional cash transfers—something India is trying to do now. Yet another example comes from the Pacific island economies, which have recently expanded financial access to both small and medium enterprises and households on remote, outer islands.

Notwithstanding Asia's impressive progress in strengthening and improving its financial sector, the region's development remains unbalanced, with the financial sector still lagging the dynamic real economy. The financial systems of developing Asia remain well behind the global finance frontier. That status in and of itself is not a first-order cause for concern, but what is more relevant is that the region's financial systems do not appear to be up to the tasks of financing badly needed infrastructure investment, innovation, and extending financial inclusion to broader segments of society.

The region largely avoided the worst of the global financial crisis of 2008–09, which battered the world economy and disrupted global financial markets to an unprecedented degree. But while the worst of that crisis has abated, and growth has revived across the region, the shadow of the crisis still looms. It has given financial reform a bad name and has made more difficult the task of upgrading the financial sector to support future growth and development.

In *From Stress to Growth: Strengthening Asia's Financial Systems in a Post-Crisis World,* scholars affiliated with the Peterson Institute for International Economics, the Asian Development Bank, and other institutions around the world, address two fundamental issues. First, what are the relationships between financial sector development and economic growth, and second, what are the necessary regulatory steps needed to ensure that the financial system delivers that growth but avoids painful crises? In separate essays, the authors argue that the quality, diversity, and resilience to shocks of developing Asian financial systems must be strengthened in order to deliver crisis-free growth in coming years.

The volume examines such phenomena as the dominant role of state-owned banks, the growth of nonbank lending (the so-called shadow banks), the need to develop local capital markets, and the need for stronger supervisory institutions to ensure stability. The People's Republic of China's large financial system is discussed, with an emphasis on what lessons from the Chinese experience might be transferable to other countries around the region. Similarly, the experiences of the United States and European Union with bank stress tests are reviewed with an eye on what lessons these experiences might usefully hold for Asia. The region needs investment to improve its infrastructure and to promote technological innovation, but the book argues that the region's financial systems are inadequate in meeting those needs. Policy recommendations are made across all of these issues of concern.

We would like to express our sincere gratitude to economists from ADB, PIIE, and the other organizations who have contributed their research to this ambitious project. We would also like to give a special thanks to ADB's Donghyun Park and PIIE's Marcus Noland, who jointly managed and coordinated the project, and to ADB's Gemma B. Estrada and April Gallega and PIIE's Madona Devasahayam, Susann Luetjen, and Steven R. Weisman for facilitating the publication of the volume. I believe that this highly informative book will be a valuable resource for analysts, investors, and policymakers in Asia and beyond as a result of their and the contributing authors' efforts.

***

The Peterson Institute for International Economics is a private nonpartisan, nonprofit institution for rigorous, intellectually open, and indepth study and discussion of international economic policy. Its purpose is to identify and analyze important issues to making globalization beneficial and sustainable for the people of the United States and the world and then to develop and communicate practical new approaches for dealing with them.

The Institute's work is funded by a highly diverse group of philanthropic foundations, private corporations, and interested individuals, as well as income on its capital fund. About 35 percent of the Institute resources in our latest fiscal year were provided by contributors from outside the United States. A list of all our financial supporters for the preceding year is posted at http://www.piie.com/supporters.cfm.

The Executive Committee of the Institute's Board of Directors bears overall responsibility for the Institute's direction, gives general guidance and approval to its research program, and evaluates its performance in pursuit of its mission. The Institute's President is responsible for the identification of topics that are likely to become important over the medium term (one to three years) that should be addressed by Institute scholars. This rolling agenda is set in close consultation with the Institute's research staff, Board of Directors, and other stakeholders.

The President makes the final decision to publish any individual Institute study, following independent internal and external review of the work. Interested readers may access the data and computations underlying Institute publications for research and replication by searching titles at www.piie.com.

The Institute hopes that its research and other activities will contribute to building a stronger foundation for international economic policy around the world. We invite readers of these publications to let us know how they think we can best accomplish this objective.

The Asian Development Bank's vision is an Asia and Pacific region free of poverty. Its mission is to help its developing member countries reduce poverty and improve the quality of life of their people. Despite the region's many successes, it remains home to the majority of the world's poor. ADB is committed to reducing poverty through inclusive economic growth, environmentally sustainable growth, and regional integration.

Based in Manila, ADB is owned by 67 members, including 48 from the region. Its main instruments for helping its developing member countries are policy dialogue, loans, equity investments, guarantees, grants, and technical assistance.

SHANG-JIN WEI
Chief Economist and Director General,
Economic Research and Regional
Cooperation Department
Asian Development Bank

ADAM S. POSEN
President
Peterson Institute for
International Economics

August 2015

Introduction

MARCUS NOLAND and DONGHYUN PARK

This volume revisits the issue of financial sector development in developing Asia. The region's real economy has grown by leaps and bounds in the past few decades. In particular, export-oriented industrialization has transformed the region into the factory of the world, and the People's Republic of China (PRC) and India have emerged as globally significant economic powers. At the same time, Asia's financial system remains underdeveloped relative to those of the advanced economies. Asia's financial weaknesses came to a head during the Asian financial crisis of 1997-98. While the region's financial sector has made tangible progress since that crisis, it remains well behind the global finance frontier. For example, Asia continues to recycle much of its abundant savings through the financial markets of the advanced economies. In light of the stark contrast between a dynamic real economy and a backward financial sector, financial sector development has long been one of the region's salient strategic challenges.

While financial development is thus hardly a new issue for Asia, at least three reasons warrant revisiting it now. Above all, financial development matters for sustaining rapid economic growth. In light of the region's growth slowdown since the global financial crisis of 2007-08, and the vital role of a sound and efficient financial system in growth, now is the perfect time to take a closer look at the role of financial development in the region's growth and development. Secondly, a more inclusive financial system will greatly abet the

Marcus Noland, executive vice president and director of studies, has been associated with the Peterson Institute for International Economics since 1985. Donghyun Park is principal economist at the Asian Development Bank.

region's quest for more inclusive growth. Finally, the region must safeguard its financial stability even as it develops its financial system since financial instability, especially financial crises, can derail growth. In short, the convergence of three strategic growth-related challenges—reigniting economic growth, tackling rising inequality, and maintaining financial stability—adds a sense of urgency to the long-standing task of building sound and efficient financial systems in developing Asia.

The visible slowdown of economic growth across developing Asia since the global financial crisis makes it imperative for the region to fully exploit all sources of economic growth. A sounder and more efficient financial sector is one such potential engine of economic growth. One may object that in the past Asia managed to grow rapidly on a sustained basis despite being saddled with a backward financial system. Some observers, in fact, interpret the coexistence of a backward financial system and dynamic real economy in Asia as evidence of the secondary importance of finance. The global financial crisis can, on its surface, serve as an indictment of financial innovation and further fuel skepticism about the benefits of financial development. However, developing Asia grew rapidly despite financial underdevelopment, not because of financial underdevelopment. With a stronger and better financial system, developing Asia may have grown even faster than it actually did. Or, it could have achieved the same level of growth with lower savings and investment—i.e., at a lower cost in terms of foregone consumption.

Therefore, a weak and inefficient financial sector is a luxury that the region can no longer afford. The loss of growth due to financial inefficiencies looms larger when an economy is growing at, say, 5 percent than at 10 percent. Equivalently, the growth dividend from a sounder and more efficient financial system matters more. In addition to a growth slowdown, the region faces the prospect of a different growth paradigm in the future. Sustained rapid growth has catapulted Asia from a capital-scarce, low-income region to an increasingly middle-income capital-abundant region. Going forward, as diminishing marginal returns to capital set in, productivity growth will become more important for economic growth, even though investment and factor accumulation will remain vital. Therefore, to support future growth, Asia's financial system will have to evolve to contribute to productivity growth, in particular R&D and other innovative activities, along with infrastructure and other long-term investments.

Sustained rapid growth has sharply reduced poverty rates in Asia, but the region now faces another difficult challenge, that of rising inequality. In countries that collectively account for over 80 percent of the region's population, the Gini coefficient—a measure of inequality—has worsened between 1990 and 2010. Financial development can affect inequality but the direction of the impact is ambiguous. If financial development creates financial products that largely benefit the rich, then financial development can widen the gap between the rich and the poor. On the other hand, if financial development promotes financial inclusion—i.e., broadens access to financial services to more households and firms—then it can mitigate inequality. For example, in many parts of Asia, only a small proportion of lower-income households have access to financial services. If the poor can borrow to finance their education or health care, they can then accumulate human capital, which, in turn, will enable them to earn more.

Financial development, innovation, and liberalization can entail substantial risk to financial stability. The global financial crisis of 2007–08 highlights the potentially enormous damage that poorly regulated and supervised financial development can inflict on financial stability. Financial crisis, in turn, can have devastating consequences for economic growth. For example, the global financial crisis almost brought the world economy and trade to its knees. Closer to home, the Asian financial crisis of 1997–98 devastated the financial systems *and* real economies of a group of high-flying East and Southeast Asian economies. A major external threat to the region's financial stability in recent times has been quantitative easing (QE) and unwinding of QE in advanced economies, as witnessed during the taper tantrums of May 2013. In addition, a number of homegrown domestic risks to financial stability, such as rapid growth of household debt and the shadow banking system, loom on the horizon. Therefore, the challenge for Asian countries is to further develop their financial sectors while safeguarding them from growth-harming financial instability.

The ten chapters in this volume explore various key dimensions of Asia's high-priority task of building sounder and more efficient financial systems—banks and capital markets—that will help the region sustain growth without sacrificing financial stability. The book is organized into roughly two parts. The first part, consisting of the next five chapters, essentially focuses on the relationship between financial development and economic growth in developing Asia. The second part, encompassing the remaining five chapters, addresses the financial regulatory issues to ensure that financial development delivers growth and not instability.

Chapter 1 by Gemma B. Estrada, Arief Ramayandi, and us provides an overview of the issues. We conclude that the financial systems of developing Asia are well within the global efficiency frontier. The issue for the low-income countries of the region is essentially a lack of finance, while for the middle-income countries the quality, not the quantity, of the financial system is more at issue. And throughout the region, inequality and financial exclusion remain issues for the poor of these societies. From a political economy perspective, addressing these issues has become more difficult, however, as the 2007–08 global financial crisis has given financial sector reform a bad name.

In chapter 2, Estrada, Park, and Ramayandi explore these issues empirically. Their research generally supports the conventional wisdom that financial development is generally good for growth but that the evidence on the relationship between financial opening, defined as increased integration with foreign financial systems, and growth is more ambiguous. They conclude that the composition of the financial system does not matter so much—both direct finance through the capital markets and indirect finance through the banking system can contribute to growth. Indeed, they find that the pro-growth effects of financial development are more pronounced at lower-income levels.

With respect to financial openness, they uncover some evidence that what matters are actual cross-border capital flows, not de jure measures of openness (i.e., nominal openness only really matters when capital begins to flow across borders), and that exchange rate flexibility increases the likelihood that those cross-border flows will support growth. But these conclusions are more provisional.

The next two chapters, by William R. Cline and Joshua Aizenman, Yothin Jinjarak, and Donghyun Park, respectively, delve into these issues in greater specificity and make comparisons between developing Asia and Latin America. In chapter 3, Cline argues that in part due to reforms undertaken in the aftermath of the 1997–98 Asian financial crisis, for the most part the region's financial systems are meeting their most essential task of avoiding crisis. This accomplishment, together with the restoration of growth following the global financial crisis, suggests that on the whole developing Asia's financial systems are performing reasonably well.

For the middle-income countries, strengthening regulatory systems, particularly with respect to nonbank financial intermediaries, is a higher priority than financial deepening per se. Cline also observes that "Clearer resolution plans would also seem prudent considering the potential too-big-to-fail problems," (p. 110) given the degree of bank concentration in some of these economies.

In chapter 4 Aizenman, Jinjarak, and Park examine the "too much finance" argument as it applies to developing Asia. Specifically they investigate the possibility that the relationship between financial sector development and growth may be nonlinear, unstable, and/or vary across different sectors of the economy. As might be expected, their results, particularly with regard to comparisons between developing Asia and Latin America, are not entirely robust. At the most general level they concur with Cline that much of developing Asia has reached the point where the quality of finance matters more than the simple expansion of the financial sector. They also find some evidence, which they term "preliminary," of a financial "Dutch disease" effect: the faster the growth of the financial sector and the wider the lending-deposit spread, the slower the growth of manufacturing.

This theme of the impact of the financial sector on nonfinancial parts of the economy is continued in the final paper of the first part of the volume. In chapter 5 Ajai Chopra addresses the issue of how to structure the financial sector to encourage productivity- and innovation-led growth in developing Asia. He starts from the simple observation that productivity increase is a multifaceted phenomenon requiring a package of interlocking policies or reforms. The particulars and priorities will vary across countries depending on specific circumstances, especially with respect to distance from the technological frontier. Examining developing Asia with regard to these issues, Chopra reaches two broad conclusions. First, given the amount of savings the region generates, the dearth of mechanisms for long-term finance (for infrastructure projects, for example) is remarkable. He makes specific recommendations for financial development in this dimension.

The second broad conclusion is actually a set of recommendations or priorities that vary by level of development. For the poorest countries of the region, conventional banking sector reforms (including the reduction of financial repression) to better mobilize and channel savings into its most productive uses should be at the top of the agenda. For the middle-income countries, capital sector reforms to encourage financial sector deepening and improve access to finance for start-ups and innovative firms and projects become more important.

Finally, for countries approaching the technological frontier, public policy interventions, which may include the encouragement of specialized finance, including public sector finance or incentives, may be more relevant. The experiences of more advanced countries in Asia and elsewhere may be salient in this regard.

The second part of the volume turns from the finance and growth nexus to the nature of financial sector regulation. In chapter 6, Adam Posen and Nicolas Véron observe that while the advanced financial systems of the West triggered the global financial crisis, "a number of Asian countries have wanted to create internationally competitive financial centers within their borders, which also require high levels of liberalization and financial innovation" (p. 230). (They advise that poorer countries may actually benefit from not being at the cutting edge of finance.) So how to square the desire to have world-class financial systems with the maintenance of stability?

The authors survey recent global financial developments and offer some guidelines for developing Asia in making these choices. In summary, these are that (1) financial systems centered around banks are not inherently more stable than ones with a greater role for direct finance; (2) domestic financial systems should be diversified in terms of available instruments and number of institutions (and therefore probably types of institutions as well); (3) financial repression should be oriented toward activities of managers and institutions, not lending-deposit spreads; (4) cross-border lending may be limited but local-currency lending and bond issuance by multinational banks' subsidiaries should be encouraged; and (5) the efficacy of macroprudential tools varies depending on circumstance, but they may be particularly useful in dealing with real estate booms/busts. Finally, Posen and Véron conclude that developing Asian policymakers, indeed policymakers globally, should carefully monitor the use and impact in finance of advances in information technology in the next few years.

In chapter 7, Michael J. Zamorski and Minsoo Lee narrow the focus to the key issue of bank supervision. They survey developments in international bank supervision standards focusing on the Bank for International Settlements' Basel Core Principles (BCP), which form the touchstone of effective bank supervision. In their analysis the authors emphasize the role of external policy anchors in leveraging domestic reform efforts. They make a number of recommendations for developing Asia, which might be summarized into four broad areas: (1) adopt international banking standards and conduct self-assessments to ensure compliance with the BCP, involving outside assessors as necessary; (2) ensure that legal powers exist to permit comprehensive assessments, including of bank affiliates and unregulated entities, both by domestic authorities broadly defined and their foreign counterparts; (3) equip domestic authorities with necessary surveillance methods to implement adequate microprudential and macroprudential risk assessments; (4) ensure that domestic authorities are adequately resourced and trained to proactively assess bank strategy and risk-taking beyond simple compliance; (5) and, reminiscent of arguments made by Cline, require that well-defined crisis management and resolution plans be in place and that domestic law provide for timely interventions and resolutions of nonviable banks.

In chapter 8, Morris Goldstein addresses the role of bank stability from another perspective, asking what developing Asia might usefully learn from the stress test exercises conducted in the United States and European Union. He derives five basic lessons: (1) stress tests are a useful tool, more flexible than the Basel Accords discussed in the previous chapter; (2) that said, the usefulness of these tests depends importantly on their design, and the general failure of stress tests conducted prior to the global financial crisis to provide early warning of bank vulnerability demonstrates that the specifics of the exercise are crucial; (3) when capital shortfalls are identified in the tests, the remedies should be implemented in a growth-consistent way, defining capital adequacy in absolute terms, and avoiding increases in capital ratios through cutting back on loans, manipulating risk weights, or fire-sale of assets; (4) because assessing risk weights is difficult and empirically leverage ratios have done a better job of identifying problem banks, these should be included in stress tests; and (5) because the Basel III capital adequacy targets are inadequate, Asian policymakers (and indeed policymakers globally) should gradually increase the capital adequacy standards in stress tests.

Chapter 9, by Nicholas Borst and Nicholas Lardy, marks a thematic departure from the previous chapters by focusing on the financial sector in a single, albeit crucial, country, the People's Republic of China. The PRC's financial sector is globally important: Its banking sector is the largest in the world, and its capital markets have approached the size of those existing in advanced countries. Certain characteristics of the financial sector (its large size at early stages of development and its orientation toward corporate rather than household borrowers) distinguish it from those prevalent in other parts of developing Asia, but Borst and Lardy derive three transferable lessons. First, it is possible to rapidly improve the efficiency of state-owned banks. (In chapter 3 Cline also notes the prevalence of and concerns about state-owned banks elsewhere in Asia.) Second, while Chinese gradualism is often held up as preferable to "big bang" type reform, there are risks to moving too slowly, and some of the problems evident in the Chinese financial system today are the result of excessively deliberate and incremental change. The final lesson, as the authors put it, is "the difficulty of rooting out implicit guarantees and moral hazard in a financial system dominated by state-owned actors" (p. 343)—a recurring theme in this volume.

Having examined banking issues in depth, the book concludes with an analysis of bond market development by John D. Burger, Francis E. Warnock, and Veronica Cacdac Warnock. Contrary to the conventional wisdom of as recently as a decade ago that emerging markets would never develop local-currency bond markets, the growth of these markets in developing Asia has been notable. This development is significant because as noted in several other chapters in this volume, robust bond markets are a component of a well-diversified financial system. Moreover, the characteristics associated with the growth of local bond markets are also associated with improved financial inclusion more generally, as well as reduced reliance on borrowing in foreign currency–denominated instruments. The latter development naturally ameliorates currency mismatches and concomitantly should reduce the likelihood of financial crisis and enhance macroeconomic stability. In short, the concluding chapter documents trends, which if sustained, augur well for the ability of developing Asia to achieve growth, inclusion, and stability.

1

Financing Asia's Growth

GEMMA B. ESTRADA, MARCUS NOLAND, DONGHYUN PARK, and ARIEF RAMAYANDI

Although it has been the fastest-growing region of the world economy for the past few decades, developing Asia is saddled with a relatively backward financial system.[1] In fact, the coexistence of a dynamic real sector and an underdeveloped financial system has been one of the region's most salient structural dichotomies. Financial sector development has long been one of the top priorities on the region's agenda.

Before the Asian financial crisis of 1997–98, large capital inflows, especially foreign currency loans, were intermediated by an inefficient financial system that channeled them into unproductive investments that did not enhance the economy's capacity to repay the loans. The predictable result was a steady deterioration of the overall quality or efficiency of investments, which

Gemma B. Estrada is senior economics officer at the Economic Research and Regional Cooperation Department of the Asian Development Bank. Marcus Noland, executive vice president and director of studies, has been associated with the Peterson Institute for International Economics since 1985. Donghyun Park is principal economist at the Asian Development Bank. Arief Ramayandi is senior economist at the Economic Research and Regional Cooperation Department of the Asian Development Bank.

1. Developing Asia refers to 45 members of the Asian Development Bank. Central Asia comprises Armenia, Azerbaijan, Georgia, Kazakhstan, the Kyrgyz Republic, Tajikistan, Turkmenistan, and Uzbekistan. East Asia comprises the People's Republic of China; Hong Kong, China; the Republic of Korea; Mongolia; and Taipei,China. South Asia comprises Afghanistan, Bangladesh, Bhutan, India, the Maldives, Nepal, Pakistan, and Sri Lanka. Southeast Asia comprises Brunei Darussalam, Cambodia, Indonesia, the Lao People's Democratic Republic, Malaysia, Myanmar, the Philippines, Singapore, Thailand, and Viet Nam. The Pacific comprises the Cook Islands, Fiji, Kiribati, the Marshall Islands, the Federated States of Micronesia, Nauru, Palau, Papua New Guinea, Samoa, Solomon Islands, Timor-Leste, Tonga, Tuvalu, and Vanuatu.

Figure 1.1   Nonperforming loans as percent of total loans in selected Asian economies, 2000–13

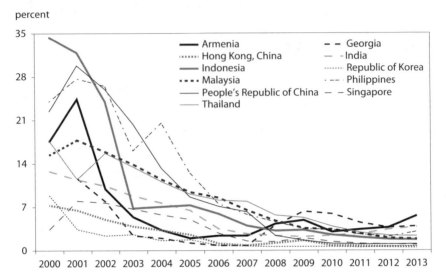

percent

Legend:
— Armenia
······· Hong Kong, China
— Indonesia
···· Malaysia
— People's Republic of China
— Thailand
– – Georgia
— · India
······· Republic of Korea
· –· Philippines
– – Singapore

Source: World Bank, *World Development Indicators* online database (accessed on September 15, 2014).

eventually led to a sudden reversal of capital flows and a financial crisis that swept across East and Southeast Asia.

Extensive restructuring and reform since the Asian crisis have strengthened and improved the region's financial systems (figures 1.1 and 1.2). But with the exception of Singapore and Hong Kong, China, Asian financial systems remain well inside the global finance frontier.

The specifics vary from country to country but are correlated with the level of development. Lower-income Asian countries that are severely underbanked and underfinanced need to quantitatively expand their financial sectors (figures 1.3 and 1.4). For the middle-income countries of the region, which have large financial sectors, improving the quality of finance—the competitiveness of the banking system, whether credit is flowing to the most productive sectors of the economy—is a more significant priority.

This relative underdevelopment explains why much of the region's ample pool of savings continues to be recycled through New York and London. Notwithstanding substantial progress since the Asian crisis, financial sector development remains very much a work in progress and a high-priority strategic objective on the region's development agenda.

Ironically, the task of strengthening the region's financial sectors was made more difficult by the global financial crisis of 2008–09, which gave financial development and innovation, and finance more generally, a bad name. To many observers, the global financial crisis was the result of too much financial innovation, which brought plenty of profits to the financial industry but

Figure 1.2 Financial sector performance in Asian crisis countries, 2000 and 2013

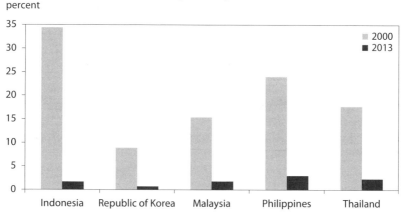

a. Nonperforming loans as percent of total loans

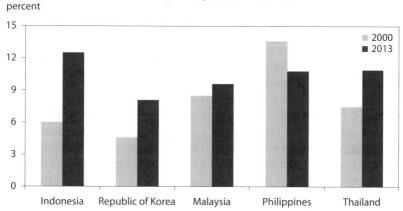

b. Bank capital as percent of total assets

Source: World Bank, *World Development Indicators* online database (accessed on September 15, 2014).

few benefits to the economy at large. A fresh wave of sophisticated financial innovations, such as mortgage-backed securities and collateralized debt obligations, masked financial institutions' reckless search for yield in the housing boom immediately preceding the global crisis. The search was reckless because the underlying transaction—the extension of mortgage loans to borrowers with subprime credit histories—was inherently risky. The global crisis was a market failure: Too much credit flowed to too many high-risk homebuyers, resulting in too much housing. Mortgage-backed securities, collateralized debt obligations, and other fancy instruments could not reduce the high level of risk associated with massive mortgage lending to subprime borrowers. The

Figure 1.3 Private credit as percent of GDP in developing Asia, 1990–2012

percent of GDP

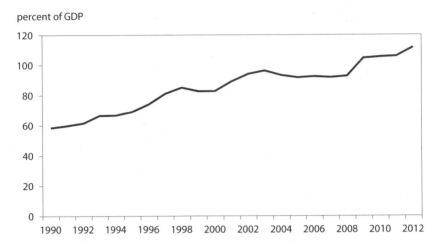

Source: Asian Development Bank estimates based on data from the World Bank, *World Development Indicators* online database (accessed on September 15, 2014).

extraordinarily clever and complex repackaging, dicing, and splicing of risk merely shifted risk from one part of banks' balance sheets to another—or off their balance sheets altogether—masking the true riskiness of these products.

The global crisis does not weaken the case for financial development in developing Asia in any way, shape, or form; indeed, it strengthens it. It would be incorrect to conclude that financial development and innovation are too dangerous and that the best course of action would therefore be to slow or reverse financial development. It was not innovation per se that precipitated the global crisis but rather the dismal failure of prudential supervision and regulation to keep pace with it. The salutary lesson for developing Asia is that even financially advanced economies are vulnerable to risks arising from esoteric products, reckless lending, and inadequate regulation.

In the context of developing Asia, financial sector development refers to the much more basic task of building sound and efficient banks and capital markets that allocate scarce resources to their most productive uses. Whatever the gains may be from cutting-edge financial sector development, there is clearly a positive and significant relationship between financial development and growth up to a certain level of financial development (Rioja and Valev 2004; Arcand, Berkes, and Panizza 2012; Cecchetti and Kharroubi 2012). Although it is possible that the relationship turns insignificant or even negative beyond some threshold, developing Asia is well short of that possible turning point. The relationship between basic financial sector development and growth is positive.

At first blush one might conclude that the coexistence of sustained rapid growth and financial underdevelopment in developing Asia implies that a

Figure 1.4   Private credit as share of GDP in developing Asian economies, 2012

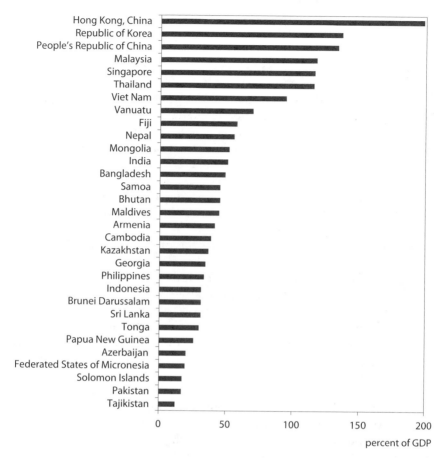

Source: World Bank, *World Development Indicators* online database (accessed on September 15, 2014).

sound and efficient financial sector is not indispensable for economic growth and development. A more considered view would be that developing Asia grew rapidly despite, not because of, financial underdevelopment. With a stronger and better financial system, it might have grown even faster or achieved the same level of growth with lower savings and investment (that is, at a lower cost in terms of forgone consumption).

These considerations loom particularly large at a time when growth is moderating and the region is giving higher priority to the quality of growth. The time is therefore opportune to revisit the issue of financial sector development in Asia, especially in the context of reigniting the region's growth momentum.

Financial Sector Development and Economic Growth in Developing Asia

How can one explain the coexistence of a dynamic real sector—East and Southeast Asia are now collectively the factory of the world—and a backward financial system? At very early stages of development, the combination of a high marginal product of capital and clear paths of industrial upgrading (from bicycles to motorcycles to automobiles, for example) means that relatively unsophisticated allocation systems can still generate significant real rates of return. However, as economies develop and approach the technological frontier, the nature of decision making by both corporate managements and their financiers becomes more demanding. The quality of investment and the quality of financial intermediation thus matter, but they may matter less in the initial stages of development than in more mature economies, where the low-hanging fruit of high marginal return projects has been picked. As the economy matures, and the plethora of profitable investment opportunities begins to shrink, the quality of financial intermediation and the quality of investment begin to loom larger in the calculus of economic growth.

In addition to low income level, low capital stock, and hence high marginal returns to capital, another factor mitigated the adverse effect of inefficient financial systems: high saving and investment rates. Relative to other parts of the developing world, developing Asia, especially East and Southeast Asia, saved a lot and invested a lot. Demographics accounts for some of this pattern: The region has benefited enormously from rapid increases in the size of the working-age population and concomitant low dependency ratios, which contributed to saving and dampened the need for social outlays. Generally speaking, the household and corporate sectors of the region were prudent, and by and large Asian governments refrained from the profligacy that characterized the public sectors of many other developing countries. Indeed, the high saving and investment rates were one of the main sources of the region's superior growth performance. Ample savings expand the pool of funds for investment and hence weaken the urgency of high-quality investments. Even if a sizable share of investment is wasted, an economy armed with abundant savings can rapidly accumulate capital and hence productive capacity. In contrast, an economy without ample savings cannot expect to grow rapidly if it wastes scarce savings on unproductive investments. At the same time, there is an intriguing possibility that plentiful savings discourage financial reform and development, because the economy can grow rapidly even in the face of low returns to savings and investment.

Although financial sector development has always mattered for developing Asia's economic growth, the slowdown of growth has added a sense of urgency to the quest for sound and efficient financial systems in the region. Growth has decelerated across the region since the global crisis, partly because of slower growth in the advanced economies (figure 1.5). Unlike most previ-

Figure 1.5   GDP growth rates in developing Asia, People's Republic of China, and India, 2000–2015

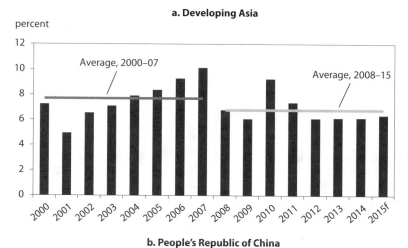

a. Developing Asia

percent

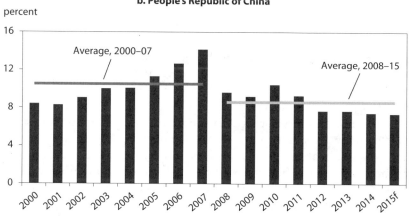

b. People's Republic of China

percent

(continued on next page)

ous financial crises, the global crisis originated in the advanced countries and hit them harder. As the United States, Europe, and Japan remain important markets for developing Asia's exporters, especially for final goods, the failure of these markets to fully recover has had adverse implications for the region's export-led growth paradigm.

In addition to a more challenging external environment, the region faces a number of homegrown structural headwinds to growth, such as population aging. The slowdown is also partly the result of the region's past success: As countries grow richer, they eventually grow at a slower pace. In the People's Republic of China (PRC) the slowdown partly reflects a healthy government-engineered transition to more sustainable growth rates. The reallocation of

Figure 1.5   GDP growth rates in developing Asia, People's Republic of China, and India, 2000–2015 (continued)

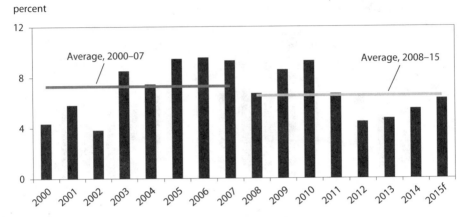

c. India

percent

f = forecast

Source: Asian Development Bank, *Asian Development Outlook* database.

surplus rural labor—that other low-hanging fruit of Asian growth—is also coming to an end in many countries. Whatever the causes, the region's slowdown means it can ill afford an inefficient financial system that wastes or increases the cost of growth.

To some extent, developing Asia is a victim of its own stunning success in the past few decades. In a very short span of time, as a result of sustained rapid growth, it matured from a largely poor region to an increasingly middle-class one. What this means in terms of its growth paradigm is that it is in the midst of a transition from growth based largely on factor accumulation, especially investment, toward growth based on both investment and productivity growth. The balance of the evidence suggests that both factor accumulation and productivity growth contributed to the region's growth in the past. Productivity growth is likely to loom larger in the coming years. To be sure, investment will remain an important source of growth in major Asian economies such as India, Indonesia, and the Philippines, where there is plenty of scope to improve the investment climate and thus raise the investment rate. Even in high-investment economies such as the PRC, there is a significant need for investment in the relatively underdeveloped central and western parts of the country. At the same time, however, precisely because past success has radically transformed developing Asia from a capital-deficient to a capital-abundant region, diminishing marginal returns to capital are likely to set in.

The key to sustaining Asia's growth in the postcrisis period lies in improving the productivity of capital, labor, and all other inputs. Transition toward knowledge-based economies will greatly contribute to productivity growth in the region. Technological progress, or the more mundane but no less important improvement in the efficiency of production, is the source of productivity growth, which comes from absorbing new knowledge and adapting it to produce new goods or services or produce existing goods or services at a lower cost. Just as diminishing marginal returns to capital set in as the stock of capital expands, the gains from copying advanced foreign technology decline as a country converges toward the global knowledge frontier.

For middle- and high-income Asian countries, transitioning toward a knowledge-based economy means investing in research and development (R&D) to create new knowledge. Some of these countries, including the PRC and the Republic of Korea, already rank among global R&D leaders. For lower-income countries without the capacity to create new technologies, the transition will be achieved by importing technologies from abroad and adapting them to local conditions.

Knowledge refers not only to revolutionary technology but also to incremental improvements in the nitty-gritty details of production. As both varieties of innovation often, although not always, come from entrepreneurs and new firms—think of Silicon Valley—financial development that provides adequate, reasonably priced credit to these groups can hasten the transition to the knowledge-based economy and spur productivity-led growth in Asia.

Addressing Financial Exclusion and Income Inequality

Within a generation sustained rapid growth in developing Asia increased income levels severalfold and lifted average living standards beyond recognition. Growth transformed Asia from a typical Third World backwater to one of the three centers of gravity of the world economy. In addition to producing much better fed, clothed, and housed citizens and catapulting the region to a much more prominent place on the global economic stage, sustained growth has lifted hundreds of millions of Asians out of poverty and given them more humane, dignified, and productive lives. The almost unprecedented reduction of poverty in developing Asia lends a great deal of empirical support to the conventional wisdom that economic growth is the most effective antidote to poverty.

The region now finds itself facing another significant social and economic challenge: rising inequality. In countries that collectively account for more than 80 percent of the region's population, the Gini coefficient, the most widely used measure of inequality, rose between 1990 and 2010 (ADB 2012).[2] These countries include the most populous countries (the PRC, India, Indonesia); high-income countries, such as the Republic of Korea; and low-income countries, such as Bangladesh. As in other parts of the world, growing inequality has fueled social discontent and popular demand for more inclusive growth.

---

2. The Gini coefficient is a number between 0 and 1, where 0 represents perfect equality and 1 represents perfect inequality.

One obvious mechanism for tackling rising inequality is fiscal policy. The government can help promote equity through both taxation (progressive personal income taxes) and expenditure policies (public spending on education and health care) (ADB 2014).

Perhaps less obviously, financial sector development can have an impact on inequality, although the direction of the impact is ambiguous. Financial development and inequality may have an inverted U shape, reducing inequality up to a certain threshold before exacerbating it (Park and Shin 2015). As with the impact of financial sector development on growth, however, developing Asia is well short of any such threshold. Financial development in the region can help mitigate inequality.

In many parts of the region, only a small proportion of lower-income groups have access to financial services (figure 1.6). If the financial system develops in a way that enables a broader segment of the population to gain access to financial services, the poor may be able to borrow to finance their education or health care (among the most important determinants of earning capacity). Doing so can help them accumulate human capital, which in turn will enable them to earn more and close the income gap with the rich. The proequity effect of such borrowing will be larger the wider the initial gap in human capital between rich and poor. In addition to human capital and productive capacity, broadening and deepening the access of the poor to financial services will help them cope better with risks and shocks. This access-broadening dimension of financial development—financial inclusion—contributes to lower inequality.

Financial inclusion is not restricted to the household sector. It extends to the corporate sector: Small and medium enterprises (SMEs) suffer from more restricted access to financial services than large companies (Ayyagari and Beck 2015; de la Torre, Martínez Pería, and Schmukler 2010). SMEs are often major sources of innovation, because they are better able to identify niche market needs.

New companies are also often full of new ideas and inject a fresh dose of competition into rigid, stagnant markets. A sound and efficient financial system facilitates entrepreneurship and private enterprise, indispensable ingredients in a dynamic and healthy market economy.

An especially pernicious form of financial exclusion is the preferential treatment of state-owned companies by state-owned financial institutions. The channeling of resources to state-owned companies on preferential terms starves more dynamic private sector firms of credit. Because the private sector tends to be more efficient, such discrimination deprives the economy of innovation and productivity growth.

Preventing Financial Instability

Asian economies experienced financial volatility when, in May 2013, US Federal Reserve Chairman Ben Bernanke signaled an intention to taper quantitative easing (figure 1.7). The episode highlighted the vulnerability of Asian

Figure 1.6 Percentage of adults in bottom 40 percent of the income distribution with an account at a formal financial institution, 2011

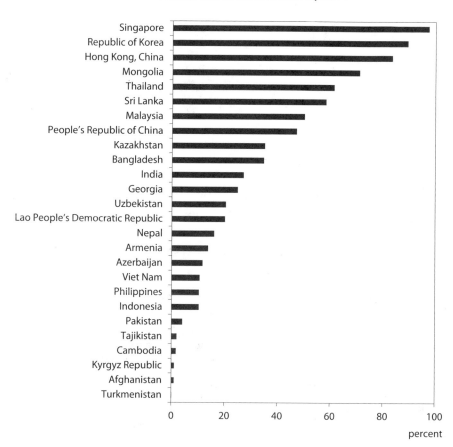

Source: Demirgüç-Kunt and Klapper (2013).

financial systems to monetary policy shocks from the advanced economies in the post–global financial crisis period.

More generally, financial development and innovation can entail substantial risk for financial stability, especially in the absence of concomitant strengthening of regulatory capacity. The global financial crisis highlights the potentially enormous damage to financial stability that poorly regulated and supervised financial development can inflict. At the height of the crisis, credit seized up and the paralyzed financial system failed to perform its core function of channeling resources to the real economy.

The potentially adverse effect of financial development on financial stability has some troubling implications about the costs and benefits of financial

Figure 1.7   Changes in nominal exchange rates in selected countries in developing Asia, May 23–June 30, 2013

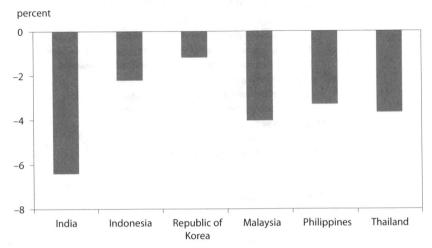

Note: Decline means depreciation.
Source: Bloomberg (accessed on September 22, 2014).

development. Financial development fosters economic growth by facilitating investment, the accumulation of capital, innovation, and productivity growth. But it can also contribute to financial instability. In particular, if financial development outpaces the capacity of prudential supervisors and regulators to keep on top of it, it can create large systemic risks, which sometimes lead to crisis.

Financial crisis can have devastating consequences for the real economy and economic growth. During the global crisis, the financial meltdown fueled widespread fears of a collapse of global output and trade. These fears were fanned by the fact that the crisis originated in the advanced economies and hit them disproportionately hard. World output did contract, albeit only marginally; world trade declined more substantially, for the only time in the post–World War II era. Only fiscal stimulus, monetary expansion, and provision of liquidity support throughout the world, by both advanced and developing economies, prevented a repeat of the Great Depression.

Although financial contagion did not spread to developing Asia, where banks had very limited exposure to US subprime assets, the region was not immune to the crisis on the real-economy front. The collapse of global trade, in particular imports by the advanced economies, crimped exports and growth.

The Asian financial crisis of 1997–98 had a devastating impact on aggregate demand and growth in developing Asia. High-flyers such as Indonesia, the Republic of Korea, Malaysia, and Thailand came crashing down to earth in the face of the sudden and massive reversal of foreign capital that had flowed in to capitalize on the region's strong growth prospects. Convulsion of

financial markets, most evident in the sharp depreciation of regional currencies, dented business and consumer confidence and spilled over into the real
economy. The contraction of output was so severe that it entailed significant
unemployment, which, in the absence of what until then had been unnecessary social safety nets, caused social problems.

It is tempting to interpret the Asian crisis as evidence of the destabilizing,
growth-destroying effect of financial development or the related but distinct
concept of external financial opening. However, it is equally accurate to view
the crisis as evidence of the substantial risks of financial underdevelopment.
The crisis was not precipitated by capital inflows per se but by the failure of a
weak and inefficient financial system to intermediate those flows to productive investments that enhance an economy's ability to produce goods and
services and hence repay foreign borrowings.

Even short of a full-blown systemic crisis, financial development can
engender financial instability, which adversely affects economic growth. This
risk is especially high if financial development is accompanied by financial liberalization and external opening in the absence of strong regulatory oversight.
More flexible and hence potentially volatile exchange rates, interest rates, and
equity prices may increase uncertainty among businesses and thus reduce
investment. Gyrations in the prices of financial assets that are detached from
fundamentals can destabilize the real economy, as can volatile short-term
capital flows.

A financial system that is tightly controlled, directed, and overregulated
by the government may seem stable on the surface but may engender instability in other ways. It may, for example, give rise to a large shadow banking
sector that serves the financial needs of companies and households the state-
directed financial system fails to serve. Shadow banking entails some benefits, but it is, by definition, beyond the realm of prudential supervision and
regulation and hence less transparent and riskier than the formal financial
sector. Furthermore, financial repression may distort incentives across institutions and projects and contribute to misallocation of investment, specifically
overinvestment in low-return projects, which may erupt into crisis when the
government eventually embarks upon financial liberalization.

More fundamentally, even if one accepts the premise that financial repression can promote financial stability, it comes at a large cost in terms of growth.
A state-dominated financial system channels resources to state-owned firms at
the expense of private sector firms even though the latter tend to be more efficient and innovative. More generally, state-directed credit allocates scarce
credit to activities, firms, and industries preferred by the government rather
than the market. Whether financial institutions are state-owned or private but
subject to extensive government guidance, a state-dominated financial system
severely distorts the allocation of resources and hampers innovation.

Ideally, financial development should proceed in a way that minimizes the
risks to financial stability while maximizing the benefits for economic growth.
Strong and effective prudential regulation is key in this regard. Such regula-

tion is an art rather than a science, as it should preempt financial instability without choking off growth-conducive financial innovation. In some cases, innovative measures such as macroprudential policies and bank stress tests can support a sound regulatory framework.

Concluding Observations

Financial sector development in developing Asia is hardly a new issue: The gap between the region's dynamic real economy and its relatively backward financial sector has existed for years. Now is an opportune time to revisit Asia's financial development, for a number of reasons. Above all, the region's growth has slowed since the global crisis, precipitated by a less benign external environment; internal structural challenges, such as population aging; and the maturing of much of the region into middle-income status. The slowdown amplifies the cost of financial underdevelopment, especially in terms of forgone growth: Wasted growth is much more costly when the economy is growing at 5 percent a year than 10 percent a year. Further reinforcing the urgency of financial development is the evolving shift in the region's growth paradigm from one based primarily on investment to one based on both investment and productivity growth. The vital role of innovation and knowledge in Asia's productivity growth and hence economic growth makes it critical that its financial system be able to channel more funds at lower cost to entrepreneurs and new firms in the future.

It is possible that financial development promotes economic growth only up to a point, that beyond a high level of financial development further development may lead to financial instability, even financial crisis, hurting economic growth. A classic example of such a possibility is the global financial crisis of 2008–09, which caused financial paralysis and nearly brought down the world economy. With the possible exceptions of the financial centers of Singapore and Hong Kong, China, however, developing Asia is at a significantly lower level of financial development than the level at which too much finance becomes a concern. Financial development in developing Asia requires building up sound and efficient banks, equity markets, and bond markets that intermediate savings into productive investments while mitigating their vulnerability to shocks.

To a large extent, the evolution in the quality of the region's growth requires evolution in the quality of its financial system. In the past the overriding priority was to grow as rapidly as possible. This priority made sense in light of the region's very low income level and grinding poverty. However, developing Asia has now become an increasingly middle-income region, where the quality of growth matters as much as the quantity of growth. A key component of higher-quality growth is more inclusive growth. Financial inclusion facilitates inclusive growth, by broadening the reach of financial services to wider swaths of the population and economy, including poorer households, smaller firms, and new firms. Some elements of financial inclusion (such as borrowing by the poor for education) have a direct positive effect on growth. Others (such as borrowing to finance consumption in the face of a natural disaster) have a less direct effect.

A sound and efficient financial system has enormous benefits for economic growth and development. Those benefits become even larger if financial development is complemented with structural and policy reforms in other areas. Reforms that improve the business climate (by, for example, reducing red tape and strengthening infrastructure) increase the benefits of financial development, which unlocks the flow of credit to new firms and entrepreneurs. Education reform that improves the quality of public schools increases the effect of financial inclusion, which improves the ability of the poor to finance their education. Better public health care also amplifies the benefits of financial inclusion. In short, financial development and inclusion work best in a policy environment that is conducive to growth and development.

References

Arcand, Jean-Louis, Enrico Berkes, and Ugo Panizza. 2012. *Too Much Finance?* IMF Working Paper WP/12/161. Washington: International Monetary Fund.

ADB (Asian Development Bank). 2012. *Asian Development Outlook 2012: Confronting Rising Inequality in Asia*. Manila.

ADB (Asian Development Bank). 2014. *Asian Development Outlook 2014: Fiscal Policy for Inclusive Growth*. Manila.

Ayyagari, Meghana, and Thorsten Beck. 2015. *Financial Inclusion in Asia: An Overview*. ADB Economics Working Paper No. 449. Manila: Asian Development Bank.

Cecchetti, Stephen G., and Enisse Kharroubi. 2012. *Reassessing the Impact of Finance on Growth*. BIS Working Paper 381. Basel: Bank for International Settlements.

de la Torre, Augusto, María Soledad Martínez Pería, and Sergio L. Schmukler. 2010. Bank Involvement with SMEs: Beyond Relationship Lending. *Journal of Banking and Finance* 34: 2280-93.

Demirgüç-Kunt, Asli, and Leora Klapper. 2013. Measuring Financial Inclusion: Explaining Variation in Use of Financial Services across and within Countries. *Brookings Papers on Economic Activity* (Spring): 279-340.

Park, Donghyun, and Kwanho Shin. 2015. *Economic Growth, Financial Development, and Income Inequality*. ADB Economics Working Paper No. 441. Manila: Asian Development Bank.

Rioja, Felix, and Neven Valev. 2004. Does One Size Fit All? A Reexamination of the Finance and Growth Relationship. *Journal of Development Economics* 74, no. 2: 429-47.

2

Financial Development, Financial Openness, and Economic Growth

GEMMA B. ESTRADA, DONGHYUN PARK, and ARIEF RAMAYANDI

A sound and efficient financial system is an indispensable ingredient of economic growth. It consists primarily of banks and capital markets, which channel savings into investments and other productive activities that contribute to economic growth and augment the economy's productive capacity.

This chapter explains the importance of financial development and openness. It sifts through the literature on the relationship between both variables and economic growth. It then reports the results and discusses some original empirical analysis. In addition to using more updated data, which extend the sample period to include some postcrisis years, the analysis examines whether country characteristics and factors such as the exchange rate regime affect the finance-growth nexus.

Why Do Financial Development and Financial Openness Matter?

A critical function of the financial system is to allocate capital to its most productive uses. Other things equal, a country with a financial system that efficiently allocates capital will grow faster than a country with a financial system that allocates capital inefficiently. The former will have more productive investments and fewer white elephants than the latter. Banks that lend on the

Gemma B. Estrada is senior economics officer at the Economic Research and Regional Cooperation Department of the Asian Development Bank. Donghyun Park is principal economist at the Asian Development Bank. Arief Ramayandi is senior economist at the Economic Research and Regional Cooperation Department of the Asian Development Bank.

basis of commercial merit will be far more efficient than banks that lend on the basis of personal relationships. As a country's financial sector develops, it will become better at allocating capital.

In addition to efficiently allocating resources, a sound and efficient financial system contributes to dynamic efficiency gains over time. Financing from venture capitalists and angel investors gave rise to Silicon Valley, the epicenter of the global information and communication technology revolution. More mundanely but more importantly, the financing of entrepreneurs and smaller firms allows new players to enter the market, which spurs new and old firms to create new products and technologies.

The concept of financial openness is related to, but distinct from, the concept of financial development. As a financial system develops and becomes more sophisticated, it often opens up to foreign capital and becomes more closely integrated with foreign financial systems. (A country can also experience financial development while maintaining a relatively closed financial system, as the experience of the People's Republic of China [PRC] shows.) Financial openness can have significant effects on financial development, both positive (participation of foreign institutional investors can benefit underdeveloped Asian bond markets) and negative (instability arising from reversal of volatile short-term capital flows can set back financial development).

Intuitively, financial openness would seem to have a positive influence on economic growth. Foreign direct investment (FDI) inflows can foster growth by bringing in advanced foreign technology, managerial skills, and other knowhow and by making domestic markets more competitive through the entry of foreign companies. Even non-FDI inflows can contribute to growth, by enabling domestic firms to access foreign savings. However, in the absence of a sound and efficient financial system, foreign capital inflows may be misallocated, resulting in growth-crippling financial crisis. For all of these factors, it is worth investigating the effect of financial openness on economic growth, in addition to the effect of financial development.

The global financial crisis of 2008–09 fueled widespread skepticism about the positive effects of financial development on economic growth and popular hostility toward the financial industry. The crisis was unprecedented in that it originated in and almost paralyzed the financial systems of the advanced economies. When the crisis spread to the real economy, it wrought havoc on global trade and growth and caused the world economy to contract, albeit marginally, for the only time in the postwar era.

Superficially, the most obvious lesson from the crisis might be that too much financial development and innovation can be harmful for financial stability and growth. After all, complex and sophisticated financial innovations such as mortgage-backed securities, structured investment vehicles, and collateralized debt obligations were the catalysts of the crisis.

The global financial crisis intensified but did not initiate doubts about whether financial development is beneficial for growth. Such doubts are consistent with empirical studies that reveal a nonlinear relationship between the two variables. These studies find that financial development contributes to economic growth—but only up to a point, after which it may even adversely affect growth. The global financial crisis is consistent with such evidence.

Concerns about too much financial development and the deleterious effect of finance on growth are much more relevant for advanced countries than developing countries. The complex financial innovations of global financial centers such as New York and London are a world away from financially underdeveloped Asia, which remains well inside the global finance frontier. For Asian countries, financial development does not refer to mortgage-backed securities, structured investment vehicles, or collateralized debt obligations but rather to the much more basic task of building sound and efficient financial systems that allocate capital to its most productive uses. In light of the vast gap between the financial development levels of Asia and the advanced economies, the wrong lesson for Asian countries to draw from the global financial crisis is that they should halt or slow down financial development.

Financial innovation is not without its risks, but financial underdevelopment carries risks of its own—as the region learned at great cost during the Asian crisis. Because financial development means fundamentally different things to advanced economies and developing countries, its effect on growth may differ for the two groups of countries. The returns to financial development are likely to be higher in developing countries, which stand to reap large efficiency gains as their banks and capital markets develop from low initial bases.

Literature Review

Several studies indicate that the depth of the financial system has a significant positive impact on growth. In particular, a larger financial system—as measured by liquid liabilities, private credit, and stock market capitalization—is associated with higher growth.

On financial openness, studies yield mixed results. Limited evidence indicates that greater financial openness leads to higher growth.

Financial Development and Economic Growth

The literature includes four types of studies on the finance-growth relationship (Demirgüç-Kunt and Levine 2008):

- pure cross-country growth regressions
- panel techniques that use both the cross-country and time series dimensions of the data
- microeconomic studies that explore the various channels through which finance may affect economic growth
- individual country case studies.

The first approach involves the application of broad cross-country growth regressions, which seek to explain growth through standard explanatory variables such as physical and human capital. These studies typically aggregate growth over long periods of time and examine the relationship between long-run growth and various measures of financial development. The second approach analyzes panel data, in an effort to mitigate some of the econometric problems associated with the pure cross-country approach. It has a number of advantages over the first approach, although it also suffers from some disadvantages. The third approach uses firm- and industry-level data to assess the impact of financial development on firm and industry performance. A positive impact would lend support to the notion that financial development is beneficial for growth. The fourth approach looks at the finance-growth relationship in a single country, usually with the aim of analyzing the impact of a specific policy change.

We focus on studies that apply cross-country growth regressions, including studies that use panel techniques, because this is the approach we used in our own empirical analysis. In earlier cross-country regression studies, economic growth is usually averaged over long periods, while financial indicators are either averaged over the same period or taken from the initial year. Several macroeconomic indicators are used as control variables.

One of the earliest studies of this type is by King and Levine (1993), who examine the relationship between financial depth (as measured by liquid liabilities) and three growth measures (real per capita GDP growth, real per capita capital stock growth, and total productivity growth), all averaged over the sample period. Using data for 77 countries over the period 1960–89, they find a statistically significant positive relationship between financial depth and the three growth measures.

Levine and Zervos (1998) analyze data for 47 countries over the period 1976–93. They find the initial level of banking development and stock market activity to have statistically significant relationships with average output growth, capital stock growth, and productivity growth.

Beck and Levine (2004) apply panel econometric techniques to new data to reexamine the relationship between stock markets, banks, and economic growth. They study whether measures of stock market and bank development have positive relationships with economic growth after controlling for simultaneity and omitted variable bias. They use data for 40 countries, over 1976–98, employing generalized method of moments estimators. They find that stock markets and banks are jointly significant in affecting economic growth, suggesting that stock markets and banks provide different financial services.

Bekaert, Harvey, and Lundblad (2005) examine financial development and financial openness, using equity market turnover and private credit as measures of financial development and equity market liberalization as an indicator of financial openness. They find that equity market liberalization led to a 1 percent increase in annual economic growth over a five-year period. Liberalization of the equity market has two effects. First, it directly reduces financing constraints, as more foreign capital becomes available. Second, it improves corporate governance, as a result of the increase in investment. The presence of financial development variables does not knock out the liberalization effect.

Čihák et al. (2012) use an updated version of the global financial development database to replicate the model of King and Levine (1993). They find similar growth-enhancing effects of financial development.

In their review of the literature, Demirgüç-Kunt and Levine (2008) note that weaknesses in measures of financial development remain. No measure adequately captures the ability of the financial system to provide financial services that facilitate the screening of firms before they are financed; the monitoring of firms after they are financed; the management of both idiosyncratic project risk and liquidity risk; or the exchange of goods, services, and financial claims. As a result, it is difficult to design suitable empirical proxies of financial development. Empirical studies—including our own and those of Rajan and Zingales (1998), Levine and Zervos (1998), and Demirgüç-Kunt and Levine (2008)—thus rely on traditional measures of financial development.

Financial Openness and Economic Growth

Various indicators have been developed to measure financial openness and integration. These indicators are often classified as de jure, de facto, and hybrid measures. The main source for most de jure indicators is the *Annual Report on Exchange Rate Arrangements and Exchange Restrictions*, published by the International Monetary Fund (IMF), which provides information on the extent and nature of rules and regulations governing external account transactions for a wide array of countries. These data have been widely used as the basis for binary measures of capital controls and financial openness (Alesina, Grilli, and Milesi-Ferretti 1994; Edison et al. 2004).

Quinn, Schindler, and Toyoda (2011) survey a wide range of indicators on financial openness, identifying their properties and how the indicators relate to one another. Among de jure measures, the KAOPEN index by Chinn and Ito (2008) and the financial openness index (FOI) by Johnston and Tamirisa (1998) and Brune and Guisinger (2006) cover the broadest range of countries and time periods. Chinn and Ito's index measures the extent of openness or restrictions in cross-border financial transactions. It is constructed using principal component analysis on four variables: the presence of multiple exchange rates, restrictions on current account transactions, restrictions on capital account transactions, and the requirement of the surrender of export proceeds.

The FOI represents the cumulative total of the binary score for 12 categories. It distinguishes between inward and outward flows and resident and nonresident transactions. It decomposes the subcomponents of capital flows in fine detail. Unlike Chinn and Ito's index, the indicators are not publicly available.

Both KAOPEN and the FOI are ideal for aggregate information. If a more disaggregated measure is needed, Schindler's (2009) KA indices may be better suited, although its sample size is smaller. Unlike other indices, the KA index provides binary codes at the level of individual types of transactions. In addition, indices can be created by asset category, residency status, and inflows versus outflows, allowing for an analysis in line with the balance of payments focus on residency as well as based on the direction of capital flows.

De jure measures are beset by limitations. They do not always reflect the actual degree of financial integration of an economy into international capital markets, as other regulations that restrict capital are not considered as such. In addition, these measures do not capture the degree of enforcement of capital controls (Quinn and Toyoda 2008; Quinn, Schindler, and Toyoda 2011; Kose et al. 2009).

An alternative way to measure financial integration is to use de facto indicators. Quantity-based measures that rely on actual flows best capture de facto integration for emerging markets and low-income developing countries. Gross flows (the sum of total inflows and total outflows) are preferred over net flows, because they provide a less volatile and more accurate picture of integration. Because gross flows tend to be volatile and prone to measurement error, however, the sum of gross stocks of foreign assets and liabilities should be expressed as a share of GDP (Kose et al. 2009). A widely used de facto indicator is Lane and Milesi-Ferretti's (2007) index, which is calculated as a country's aggregate assets plus liabilities relative to its GDP. This measure includes portfolio equity, FDI, debt, and financial derivatives.

An important limitation of de facto indicators is the inconsistent reporting and treatment of FDI across countries and over time. De facto measures may also fail to accurately reflect a government's policy stance. Some firms may invest in some countries because of capital account restrictions. De jure restrictions can thus affect capital flows.

Comparing both de jure and de facto indicators, Kose et al. (2009) find that average de jure openness did not change much over the last two decades but de facto integration increased dramatically. This finding reflects the fact that the information in the two types of integration can differ. It is important to take these differences into account.

Studies of the relationship between financial openness and growth reveal mixed results or provide little evidence on developing countries (Kose et al. 2009; Obstfeld 2009; Quinn and Toyoda 2008; Quinn, Schindler, and Toyoda 2011). Differences in the type of openness measure, the sample period, country coverage, and the choice of empirical methodology are the main reasons for the diverse findings in the literature.

The positive relationship between capital account liberalization and growth appears to have declined over time, as studies undertaken using data from the 1980s and 1990s or 1960s–90s are more likely to indicate a positive effect than studies undertaken more recently. Another issue that weakens results is endogeneity—the fact that countries may decide to open their financial sector when growth prospects become more favorable (Bartolini and Drazen 1997; Rodrik 1998). Changes in the policy environments or institutions that simultaneously drive additional reforms may also affect financial openness.

Finding robust evidence that financial integration systematically increases growth has remained difficult. But studying longer time periods, researchers have found a positive link between the two variables, especially when financial integration is measured using de facto or finer de jure measures and interaction terms accounting for supportive conditions such as good policies and institutions are properly included.

Despite limited evidence, countries have pursued greater financial openness, as a growing financial sector cannot afford to be insulated from cross-border financial flows. Financial opening is likely to promote a more competitive and resilient domestic financial system. Financial liberalization can yield collateral benefits that spur growth and make an open financial account less prone to crises.

For financial openness to generate growth benefits, however, a well-developed and well-supervised financial sector, good institutions, and sound macroeconomic policies need to be in place (Kose et al. 2009). Countries are more likely to gain from financial openness when it is implemented in a phased manner, starting with an opening up to FDI, which has the biggest positive effect on domestic investment and growth. This step may be followed by liberalizing portfolio equity flows, in parallel with a growing local financial market. Restrictions on longer-term debt flows can then be eased. Short-maturity flows should be liberalized last (Obstfeld 2009).

Empirical Framework and Data

This section lays out the econometric framework used in our empirical analysis. It also describes the data used.

Baseline Regression

The general approach in the literature is to estimate growth regressions that explicitly include financial development and openness in the set of determinants of economic growth. The basic structure of the regression equation is as follows:

$$Y_{i,t} = \alpha + \beta_1 [FD]_{i,t} + \beta_2 [FO]_{i,t} + \gamma [ER]_{i,t} + \lambda [Other]_{i,t} + v_i + \varepsilon_{i,t} \qquad (2.1)$$

where financial sector development [FD] indicators, measures of financial openness [FO], the exchange rate regime [ER], and a number of nonfinancial control variables [Other] are assumed to affect economic growth (Y). For measures of economic growth, we use a series of nonoverlapping five-year average of GDP per capita growth for each of the sample countries. The depth of the financial sector is commonly used as an empirical proxy for financial develop-

Figure 2.1   Liquid liabilities and lending-deposit spreads, selected years

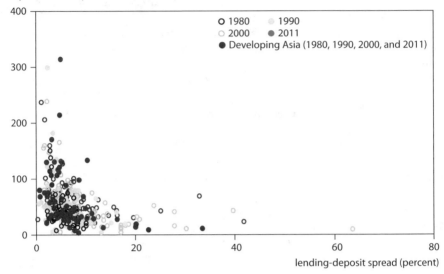

liquid liabilities (percent of GDP)

Sources: Beck, Demirgüç-Kunt, and Levine (2000, 2009); Čihák et al. (2012).

ment. The notion of financial development, however, goes beyond mere depth. A more developed financial sector is expected to promote economic growth through its greater efficiency in channeling funds to support economic activities. Financial efficiency can be gauged by lending-deposit spreads and banks' overhead costs, which are lower in broader and more advanced financial systems.[1] Data on these indicators tend to be more limited than data on financial depth.

The relationship between lending-deposit spreads and liquid liabilities (figure 2.1) and overhead costs and liquid liabilities (figure 2.2) is somewhat curvilinear. Lower lending-deposit spreads and overhead costs are associated with larger financial sectors, confirming the widely held view that deeper financial markets tend to be more efficient. This relationship may justify the use of financial depth indicators as proxies for financial development. We use three indicators of financial development in this chapter:

- Total liquid liabilities as a share of GDP measures relative overall financial depth. It consists of currency plus demand and interest-bearing liabilities of banks and nonbank financial intermediaries. It is the broadest measure of financial intermediation activity, as it covers all banks, central banks, and nonfinancial intermediary activities.

---

1. See the Financial Development and Structure Dataset (Beck, Demirgüç-Kunt, and Levine 2000, 2009; Čihák et al. 2012). Data on lending-deposit spreads are available for 1980–2011. Data on overhead costs are available for 1998–2011.

Figure 2.2 Liquid liabilities and overhead costs

liquid liabilities (percent of GDP)

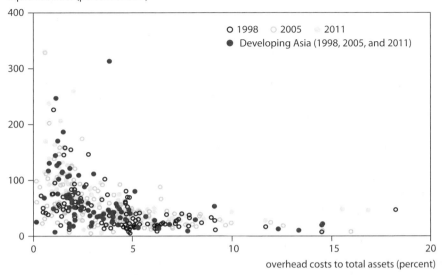

Sources: Beck, Demirgüç-Kunt, and Levine (2000, 2009); Čihák et al. (2012).

- Private credit by deposit money banks as a share of GDP isolates the impact of the banking sector.
- Stock market capitalization as a share of GDP gauges the relative size of the equity market in an economy.

Data on liquid liabilities come from the Financial Development and Structure Dataset of Beck, Demirgüç-Kunt, and Levine (2000, 2009) and Čihák et al. (2012), which was updated in November 2013. Data on private credit and stock market capitalization come from the World Bank's *World Development Indicators* online database.

We rely on three measures of financial openness, two de facto and one de jure indicator. The first de facto measure is total capital flows, estimated from Haver Analytics data, as a share of GDP. This measure is the sum of inflows and outflows of direct investment, equity investment, debt securities, financial derivatives, and other investment. It accounts for capital account transactions of both residents and nonresidents in a given year.

The second de facto measure is the updated and extended version of a dataset constructed by Lane and Milesi-Ferretti (2007) that includes data for 188 countries. This widely used de facto indicator is calculated as a country's aggregate assets plus liabilities as a share of its GDP. It includes portfolio equity, FDI, debt, and financial derivatives. The dataset employs a common methodology to construct estimates of foreign asset and liability positions of a large set of countries, relying on both direct measures of stocks and cumulative flows with valuation adjustments. For most countries, the benchmark used is the official international investment position (IIP) estimates for recent years. Lane and Milesi-Ferretti then work backward with data on capital flows and estimates for capital gains and losses to calculate stock positions for earlier years. Recognizing the large cross-country variation in the reliability of data on capital flows and estimated stock positions, they use various techniques to derive the most suitable series for each country.

The third type of capital openness measure is the de jure index constructed by Chinn and Ito (2008). Their measure of the extent of openness uses data from the IMF's *Annual Report on Exchange Rate Arrangements and Exchange Restrictions*, which provides information on the extent and nature of rules and regulations governing external account transactions for a wide array of countries.

For exchange rate regimes, we consider both the de facto classification and the official IMF classification constructed by Reinhart and Rogoff (2004) and updated by Ilzetzki, Reinhart, and Rogoff (2011). The de facto classification starts by using country chronologies to identify countries with official, dual, or multiple rates or active parallel (black) markets. In the absence of a dual or parallel market, the authors check any official preannounced arrangement and verify it by examining exchange rate movements. If there is no preannounced exchange rate regime or the announced regime cannot be verified by data and the 12-month inflation rate is below 40 percent, they classify a country by examining the exchange rate behavior. Their judgment is based on exchange rate variability of monthly observations (measured through mean absolute change), averaged over two-year and five-year rolling windows. To determine whether exchange rate changes are kept within a band, they calculate the probabilities that the exchange rate remains within +/- 1, 2, and 5 percent bands over two-year and five-year rolling windows.

Countries are classified as de facto freefalling on the basis of two criteria. One is having a 12-month rate of inflation of at least 40 percent, unless the regime can be classified as a preannounced peg or preannounced narrow band. The other is whether in the six months following a currency crisis the country moves from a fixed or quasi-fixed regime to a managed or independently floating regime or a large change in the exchange rate reflects a loss of credibility and persistent speculative attacks rather than a policy change.

Reinhart and Rogoff (2004) and Ilzetzki, Reinhart, and Rogoff (2011) construct the official IMF classification based on the information submitted by member countries and reported in the *Annual Report on Exchange Rate Arrangements and Exchange Restrictions*. The coarse classifications are recategorized into four regimes: fixed, managed, flexible, and freely falling or dual markets with missing parallel market data (appendix 2A). The regimes follow the initial year of each five-year period.

Several control variables are included to account for other factors affecting growth. The choice of these variables closely follows the variables used in many growth regression analyses (Levine and Zervos 1998; Beck, Levine, and

Loayza 2000; Edison et al. 2002). Initial GDP per capita from the World Bank's *World Development Indicators* online database is included to account for the growth convergence effect. Years of schooling from Barro and Lee (2010) are included to represent the impact of human capital accumulation on growth. Other standard growth determinants controlled for include relative trade openness, inflation, and government consumption, all taken from the *World Development Indicators* online database. The control variables were averaged for each five-year period, except initial GDP, for which the value at $t - 5$ is used.

Appendix table 2B.1 shows the correlation coefficients for an initial examination of the associations among variables, especially financial development, financial openness, and growth. It shows positive correlations between measures of financial development and growth, which are higher than the correlations between measures of financial openness and growth.

For the empirical estimation, we apply the Arellano-Bond generalized method of moments to the panel dataset. The full sample of the GDP per capita growth regression is a cross-country panel dataset covering 108 economies (of which 20 are developing Asian economies) with five nonoverlapping five-year periods between 1977 and 2011.[2] Arellano and Bond (1991) suggest first-differencing the regression equation to eliminate the country-specific effect, as follows:

$$\Delta Y_{i,t} = \Delta \beta_1 [FD]_{i,t} + \Delta \beta_2 [FO]_{i,t} + \Delta \gamma [ER]_{i,t} + \Delta \lambda [Others]_{i,t} + \Delta u_{i,t} \qquad (2.2)$$

where $\Delta u_{i,t} = \Delta v_i + \Delta \varepsilon_{i,t} = (v_i - v_i) + (\varepsilon_{i,t} - \varepsilon_{i,t-1}) = (\varepsilon_{i,t} - \varepsilon_{i,t-1})$.

First-differencing removes the fixed country-specific effect. The first-differenced dependent variables, which are assumed to be endogenous, can then be instrumented with their past levels. The estimation method addresses possible endogeneity problems that arise because of the possibility of two-way causation between financial development and openness.

The equation represents our baseline regression, which includes the financial development and openness indicators, the exchange rate regime dummies, and the standard determinants of growth used in empirical growth regressions. The main focus of the analysis is the effect of financial development and financial openness on economic growth. Other explanatory variables are included to control for their influence on the growth rate.

Extended Analysis

We extend the analysis by asking several additional questions. Is the growth effect of the financial variables different for developing countries? Would a different level of financial openness or development alter the effect of the other financial variables on growth? Does the foreign exchange regime interfere with the way financial variables affect economic growth?

---

2. Appendix 2C lists the economies included in the regressions. The five-year periods are 1977–81, 1982–86, 1987–91, 1992–96, 1997–2001, 2002–06, and 2007–11.

Partial scatter plots of these indicators show the marginal contribution of openness or financial development indicator to GDP per capita growth while controlling for other variables in the model. GDP per capita growth, openness, and financial development indicators are regressed against the other predictor variables, and the residuals are obtained from each estimation. Estimations were done using pooled panel regressions. The residuals from regressing GDP per capita growth against the other explanatory variables are shown on the vertical axis; the residuals from regressing openness or financial development against the other variables are shown on the horizontal axis. The plots are used to identify the nature of the relationship between two indicators given the effect of the other independent variables in the model. We first explored the plots using separate models for de facto and de jure foreign exchange regimes. As plots in both types of regime show strong resemblance, we show only the plots with de facto regimes.

We investigate the likely relationship using the three measures of openness: total capital flows, Lane and Milesi-Ferretti's openness measure, and Chinn and Ito's openness indicator (figure 2.3). The plot for total capital flows indicates a flat marginal contribution from openness, indicating no clear positive or negative linear relationship. When Lane and Milesi-Ferretti's openness measure is used, an apparent negative linear relationship is seen. As with total capital flows, Chinn and Ito's measure does not show a clear negative or positive linear association with output growth.

We perform the same analysis for FDI and non-FDI flows, using computed total flows and Lane and Milesi-Ferretti's measure (figure 2.4). The residuals for FDI indicate a positive linear pattern when using total flows data. The trend is not evident when using Lane and Milesi-Ferretti's measure. An almost flat pattern is seen for total non-FDI flows, suggesting no clear positive or negative linear association. With Lane and Milesi-Ferretti's measure of non-FDI, there is an obvious negative linear relationship.

For financial development, we use data on liquid liabilities, private credit, and stock market capitalization (figure 2.5). The plots indicate that growth is positively associated with liquid liabilities and private credit. There is no clear relationship between output growth and stock market capitalization.

There appears to be an outlier, which has a residual of less than –15 from the growth regression. Removing it from the sample does not strongly influence the nature of the relationship between the variables.

Empirical Results

Correlations and scatter plots are useful in understanding the relationships between growth and openness measures and between growth and financial development. A more rigorous analytical method is required to assess the robustness of such relationships. This section presents our results from applying the Arellano-Bond generalized method of moments estimation.

Figure 2.3 GDP per capita growth and total openness, with liquid liabilities as financial development indicator and under de facto foreign exchange rate regime

a. Total capital flows

residuals (GDP per capita growth as DV)

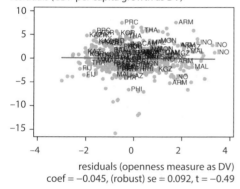

residuals (openness measure as DV)
coef = 0.055, (robust) se = 0.166, t = 0.33

b. Lane and Milesi-Ferretti's openness measure

residuals (GDP per capita growth as DV)

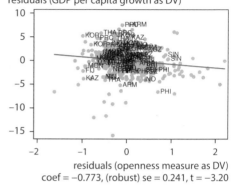

residuals (openness measure as DV)
coef = −0.773, (robust) se = 0.241, t = −3.20

c. Chinn and Ito's openness measure

residuals (GDP per capita growth as DV)

residuals (openness measure as DV)
coef = −0.045, (robust) se = 0.092, t = −0.49

DV = dependent variable

ARM = Armenia; BAN = Bangladesh; CAM = Cambodia; FIJ = Fiji; IND = India; INO = Indonesia; KAZ = Kazakhstan; KGZ = Kyrgyz Republic; KOR = Republic of Korea; MAL = Malaysia; MON = Mongolia; NEP = Nepal; PAK = Pakistan; PHI = Philippines; PRC = People's Republic of China; SIN = Singapore; SRI = Sri Lanka; TAJ = Tajikistan; THA = Thailand; VIE = Viet Nam

Sources: Authors' estimates based on data from Chinn and Ito (2008); Haver Analytics (accessed on October 7, 2014); Lane and Milesi-Ferretti (2007); Reinhart and Rogoff (2004); Ilzetzki, Reinhart, and Rogoff (2011); and World Bank, *World Development Indicators* online database (accessed on September 15, 2014).

Baseline Results

Table 2.1 displays the results of our baseline regressions. They are consistent with economic intuition as well as the findings of the previous empirical literature. We apply time dummies to account for possible unobserved heterogeneity across time in the sample.

Figure 2.4 GDP per capita growth and total FDI, with liquid liabilities as financial development indicator and under de facto foreign exchange rate regime

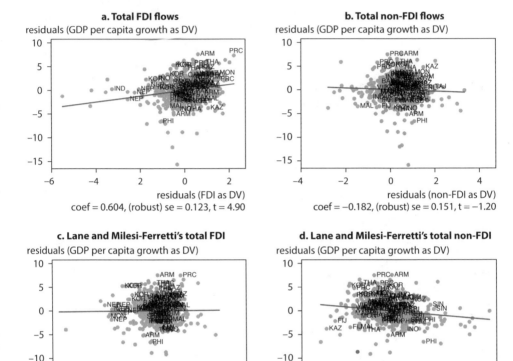

a. Total FDI flows

residuals (GDP per capita growth as DV)

coef = 0.604, (robust) se = 0.123, t = 4.90

b. Total non-FDI flows

residuals (GDP per capita growth as DV)

coef = −0.182, (robust) se = 0.151, t = −1.20

c. Lane and Milesi-Ferretti's total FDI

residuals (GDP per capita growth as DV)

coef = 0.044, (robust) se = 0.167, t = 0.26

d. Lane and Milesi-Ferretti's total non-FDI

residuals (GDP per capita growth as DV)

coef = −0.806, (robust) se = 0.215, t = −3.75

FDI = foreign direct investment; DV = dependent variable

ARM = Armenia; BAN = Bangladesh; CAM = Cambodia; FIJ = Fiji; IND = India; INO = Indonesia; KAZ = Kazakhstan; KGZ = Kyrgyz Republic; KOR = Republic of Korea; MAL = Malaysia; MON = Mongolia; NEP = Nepal; PAK = Pakistan; PHI = Philippines; PRC = People's Republic of China; SIN = Singapore; SRI = Sri Lanka; TAJ = Tajikistan; THA = Thailand; VIE = Viet Nam

Sources: Authors' estimates based on data from Haver Analytics (accessed on October 7, 2014); Lane and Milesi-Ferretti (2007); Reinhart and Rogoff (2004); Ilzetzki, Reinhart, and Rogoff (2011); and World Bank, *World Development Indicators* online database (accessed on September 15, 2014).

The results on the standard determinants of growth are consistent with the empirical findings in the growth literature, with the coefficients relatively stable over different regression specifications. Initial per capita GDP exhibits a negative and significant effect on growth of GDP per capita, suggesting conditional convergence. Trade has the expected significant and positive signs: per

Figure 2.5 GDP per capita growth and financial development measures, with total capital flows as openness indicator and under de facto foreign exchange rate regime

a. Liquid liabilities

residuals (GDP per capita growth as DV)

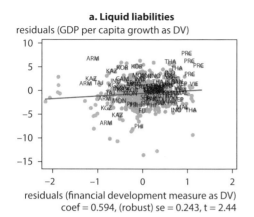

residuals (financial development measure as DV)
coef = 0.594, (robust) se = 0.243, t = 2.44

b. Private credit

residuals (GDP per capita growth as DV)

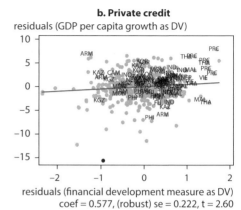

residuals (financial development measure as DV)
coef = 0.577, (robust) se = 0.222, t = 2.60

c. Stock market capitalization

residuals (GDP per capita growth as DV)

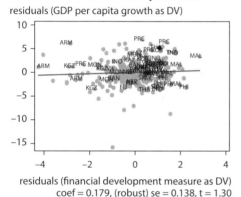

residuals (financial development measure as DV)
coef = 0.179, (robust) se = 0.138, t = 1.30

DV = dependent variable

ARM = Armenia; BAN = Bangladesh; CAM = Cambodia; FIJ = Fiji; IND = India; INO = Indonesia; KAZ = Kazakhstan; KGZ = Kyrgyz Republic; KOR = Republic of Korea; MAL = Malaysia; MON = Mongolia; NEP = Nepal; PAK = Pakistan; PHI = Philippines; PRC = People's Republic of China; SIN = Singapore; SRI = Sri Lanka; TAJ = Tajikistan; THA = Thailand; VIE = Viet Nam

Sources: Authors' estimates based on data from Haver Analytics (accessed on October 7, 2014); Reinhart and Rogoff (2004); Ilzetzki, Reinhart, and Rogoff (2011); and World Bank, *World Development Indicators* online database (accessed on September 15, 2014).

capita economic growth is higher in countries that are more open to trade. Inflation and government size tend to affect growth negatively, suggesting that macroeconomic instability and smaller private sector involvement in economic activities could be harmful for medium- to long-term growth. The findings are qualitatively similar to those of Estrada, Park, and Ramayandi

Table 2.1 Baseline results (financial development indicator: liquid liabilities)

	Ilzetzki, Reinhart, and Rogoff de facto indicator			IMF de jure indicator		
	Total capital flows	Lane and Milesi-Ferretti	Chinn and Ito	Total capital flows	Lane and Milesi-Ferretti	Chinn and Ito
Variable	(1)	(2)	(3)	(4)	(5)	(6)
Financial openness	2.146***	2.244***	-0.255	2.250***	2.475***	-0.171
	(0.714)	(0.849)	(0.309)	(0.696)	(0.844)	(0.295)
Liquid liabilities (percent of GDP)	2.723**	2.778*	3.033**	2.612**	2.854*	2.797*
	(1.360)	(1.534)	(1.484)	(1.296)	(1.485)	(1.434)
Initial real per capita GDP	-12.53***	-13.14***	-11.75***	-12.46***	-13.18***	-11.85***
	(1.679)	(1.528)	(1.502)	(1.688)	(1.527)	(1.461)
Government spending (percent of GDP)	-2.843***	-1.785*	-2.110**	-3.051***	-2.138**	-2.300**
	(1.003)	(0.984)	(0.921)	(0.992)	(0.992)	(0.899)
Inflation	-1.570***	-1.382***	-1.762***	-1.668***	-1.478***	-1.556***
	(0.484)	(0.427)	(0.415)	(0.433)	(0.390)	(0.375)
Years of schooling	-0.548	0.957	-1.766	0.334	1.581	-1.624
	(2.769)	(3.051)	(2.196)	(2.843)	(3.120)	(2.184)
Trade openness (percent of GDP)	1.601*	1.905**	2.922***	1.842**	2.003**	2.950***
	(0.888)	(0.955)	(0.811)	(0.924)	(1.003)	(0.830)
Managed exchange rate regime	0.344	0.173	-0.0321	-0.186	-0.137	-0.216
	(0.349)	(0.354)	(0.415)	(0.335)	(0.314)	(0.305)
Flexible exchange rate regime	-0.062	0.177	0.162	-0.710*	-0.705*	-0.711*
	(0.627)	(0.755)	(0.629)	(0.385)	(0.373)	(0.375)
Freefalling/dual exchange rate regime	0.545	0.276	0.629			
	(0.772)	(0.807)	(0.778)			

Period 2	-0.159	-1.117	-0.273	-0.237	-1.250*	-0.182
	(0.553)	(0.699)	(0.447)	(0.555)	(0.702)	(0.437)
Period 3	0.482	-0.703	0.738	0.340	-0.886	0.907
	(0.921)	(1.169)	(0.737)	(0.917)	(1.166)	(0.699)
Period 4	0.408	-0.607	1.273	0.237	-0.760	1.563*
	(1.289)	(1.472)	(0.977)	(1.288)	(1.488)	(0.930)
Period 5	-0.121	-1.087	1.173	-0.563	-1.514	1.481
	(1.755)	(1.934)	(1.214)	(1.760)	(1.965)	(1.152)
Period 6	1.247	0.264	2.755*	0.575	-0.421	2.926**
	(2.058)	(2.221)	(1.457)	(2.073)	(2.254)	(1.396)
Period 7	1.533	0.601	3.120*	0.778	-0.152	3.274*
	(2.323)	(2.486)	(1.668)	(2.369)	(2.564)	(1.657)
Number of observations	474	479	477	467	472	470
Number of groups	108	108	108	108	108	108
Number of instruments	72	72	72	71	71	71
Serial correlation test (p-value)	0.140	0.132	0.020	0.220	0.231	0.051
Hansen test of overidentifying restrictions (p-value)	0.194	0.153	0.183	0.202	0.075	0.177

Note: Robust standard errors in parentheses. * $p < 0.1$, ** $p < 0.05$, *** $p < 0.01$. Total capital flows, Lane and Milesi-Ferretti's measure of openness, liquid liabilities, initial real GDP per capita, inflation, and years of schooling are expressed in natural logarithms.

Source: Authors' estimates.

(2010), who apply a panel fixed effects approach. We find, however, that the year of schooling variable has an insignificant effect on medium- to long-term growth. This result is similar to the findings of Quinn and Toyoda (2008), who use the same indicator in their growth regressions using panel data. These results are robust over alternative regression specifications.

The level of financial development, as represented by the level of a country's liquid liabilities relative to its GDP, is positive and significant for all of the specifications reported in table 2.1 (also positive and significant are the relative size of private sector credit to GDP [see appendix table 2D.1] and the relative size of stock market capitalization to GDP [see appendix table 2E.1]). These findings suggest that our estimated parameters are robust. Our findings are very much in line with the empirical literature that suggests that financial sector development—as measured by financial depth—leads to higher growth. They also suggest that both the banking sector and capital markets are beneficial for growth. Regardless of its structure, overall financial development always contributes to economic growth. Therefore, deepening the financial sector should always be on the agenda of pro-growth policymakers.

The actual level of financial openness also appears to have direct positive and significant effects on economic growth. This finding holds for both the total volume and the Lane and Milesi-Ferretti measure of capital flows. In contrast, the de jure measure of capital flows by Chinn and Ito does not appear to have significant effects on growth. Although the evidence about the link between economic growth and financial openness is inconclusive, our results suggest that a country's commitment to an open domestic financial sector does not necessarily foster economic growth until it actually facilitates flows of capital to the economy.[3]

Our results also provide insights into whether different exchange rate regimes matter for growth. We use two definitions of exchange rate regimes, the de jure one based on the IMF classification and the de facto one constructed by Ilzetzki, Reinhart, and Rogoff. For our sample, the two definitions differ substantially. The IMF definition includes no observation of freefalling currency regimes; the Ilzetzki, Reinhart, and Rogoff definition does.

There is no robust evidence on the effect of exchange rate regimes on growth, although there are some indications of a consistent negative association between a flexible exchange rate regime under the IMF classification and growth. The negative and significant coefficients of the flexible exchange rate regime under the IMF classification may capture the fact that many developed countries in the sample, which tend to have lower growth rates, adopted flexible exchange rate regimes. It may also reflect the fact that the larger number of exchange rate fluctuations in countries adopting flexible exchange rate regimes may create more uncertainty, which reduces their growth potential.

---

3. See, for example, the discussion in Kose et al. (2009) and Bussière and Fratzscher (2008).

Evidence from Developing Countries

To produce our results on developing countries, we interacted the financial openness and financial development indicators with a dummy variable that takes a value of 1 for a developing country (non-OECD member) and added the interactions to our baseline specifications. We also added interactions between financial indicators and a developing Asia country dummy variable (that is, the Asian Development Bank's developing member countries) to see whether the financial variables' effect on growth in Asia was any different.

Once we add the interaction dummies for developing countries, the coefficients for the financial development indicator generally turn from positive to negative (table 2.2). In contrast, the coefficients on the interaction between financial development and the developing-country dummy are positive, significant, and robust across specifications. A similar trend is observed for the ratio of private credit to GDP but not for the ratio of stock market capitalization to GDP (appendix tables 2D.2 and 2E.2).[4] Positive effects of financial sector development on growth are particularly evident in developing countries, and the effects are even stronger in developing Asia. This finding reinforces the need to promote financial development to foster economic growth, particularly in light of the moderating trend of growth rate in the region since the global financial crisis.

The effect of financial openness on growth tends to be lower in developing countries than elsewhere, with some evidence of exceptions for developing Asian countries when financial development is represented by the ratio of private credit to GDP. Financial openness may bring about potential financial instability, which in turn may constrain economic growth. This interpretation is in line with the argument about the importance of a sound regulatory setup for the financial sector (Jeanne et al. 2014). Because mature regulatory systems in developing countries are less mature than in developed countries, more financial openness tends to be associated with more volatility, which elevates the risks for investments, particularly in light of possible sudden reversals of capital flows.[5]

Degree of Financial Development and Openness

To assess the effect of financial development and openness on growth, we extend our baseline specification in two ways. The first is by adding an in-

---

4. For the ratio of stock market capitalization to GDP, the coefficients for the financial sector development indicator remain positive and the coefficients on the interaction with the developing-country dummy turn negative. The implications of this finding are the opposite of the implications of the other financial development indicators.

5. Countries need to carefully weigh the degree of effectiveness of their options for regulating the financial sector. Rojas-Suarez (2008) argues that regulations that incentivize financial institutions to avoid excessive risk-taking activities may work better in containing the risks of increased volatility in capital flows than regulations that directly control financial aggregates, such as liquidity expansion and credit growth.

Table 2.2   Results on whether effects in developing countries and developing Asia differ (financial development indicator: liquid liabilities)

Variable	Ilzetzki, Reinhart, and Rogoff de facto indicator			IMF de jure indicator		
	Total capital flows	Lane and Milesi-Ferretti	Chinn and Ito	Total capital flows	Lane and Milesi-Ferretti	Chinn and Ito
	(1)	(2)	(3)	(4)	(5)	(6)
Financial openness	2.943**	3.936**	0.391	2.872**	4.076**	0.0467
	(1.210)	(1.911)	(0.888)	(1.160)	(1.877)	(0.820)
Liquid liabilities (percent of GDP)	−6.858**	−8.788**	−5.113	−7.144**	−9.242**	−5.849*
	(2.981)	(4.217)	(3.318)	(2.912)	(4.372)	(2.993)
Financial openness x developing country	−2.166*	−3.948**	−0.602	−2.029*	−4.054**	−0.211
	(1.203)	(1.780)	(0.831)	(1.166)	(1.758)	(0.768)
Liquid liabilities x developing country	5.492*	7.564*	3.807	5.894**	8.097*	4.792*
	(2.815)	(4.049)	(2.855)	(2.823)	(4.224)	(2.641)
Financial openness x developing Asia	0.872	1.901	0.570	0.817	2.127	0.660
	(1.044)	(1.671)	(0.495)	(1.043)	(1.745)	(0.489)
Liquid liabilities x developing Asia	5.033***	4.536***	4.638***	5.148***	4.650***	4.605***
	(1.510)	(1.561)	(1.143)	(1.617)	(1.696)	(1.230)
Number of instruments	76	76	76	75	75	75
Serial correlation test (p-value)	0.129	0.150	0.044	0.148	0.161	0.074
Hansen test of overidentifying restrictions (p-value)	0.591	0.238	0.260	0.382	0.283	0.331

Note: Robust standard errors in parentheses. * $p < 0.1$, ** $p < 0.05$, *** $p < 0.01$. Control variables, including period dummy variables indicated in table 2.1, are included in the estimation but not reported here. Total capital flows, Lane and Milesi-Ferretti's measure of openness, and liquid liabilities are expressed in natural logarithms.

Source: Authors' estimates.

teraction of the financial openness indicator with a dummy of higher degree of financial development, defined to take a value of 1 if a country's degree of financial development is higher than the sample median. The second applies a similar approach to investigate the reverse concept, whether the effect of financial development on growth differs for countries with greater financial openness.

The effect of financial openness on growth tends to be lower in countries with higher levels of financial development (table 2.3). The other specification also shows that the effect of financial development tends to be weaker in countries with a higher degree of financial openness. These two complementary observations suggest that a combination of a high degree of financial sector development and financial openness could potentially limit growth potential, because they may expose countries to greater financial market volatility and higher risks for capital flow reversals. These findings reinforce the need for sound financial sector regulation that could reduce the sector's volatility, particularly when the size of the domestic financial sector grows and its connection to the global financial system is enhanced.

Effect of the Exchange Rate Regime

To determine the effect of the exchange rate regime, we interacted dummy variables of different regimes with financial development variables. The results in table 2.4 do not robustly indicate a statistically significant effect of managed and floating exchange rate regime on economic growth. This result is consistent with that of Ghosh et al. (1997), who find that growth varies only slightly across regimes.

Table 2.4 also shows some evidence that the effect of financial openness on growth is milder when coupled with a more flexible exchange rate regime, particularly under the IMF exchange rate regime definition and the Lane and Milesi-Ferretti definition of capital openness. This finding suggests that a more flexible exchange rate regime may reduce the effectiveness of financial openness in promoting economic growth. Table 2.4 also shows some evidence that financial sector development has a stronger effect on growth under a managed floating exchange rate regime. As long as it is credible, such a regime may offer more certainty for investment decisions, which could eventually enhance growth.

Differences between FDI and Non-FDI

FDI flows are often thought to increase growth more than other types of capital flows, for at least two reasons. First, FDI tends to be long term and hence less volatile than other types of capital flow. Second, FDI may have a stronger positive association with domestic investment relative to other types of capital flows and hence be more effective in promoting economic growth (see, for example, Bosworth and Collins 1999 and Mody and Murshid 2005). This section

Table 2.3 Results on whether growth effects vary with level of financial development and openness (financial development indicator: liquid liabilities)

| | Ilzetzki, Reinhart, and Rogoff de facto indicator | | | | IMF de jure indicator | | | |
| | Total capital flows | | Lane and Milesi-Ferretti | | Total capital flows | | Lane and Milesi-Ferretti | |
Variable	(1)	(2)	(3)	(4)	(5)	(6)	(7)	(8)
Financial openness	2.459***	2.592***	2.012**	2.757***	2.452***	2.625***	2.109**	2.874***
	(0.858)	(0.845)	(0.852)	(0.977)	(0.839)	(0.791)	(0.838)	(0.968)
Liquid liabilities (percent of GDP)	3.221**	2.343*	3.788**	3.316**	2.992**	2.155	3.475**	3.166**
	(1.549)	(1.376)	(1.691)	(1.632)	(1.485)	(1.307)	(1.585)	(1.559)
High financial development interacted with financial openness level	-0.637**		-0.329***		-0.639**		-0.321***	
	(0.276)		(0.115)		(0.265)		(0.111)	
High financial openness interacted with financial development level		-0.288**		-0.354***		-0.302**		-0.379***
		(0.135)		(0.119)		(0.122)		(0.117)
Number of instruments	73	73	73	73	72	72	72	72
Serial correlation test (p-value)	0.093	0.043	0.074	0.033	0.160	0.070	0.136	0.055
Hansen test of overidentifying restrictions (p-value)	0.215	0.132	0.143	0.098	0.233	0.142	0.101	0.052

Note: Robust standard errors in parentheses. * $p < 0.1$, ** $p < 0.05$, *** $p < 0.01$. Control variables, including period dummy variables indicated in table 2.1, are included in the estimation but not reported here. Total capital flows, Lane and Milesi-Ferretti's measure of openness, and liquid liabilities are expressed in natural logarithms. Results of private credit and stock market capitalization as financial development indicators are shown in appendix tables 2D.3 and 2E.3, respectively.

Source: Authors' estimates.

Table 2.4 Results on whether foreign exchange rate regimes matter (financial development indicator: liquid liabilities)

Variable	Ilzetzki, Reinhart, and Rogoff de facto indicator			IMF de jure indicator		
	Total capital flows	Lane and Milesi-Ferretti	Chinn and Ito	Total capital flows	Lane and Milesi-Ferretti	Chinn and Ito
	(1)	(2)	(3)	(4)	(5)	(6)
Financial openness	2.071*	2.205**	−0.221	2.099**	3.149***	−0.129
	(1.213)	(0.983)	(0.431)	(0.848)	(0.951)	(0.357)
Liquid liabilities	2.504	2.096	2.155	2.203*	1.859	2.183
(percent of GDP)	(1.691)	(1.728)	(1.807)	(1.303)	(1.438)	(1.433)
Managed exchange	1.789	3.413	0.015	−0.936	1.603	−1.188
rate regime	(2.818)	(3.470)	(2.972)	(1.716)	(2.163)	(1.659)
Flexible exchange	−1.250	1.917	−4.136	0.316	3.624	−1.404
rate regime	(4.947)	(6.505)	(6.337)	(1.921)	(3.215)	(2.018)
Freefalling/dual	7.521	0.243	1.242			
exchange rate regime	(5.219)	(6.179)	(4.536)			
Financial openness x	−0.755	−0.875	−0.073	−0.254	−1.121**	0.146
managed exchange	(0.843)	(0.574)	(0.323)	(0.457)	(0.476)	(0.233)
rate regime						
Financial openness x	−0.632	−1.533	−0.082	−1.099*	−1.393*	−0.295
flexible exchange	(1.044)	(1.225)	(0.637)	(0.618)	(0.719)	(0.271)
rate regime						
Financial openness x	−2.189*	0.086	−0.500			
freefalling/dual	(1.134)	(1.010)	(0.550)			
exchange rate regime						
Liquid liabilities x	0.083	0.256	0.001	0.397	1.039**	0.240
managed exchange	(0.786)	(0.723)	(0.821)	(0.518)	(0.466)	(0.426)
rate regime						
Liquid liabilities x	0.784	1.496	1.134	0.464	0.686	0.231
flexible exchange	(1.273)	(1.398)	(1.778)	(0.522)	(0.608)	(0.546)
rate regime						
Liquid liabilities x	−0.722	−0.122	−0.357			
freefalling/dual	(1.342)	(1.247)	(1.360)			
exchange rate regime						
Number of instruments	78	78	78	75	75	75
Serial correlation test	0.191	0.153	0.029	0.143	0.158	0.028
(p-value)						
Hansen test of	0.198	0.121	0.142	0.203	0.096	0.164
overidentifying						
restrictions (p-value)						

Note: Robust standard errors in parentheses. * $p < 0.1$, ** $p < 0.05$, *** $p < 0.01$. Control variables, including period dummy variables indicated in table 2.1, are included in the estimation but not reported here. Total capital flows, Lane and Milesi-Ferretti's measure of openness, and liquid liabilities are expressed in natural logarithms. Results of private credit and stock market capitalization as financial development indicators are shown in appendix tables 2D.4 and 2E.4, respectively.

Source: Authors' estimates.

revisits the issue by including FDI and non-FDI components of financial flow separately in the growth regressions.

Table 2.5 shows that FDI is positively associated with per capita economic growth, in terms of both total flows and stocks based on the Lane and Milesi-Ferretti definition. In contrast, the non-FDI components of capital flow appear to be positive and significant in terms of stocks based only on the Lane and Milesi-Ferretti definition. This finding suggests that in general, both FDI and non-FDI components of capital flow tend to be positively associated with economic growth but that evidence of positive effects of non-FDI flows on growth is weak.

We also investigate whether these effects are different in developing countries. The results show some positive effect of the FDI component on growth and weak evidence of the effect of non-FDI components (table 2.6). Among developing countries, the effect of FDI on growth tends to be stronger in Asian countries.

Concluding Observations

This chapter examines the empirical relationship between financial development and economic growth. The relationship has been studied extensively in the past. Now is a particularly good time to revisit it for a number of reasons. First, the global financial crisis has provoked widespread hostility toward the financial industry and widespread skepticism about its benefits for growth. Although such concerns are less relevant for developing countries, where financial systems are generally much less developed, they nevertheless provide compelling grounds for taking another look at the effect of financial development on growth. Second, because their financial systems are underdeveloped, building up a sounder and more efficient financial system can increase growth in developing countries. Growth considerations are always important for developing countries, but they have gained significance in light of the global slowdown since the financial crisis. In the case of developing Asia, a gap between backward financial systems and dynamic real economies strengthens the case for financial development.

A large body of empirical literature examines the effects of financial development and financial openness on growth. Much of the evidence on financial development finds a positive and significant effect; the evidence on the effect of financial openness is much more mixed.

Our empirical analysis is rooted in and follows the literature but extends it in incremental ways. First, we update the sample period to 2011, to include a number of post–global crisis years. Second, we introduce several interaction variables, in order to investigate the impact of country characteristics on the finance-growth nexus. In particular, we are interested in whether the effect of financial development on growth differs in advanced versus developing countries. Third, we introduce additional variables, including the exchange rate regime, that might influence the finance-growth nexus. Fourth, we use

Table 2.5 Baseline results on impact of FDI and non-FDI on growth

| Variable | Ilzetzki, Reinhart, and Rogoff de facto indicator | | IMF de jure indicator | |
| | Total flows | Lane and Milesi-Ferretti | Total flows | Lane and Milesi-Ferretti |
	(1)	(2)	(3)	(4)
Foreign direct investment (FDI)	0.920**	1.288**	0.968***	1.410**
	(0.378)	(0.585)	(0.368)	(0.611)
Non-FDI	0.706	1.417**	0.879	1.510**
	(0.806)	(0.689)	(0.802)	(0.713)
Liquid liabilities (percent of GDP)	2.200	2.242	2.330*	2.551*
	(1.413)	(1.435)	(1.345)	(1.401)
Initial real per capita GDP	−11.49***	−13.10***	−11.50***	−13.31***
	(1.613)	(1.588)	(1.640)	(1.556)
Government spending (percent of GDP)	−2.784**	−1.570	−3.246***	−1.987*
	(1.102)	(1.008)	(1.080)	(1.020)
Inflation	−1.327***	−1.076**	−1.509***	−1.167***
	(0.447)	(0.444)	(0.427)	(0.420)
Years of schooling	−1.164	1.223	−0.517	1.721
	(2.933)	(3.068)	(3.258)	(3.081)
Trade openness (percent of GDP)	1.463*	1.171	1.713**	1.366
	(0.823)	(0.951)	(0.843)	(0.982)
Managed exchange rate regime	0.156	0.185	−0.182	−0.166
	(0.396)	(0.344)	(0.331)	(0.324)
Flexible exchange rate regime	0.422	0.381	−0.718*	−0.779**
	(0.727)	(0.752)	(0.425)	(0.369)
Freefalling/dual exchange rate regime	0.066	−0.027		
	(0.722)	(0.708)		
Period 2	−0.211	−1.032	−0.278	−1.128
	(0.538)	(0.703)	(0.564)	(0.704)
Period 3	0.405	−0.801	0.279	−0.920
	(0.941)	(1.184)	(0.993)	(1.171)
Period 4	0.207	−0.834	0.044	−0.944
	(1.345)	(1.509)	(1.434)	(1.500)
Period 5	−0.267	−1.499	−0.774	−1.877
	(1.890)	(1.990)	(2.040)	(1.965)
Period 6	1.265	−0.240	0.509	−0.874
	(2.223)	(2.266)	(2.377)	(2.224)
Period 7	1.423	−0.010	0.600	−0.735
	(2.450)	(2.499)	(2.646)	(2.490)
Number of observations	455	477	448	470
Number of groups	108	108	108	108
Number of instruments	84	84	83	83
Serial correlation test (p-value)	0.029	0.179	0.055	0.372
Hansen test of overidentifying restrictions (p-value)	0.169	0.222	0.157	0.232

Note: Robust standard errors in parentheses. * $p < 0.1$, ** $p < 0.05$, *** $p < 0.01$. Control variables, including period dummy variables indicated in table 2.1, are included in the estimation but not reported here. FDI, non-FDI, liquid liabilities, initial real GDP per capita, inflation, and years of schooling are expressed in natural logarithms.

Source: Authors' estimates.

Table 2.6 Results on whether effects of FDI and non-FDI on growth differ in developing countries and developing Asia

Variable	Ilzetzki, Reinhart, and Rogoff de facto indicator		IMF de jure indicator	
	Total flows	Lane and Milesi-Ferretti	Total flows	Lane and Milesi-Ferretti
	(1)	(2)	(3)	(4)
Foreign direct investment (FDI)	2.344**	0.698	2.006*	1.013
	(1.127)	(1.664)	(1.125)	(1.697)
Non-FDI	−1.852	2.740	−1.469	2.007
	(1.752)	(2.431)	(1.637)	(2.366)
FDI x developing country	−1.910*	0.128	−1.553	−0.209
	(1.116)	(1.451)	(1.103)	(1.484)
Non-FDI x developing country	1.887	−3.597	1.488	−2.868
	(1.767)	(2.292)	(1.661)	(2.246)
Liquid liabilities x developing country	1.127	3.411	1.392	3.931
	(2.819)	(3.762)	(2.631)	(3.568)
FDI x developing Asia	0.901**	1.128	0.887*	1.352*
	(0.447)	(0.735)	(0.461)	(0.780)
Non-FDI x developing Asia	0.227	0.823	0.254	0.821
	(0.740)	(1.357)	(0.772)	(1.343)
Liquid liabilities x developing Asia	3.561**	3.859**	3.690**	3.864**
	(1.490)	(1.576)	(1.585)	(1.641)
Number of instruments	78	78	77	77
Serial correlation test (p-value)	0.155	0.223	0.163	0.238
Hansen test of overidentifying restrictions (p-value)	0.161	0.08	0.092	0.056

Note: Robust standard errors in parentheses. * $p < 0.1$, ** $p < 0.05$, *** $p < 0.01$. Control variables, including period dummy variables indicated in table 2.1, are included in the estimation but not reported here. FDI and non-FDI, and liquid liabilities are expressed in natural logarithms.

Source: Authors' estimates.

generalized method of moments estimation to tackle potential simultaneity problems (the fact that causality from economic growth to both financial development and financial openness may run in both directions). For example, rapid growth of the middle class fuels demand for financial services, and a country's strong growth performance and prospects attract foreign capital inflows.

Most of our findings are consistent with earlier studies. Above all, we find that it is overall financial development, rather than the composition of the financial system, that matters for growth. The shares of both the banking sector and stock market activities relative to GDP are positively associated with economic growth. It is thus not the development of banks, stock markets, or specific components of the financial system but rather the development of the financial system as a whole that contributes to growth.

An important additional finding is that the positive effect of financial development on growth is stronger in developing countries than in advanced economies. The effect is especially pronounced in developing Asia. These findings are consistent with our earlier conjecture that post–global financial crisis concerns about excessive finance and a potentially harmful impact of finance on growth are more relevant for advanced economies than for developing countries. They also reinforce our hunch that developing Asia stands to reap large gains from correcting the imbalance between its financial backwardness and real-economy dynamism. The overriding policy implication of our evidence is that financial development can serve as an engine of growth for developing countries, especially in Asia. For middle- and upper-middle-income Asian countries with mature banking sectors, a top priority is to broaden and deepen capital markets, especially bond markets. For lower-income Asian countries, a higher priority is to develop and strengthen the banking sector.

Our evidence on the relationship between financial openness and economic growth is mixed, in line with the inconclusive evidence of previous studies. We find that actual financial openness has a positive and significant effect on economic growth but de jure measures do not. This finding implies that a commitment to open up the domestic financial system to foreign capital inflows does not benefit growth until it stimulates actual inflows. In addition, we find that the effect of financial openness on growth tends to be weaker in developing countries. One possible interpretation is that the financial systems of the advanced economies are better able to allocate foreign capital inflows to productive uses. The Asian crisis underlined the devastating consequences of the failure of developing-country financial systems to efficiently allocate foreign capital. But somewhat paradoxically, we also find that the effect of financial openness on growth tends to be weaker in financially more developed countries. This finding may reflect the facts that our measure of financial development is a quantitative indicator that captures the relative size of the financial sector and that the potential for capital inflows to destabilize the real economy is greater in a larger financial sector.

Our analysis fails to yield robust evidence about the direct effect of the exchange rate regime on economic growth. It does, however, find some evidence that a more flexible exchange rate regime can have a greater indirect effect on growth through both financial openness and financial development.

Although our empirical analysis reconfirms the positive and significant impact of financial development on growth, it is far from perfect. Future research can extend and strengthen the analytical framework in various ways. Perhaps the single biggest shortcoming of our analysis is the measures of financial development. Although our indices of financial development are standard indices widely used in earlier studies in the literature, they measure the relative size of the financial sector rather than its soundness and efficiency. It would be more illuminating to directly examine the relationship between a measure of the quality of finance and growth. Future research could devise a conceptually sound measure of quality of finance that is empirically testable (that is, for which data are available).

Finally, our analysis examines financial development and growth. Financial stability also has implications for growth. Financial instability in general and financial crisis in particular can adversely affect growth and even cause economic crises, as evident in the impact of the global and Asian financial crises. Future research could focus on this issue.

Appendix 2A Reclassification of classification codes

Table 2A.1 Reclassification of coarse classification codes of Ilzetzki, Reinhart, and Rogoff (2011)

Coarse classification	Reclassification
1 No separate legal tender	1 Fixed
1 Preannounced peg or currency board arrangement	1 Fixed
1 Preannounced horizontal band that is narrower than or equal to +/–2 percent	1 Fixed
1 De facto peg	1 Fixed
2 Preannounced crawling peg	2 Managed
2 Preannounced crawling band that is narrower than or equal to +/–2 percent	2 Managed
2 De facto crawling peg	2 Managed
2 De facto crawling band that is narrower than or equal to +/–2 percent	2 Managed
3 Preannounced crawling band that is wider than or equal to +/–2 percent	2 Managed
3 De facto crawling band that is narrower than or equal to +/–5 percent	2 Managed
3 Moving band that is narrower than or equal to +/–2 percent (that is, allows for both appreciation and depreciation over time)	2 Managed
3 Managed floating	2 Managed
4 Freely floating	3 Flexible
5 Freely falling	4 Freely falling/dual market
6 Dual market in which parallel market data are missing	4 Freely falling/dual market

Source: Authors' compilation based on Ilzetzki, Reinhart, and Rogoff (2011).

Appendix 2B Correlation coefficients of variables

Table 2B.1 Correlation coefficients of variables

	GDP per capita growth	Total capital flows	Openness indicator, Lane and Milesi-Ferretti	Openness indicator, Chinn and Ito	Liquid Liabilities (percent of GDP)	Private credit (percent of GDP)	Stock market capitalization (percent of GDP)	Initial GDP per capita
GDP per capita growth	1.00							
Total capital flows	0.09	1.00						
Openness indicator, Lane and Milesi-Ferretti	-0.02	0.70	1.00					
Openness indicator, Chinn and Ito	0.09	0.48	0.49	1.00				
Liquid liabilities (percent of GDP)	0.17	0.26	0.36	0.37	1.00			
Private credit (percent of GDP)	0.13	0.33	0.38	0.45	0.79	1.00		
Stock market capitalization (percent of GDP)	0.02	0.35	0.43	0.32	0.61	0.63	1.00	
Initial GDP per capita	-0.02	0.37	0.35	0.55	0.56	0.69	0.55	1.00

(continued on next page)

Table 2B.1 Correlation coefficients of variables *(continued)*

	GDP per capita growth	Total capital flows	Openness indicator, Lane and Milesi-Ferretti	Openness indicator, Chinn and Ito	Liquid liabilities (percent of GDP)	Private credit (percent of GDP)	Stock market capitalization (percent of GDP)	Initial GDP per capita	Years of schooling	Government spending (percent of GDP)	Inflation	Trade openness (percent of GDP)	Fixed exchange rate regime: Ilzetzki, Reinhart, and Rogoff de facto indicator	Managed exchange rate regime: Ilzetzki, Reinhart, and Rogoff de facto indicator	Flexible exchange rate regime: Ilzetzki, Reinhart, and Rogoff de facto indicator	Freefalling/dual exchange rate regime: Ilzetzki, Reinhart, and Rogoff de facto indicator	Fixed exchange rate regime: IMF de jure	Managed exchange rate regime: IMF de jure	Flexible exchange rate regime: IMF de jure
Years of schooling	0.17	0.40	0.31	0.48	0.43	0.49	0.35	0.69	1.00										
Government spending (percent of GDP)	−0.13	0.22	0.32	0.22	0.32	0.31	0.30	0.44	0.28	1.00									
Inflation	−0.25	−0.31	−0.41	−0.43	−0.48	−0.43	−0.50	−0.31	−0.17	−0.18	1.00								
Trade openness (percent of GDP)	0.10	0.48	0.56	0.19	0.14	0.14	0.05	0.08	0.24	0.24	−0.21	1.00							
Fixed exchange rate regime: Ilzetzki, Reinhart, and Rogoff de facto indicator	−0.08	0.26	0.25	0.07	−0.01	0.07	0.18	−0.02	−0.17	0.11	−0.29	0.26	1.00						
Managed exchange rate regime: Ilzetzki, Reinhart, and Rogoff de facto indicator	0.21	−0.20	−0.16	−0.02	0.11	0.03	−0.14	−0.01	0.09	−0.10	−0.04	−0.05	−0.74	1.00					

Flexible exchange rate regime: Ilzetzki, Reinhart, and Rogoff de facto indicator	−0.02	0.02	0.04	0.17	0.16	0.13	0.23	0.16	0.13	0.05	−0.12	−0.22	−0.16	−0.24	1.00				
Freefalling/dual exchange rate regime: Ilzetzki, Reinhart, and Rogoff de facto indicator	−0.22	−0.10	−0.16	−0.19	−0.30	−0.27	−0.25	−0.08	0.02	−0.05	0.61	−0.16	−0.22	−0.34	−0.07	1.00			
Fixed exchange rate regime: IMF de jure	−0.18	−0.01	0.02	−0.24	−0.18	−0.17	−0.01	−0.20	−0.30	0.10	0.02	0.14	0.40	−0.26	−0.13	−0.10	1.00		
Managed exchange rate regime: IMF de jure	0.19	−0.02	−0.04	0.05	0.11	0.11	−0.03	0.10	0.12	−0.06	−0.01	−0.02	−0.18	0.21	−0.10	0.00	−0.63	1.00	
Flexible exchange rate regime: IMF de jure	−0.01	0.04	0.02	0.23	0.09	0.07	0.04	0.13	0.23	−0.06	−0.01	−0.15	−0.27	0.08	0.27	0.10	−0.47	−0.39	1.00

Source: Authors' estimates.

Appendix 2C List of economies in the sample

Developing Asia (20)

1	Armenia	11	Malaysia
2	Bangladesh	12	Mongolia
3	Cambodia	13	Nepal
4	People's Republic of China	14	Pakistan
5	Fiji	15	Philippines
6	India	16	Singapore
7	Indonesia	17	Sri Lanka
8	Kazakhstan	18	Tajikistan
9	Republic of Korea	19	Thailand
10	Kyrgyz Republic	20	Viet Nam

Other economies (88)

1	Albania	26	Finland
2	Australia	27	France
3	Austria	28	Gabon
4	Bahrain	29	Gambia, The
5	Belgium	30	Germany
6	Benin	31	Ghana
7	Bolivia	32	Greece
8	Botswana	33	Guatemala
9	Brazil	34	Guyana
10	Bulgaria	35	Honduras
11	Burundi	36	Hungary
12	Cameroon	37	Iran, Islamic Republic of
13	Canada	38	Ireland
14	Colombia	39	Israel
15	Congo, Republic of	40	Italy
16	Costa Rica	41	Japan
17	Côte d'Ivoire	42	Jordan
18	Croatia	43	Kenya
19	Cyprus	44	Kuwait
20	Czech Republic	45	Latvia
21	Denmark	46	Lesotho
22	Dominican Republic	47	Liberia
23	Ecuador	48	Lithuania
24	Egypt, Arab Republic of	49	Malawi
25	El Salvador	50	Mali

51	Mexico	70	South Africa
52	Moldova	71	Spain
53	Morocco	72	Sudan
54	Mozambique	73	Swaziland
55	Namibia	74	Sweden
56	Netherlands	75	Switzerland
57	New Zealand	76	Syrian Arab Republic
58	Nicaragua	77	Tanzania
59	Niger	78	Togo
60	Norway	79	Trinidad and Tobago
61	Panama	80	Tunisia
62	Paraguay	81	Turkey
63	Peru	82	Uganda
64	Poland	83	Ukraine
65	Portugal	84	United Kingdom
66	Russian Federation	85	United States
67	Saudi Arabia	86	Uruguay
68	Senegal	87	Zambia
69	Slovenia	88	Zimbabwe

Source: Authors.

Appendix 2D Regression results for private credit as financial development indicator

Table 2D.1 Baseline results (financial development indicator: private credit)

Variable	Ilzetzki, Reinhart, and Rogoff de facto indicator			IMF de jure indicator		
	Total capital flows	Lane and Milesi-Ferretti	Chinn and Ito	Total flows	Lane and Milesi-Ferretti	Chinn and Ito
	(1)	(2)	(3)	(4)	(5)	(6)
Financial openness	1.780**	2.146**	−0.221	1.823**	2.293**	−0.187
	(0.727)	(0.942)	(0.330)	(0.760)	(0.951)	(0.310)
Private credit (percent of GDP)	1.509*	1.507*	1.608**	1.525*	1.748**	1.745**
	(0.821)	(0.774)	(0.715)	(0.837)	(0.832)	(0.729)
Initial real per capita GDP	−12.36***	−12.90***	−11.79***	−12.20***	−13.02***	−11.87***
	(1.823)	(1.582)	(1.642)	(1.811)	(1.608)	(1.631)
Government spending (percent of GDP)	−2.608**	−1.700*	−1.840*	−2.875***	−2.073**	−2.162**
	(0.999)	(0.992)	(0.944)	(0.959)	(0.968)	(0.911)
Inflation	−1.696***	−1.592***	−1.747***	−1.931***	−1.760***	−1.785***
	(0.506)	(0.437)	(0.445)	(0.437)	(0.362)	(0.369)
Years of schooling	0.165	2.118	−0.854	1.589	3.062	−0.081
	(2.859)	(3.396)	(2.234)	(2.950)	(3.486)	(2.294)
Trade openness (percent of GDP)	1.510*	1.646*	2.655***	1.834**	1.717*	2.809***
	(0.859)	(0.960)	(0.850)	(0.875)	(0.973)	(0.855)
Managed exchange rate regime	0.486*	0.234	0.125	−0.0324	−0.124	−0.180
	(0.289)	(0.325)	(0.320)	(0.334)	(0.301)	(0.299)
Flexible exchange rate regime	−0.278	−0.042	−0.074	−0.688*	−0.693*	−0.658*
	(0.587)	(0.694)	(0.591)	(0.371)	(0.351)	(0.363)
Freefalling/dual exchange rate regime	0.375	0.050	0.176			
	(0.859)	(0.874)	(0.853)			

(continued on next page)

Table 2D.1 Baseline results (financial development indicator: private credit) *(continued)*

Variable	Ilzetzki, Reinhart, and Rogoff de facto indicator			IMF de jure indicator		
	Total capital flows	Lane and Milesi-Ferretti	Chinn and Ito	Total flows	Lane and Milesi-Ferretti	Chinn and Ito
	(1)	(2)	(3)	(4)	(5)	(6)
Period 2	−0.241	−1.202	−0.309	−0.448	−1.380*	−0.392
	(0.562)	(0.833)	(0.475)	(0.551)	(0.828)	(0.451)
Period 3	0.346	−0.935	0.618	−0.010	−1.203	0.495
	(0.972)	(1.400)	(0.796)	(0.941)	(1.386)	(0.756)
Period 4	0.272	−0.955	1.117	−0.208	−1.253	0.986
	(1.401)	(1.774)	(1.057)	(1.370)	(1.758)	(1.010)
Period 5	−0.305	−1.675	0.942	−1.192	−2.264	0.629
	(2.008)	(2.425)	(1.401)	(1.971)	(2.399)	(1.336)
Period 6	1.093	−0.330	2.560	−0.073	−1.191	2.027
	(2.318)	(2.772)	(1.642)	(2.293)	(2.757)	(1.587)
Period 7	1.515	0.091	3.060	0.217	−0.876	2.435
	(2.563)	(3.053)	(1.850)	(2.564)	(3.083)	(1.843)
Number of observations	476	481	479	469	474	472
Number of groups	108	108	108	108	108	108
Number of instruments	72	72	72	71	71	71
Serial correlation test (*p*-value)	0.270	0.243	0.050	0.340	0.370	0.092
Hansen test of overidentifying restrictions (*p*-value)	0.077	0.112	0.116	0.059	0.078	0.170

Note: Robust standard errors in parentheses. * $p < 0.1$, ** $p < 0.05$, *** $p < 0.01$. Total capital flows, Lane and Milesi-Ferretti's measure of openness, private credit, initial real GDP per capita, inflation, and years of schooling are expressed in natural logarithms.

Source: Authors' estimates.

Table 2D.2 Results on whether effects in developing countries and developing Asia differ (financial development indicator: private credit)

Variable	Ilzetzki, Reinhart, and Rogoff de facto indicator			IMF de jure indicator		
	Total capital flows	Lane and Milesi-Ferretti	Chinn and Ito	Total capital flows	Lane and Milesi-Ferretti	Chinn and Ito
	(1)	(2)	(3)	(4)	(5)	(6)
Financial openness	2.522**	3.358	0.591	2.810**	3.350	0.561
	(1.226)	(2.276)	(0.767)	(1.288)	(2.278)	(0.801)
Private credit (percent of GDP)	−8.069***	−7.565**	−3.653	−8.208***	−7.687**	−3.573
	(2.845)	(3.058)	(2.509)	(2.814)	(3.074)	(2.473)
Financial openness × developing country	−2.141*	−3.955*	−0.874	−2.301*	−3.927*	−0.833
	(1.212)	(2.076)	(0.761)	(1.294)	(2.113)	(0.814)
Private credit × developing country	8.243***	8.135***	3.959*	8.326***	8.242***	3.891*
	(2.704)	(3.054)	(2.314)	(2.674)	(3.073)	(2.293)
Financial openness × developing Asia	2.409**	3.571**	0.995*	2.358**	3.745**	1.065*
	(1.118)	(1.504)	(0.565)	(1.139)	(1.563)	(0.572)
Private credit × developing Asia	0.970	0.867	1.763**	1.065	0.863	1.760**
	(1.056)	(0.897)	(0.826)	(1.056)	(0.914)	(0.815)
Number of instruments	76	76	76	75	75	75
Serial correlation test (p-value)	0.139	0.124	0.062	0.175	0.169	0.100
Hansen test of overidentifying restrictions (p-value)	0.248	0.080	0.081	0.295	0.070	0.102

Note: Robust standard errors in parentheses. * $p < 0.1$, ** $p < 0.05$, *** $p < 0.01$. Control variables, including period dummy variables indicated in table 2.1, are included in the estimation but not reported here. Total capital flows, Lane and Milesi-Ferretti's measure of openness, and private credit are expressed in natural logarithms.

Source: Authors' estimates.

Table 2D.3   Results on whether growth effects vary with level of financial development and openness (financial development indicator: private credit)

Variable	Ilzetzki, Reinhart, and Rogoff de facto indicator				IMF de jure indicator			
	Total capital flows		Lane and Milesi-Ferretti		Total capital flows		Lane and Milesi-Ferretti	
	(1)	(2)	(3)	(4)	(1)	(2)	(3)	(4)
Financial openness	2.059**	2.218**	1.878**	2.576**	1.975**	2.116**	1.949**	2.651**
	(0.792)	(0.906)	(0.919)	(1.090)	(0.776)	(0.890)	(0.944)	(1.103)
Private credit (percent of GDP)	1.828**	1.661**	2.072**	1.942**	1.776**	1.589**	2.141**	1.966**
	(0.864)	(0.809)	(0.878)	(0.782)	(0.848)	(0.787)	(0.885)	(0.791)
High financial development interacted with financial openness level	−0.468**		−0.192		−0.456*		−0.196	
	(0.234)		(0.119)		(0.245)		(0.121)	
High financial openness interacted with financial development level		−0.274*		−0.365***		−0.271*		−0.390***
		(0.144)		(0.131)		(0.137)		(0.129)
Number of instruments	73	73	73	73	72	72	72	72
Serial correlation test (p-value)	0.071	0.062	0.079	0.042	0.102	0.081	0.139	0.068
Hansen test of overidentifying restrictions (p-value)	0.092	0.044	0.094	0.040	0.090	0.056	0.171	0.066

Note: Robust standard errors in parentheses. * $p < 0.1$, ** $p < 0.05$, *** $p < 0.01$. Control variables, including period dummy variables indicated in table 2.1, are included in the estimation but not reported here. Total capital flows, Lane and Milesi-Ferretti's measure of openness, and private credit are expressed in natural logarithms.

Source: Authors' estimates.

Table 2D.4   Results on whether foreign exchange rate regimes matter (financial development indicator: private credit)

	Ilzetzki, Reinhart, and Rogoff de facto			IMF de jure		
	Total capital flows	Lane and Milesi-Ferretti	Chinn and Ito	Total capital flows	Lane and Milesi-Ferretti	Chinn and Ito
Variable	(1)	(2)	(3)	(4)	(5)	(6)
Financial openness	1.743	2.411**	−0.158	1.622*	3.142***	−0.0576
	(1.359)	(1.191)	(0.519)	(0.906)	(1.071)	(0.399)
Private credit (percent of GDP)	0.356	0.163	−0.073	1.050	0.663	0.753
	(0.878)	(0.984)	(0.875)	(0.901)	(1.023)	(0.824)
Managed exchange rate regime	0.378	3.768	−2.583	−1.085	1.711	−3.113**
	(2.236)	(2.967)	(2.783)	(1.376)	(1.764)	(1.491)
Flexible exchange rate regime	−1.482	3.704	−5.782	−0.077	4.248	−2.937*
	(3.153)	(5.370)	(4.027)	(1.486)	(2.728)	(1.578)
Freefalling/dual exchange rate regime	0.669	−4.275	−5.383			
	(3.198)	(5.300)	(3.696)			
Financial openness × managed exchange rate regime	−0.709	−1.307*	−0.293	−0.132	−1.215**	−0.043
	(0.978)	(0.702)	(0.434)	(0.496)	(0.474)	(0.259)
Financial openness × flexible exchange rate regime	−0.503	−1.705	−0.666	−1.072*	−1.679**	−0.517*
	(0.968)	(1.349)	(0.829)	(0.633)	(0.693)	(0.292)
Financial openness × freefalling/dual exchange rate regime	−1.838	−0.058	−0.482			
	(1.138)	(1.175)	(0.571)			
Private credit × managed exchange rate regime	0.464	0.743	0.748	0.404	1.182**	0.814**
	(0.834)	(0.742)	(0.791)	(0.525)	(0.464)	(0.401)
Private credit × flexible exchange rate regime	0.817	1.371	1.775	0.587	0.933*	0.714
	(0.930)	(0.961)	(1.265)	(0.535)	(0.503)	(0.463)
Private credit × freefalling/dual exchange rate regime	1.240	1.613	1.779			
	(1.275)	(1.233)	(1.314)			
Number of instruments	78	78	78	75	75	75
Serial correlation test (p-value)	0.402	0.415	0.104	0.199	0.232	0.061
Hansen test of overidentifying restrictions (p-value)	0.047	0.114	0.116	0.060	0.079	0.195

Note: Robust standard errors in parentheses. * $p < 0.1$, ** $p < 0.05$, *** $p < 0.01$. Control variables, including period dummy variables indicated in table 2.1, are included in the estimation but not reported here. Total capital flows, Lane and Milesi-Ferretti's measure of openness, and private credit are expressed in natural logarithms.

Source: Authors' estimates.

Appendix 2E Regression results for stock market capitalization as financial development indicator

Table 2E.1 Baseline results (financial development indicator: stock market capitalization)

	Ilzetzki, Reinhart, and Rogoff de facto indicator			IMF de jure indicator		
	Total capital flows	Lane and Milesi-Ferretti	Chinn and Ito	Total capital flows	Lane and Milesi-Ferretti	Chinn and Ito
Variable	(1)	(2)	(3)	(4)	(5)	(6)
Financial openness	0.675	2.021*	−0.972**	0.857	2.224*	−1.015**
	(0.852)	(1.157)	(0.437)	(0.825)	(1.194)	(0.425)
Stock market capitalization (percent of GDP)	2.799***	2.337***	3.151***	2.746***	2.331***	3.113***
	(0.522)	(0.413)	(0.535)	(0.524)	(0.385)	(0.537)
Initial real per capita GDP	−12.70***	−12.46***	−12.31***	−12.54***	−12.28***	−12.18***
	(1.641)	(1.441)	(1.509)	(1.673)	(1.426)	(1.506)
Government spending (percent of GDP)	−1.027	−1.298	−0.616	−1.426	−1.627	−0.659
	(1.394)	(1.295)	(1.415)	(1.444)	(1.333)	(1.400)
Inflation	−0.278	−0.655*	−0.881	−0.386	−0.799**	−0.813
	(0.434)	(0.387)	(0.591)	(0.434)	(0.396)	(0.566)
Years of schooling	−2.461	3.162	−5.159	−1.516	4.140	−4.656
	(3.997)	(4.706)	(3.764)	(4.105)	(4.966)	(3.853)
Trade openness (percent of GDP)	−0.864	−1.174	−0.379	−0.890	−1.202	−0.478
	(1.395)	(1.434)	(1.333)	(1.428)	(1.408)	(1.359)
Managed exchange rate regime	0.427	0.479	0.311	0.316	0.415	0.481
	(0.422)	(0.404)	(0.425)	(0.399)	(0.396)	(0.379)
Flexible exchange rate regime	−0.860	−0.487	0.010	0.285	0.323	0.516
	(0.931)	(0.985)	(0.897)	(0.460)	(0.428)	(0.477)
Freefalling/dual exchange rate regime	0.304	0.307	0.721			
	(0.966)	(0.886)	(1.020)			

(continued on next page)

Table 2E.1 Baseline results (financial development indicator: stock market capitalization) (continued)

| | Ilzetzki, Reinhart, and Rogoff de facto indicator | | | IMF de jure indicator | | |
| | Total capital flows | Lane and Milesi-Ferretti | Chinn and Ito | Total capital flows | Lane and Milesi-Ferretti | Chinn and Ito |
Variable	(1)	(2)	(3)	(4)	(5)	(6)
Period 3	-0.521	-0.658	-2.927***	-1.103	1.009	-0.037
	(0.696)	(1.474)	(1.042)	(1.763)	(2.105)	(0.493)
Period 4	-0.421	-1.402	-2.676***	-1.865	-0.157	
	(1.160)	(0.875)	(0.649)	(1.226)	(1.537)	
Period 5	1.345	-0.114	-0.645*	-2.012***	-1.221	0.123
	(1.520)	(0.472)	(0.375)	(0.736)	(0.872)	(0.866)
Period 6	1.753			-0.314	-0.014	2.165*
	(1.795)			(0.407)	(0.471)	(1.154)
Period 7		0.254	-2.973**			2.737**
		(1.972)	(1.329)			(1.344)
Number of observations	271	273	272	266	268	267
Number of groups	86	86	86	86	86	86
Number of instruments	60	60	60	59	59	59
Serial correlation test (p-value)	0.384	0.444	0.366	0.401	0.531	0.339
Hansen test of overidentifying restrictions (p-value)	0.116	0.042	0.131	0.901	0.089	0.141

Note: Robust standard errors in parentheses. * $p < 0.1$, ** $p < 0.05$, *** $p < 0.01$. Total capital flows, Lane and Milesi-Ferretti's measure of openness, stock market capitalization, initial real GDP per capita, inflation, and years of schooling are expressed in natural logarithms.

Source: Authors' estimates.

Table 2E.2 Results on whether effects in developing countries and developing Asia differ (financial development indicator: stock market capitalization)

	Ilzetzki, Reinhart, and Rogoff de facto indicator			IMF de jure indicator		
	Total capital flows	Lane and Milesi-Ferretti	Chinn and Ito	Total capital flows	Lane and Milesi-Ferretti	Chinn and Ito
Variable	(1)	(2)	(3)	(4)	(5)	(6)
Financial openness	−2.082	−1.670	0.654	−2.169	−0.657	0.123
	(1.990)	(1.949)	(0.975)	(1.742)	(1.774)	(0.883)
Stock market capitalization (percent of GDP)	5.146***	4.759***	3.290***	5.237***	4.670***	3.839***
	(1.753)	(1.236)	(1.228)	(1.654)	(1.175)	(1.117)
Financial openness × developing country	2.645	2.125	−0.720	2.740	1.026	−0.333
	(1.943)	(1.744)	(0.974)	(1.696)	(1.549)	(0.883)
Stock market capitalization × developing country	−4.157**	−3.739***	−2.143	−4.299**	−3.559***	−2.735**
	(1.749)	(1.224)	(1.323)	(1.647)	(1.143)	(1.190)
Financial openness × developing Asia	0.654	3.003*	0.107	0.799	3.292**	0.279
	(1.118)	(1.708)	(0.712)	(1.061)	(1.647)	(0.686)
Stock market capitalization × developing Asia	1.733***	1.639***	1.866***	1.772***	1.615***	1.871***
	(0.562)	(0.489)	(0.554)	(0.541)	(0.488)	(0.525)
Number of instruments	64	64	64	63	63	63
Serial correlation test (p-value)	0.171	0.474	0.800	0.176	0.653	0.713
Hansen test of overidentifying restrictions (p-value)	0.218	0.342	0.299	0.395	0.430	0.244

Note: Robust standard errors in parentheses. * $p < 0.1$, ** $p < 0.05$, *** $p < 0.01$. Control variables, including period dummy variables indicated in table 2.1, are included in the estimation but not reported here. Total capital flows, Lane and Milesi-Ferretti's measure of openness, and stock market capitalization are expressed in natural logarithms.

Source: Authors' estimates.

Table 2E.3 Results on whether growth effects vary with level of financial development and openness (financial development indicator: stock market capitalization)

Variable	Ilzetzki, Reinhart, and Rogoff de facto indicator				IMF de jure indicator			
	Total capital flows		Lane and Milesi-Ferretti		Total capital flows		Lane and Milesi-Ferretti	
	(1)	(2)	(3)	(4)	(1)	(2)	(3)	(4)
Financial openness	1.205	0.921	1.693	2.579**	1.260	0.733	1.998*	2.824**
	(0.946)	(1.063)	(1.181)	(1.293)	(0.963)	(0.963)	(1.187)	(1.289)
Stock market capitalization (percent of GDP)	2.784***	2.879***	2.485***	2.694***	2.763***	2.812***	2.440***	2.621***
	(0.574)	(0.522)	(0.472)	(0.431)	(0.571)	(0.526)	(0.438)	(0.384)
High financial development interacted with financial openness level	-0.437**		-0.221**		-0.473**		-0.235***	
	(0.210)		(0.087)		(0.211)		(0.0832)	
High financial openness interacted with financial development level		-0.357		-0.439***		-0.323		-0.455***
		(0.217)		(0.151)		(0.200)		(0.147)
Number of instruments	61	61	61	61	60	60	60	60
Serial correlation test (p-value)	0.069	0.294	0.184	0.234	0.086	0.337	0.252	0.279
Hansen test of overidentifying restrictions (p-value)	0.067	0.068	0.098	0.086	0.071	0.065	0.126	0.084

Note: Robust standard errors in parentheses. * $p < 0.1$, ** $p < 0.05$, *** $p < 0.01$. Control variables, including period dummy variables indicated in table 2.1, are included in the estimation but not reported here. Total capital flows, Lane and Milesi-Ferretti's measure of openness, and stock market capitalization are expressed in natural logarithms.

Source: Authors' estimates.

Table 2E.4 Results on whether foreign exchange rate regimes matter (financial development indicator: stock market capitalization)

Variable	Ilzetzki, Reinhart, and Rogoff de facto indicator			IMF de jure indicator		
	Total capital flows	Lane and Milesi-Ferretti	Chinn and Ito	Total capital flows	Lane and Milesi-Ferretti	Chinn and Ito
	(1)	(2)	(3)	(4)	(5)	(6)
Financial openness	1.562	1.261	−0.617	−0.497	2.050	−1.239***
	(1.141)	(1.452)	(0.502)	(1.185)	(1.402)	(0.429)
Stock market capitalization (percent of GDP)	1.485*	1.341*	2.252***	3.028***	2.400***	3.516***
	(0.796)	(0.792)	(0.752)	(0.530)	(0.439)	(0.656)
Managed exchange rate regime	0.556	2.227	0.248	−0.377	1.882	2.579*
	(2.414)	(3.311)	(2.095)	(2.181)	(2.082)	(1.437)
Flexible exchange rate regime	−1.139	−0.305	−2.098	2.573	3.921	3.801**
	(3.348)	(5.626)	(3.142)	(2.167)	(3.234)	(1.699)
Freefalling/dual exchange rate regime	2.732	−4.519	1.218	−2.200		
	(3.554)	(9.062)	(2.433)	(1.514)		
Financial openness × managed exchange rate regime	−0.613	−0.792	0.118	0.776	−0.268	0.837***
	(0.736)	(0.613)	(0.411)	(0.772)	(0.466)	(0.248)
Financial openness × flexible exchange rate regime	−1.054	−0.626	1.195**	0.0147	−0.415	0.486
	(1.090)	(1.500)	(0.502)	(0.873)	(0.720)	(0.307)
Financial openness × freefalling/dual exchange rate regime	−1.527	0.755	−0.435			
	(1.199)	(1.840)	(0.609)			
Stock market capitalization × managed exchange rate regime	0.419	0.578	−0.041	−0.465	0.007	−0.860*
	(0.687)	(0.631)	(0.685)	(0.385)	(0.365)	(0.438)
Stock market capitalization × flexible exchange rate regime	0.780	0.588	0.069	−0.870*	−0.506	−1.244**
	(0.837)	(0.901)	(0.904)	(0.522)	(0.459)	(0.516)
Stock market capitalization × freefalling/dual exchange rate regime	0.003	0.195	−0.795			
	(0.756)	(0.659)	(0.820)			
Number of instruments	66	66	66	63	63	63
Serial correlation test (p-value)	0.567	0.404	0.272	0.311	0.575	0.350
Hansen test of overidentifying restrictions (p-value)	0.059	0.043	0.108	0.056	0.072	0.319

Note: Robust standard errors in parentheses. * $p < 0.1$, ** $p < 0.05$, *** $p < 0.01$. Control variables, including period dummy variables indicated in table 2.1, are included in the estimation but not reported here. Total capital flows, Lane and Milesi-Ferretti's measure of openness, and stock market capitalization are expressed in natural logarithms.

Source: Authors' estimates.

References

Alesina, Alberto F., Vittorio Grilli, and Gian Maria Milesi-Ferretti. 1994. The Political Economy of Capital Controls. In *Capital Mobility: The Impact on Consumption, Investment, and Growth*, ed. L. Leiderman and A. Razin. New York: Cambridge University Press.

Arellano, Manuel, and Stephen Bond. 1991. Some Tests of Specification for Panel Data: Monte Carlo Evidence and an Application to Employment Equations. *Review of Economic Studies* 58, no. 2: 277–97.

Barro, Robert, and Jong-Wha Lee. 2010. A New Data Set of Educational Attainment in the World, 1950–2010. *Journal of Development Economics* 104: 184–98.

Bartolini, Leonardo, and Allan Drazen. 1997. When Liberal Policies Reflect External Shocks, What Do We Learn? *Journal of International Economics* 42, no. 3–4: 249–73.

Beck, Thorsten, Asli Demirgüç-Kunt, and Ross Levine. 2000. A New Database on Financial Development and Structure. *World Bank Economic Review* 14: 597–605.

Beck, Thorsten, Asli Demirgüç-Kunt, and Ross Levine. 2009. *Financial Institutions and Markets across Countries and over Time: Data and Analysis*. World Bank Policy Research Working Paper 4943. Washington: World Bank.

Beck, Thorsten, and Ross Levine. 2004. Stock Markets, Banks and Growth: Panel Evidence. *Journal of Banking and Finance* 28, no. 3: 423–42.

Beck, Thorsten, Ross Levine, and Norman Loayza. 2000. Finance and Sources of Growth. *Journal of Financial Economics* 58: 261–300.

Bekaert, Geert, Campbell R. Harvey, and Christian Lundblad. 2005. Does Financial Liberalization Spur Growth? *Journal of Financial Economics* 77, no. 1: 3–55.

Bosworth, Barry P., and Susan M. Collins. 1999. Capital Flows to Developing Economies: Implications for Saving and Investment. *Brookings Papers on Economic Activity* 1. Washington: Brookings Institution.

Brune, Nancy E., and Alexandra Guisinger. 2006. *Myth or Reality? The Diffusion of Financial Liberalization in Developing Countries*. Available at ncgg.princeton.edu/IPES/2006/papers/brune_guisinger_F900_1.pdf (accessed on October 15, 2014).

Bussière, Matthieu, and Marcel Fratzscher. 2008. Financial Openness and Growth: Short-run Gain, Long-run Pain? *Review of International Economics* 16, no. 1: 69–95.

Chinn, Menzie D., and Hiro Ito. 2008. A New Measure of Financial Openness. *Journal of Comparative Policy Analysis* 10: 309–22.

Čihák, Martin, Asli Demirgüç-Kunt, Eric Feyen, and Ross Levine. 2012. *Benchmarking Financial Systems around the World*. World Bank Policy Research Working Paper 6175. Washington: World Bank.

Demirgüç-Kunt, Asli, and Ross Levine. 2008. *Finance, Financial Sector Policies, and Long-Run Growth*. World Bank Policy Research Working Paper 4469. Washington: World Bank.

Edison, Hali J., Michael W. Klein, Luca Antonio Ricci, and Torsten Sløk. 2004. Capital Account Liberalization and Economic Performance: Survey and Synthesis. *IMF Staff Papers* 51, no. 2: 22–56.

Edison, Hali J., Ross Levine, Luca Ricci, and T. Sløk. 2002. International Financial Integration and Economic Growth. *Journal of International Money and Finance* 21, no. 6: 749–76.

Estrada, Gemma, Donghyun Park, and Arief Ramayandi. 2010. *Financial Development and Economic Growth in Developing Asia*. ADB Economics Working Paper Series No. 233. Manila: Asian Development Bank.

Ghosh, Atish R., Anne-Marie Gulde, Jonathan D. Ostry, and Holger C. Wolf. 1997. *Does the Nominal Exchange Rate Regime Matter?* NBER Working Paper 5874. Cambridge, MA: National Bureau for Economic Research.

Ilzetzki, Ethan, Carmen M. Reinhart, and Kenneth S. Rogoff. 2011. The Country Chronologies and Background Material to Exchange Rate Arrangements into the 21st Century: Will the Anchor Currency Hold? Available at personal.lse.ac.uk/ilzetzki/data/ERA-Country_ Chronologies_2011.pdf (accessed on September 15, 2014).

Jeanne, Olivier, Marcus Noland, Arvind Subramanian, and John Williamson. 2014. Financial Globalization and Long-Run Growth: Is Asia Different? In *Asian Capital Market Development and Integration.* Asian Development Bank and Korea Capital Market Institute. Delhi: Oxford University Press.

Johnston, R. Barry, and Natalia T. Tamirisa. 1998. *Why Do Countries Use Capital Controls?* IMF Working Paper 98/181. Washington: International Monetary Fund.

King, Robert G., and Ross Levine. 1993. Finance, Entrepreneurship, and Growth: Theory and Evidence. *Journal of Monetary Economics* 32: 513–42.

Kose, M. Ayhan, Eswar Prasad, Kenneth Rogoff, and Shang-Jin Wei. 2009. Financial Globalization: A Reappraisal. *IMF Staff Papers* 56, no. 1: 8–62.

Lane, Philip R., and Gian Maria Milesi-Ferretti. 2007. The External Wealth of Nations, Mark II: Revised and Extended Estimates of Foreign Assets and Liabilities, 1970–2004. *Journal of International Economics* 73: 223–50.

Levine, Ross, and Sara Zervos. 1998. Stock Markets, Banks, and Economic Growth. *American Economic Review* 88, no. 3: 537–58.

Mody, Ashoka, and Antu Panini Murshid. 2005. Growing Up with Capital Flows. *Journal of International Economics* 65, no. 1: 249–66.

Obstfeld, Maurice 2009. International Finance and Growth in Developing Countries: What Have We Learned? *IMF Staff Papers* 56, no. 1. Washington: International Monetary Fund.

Quinn, Dennis P., and A. Maria Toyoda. 2008. Does Capital Account Liberalization Lead to Growth? *Review of Financial Studies* 21: 1403–49.

Quinn, Dennis, Martin Schindler, and A. Maria Toyoda. 2011. Assessing Measures of Financial Openness and Integration. *IMF Economic Review* 59, no. 3: 488–522.

Rajan, Raghuram G., and Luigi Zingales. 1998. Financial Dependence and Growth. *American Economic Review* 88, no. 3: 559–86.

Reinhart, Carmen M., and Kenneth S. Rogoff. 2004. The Modern History of Exchange Rate Arrangements: A Reinterpretation. *Quarterly Journal of Economics* 119, no. 1: 1–48.

Rodrik, Dani. 1998. Who Needs Capital-Account Convertibility? In *Should the IMF Pursue Capital-Account Convertibility?* ed. Stanley Fischer, Richard N. Cooper, Rudiger Dornbusch, Peter M. Garber, Carlos Massad, Jacques J. Polak, Dani Rodrik, and Savak S. Tarapore. *Essays in International Finance* May, no. 207, International Finance Section, Department of Economics, Princeton University. Available at www.princeton.edu/~ies/IES_Essays/E207.pdf (accessed on August 12, 2014).

Rojas-Suarez, Liliana. 2008. Domestic Financial Regulations in Developing Countries: Can They Effectively Limit the Impact of Capital Account Volatility? In *Capital Market Liberalization and Development,* ed. José Antonio Ocampo and Joseph E. Stiglitz. New York: Oxford University Press.

Schindler, Martin. 2009. Measuring Financial Integration: A New Data Set. *IMF Staff Papers* 56: 222–38. Washington: International Monetary Fund.

3

The Financial Sector and Growth in Emerging Asian Economies

WILLIAM R. CLINE

This chapter takes a broad look at the strengths and weaknesses of the financial sectors in Asian emerging-market economies and draws inferences regarding possible institutional and policy changes that could enhance the contribution of these sectors to economic growth going forward. The first section reviews economic growth theory and the role for the financial sector as it has been featured in the growth literature. The second section considers summary evidence on actual growth performance in recent years in the main Asian emerging-market economies and, for comparison, their counterparts in Latin America as well as the three largest industrial economies. The third section attempts to compile data that provide a profile of the depth and structure of financial sectors in the same set of economies. The fourth section addresses the specific issue of financial sector openness and the balance between risks and opportunities associated with financial globalization. The fifth section briefly summarizes recent patterns encountered in IMF/World Bank financial sector reviews for the Asian emerging-market economies, reported in appendices A and B. The sixth section summarizes the implications for institutions and policies, and the final section recapitulates the conclusions.

William R. Cline, senior fellow, has been associated with the Peterson Institute for International Economics since its inception in 1981. He thanks Abir Varma for research assistance and, without implicating, Ajai Chopra, Morris Goldstein, Nicholas Lardy, Marcus Noland, and Arvind Subramanian, who provided valuable comments on an earlier draft, and Chang-Tai Hsieh, who provided insight on the Chinese banking system.

Growth Theory and the Financial Sector

Capital Accumulation and Factor Productivity

Classic growth theory emphasizes the accumulation of capital as the driving force in raising output, and hence output per worker and GDP per capita. The early economic development literature prominently featured the Harrod-Domar model (Harrod 1939, Domar 1946), in which GDP was equal to the amount of capital divided by the capital-output ratio. Because the amount of capital increased by the amount of investment, and the amount of investment was equal to the amount of savings, and the amount of savings in absolute terms was equal to the saving rate multiplied by GDP (or output), it followed that the growth rate would be equal to the saving rate divided by the capital-output ratio.[1] Growth could thus be increased by increasing the saving rate, or by making production more efficient and thereby reducing the capital-output ratio, or both. Although the Harrod-Domar model had been developed in the context of concern about Keynesian unemployment and an excess of saving over desired investment in advanced countries, in the development context it was natural instead to focus on the model's implications for the need to raise capital to increase productive capacity. In this context raising the saving rate was seen as the central challenge of economic development.

The "surplus labor" model of W. Arthur Lewis (1954) formalized this approach by arguing that so long as there was a large pool of rural labor willing to enter the industrial labor force at a constant (and low) institutional wage, the modern sector would behave in a Harrod-Domar fashion with output rising in proportion to the amount of capital in the modern sector. Capital in the modern sector would rise from reinvested profits, boosting the share of saving and investment in the economy as a whole because of the much higher rate in the modern sector. Only when surplus labor from the countryside was exhausted would wages begin to rise in the modern sector, at the "turning point" at which the rising marginal product of labor and falling ratio of labor to capital would make the modern sector begin to behave in a neoclassical fashion (with output constrained by both capital and labor) instead of a fixed-coefficient relationship to capital as the only constraint. Even today the development of the People's Republic of China in particular is sometimes depicted as largely still being consistent with the surplus labor model, and the question has been whether the turning point has arrived, or when it will (see, for example, Das and N'Diaye 2013).

The alternative growth model was the neoclassical model, which emphasized both capital and labor as well as technological change as the sources of growth. In the famous formulation by Robert Solow (1956), output grows at

---

1. With $Q = K/B$, $\Delta Q = \Delta K/B$, where Q is output, K is capital, and B is the capital-output ratio. The change in capital equals the amount of saving: $\Delta K = S = sQ$, where s is the saving rate. It follows that the growth rate, $g \equiv (\Delta Q)/Q$, will be: $g = (\Delta K/B)/Q = ([sQ]/B)/Q = s/B$.

a rate equal to the sum of proportionate growth of each factor multiplied by its "factor share," plus a residual attributable to technological change. The weighting of each factor's growth by its share in output stems from the assumption that each factor is paid its marginal product.[2] Sometimes the model was formulated to treat human capital as a third distinguishable factor of production (Mankiw, Romer, and Weil 1992).

The natural role for the financial sector in growth in either the Harrod-Domar or the neoclassical model is as an institution that helps mobilize saving for investment, boosting capital, or technological change, reducing the capital required per unit of output (Harrod-Domar), or increasing the growth residual (neoclassical). Finance could also be thought of as facilitating investment in human capital, another factor in the neoclassical framework.

Finance and Growth: Theory

Joseph A. Schumpeter (1911) emphasized his "heresy" that money and credit matter because they were crucial to the process of creative destruction as resources are bid away from the old sectors and channeled to new sectors with new technologies. In the late 1960s, Raymond W. Goldsmith (1969) emphasized the role of finance in economic development (as discussed below). Ronald I. McKinnon (1973) attacked "financial repression" in developing countries, the practice of imposing official ceilings on interest rates. Although the objective of such restrictions was to boost investment, instead the result was to discourage saving and the channeling of resources to productive investment. "Financial liberalization" came to mean the freeing of interest rates to reach market-clearing levels, as well as a shift away from directed lending by state banks toward market-based lending.

Ross Levine (2004) emphasizes that the theoretical approaches to the relationship between the financial system and growth are premised on the role of the financial sector in reducing information and transaction costs. Creditors may have insufficient information on the ability of debtors to repay to make the credit transaction possible. Raghuram G. Rajan and Luigi Zingales (2003) more specifically emphasize the Schumpeterian consideration: the ability of the financial system to finance innovation, regardless of whether the entrepreneur is connected to existing circles of firms (Bertocco 2006).

---

2. In a neoclassical production function, the elasticity of output with respect to the factor (say, N, for labor) can be shown to equal the factor share of output as follows. The factor is paid its marginal product (MP_N), so total payment to labor is $MP_N \times N$, and labor's share in total output is $(MP_N \times N)/Q$. The elasticity of output with respect to labor is: $\frac{\partial Q/Q}{\partial N/N}$, which can be rewritten as $\frac{\partial Q/\partial N}{Q/N}$, which in turn can be rearranged into $(MP_N \times N)/Q$ (that is, by definition $\partial Q/\partial N = MP_N$). The total percent change in output will equal the sum of the percent increases in each of the factors times its respective output elasticity (or factor share).

The Financial Sector and Macroeconomic Stability

Beyond its influence on business-as-usual growth through facilitating capital accumulation and technological change, the financial sector has featured prominently in influencing susceptibility to business cycles. Crises in the financial sector have disrupted macroeconomic stability in emerging-market economies with sufficient frequency, and more recently in the advanced economies, that it can be argued that what might be called the "Hippocratic theory of finance" is the most important. This theory would posit simply that the most important function of the financial sector is to do no harm to the macroeconomy.

Weak financial sectors were a driving force in the East Asian crisis of the late 1990s. Although Argentina's 2001–02 crisis had mainly fiscal (and political) origins, the freeze in bank deposits in the crisis brought a downward spiral to the economy. Public sector costs of restructuring financial sectors in the crises of the late 1990s reached as high as 57 percent of GDP in Indonesia, 31 percent in the Republic of Korea, 44 percent in Thailand, 22 percent in Ecuador, 32 percent in Turkey, and 16 percent in Malaysia (Laeven and Valencia 2013, appendix A1). More recently, the banking crisis in Ireland imposed direct fiscal costs amounting to 40 percent of GDP (Ahearne 2012, 43).

Excessive credit expansion has frequently characterized the run-ups to financial crises in international historical experience. For emerging-market economies, an iconic application of the financial boom-bust syndrome is the concept of the "sudden stop," a term coined by Guillermo A. Calvo (1998). The term refers to the switch from the euphoric phase to the panic phase in the flows of foreign capital. The sudden stop featured prominently in the three major sovereign debt crises of the past three decades: the Latin American crisis of the 1980s, the East Asian financial crisis of the late 1990s, and the sovereign debt crisis of the euro area periphery in 2010–13 (Cline 2013a, 2014).

For both advanced and emerging-market economies, Enrique G. Mendoza and Marco E. Terrones (2008) find that in 1960–2006, credit booms were associated with periods of economic expansion, rising equity and housing prices, and real exchange rate appreciations, dynamics that reversed in subsequent downswings. They find that many of the recent emerging-market crises were associated with credit booms. Researchers at the International Monetary Fund (IMF) estimated that about one-third of credit booms wind up in financial crises, but also found that many credit booms resulted in permanent financial deepening beneficial to longer-term growth (Dell'Ariccia et al. 2012).[3]

The Great Recession centered in the United States in 2008–09 is the most conspicuous case in recent history of macroeconomic disruption triggered

---

3. However, Mathias Drehmann, Claudio Borio, and Kostas Tsatsaronis (2012, 11) find that a much closer linkage of financial crisis to credit cycles is obtained if in addition residential property price cycles are jointly incorporated with credit.

by financial sector weakness. Breakdowns in the financial sector, notably in the highly leveraged investment banking sector, sharply intensified the recessionary pressures from the downturn in the housing market. The most relevant conceptual framework pertaining to financial crises is probably that of Hyman Minsky (1986, 1992), albeit his approach was less formal than that of the Harrod-Domar or neoclassical growth models. Minsky argued that in periods of prolonged prosperity, complacency induces the financial sector to transit from stabilizing "hedge finance" (in which operating income is sufficient to cover both interest and principal) toward "speculative finance" (expected operating income covers interest but not principal) to "Ponzi finance" (operating income insufficient to cover all interest). Charles P. Kindleberger (1978) similarly emphasized widespread historical episodes of boom and bust associated with initial phases of financial euphoria followed by panic.

The US crisis had some features that accord with the Minsky-Kindleberger framework, but others that did not. The equity and commodity markets had not reached extreme states of euphoria in 2007.[4] The housing market turned out to be in a bubble, however. US housing prices doubled from 2000 to 2006. They then fell by one-third over the following three years (Cline 2010, appendix 4B). However, it was the combination of this sea change from rising to declining housing prices with several other major factors that brought the crisis. One important influence was the unanticipated vulnerability from financial engineering in the form of securitized subprime mortgages (and associated perverse incentives to rating agencies). For purposes of this review, however, it is appropriate to emphasize another influence: the extremely high leverage ratios of the shadow banking sector and the short-term nature of its financing. Whereas banks had asset to capital ratios on the order of 10 to 1, investment banks had ratios of 20 or 30 to 1.[5] The "Minsky moment" arrived in the fall of 2008 when Lehman Brothers failed. Lehman was deeply insolvent, so the Federal Reserve could not provide the same financial backstop it had made available for the earlier takeover of Bear Stearns (Cline and Gagnon 2013; Geithner 2014, 207). For emerging-market economies, a key lesson is the importance of capital adequacy and regulatory supervision. More specifically, a key responsibility of economic policymakers is to ensure macroprudentiality. This task requires ensuring that highly interconnected financial institutions with systemic consequences (for the economy) have robust capitalization and supervision.

---

4. The trailing 12-month price-earnings ratio for the Standard & Poor's 500 Index (operating earnings) stood at 17.8 at the end of 2007, well below its level of 29.6 at the end of 1999 in the tech boom (Standard and Poor's 2014).

5. Leverage was far higher at the London investment bank unit of insurer AIG, which wrote one-way bets on credit default swaps for collateralized debt obligations with a notional value of some $500 billion. Gretchen Morgenstern, "Behind Insurer's Crisis, Blind Eye to a Web of Risk," *New York Times*, September 27, 2008. The Federal Reserve and US Treasury would wind up providing some $150 billion in emergency support to AIG (Cline 2010, 273–75).

Finance and Growth: Evidence

Goldsmith (1969) argued that there were systematic patterns in financial and economic development in which the ratio of all financial assets to underlying tangible net national wealth increases. He found that the "financial interrelationships ratio" tended to rise to about 100 to 150 percent and then level off, and was about the same for the United States in the 1960s as in the 1920s. In contrast, the ratio was only about 30 to 60 percent in developing countries. However, he judged that it could not be established "with confidence whether financial factors were responsible for the acceleration of economic development" (1969, 48).

Robert G. King and Ross Levine (1993) applied statistical tests for 77 countries for the period 1960–89 to estimate the influence of finance on development. They found that financial depth, measured by the ratio of liquid liabilities of the financial system to GDP, was a good predictor of growth. The bottom quartile of countries by growth performance had mean financial depth of 0.2, compared with 0.6 for the top quartile. The estimated coefficient implied that the expected difference in growth between the two groups would amount to 1 percent annually. Subsequently Levine, Norman Loayza, and Thorsten Beck (2000) applied instrumental variable and dynamic panel techniques to confirm exogeneity in the influence of financial intermediary development on economic growth, as well as the influence of legal rights for creditors and accounting systems in determining financial development.

More recently, however, in work for the Bank for International Settlements, Stephen G. Cecchetti and Enisse Kharroubi (2012) find that there can be too much of a good thing: Beyond a certain level, financial deepening is associated with slower rather than faster growth. Using data for 50 advanced and emerging-market economies for 1980–2009, they find that when private credit exceeds GDP, it becomes a drag on productivity growth. Similarly, when the financial sector comprises more than 3.5 percent of total employment, further increases in financial sector size are detrimental to growth. Moreover, they find that more rapid financial sector expansion affects growth adversely. For 21 OECD countries, the authors find an elasticity of –0.33 relating annual growth in output per worker to the annual percentage growth rate in the share of employment in the financial sector.[6]

Similarly, Jean-Louis Arcand, Enrico Berkes, and Ugo Panizza (2012) find negative effects of additional financial deepening when credit to the private sector exceeds 100 percent of GDP. They argue that the usual specification in earlier estimates (growth rate on the logarithm of the credit/GDP ratio) failed to allow for the possibility of a reversal of the sign (by being "monotone").

---

6. Thus, a country with the financial sector employment share growing at 1.6 percent annually (the sample median among countries with rising employment shares in the sector) would experience approximately 0.5 percentage point slower growth annually in labor productivity.

They use instead a quadratic formulation, and the coefficient on the squared term is negative.

These estimates should probably be taken with a large grain of salt, particularly such conclusions as the Cecchetti-Kharroubi estimates that Canada would grow faster by 1.3 percent annually, and Switzerland by 0.7 percent, if each were to shrink the size of its financial sector back to the growth-maximizing point. Except for a casual reference to diverting the brightest from rocket science to finance, there is little motivation of a causal mechanism for the impact of financial deepening on growth to turn negative. Arcand, Berkes, and Panizza (2012) may have a better argument in linking their findings to earlier findings about thresholds at which financial crises become more likely. Nonetheless, cross-country studies such as these are inherently subject to questions of specification and, especially, causality.[7]

If the threshold of 100 percent of GDP were taken seriously, the implications would be fairly negative for some of the key Asian emerging-market economies. Thus, the ratio of credit to the private sector to GDP at the end of 2013 stood at 140 percent in the PRC, 135 percent in the Republic of Korea, 122 percent in Malaysia, and 121 percent in Thailand.[8] However, it simply flouts common sense to conclude that the most important financial sector policy in these four countries should be to reduce aggressively the level of credit. (Others in the region would be spared, as the ratios stand at 97 percent in Viet Nam, 51 percent in India, 36 percent in the Philippines, and 34 percent in Indonesia.) A more meaningful policy inference could be simply that in the first four countries, the objective of policy should no longer be primarily to further raise total depth of credit to GDP, but instead ensure that the credit is of high quality in the sense that it is directed to the highest-return activities and that it is safe, in the sense that excessive leverage is not being pursued nor is a boom-bust credit cycle taking place.

Growth Performance, 2000–2013

Before examining financial sector development, it is useful to recapitulate the actual growth performance of the major emerging-market economies in Asia so far in the new century. For perspective, it is also useful to compare their growth results with those of peer emerging-market economies in Latin America as well as those of the largest industrial countries. Table 3.1 reports annual real GDP growth rates for 2000–2013 for nine emerging Asian economies and seven Latin American economies with populations of 18 million or more and

---

7. Consider the influence of the typically higher credit ratios in richer countries, combined with the fact that growth convergence means growth tends to be faster at lower income levels. Unless the control variables give a fully accurate treatment of the convergence effect, there could be a spurious attribution of a negative growth rate influence of rising credit.

8. Using the IMF's data series for credit to the private sector, category 32D, the concept applied in Arcand, Berkes, and Panizza (2012) and IMF (2014b).

Table 3.1 Growth performance, 2000–13

Country	Population (millions)	PPP GDP per capita (thousands of US dollars, 2013)	Real GDP (percent annual growth)	Population, ages 15–64 (percent annual change)	Real GDP relative to potential labor force (percent annual) (C – D)	Rank (E)	Investment (percent of GDP)	ICOR (G/C)	Rank (H)
	(A)	(B)	(C)	(D)	(E)	(F)	(G)	(H)	(I)
Asia									
People's Republic of China	1,386	9.8	9.93	1.09	8.84	1	43.3	4.36	3
India	1,252	4.1	7.27	1.90	5.37	2	32.4	4.46	4
Indonesia	250	5.2	5.41	1.50	3.91	6	27.4	5.06	10
Republic of Korea	49	33.2	3.78	0.51	3.28	8	29.1	7.70	15
Malaysia	30	17.7	4.75	2.21	2.54	12	23.5	4.95	8
Philippines	98	4.7	4.88	2.42	2.46	13	20.1	4.12	2
Sri Lanka	21	6.5	5.67	0.97	4.70	3	26.7	4.71	7
Thailand	67	9.9	3.98	0.88	3.10	9	26.5	6.66	14
Viet Nam	92	4.0	6.41	2.12	4.29	5	33.1	5.16	11
Latin America									
Argentina	41	18.7	4.56	1.17	3.39	7	20.7	4.54	5
Brazil	200	12.2	3.55	1.48	2.07	14	17.9	5.04	9
Chile	18	19.1	4.30	1.44	2.87	10	22.4	5.21	12
Colombia	48	11.2	4.45	1.82	2.62	11	20.8	4.67	6

Mexico	122	15.6	2.23	1.80	0.43	19	23.1	10.36	16
Peru	30	11.1	6.09	1.69	4.40	4	21.9	3.60	1
Venezuela	30	13.6	4.07	2.01	2.06	15	24.2	5.95	13
Industrial 3									
Germany	83	40.0	1.13	-0.32	1.45	16	18.3	16.19	18
Japan	127	36.9	0.7	-0.71	1.41	17	22.1	31.57	19
United States	320	53.1	1.68	0.91	0.77	18	21.0	12.50	17

PPP = purchasing power parity; ICOR = incremental capital-output ratio

Sources: Columns A, B, C, and G: IMF (2014a); column D: US Census Bureau (2014).

purchasing power parity (PPP) per capita incomes of $4,000 or more in 2013 (UN 2012, IMF 2014a).[9]

Asian emerging-market economies have led world growth in this period. Unweighted average growth rates were 5.8 percent for the nine emerging Asian economies, 4.2 percent for the seven Latin America economies, and 1.2 percent for the three large industrial countries (column C in table 3.1). To consider relative growth performance, it is important to take account of growth of the potential labor force. Column D reports the average annual growth of the population aged 15 to 64 years for 2000–2013 (US Census Bureau 2014). Malaysia, the Philippines, and Viet Nam were notable for high growth of this age group (over 2 percent annually), and even India was relatively high (1.9 percent); Germany and Japan were notable for significant declines in the number of persons in this age group.

Column E of table 3.1 provides a summary indicator of growth performance: the annual real GDP growth rate minus the average annual growth of the working-age population. Column F shows country rankings on this measure. Not surprisingly, the PRC ranks first. Somewhat less well known, India ranks second, and Sri Lanka, third. The only Latin American country close to this group is Peru, which ranks fourth. Among the three large rich countries, on this measure both Germany and Japan outperformed the United States. Growth of output per working-age population was about 1.4 percent annually in Germany and Japan, versus about 0.8 percent in the United States. These results reflect the fact that the United States was the epicenter of the Great Recession. As expected, nearly all of the emerging-market economies outperformed the three rich countries, the sole exception being Mexico. The outcome for Mexico likely reflects its extreme sensitivity to the US economy.

Finally, the table shows the average rate of gross investment as a percent of GDP in this period. For the Asian emerging-market economies, the unweighted average of the gross investment rate was 29.1 percent; for the Latin American economies, 21.6 percent; and for the three rich economies, 20.5 percent. The results for this period confirm the broadly accepted view that higher growth in emerging Asia than in Latin America reflects higher investment rates, with the PRC in particular at an extremely high average investment rate of 43 percent. Investment was also especially high in Viet Nam (33 percent), India (32 percent), and the Republic of Korea (29 percent).

Figure 3.1 displays the growth and investment data from table 3.1 for the 16 emerging-market economies. There is a clear correlation between the gross

---

9. The growth rates are estimated from log-linear regressions of real GDP on time. For Argentina, IMF (2014a) data are used through 2007. Thereafter, estimates are based on Coremberg (2014), who calculates that the official data overstated GDP by 12.2 percent in 2012. Note further that the per capita GDP screen means that four large, low-income countries in Asia are excluded from table 3.1: Bangladesh, Myanmar, Nepal, and Pakistan.

Figure 3.1 Gross investment and average growth, 2000–2013

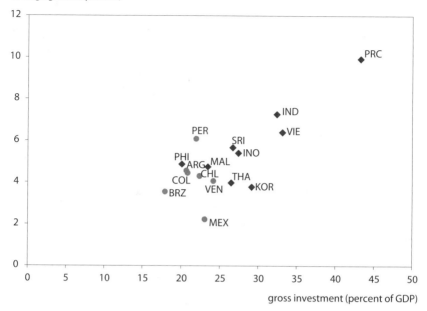

average growth (percent)

ARG = Argentina; BRZ = Brazil; CHL = Chile; COL = Colombia; IND = India; INO = Indonesia; KOR = Republic of Korea; MAL = Malaysia; MEX = Mexico; PHI = Philippines; PER = Peru; PRC = People's Republic of China; SRI = Sri Lanka; THA = Thailand; VEN = Venezuela; VIE = Viet Nam

Source: IMF (2014a).

investment rate and the real GDP growth rate.[10] At a broad level, then, classic Harrod-Domar and Lewis growth models based on capital accumulation do relatively well in explaining differing growth outcomes. At the most basic level, the implicit question for the financial sector is: What kind of financial sector is most successful at mobilizing investment? Because efficiency also matters, however, an important corollary question is: What kind of financial sector leads toward efficient investment? In figure 3.1, the first question pertains simply to how far the country observation is to the right-hand side. Again, the PRC, India, and Viet Nam led in capital mobilization, and more broadly the strong dominance of the Asian over the Latin American economies is evident in the predominance of diamond-shaped observations to the right and circular ones to the left.

As for the second question, investment efficiency, the relevant information in figure 3.1 is the extent to which the country observation is found above the trend line (higher than average efficiency) rather than below the line

10. A simple regression of the full-period growth rates on average investment rates yields: $g = -0.58 \ (-0.5) + 0.219 \ (4.7) \ I$; adj. $R^2 = 0.59$, where g is the growth rate, I is the gross investment rate, and t-statistics are in parentheses.

(lower efficiency). In this dimension, Peru stands out favorably (with a gross incremental capital-output ratio [ICOR] of 3.6), and Mexico unfavorably (at 10.4).[11] Among the Asian emerging-market economies, the investment efficiency outcome was most favorable for the Philippines (ICOR = 4.1) and the PRC (4.4), and least favorable for the Republic of Korea (7.7).[12] Lower return on investment in the Republic of Korea is consistent, however, with its much more advanced level of development (with PPP per capita GDP close to that of Japan and about three times that of the PRC and eight times that of India; table 3.1, column B).[13]

Financial Sector Structure

Banks

In most economies the banking sector is the main source of financing to the private sector. A review of financial sector health appropriately begins with the banks. One's prior expectations for the sector in the main emerging-market economies would be roughly along the following lines. First, in part because of reforms following earlier crises, the expectation would be that banks are in relatively sound condition in economies such as Chile, Indonesia, the Republic of Korea, and Thailand. Second, one would not expect the depth of banking finance to be as great in the emerging-market economies as in the advanced economies. Third, where the state sector owns a large portion of the banking sector, as in the PRC, the expectation would be that banking fragility would be less of a concern because of the assured backstopping by the state. Fourth, however, state banks tend to be less efficient, so that conscious plans for either phasing down their share of the system or introducing means to improve their performance are likely to be needed. Fifth, it is an open question what one might expect regarding bank capitalization relative to that in advanced economies. The general presumption of lesser development in emerging-market economies might point to lower capitalization, but the likelihood of greater sophistication of financial engineering in advanced economies could ironically lead to the opposite. Sixth, among advanced economies, the expectation is that banking plays a more dominant role in Europe and Japan whereas the nonbank financial sector is more dominant in the United States.

---

11. The ICOR is the ratio of investment as a percent of GDP to the growth rate.

12. My colleague Nicholas Lardy points out, however, that the PRC's performance divides into a more favorable period (2000–2007) and less favorable period (2008–14). In the former period growth averaged 10.5 percent annually; in the latter, 8.8 percent (IMF 2014a). Conversely, the investment ratio was lower in the first period (37.8 percent) than in the later period (44.7 percent; IMF 2014b). So the ICOR was considerably lower in 2000–2007 (at 3.6) than in 2008–14 (5.1).

13. The ICOR was even higher in the three rich countries, at a simple average of 20. Note that the ICOR for investment net of capital consumption would be lower. Data are incomplete for capital consumption, however.

Table 3.2 reports selected indicators for the banking systems of the same countries just considered with regard to growth outcomes. Somewhat surprisingly, the banking sectors are larger than might have been expected in several of the Asian emerging-market countries, especially the PRC, the Republic of Korea, Malaysia, and Thailand. In all four cases bank assets are over 200 percent of GDP.[14] The poorest economy shown, Viet Nam, has surprisingly high bank assets at well above 100 percent of GDP. In contrast, the Latin American economies with the highest bank assets, Brazil and Chile, both have only about 110 percent of GDP in bank assets. The three advanced economies have the expected pattern, though the differences are perhaps more than might have been anticipated, with US bank assets relative to GDP only about one-fourth those in Japan. In broad terms, the data suggest that the Asian emerging-market economies do not suffer from underbanked financial sectors. The more relevant question may be whether in some cases the sector is overdimensioned.[15]

The next three columns in table 3.2 in principle provide information about the health of the banking sectors. Concentration of bank assets in the five largest banks represents potential "too big to fail" risks. The five largest banks account for about three-fourths or more of bank assets in Sri Lanka, Malaysia, Brazil, Chile, Colombia, and Peru.[16] In the advanced economies, the top five banks hold about two-thirds of assets in the United States but considerably less in Germany and Japan. The combined influence of concentration and overall bank assets indicates that on average each of the five largest banks has assets equal to 32 percent of GDP in Malaysia, 27 percent in Japan, 26 percent in Germany, 20 percent in the Republic of Korea, 19 percent in Thailand, and 18 percent in Brazil. Considering that the corresponding number is only 11 percent of GDP for the United States, where concerns remain about too big to fail, the implication would seem to be that there are grounds for this concern in several other major economies as well.

The third column in table 3.2 provides a direct market indicator of banking sector health: the average credit default swap (CDS) rate on five-year dollar

---

14. Data are from IMF (2014b) for depository institutions. The most recent available data are used, usually for March 2014 or December 2013. The PRC's 280 percent of GDP for bank assets is twice the 140 percent ratio of private sector credit to GDP. Only a part of the difference can be explained by claims on the government sector. (In 2013, central government debt was 17.9 percent of GDP, and local government debt, 35.8 percent; see IMF 2014l, 51). The rest of the difference apparently reflects the fact that claims in table 3.2 include claims on other financial institutions.

15. The principal case of the opposite possibility appears to be Argentina, where bank assets are only about one-third of GDP. This level may reflect the aftermath of the severe banking crisis in 2001–03.

16. Data on individual bank assets were obtained from Bloomberg, bank websites, and Banco Central (2014) for Brazil. Note that in Brazil the large state development bank, BNDES, is not included in the depository bank data.

Table 3.2 Banking sector indicators

Country	Bank assets (percent of GDP)	Largest 5 share (percent)	Average CDS rate of 3 largest (basis points)	Capital/ assets (percent)	Government- owned (percent)	Foreign- owned (percent)
Asia						
People's Republic of China	280.5	45.3	136	6.3	90e	2
India	94.7	28.4	204	6.9	74	7
Indonesia	56.4	47.3	n.a.	12.5	38	34
Republic of Korea	241.6	42.2	67	8.1	22	77
Malaysia	207.7	76.3	97	9.6	0	22
Philippines	93.1	44.9	n.a.	10.8	13	11
Sri Lanka	50.9	79.9	n.a.	8.2	59	14
Thailand	203.8	45.8	92*	10.9	18	7
Viet Nam	125.5	54.3	n.a.	9.9	49e	n.a.
Latin America						
Argentina	34	38.3	n.a.	12.1	44	26
Brazil	112.2	79.3	197	9.3	44	18
Chile	109.1	76.3	92*	8.1	20	39
Colombia	66	73.9	201*	14.8	6	20

Mexico	66.4	41.6	78*	10.4	13	85
Peru	51.2	80.7	n.a.	10.1	0	49
Venezuela	59.8	48.1	n.a.	10.9	33	17
Industrial 3						
Germany	274.6	46.7	83	5.5	32	12
Japan	363.6	37.8	62	5.5	n.a.	n.a.
United States	85.4	62.7	65	11.8	0	n.a.

e = estimate; CDS = credit default swap; * = data for only one bank; n.a. = not available

Note: Dates for the data are as follows: Bank assets and largest five shares, end-2013 or March 2014; CDS rates, July 2014; capital/assets, 2013; ownership, 2010 (PRC: 2012).

Sources: Barth, Caprio, and Levine (2013); Bloomberg; Datastream; EY (2014); FRBSF (2011); IMF (2014b); World Bank (2013, 2014).

obligations for the three largest banks.[17] All of these spreads are relatively modest, with the exceptions of India, Brazil, and Colombia (all at about 200 basis points), and possibly the PRC as well (about 135 basis points). Typically the banks will not enjoy a narrower credit default swap spread than does the sovereign in question. Recent five-year sovereign CDS rates for these four countries have been around 160 basis points for India, 145 for Brazil, 90 for Colombia, and 80 for the PRC.[18] So at least for Brazil and India the rates may be more a reflection of each economy's sovereign risk than any differential risk of the banking sector itself.

The fourth column reports the average ratio of bank capital to assets, as reported in the World Bank's *World Development Indicators* (2014). The measure for capital is total capital and reserves.[19] The measure for assets is total assets, not risk-weighted. These capital ratios are thus essentially the inverse of asset/capital leverage ratios. They suggest that among the Asian emerging-market economies, the PRC and India in particular may be on the low side in terms of bank capitalization, at 6 to 7 percent ratios of capital to unweighted assets (leverage of about 15 to 1). In contrast, the capital-assets ratio is typically 10 percent or more in Latin America (with Brazil slightly lower and Chile at about 8 percent but Colombia nearly 15 percent).

The lower capitalization ratios for banks in the PRC and India should be considered in light of the fact that in both economies much of the banking sector is owned by the government (an estimated 90 percent in the PRC and 74 percent in India; next-to-last column).[20] If banks are in fact relatively less capitalized, the implications might be less important than in many other economies because of the presumption that the governments would be capable of supporting additional bank capitalization. For the PRC this assumption would seem to be especially warranted given the fact that the general government is a net creditor.[21] For India the presumption of government backing might be less robust, considering that public debt is not particularly low for an emerging-market economy.[22]

---

17. Data are from Datastream and Bloomberg.

18. Bloomberg, July 31, 2014.

19. Including tier 1 paid-up shares and common stock, and other regulatory capital in the form of subordinated debt that need not be repaid if funds are required to meet minimum capital needs (tier 2 and tier 3 capital). A better measure would be tier 1 capital (predominantly common shares and retained earnings; BIS 2010, 2), but cross-country data are not as readily available for this measure.

20. The estimate for the PRC is by Barth, Caprio, and Levine (2013, 7), who also report that in 2007 just the four largest state banks accounted for about 70 percent of bank assets.

21. The PRC's general government gross debt in 2013 was only 22 percent of GDP (IMF 2014a). Considering that its external reserves amount to 43 percent of GDP (IMF 2014b), the government is a net creditor rather than net debtor.

22. General government gross debt stood at 67 percent of GDP in 2013 (IMF 2014a). International reserves were 15 percent of GDP (IMF 2014b).

Table 3.2 also reports the bank capital to assets ratios for Germany, Japan, and the United States. It is striking that this ratio is only half as high in Germany and Japan as in the United States. The difference in part likely reflects the use of International Financial Reporting Standards (IFRS) in Europe versus Generally Accepted Accounting Principles (GAAP) in the United States. The IFRS allow much less netting of derivatives.[23] Note also that the high capital to assets ratio for the United States reflects the inclusion of all capital; when only tangible capital is included, the ratio is only about half as large. This same consideration suggests that the frequency of capital to assets ratios on the order of 10 percent or above for the emerging-market economies in the table might also be taken with a grain of salt.

Basel III international rules for bank capitalization focus mainly on risk-weighted assets (RWAs). Banks are to hold 4.5 percent of RWAs in common equity and an additional 2.5 percent capital conservation buffer, for 7 percent total by 2019 (BIS 2010, 69). However, risk weighting reduces the reported value of assets by about half for the large banks, under GAAP, and even more under IFRS.[24] Basel III introduces only a modest leverage ratio of 3 percent for capital relative to total assets. With the benefit of experience in the Great Recession, however, emerging-market economies would seem better advised to evaluate banking strength against total assets rather than RWAs.[25] It would also seem prudent for policymakers to seek capitalization levels *at least* as high as the Basel III requirements. A fruitful debate in the region could address whether the current capital-assets ratios of 11 to 12 percent in Indonesia, the Philippines, and Thailand are too high, or the ratios of 6 to 7 percent in India and the PRC are too low. Given the prospect of increasing regional integration, moreover, the answer to this question would presumably affect competitiveness of banks within a more open regional trading regime. Indeed, a key original motivation for Basel capital requirements was to reduce the competitive advantage of Japan's banks (with relatively low capital ratios) against those of the United States and Europe (where capital requirements were higher).

The final two columns of table 3.2 report the share of bank assets held by banks that are majority owned by the government (next-to-last column) or by foreigners (last column). In Asia, government ownership of banks is high

---

23. Hoenig (2013) estimates that whereas eight large global systemically important banks (GSIBs) in the United States have tangible capital amounting to 6.2 percent of total assets under GAAP, the ratio is only 3.9 percent using IFRS treatment of derivatives. He calculates that this ratio is only 1.5 percent for the one GSIB in Germany, but the average for non-US GSIBs is 3.7 percent.

24. For the fourth quarter of 2012, the eight GSIBs in the United States had a total of $5.4 trillion in RWAs, $10.2 trillion in total assets under GAAP, and $15.9 trillion in total assets under IFRS. For 16 foreign GSIBs (almost all based in Europe), RWAs were a total of $9.1 trillion whereas IFRS total assets were $27.5 trillion (Hoenig 2013).

25. Low-risk weights for mortgages based on past history turned out to be misleading for the United States; zero-risk weights for loans to sovereigns turned out to be misleading for banks in the euro area.

in the PRC, India, Sri Lanka, and (to a lesser degree) Viet Nam. Government ownership is intermediate in Indonesia and the Republic of Korea, but low in Thailand, the Philippines, and especially Malaysia. In contrast, Latin America shows only intermediate government ownership (Argentina, Brazil, Chile, and Venezuela) or low government ownership (Colombia and Mexico). Foreign ownership is exceptionally high in the Republic of Korea and Mexico (at about 80 percent of bank assets each). Foreign ownership is in an intermediate range of one-fourth to one-half in Indonesia, Malaysia, Argentina, Chile, and Peru. It is extremely low in the PRC, India, and Thailand (below 10 percent) and moderately low in Brazil, Colombia, and Venezuela (17 to 20 percent). Aside from the two cases of the PRC and India, there is no correlation between the level of bank capitalization (capital-assets ratio) and the degree of foreign ownership.

Nonbank Finance

Financial sector development involves expansion of not only the banks but also nonbank financial institutions as well as the equity and bond markets. It is relatively well known that emerging-market economies have made major progress in shifting government borrowing away from international bond markets toward domestic bond markets, often with increasing shares of foreign holdings of domestically issued government bonds. Thus, from 2000 to 2010, the share of outstanding public debt issued domestically rose from 10 to 91 percent in Chile, from 23 to 63 percent in Thailand, and similarly by 20 to 30 percentage points in Colombia, Mexico, Peru, the Republic of Korea, and the Philippines, and nearly 20 percentage points in Brazil, India, and Malaysia (Cline 2013a, 299).[26] It is less clear whether domestic bond markets have become substantially more important as a source of financing for the private sector. Similarly, although it is widely perceived that emerging equity markets have expanded sharply in recent years (and have been increasingly correlated with industrial-country equity markets), it is less clear how important they have become relative to the more traditional source of financing, the banking sector.

Table 3.3 seeks to shed light on the recent structural profiles of financial sector intermediation in financing the private sectors in major emerging-market economies. The table divides the sector into four categories: loans from banks, loans from nondepository financial institutions, bonds and other debt securities, and equity markets. The first three categories fit easily into treatment as alternative sources of debt finance. For equity finance, the table reports market capitalization. If there were no retained earnings and no difference between the market price and book value, the market capitalization would equal cumulative paid-in capital from shares issued, the narrow equivalent of alternative financing from debt. Market capitalization will thus overstate the relative role of equity markets in raising capital but nonetheless

---

26. The PRC was a major exception, with a decline from 56 percent in 2000 to 51 percent in 2010.

Table 3.3   Structure of financing to the nongovernment economy (percent of GDP)

Country	Loans, 2013		Bonds, debt securities, 2013	Stock market capitalization, 2012	Total	Depth	Type
	Banks	Nonbanks					
Asia							
People's Republic of China	146.1[a]	47.9	28.1	44.9	267.0	H	B
India	50.9	n.a.	n.a.	68.0	118.9	M	D
Indonesia	34.2[a]	3.8[a]	2.3	45.3	85.6	L	D
Republic of Korea	135	n.a.	77.5	96.5	309	H	D
Malaysia	122.2	n.a.	58.5	156.2	336.9	H	P
Philippines	35.8	n.a.	1.1	105.6	142.5	M	P
Sri Lanka	29	n.a.	n.a.	28.7	57.7	L	B
Thailand	122.1[a]	33.4[a]	44.2	104.7	304.4	H	D
Viet Nam	96.8	n.a.	n.a.	21.1	117.9	M	B
Latin America							
Argentina	15.7[a]	0.5	3.0	5.7	24.9	L	B
Brazil	74.5[a]	6.9	32.3	54.7	168.4	M	D
Chile	77	25.4	36.3	117.7	256.4	H	P
Colombia	41[a]	10.4	0.6	70.8	122.8	M	D

(continued on next page)

Table 3.3   Structure of financing to the nongovernment economy (percent of GDP) *(continued)*

Country	Loans, 2013		Bonds, debt securities, 2013	Stock market capitalization, 2012	Total	Depth	Type
	Banks	Nonbanks					
Latin America							
Mexico	22.2[a]	8.2	17.5	44.3	92.2	L	P
Peru	32.3	n.a.	6.1	50.3	88.7	L	P
Venezuela	27.6[a]	n.a.	n.a.	6.6	34.2	L	B
Industrial 3							
Germany	95.7[a]	n.a.	57.8	43.4	196.9	M	D
Japan	113.1	75.9	61.7	62	312.7	H	D
United States	58.6	139.5	131.7	114.9	444.7	H	D

n.a. = not available; L: low; M: medium; H: high; B: bank; P: portfolio; D: diversified

a. March 2014.

Sources: BIS (2014); IMF (2014b); World Bank (2014).

provides a rough guide to the relative importance of equity compared with debt.

In the table, data on loans to the private (or nongovernment) sector from depository institutions (banks) and nondepository financial institutions (nonbanks) are from IMF (2014b) and refer to end-2013 or March 2014.[27] They are expressed as a percent of 2013 GDP. Data for bonds and debt securities are from the Bank for International Settlements (BIS 2014). Market capitalization data are from the *World Development Indicators* (World Bank 2014) and refer to 2012.

Despite the caveat on overstatement of equity finance from total market capitalization, table 3.3 classifies the type of financial sector structure in each economy based on the simple sum of the four columns. An economy is first identified as having low, high, or medium financial intermediation (next-to-last column) based on whether the total of the four categories is less than 100 percent of GDP, more than 250 percent of GDP, or in between. The final column further classifies the country based on the relative importance of each category of finance. If outstanding bank loans exceed one-half of the sum for the four categories, the classification is "bank" (B). If bond finance plus equity market capitalization exceed 60 percent of the total, the classification is "portfolio" (P). If neither threshold is met, the country is considered "diversified" (D).

As expected, the depth of industrial-country financial intermediation tends to be higher than that of the emerging markets. The unweighted average for total financial intermediation is 318 percent of GDP for the three industrial countries, compared with 193 percent for the nine emerging Asian economies and 113 percent for the seven Latin American economies. Among the Asian emerging-market economies, Malaysia stands out as having the highest equity market capitalization, at 156 percent of GDP, considerably higher than even that of the United States (115 percent). Equity market capitalization is also high in the Philippines (106 percent), Thailand (105 percent), and Chile (118 percent). Overall depth of financial intermediation is found to be low in only two of the Asian emerging-market economies, Indonesia and Sri Lanka. In contrast, intermediation is low in four of the seven Latin American economies (Argentina, Mexico, Peru, and Venezuela). The high intermediation threshold is reached in four Asian emerging-market economies (the PRC, the Republic of Korea, Malaysia, and Thailand) and only one Latin American economy (Chile).

As for classification of structural type, surprisingly only five economies turn out to be bank dominated in finance to the private sector: the PRC, Sri Lanka, Viet Nam, Venezuela, and Argentina. In all other economies in the

---

27. However, nonbank credit for the PRC is not available from the IMF, and instead is based on the estimate of the Chinese Academy of Social Sciences for the shadow banking sector in 2013 (Agence France Presse, "China's Shadow Banking Sector is Now Worth $4.4 Trillion," May 13, 2014). At nearly 50 percent of GDP, this estimate may be understated because of further rapid expansion in 2014 but may be overstated because of some double counting with bonds and other securities in the BIS database.

table, bank loans account for less than 50 percent of the financial intermediation total. The presence of bond and equity finance is high enough to categorize the following economies as "portfolio": Malaysia, the Philippines, Chile, Mexico, and Peru. Among the three industrial countries, the table confirms the general perception of the greater relative importance of banks in Germany and Japan versus nonbanks, bonds, and the equity market in the United States.

The broad implication of table 3.3 is that there is already a surprisingly strong presence of bond, equity, and to a lesser extent nonbank loan financing in most of the emerging-market economies, rather than an exclusive reliance on the traditional banking sector.[28] The exceptions are the lower-income Asian economies shown in the table (Indonesia, Sri Lanka, and Viet Nam), and the two Latin American economies where institutional distortions have severely curbed markets (Argentina and Venezuela).

Appendix 3D provides time series information for the nine Asian emerging-market economies considered here. Figure 3D.1 reveals that high levels of banking intermediation have been a persistent pattern in the PRC, Malaysia, and Thailand, with all three showing bank assets of 100 to 120 percent of GDP already in 2000. The Republic of Korea began the decade at only about 70 percent, but by 2012 was on a par with the PRC at near 140 percent. Bank intermediation has been considerably lower and has grown more slowly in India, Indonesia, the Philippines, and Sri Lanka, at 20 to 40 percent of GDP in 2000 and rising to 25 to 50 percent by 2012. Viet Nam is an exception, as its bank assets relative to GDP began the decade in a range similar to the other four lower-income peers but by 2012 had reached the 100 percent of GDP range characteristic of the higher-income emerging-market economies of the region.

Figure 3D.2 shows that in bonds and other debt securities financing the nongovernment sector, the Republic of Korea and Malaysia stand out, rising from 30 to 50 percent of GDP at the beginning of the 2000s to 70 to 80 percent by 2012. The PRC began considerably lower (about 10 percent) and reached only about 30 percent. Thailand showed remarkable growth, from 10 percent early in the decade to about 50 percent by 2010–12. The lower-income economies show far lower levels of bond financing, with outstanding amounts reaching only 5 percent of GDP late in the period in India and even less in Indonesia and the Philippines.

Figure 3D.3 shows corresponding trends in equity market capitalization. Malaysia stands out as persistently having the highest capitalization, at 120 to 140 percent of GDP even early in the period. The Philippines, the Republic of Korea, and Thailand all showed relatively steady progress from capitalization of about 30 percent of GDP in 2000 to about 100 percent by 2012. Similar broad increases along a lower path were also present in Indonesia and Sri

---

28. A caveat is that in cross-country firm-level data, Tatiana Didier, Ross Levine, and Sergio L. Schmukler (2014) find that a high degree of concentration by firms receiving financing by equity and bonds means that these forms of financial intermediation may be considerably less significant as a source of financing for most firms than implied by the country aggregates.

Lanka (from 10 to 20 percent of GDP in 2000 to 30 to 50 percent by 2012). In contrast, stock market boom-bust dynamics characterized market capitalization in both India and the PRC, as market cap rose from about 40 percent of GDP in 2003 to 140 to 180 percent in 2007 before plunging to around 40 to 60 percent by 2012.

Figure 3D.4 shows that real stock market indices (deflating by consumer prices) registered the boom-bust pattern in the PRC and India. With January 2006 as 100, real stock prices soared to peaks in 2007 of 450 in the PRC and about 300 in Viet Nam. The stock market crash in the PRC seems likely to have been a major driver in the subsequent real estate boom, as a result of investors' seeking alternative assets. A reasonable question is whether the equity market can soon again play a major role in these two economies in the aftermath of this experience. Otherwise, the real stock price index patterns in figure 3D.4 not surprisingly show the similar (but far less dramatic) boom and bust in 2007 and 2009, respectively, in sympathy with international asset prices during the Great Recession. There is also some evidence of the "taper tantrum" of May to December 2013 in the temporary declines of markets in some economies (Thailand, Indonesia, and the Philippines). In contrast, there is no such adverse impact for the Republic of Korea, suggesting that it turned out to be something of a regional safe haven in the taper shock experience.

Role of External Finance[29]

Levine (2001) emphasizes the role of liberalization to entry by foreign capital in increasing efficiency and total factor productivity growth of the domestic financial sector. He finds statistically significant positive effects of capital market opening on the value of share trading relative to GDP in emerging-market economies. Based on other results relating growth positively to stock market liquidity, he infers a positive growth effect of the opening of portfolio equity inflows. Geert Bekaert and Campbell R. Harvey (2005) and Peter B. Henry (2000) directly examine the influence of portfolio equity opening to foreign capital on growth and find strong positive effects.

Levine (2001) also examines the influence of financial openness on banking sector efficiency. He argues that superior skills, management techniques, technology, and products of foreign banks spur domestic competition in the sector. He confirms earlier statistical results of Asli Demirgüç-Kunt and Enrica Detragiache (1998) indicating that foreign bank entry reduces the ratio of overhead costs to assets as well as profit to asset ratios, reflecting greater competition.

Alessandra Bonfiglioli and Caterina Mendicino (2004) find a high responsiveness of financial sector development, as measured by the ratio of private credit to GDP, to capital account openness as measured by the Quinn index (discussed below). Ellen Vanassche (2004) finds that for 43 developing

---

29. This section draws on Cline (2010, chapter 2).

countries in the period 1980–95, there was a statistically significant positive effect of capital account openness (based on the IMF's *Annual Report on Exchange Arrangements and Exchange Restrictions* [AREAER]) on domestic financial development.

As shown in table 3.2, foreign ownership of banks is particularly high in the Republic of Korea (77 percent by assets) and Mexico (85 percent). It is useful to consider whether the strong foreign presence is generally seen as having been positive or negative. For Mexico, the strength of the foreign banks has recently been underscored by the fact that they have turned out to be in a better position than their holding company parents, and a portion of equity has been sold to bolster the home parent in one case (the Mexican subsidiary of Spain's Banco Santander).[30] One recent study argues that the Mexican banking system is stronger than ever before, following three decades in which it was extraordinarily unstable. The authors attribute this outcome to the decision of President Ernesto Zedillo following the 1995–96 banking crisis to choose a set of large, foreign-owned banks as the government's de facto banking partners, in contrast to the decision to exclude foreign owners in the earlier 1991–92 bank privatization (Haber and Musacchio 2013).[31]

For the Republic of Korea, Insill Yi, Stephen M. Miller, and Yongil Jeon (2009, 132) state that the government liberalized foreign entry in the wake of the 1998 financial crisis (including allowing 100 percent ownership) to strengthen the financial system. By 2006, only one of the seven largest banks was not majority-owned by foreign holders. The authors conduct statistical tests and find that increased foreign ownership does not increase loans to large firms or reduce loans to small and medium firms. They find that foreign banks engage more in foreign-related activities and less in derivative activities, which they interpret as a preference for safer bank management. They find no influence of foreign ownership on return on assets, but a negative relationship with return on equity, which they interpret as consistent with earlier findings in the literature regarding increased competition in the sector after foreign entry.

Stijn Claessens and Neeltje van Horen (2010) use a new dataset on more than 5,000 banks in 137 countries, for 1995–2009, to examine the influence of foreign ownership. They find that for OECD countries and emerging markets, there is no evidence of an influence of foreign ownership on the ratio of private credit to GDP (after taking account of several control variables). For developing (i.e., poorer) countries, however, there is a significant negative relationship.[32] However, they "cannot claim the direction of causality" (2010, 16).

---

30. Similarly, in 2012 the Mexican subsidiaries of BBVA, Citibank, and Santander all had better ratings than their parents. See "From Tequila Crisis to Sunrise," *Economist*, September 22, 2012.

31. The López Portillo government had nationalized the banks in 1982 at the time of the debt crisis. The Salinas government reprivatized them as part of a broader program of privatization but excluded foreign purchasers.

32. A result also found by Detragiache, Tressel, and Gupta (2008).

In view of heightened concerns after the Great Recession that foreign banks might reduce credit in host countries in response to crisis, they conduct relevant tests. They do find such a pattern overall in the crisis year of 2009 but also find that where foreign banks are dominant their maintenance of credit was more stable than that of domestic banks. They also find that foreign banks relying mainly on funding from local deposits were much less likely to reduce lending.

In the most recent major economic crisis, that of the euro area periphery in 2010–13, foreign banks did indeed contribute to destabilization in the form of sudden stop and exit. International banks' cross-border claims on the five periphery economies (Greece, Ireland, Italy, Portugal, and Spain) fell by 43 percent from end-2009 to end-2013. Foreign banks' claims on domestic banks fell even more sharply: by 91 percent in Greece; 66 percent each in Ireland, Portugal, and Spain; and 47 percent in Italy (Cline 2014, 60–61). However, for most emerging-market economies the nature of foreign bank involvement in the financial sector likely goes well beyond the portfolio holdings that characterized these outflows. Foreign bank presence is in the form of direct investment for ongoing presence. Foreign bank loans to sovereigns were predominant in the Latin American debt crisis of the 1980s, but thereafter sovereign finance shifted heavily back to bonds (the dominant form before the Great Depression). Loans from foreign to domestic banks (but not sovereigns) had featured centrally in the East Asian crisis of the late 1990s. In perhaps the most conspicuous case, that of the Republic of Korea, the postcrisis involvement of foreign banks has instead been much more in the form of ongoing corporate presence, as just described. Even so, the recent euro area experience can reasonably be read as a cautionary tale about heavy reliance on loans and portfolio investment by foreign banks, as opposed to openness to their ongoing corporate presence in the economy.

On the broader question of the influence of financial globalization, Cline (2010) surveys 76 studies.[33] Of those conducted at the general level (about one-third), studies with statistically significant results almost uniformly find a positive effect on financial openness on growth.[34] Typically the impact identified is that a move from complete financial closure to complete openness is associated with an increase in the annual growth rate by 1.5 to 2 percentage points.[35] The study arrives at a more conservative benchmark of a 0.5 percentage point growth impact for the difference between complete openness and

---

33. For a synopsis and partial update, see Cline (2013b).

34. Other categories include the influence on financial development, impact of direct investment, portfolio equity, crisis effects, institutional discipline, sector-level studies, and calibrated theoretical studies.

35. A popular skeptical survey (Edison et al. 2004) found that earlier significant results turned insignificant when a variable for government reputation was included, but Cline (2010, appendix 2D) shows that this variable itself is explained by prior country growth. Although Edison et al. (2002) found endogeneity, the resulting correction of impact coefficients reduced them by only about one-fourth (Cline 2010, 9).

complete closure, after applying statistical meta-analysis (Hedges and Olkin 1985) both across studies and within them (among various models included in each).[36] Even applying this conservative estimate, the study finds that about 8 percent of current GDP levels in industrial countries can be attributed to the cumulative effect of financial openness since 1980 (given actual openness levels) and about 2 percent of present GDP in emerging-market economies (where openness was lower and other sources of growth were higher).

Nor does consideration of risks from financial crises reverse the growth verdict on financial openness. Using evidence on currency and banking crises compiled by Michael Hutchison and Ilan Noy (2005) in comparison to the financial openness index of Dennis Quinn and Maria Toyoda (2008), Cline (2010, 99) finds that crises have tended to be somewhat more frequent in countries with low openness than in those with high openness. In a calibrated model considering the probability and severity of banking and currency crises, the study estimates that the odds are 20 to 1 in favor of the secular gains from financial openness exceeding the losses from any increased chance of crisis (Cline 2010, 101). In actual experience in the Great Recession, declines in equity markets in 2008–09 were no greater for more financially open emerging-market economies than for those that were more closed (Cline 2010, 258–59).

More recently, the "taper shock" after the May 2013 announcement that the US Federal Reserve would reduce quantitative easing induced yet another episode of turbulence in emerging markets. Rather than having long-lasting adverse effects, however, the shock had the salutary effect of reducing the overvaluation of several emerging-market currencies.[37] It remains to be seen whether the future actual arrival of higher real interest rates in the United States and other industrial economies will cause new and lasting pressures on emerging markets. The IMF has emphasized potential vulnerability associated with the large increase in corporate debt in emerging-market economies since 2008 in the context of low international interest rates, noting susceptibility in Argentina, Turkey, India, and Brazil in particular. It notes that larger foreign participation in local markets can transmit new instability and that investor herding continues. Nonetheless, it finds that "the progress made by emerging markets toward strengthening their financial systems reduces their financial asset prices' sensitivity to global financial shocks" (IMF 2014c, 25, 67).

In December 2012, the IMF adopted a new policy view approving the use of capital flow management measures (CFMs) under certain circumstances.[38] The staff document underlying the change emphasized that capital flows can have substantial benefits and that capital restrictions should not be substitutes for sound macroeconomic policies (IMF 2012a). It indicated that in the face of large capital inflows, countries should usually adopt macroeconomic policy

---

36. In meta-analysis results are weighted by the inverse of the variance of the estimate.

37. Those of Turkey, South Africa, Brazil, India, and Indonesia (Cline 2013c).

38. Sandrine Rastello, "IMF Officially Endorses Capital Controls in Reversal," Bloomberg, December 3, 2012.

adjustments, including lower interest rates, increased holdings of reserves, and currency appreciation. But the report endorsed a role for CFMs "when the room for adjusting macroeconomic policies is limited" (p. 18), for example, because the economy is overheating, the exchange rate is overvalued, and further reserve accumulation would be inappropriate or costly. It argued that restrictions should be temporary and took a less permissive view on capital outflow restrictions (e.g., they "should always be part of a broader policy package that includes macroeconomic, financial sector, and structural adjustment to address the fundamental causes of the crisis" [p. 26]). The report specifically cited Brazilian taxes on certain types of capital inflows and Korean leverage caps on banks' derivatives positions as examples of potentially appropriate measures (p. 17). For economies with long-standing capital restrictions, the report recommended that the sequence of liberalization begin with direct investment inflows, followed by direct investment outflows and long-term portfolio flows, and finally short-term portfolio flows, with the phase-in linked to strengthening of legal, accounting, regulatory, and supervisory institutions.

Although the IMF guidelines emphasize the temporary nature of appropriate capital controls and the importance of correct underlying macroeconomic policies, there is some risk that the policy signal may be read as a relatively relaxed attitude toward controls that may not be in the best interest of longer-term growth. The framing of the view in terms of staged domestic maturing of institutions would also seem to lend itself to interpretation by a country's officials that their economy is never quite ready to liberalize.[39] In the case of Brazil, domestic distortions have made it necessary to maintain a high interest rate (averaging 4.5 percent in real terms for the short-term policy rate in 2008–14Q1)[40] that provides a strong incentive for capital inflows. International policy advice would seem better oriented to address these distortions rather than commend the capital inflow tax.[41]

Trends in Financial Openness

The Chinn-Ito de jure index of financial openness provides a useful basis for tracking trends in financial openness in major emerging-market econo-

---

39. Note in particular that special tests in Cline (2010, 42–44) did not find support for the proposition that whereas direct investment openness is good for growth, openness to bond and bank flows is not.

40. In this period inflation averaged 5.7 percent and the policy interest rate 10.2 percent (IMF 2014b).

41. The distortions include the need for stronger fiscal performance to weigh against Brazil's historic memory of hyperinflation, as well as the presence of low-interest credit from the state development bank that eases borrowing costs for industry, thereby facilitating maintenance of the high policy interest rates that attract foreign capital. For its part, the Fund seems to endorse the capital inflow tax (IMF 2013k, 13–14).

mies (Ito and Chinn 2013).[42] The index is based on the IMF's AREAER, with variables pertaining to regulatory controls over current or capital account transactions, the presence of multiple exchange rates, and requirements for surrendering export proceeds.[43] In the 2011 version the maximum value for the financial openness variable was 2.44 ("most financially open") and applied to 54 countries; the minimum value was –1.86 and applied to 13 countries (of a total of 182 countries). Figure 3.2 shows the path of the index for the 16 emerging-market economies considered in this paper, for 2002–11.

Panel A in figure 3.2 shows that the PRC and India were systematically relatively closed (index value of –1.17) during the entire period. Venezuela began more open but became the most closed of the 16 countries by 2009 and after (index of –1.86 by 2010). Thailand also began relatively open (at –0.11) but in 2007 and after switched to the same degree of closedness as the PRC and India. Argentina is also in the relatively closed group, and its index would likely show an even more closed level if the period extended to 2012, when a de facto dual exchange rate policy took force.[44] The only country in the first panel that shifted from closed to more open was Viet Nam, which had the same index score as the PRC and India during 2002–07 but then shifted to intermediate openness (index at –0.11) in 2008 and after.

Panel B (with an average index of –0.1 for the six countries over 10 years) includes Colombia and Brazil from Latin America and four Asian emerging economies. Sri Lanka maintained an unchanging intermediate openness through the period, but Malaysia and the Philippines showed a substantial move toward closure in 2010–11. Only the Republic of Korea in this group showed an opening trend toward the end of the period.

Panel C shows four relatively open economies. Peru systematically maintains the highest openness score possible. Openness is also at the maximum for Chile in 2004–06 but more moderate by 2010–11. Mexico and Indonesia are both relatively open (index of 1.1) through most of the period, although there is a move toward less openness by Indonesia in 2011.

The recent trends for Asian emerging-market economies are sobering. Through 2011 they show no opening in the relatively closed cases of the PRC and India. Thailand, Malaysia, and the Philippines all moved toward closedness at the PRC-India level by 2010–11. Even Indonesia joined the closing trend albeit to a lesser degree. Only the Republic of Korea and Viet Nam moved in an opening direction (although Sri Lanka maintained a steady intermediate openness). The more dominant trend toward closing may reflect a response to capital inflow pressures associated with the extremely low

---

42. For problematic aspects of the alternative of de facto measures, such as gross capital flows as a percent of GDP, see the discussion in Cline (2010, 177–78).

43. The index is the first principal component of these variables and is recalculated for the entire sample for each year's new set of data.

44. Hilary Burke, "Analysis: Argentina Currency Policy Creates Multi-headed Monster," Reuters, September 12, 2012.

Figure 3.2   Chinn-Ito index of financial openness, 2002–11

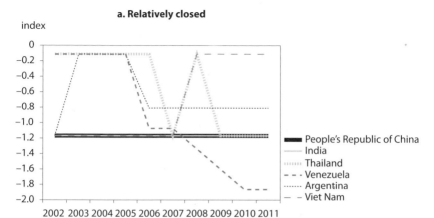

a. Relatively closed

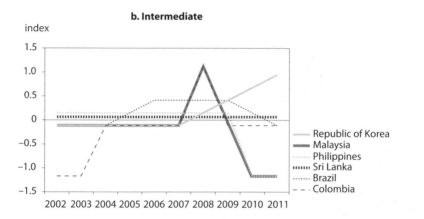

b. Intermediate

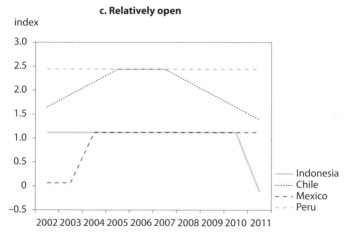

c. Relatively open

Source: Ito and Chinn (2013).

interest rate environment in the United States (and eurozone, aside from the debt-afflicted periphery). The Republic of Korea's opening could then be seen as an exception that proved the rule, considering that it adopted controls on currency derivatives that were not of the more usual type captured by the Chinn-Ito index.

As a final note on these data, it is suggestive that the country with unambiguously the highest persistent financial openness, Peru, is also the country that has the highest efficiency in the use of capital in figure 3.1.[45]

Principal Strengths in Asia

For the nine Asian emerging-market economies considered in this study, appendix 3A reviews recent financial sector conditions as described in the most recent available Financial Sector Assessment Program (FSAP) and IMF Article IV reports. The qualitative message that emerges from these reports can be read as a sound bill of health for especially the financial sectors in Malaysia and the Republic of Korea and relatively robust sectors in the Philippines, Thailand, and Indonesia. It is likely no coincidence that all five of these economies were at the epicenter of the East Asian crisis of the late 1990s and that this crisis was centered in the financial sector rather than in the sovereigns. Reform and restructuring of the traumatized sectors seems to have left them much stronger. Even within this group there are key differences in strategies. The Republic of Korea has chosen the route of importing financial strength through dominant presence of foreign banks. Malaysia instead has a considerably greater role of the government, direct and indirect.

A second major pattern is revealed by omission of comment in the international reviews: Economies with state-dominated financial sectors do not face the usual financial sector risk of bank runs, because the sovereigns stand behind their banks. This is the case for four economies with socialist traditions: the PRC and India, where the state owns the great bulk of the banking system; Sri Lanka, where it owns well more than half; and Viet Nam, where it owns about half (table 3.2). The FSAP and Article IV concerns for the state-dominated sectors are focused more on the termites-in-the-woodwork (as opposed to sudden-catastrophic) risk that poor banking practices will result in losses that add to government debt.

Overall, the combination of reform-after-crisis for the five East Asian economies and state-sector-backstop for the PRC, India, and Viet Nam suggests that the region has relatively good prospects of continuing to achieve the first responsibility of the financial sector: do no harm, in the sense of avoiding severe crises like those that (most recently) afflicted the United States, Ireland, and to a lesser extent the United Kingdom and Spain.

---

45. In the simple regression reported above, Peru has the highest positive residual (actual average growth at 1.86 percent per year in excess of the level predicted by the regression of growth on the investment rate).

Principal Challenges in Asia

The region nonetheless faces financial sector challenges. For the state-oriented sectors, the other side of the safety coin is the potential problem of inefficiency and poor allocation of credit. From the macroeconomic outcomes, this problem is not directly evident in the PRC and India, because their residual growth performance has been positive and the amount of investment mobilized in the economies (either because of or despite the financial sector structures) has been high (figure 3.1).[46] Even so, one suspects that such features as preference for lending to state-owned enterprises (SOEs) has meant the state-dominated systems tend to inhibit rather than stimulate efficient growth (see the discussion of the Chinese and Indian cases in appendix 3C). The policy considerations below thus suggest that a conscious long-term plan should be articulated for the future path of the state banking sector in those economies where it is predominant.

There are also conjunctural issues, and in particular what appears to be excessive credit to an overextended housing sector in the PRC (a pattern familiar from the US, Irish, and Spanish crises). A new problem that seems to be brewing in the PRC concerns the nonbank sector, in particular the wealth management product sector with questions of opacity and possibly excessive leverage. This problem in turn has been aggravated by the distortions caused by interest rate ceilings (in turn associated with the strategy of exchange rate intervention).[47]

Of the various problems enumerated in the FSAPs and Article IV reviews, a particularly sobering one is the specific mention of legal vulnerability of supervisors in three cases: Indonesia, the Philippines, and Viet Nam.

In all of the economies, an important challenge going forward will be to arrive at the right balance in setting capital requirements, for the banks, and enforcing regulation and supervision as well as setting appropriate capital requirements in the emerging nonbank sectors. The US experience with financial engineering gone wrong can be a useful cautionary tale in this regard. Especially in view of the dangers of high leverage revealed in the US experience, the Asian emerging-market economies might do well to treat the Basel III capital targets as minimum goals rather than state of the art goals for ensuring sound finance (see Hoenig 2013).

---

46. Applying the regression line for the observations in figure 3.1, the PRC has a positive growth residual of 1 percent per year and India a positive residual of 0.7 percent per year.

47. Thus, Nicholas Lardy (2013, 21) argues that "economic growth based on a super-elevated level of investment and systematic suppression of private consumption is not a viable long-run growth model. . . . Reform of the financial sector is the single most important prerequisite for sustained economic rebalancing in favor of consumption. The key element of financial reform . . . [is] eliminating the remaining government controls on interest rates on both deposits and loans."

Low-Income Economies

This study primarily examines the main emerging-market economies in Asia. However, appendix 3B briefly reviews financial sector conditions in four major low-income economies in the region: Bangladesh, Pakistan, Myanmar, and Nepal. Governance issues appear to be more serious in at least some of these cases. There may be a greater structural tradeoff for the advantages and disadvantages of state-dominated systems, because of greater vulnerability to fraud and poor control in state systems (IMF 2013h, 19), in addition to the more questionable solvency status of the sovereign and hence greater risk of losses socialized from the banking sector. These considerations suggest that the potential confidence ("no-run") advantage of a state sector may be lesser. Opening to strong foreign banks to bolster the system may accordingly be more attractive.

Implications for Institutions and Policies

There are large differences among the Asian emerging-market economies in levels of development, economic structure, and strengths and weaknesses of financial sectors. Nevertheless, it is important to seek to identify principal patterns in the policies and institutions needed to further develop their financial sectors. These sectors are not necessarily seriously lagging, even though by comparison with dynamic manufacturing export sectors (for example) they might seem to be so. Indeed, financial depth in the main economies is surprisingly high. The lines of action suggested here thus represent approaches meant to consolidate areas of strength and reduce areas of vulnerability.

Articulate Long-Term Plans for the State-Owned Banking Sector. Central planning for economic development has long been out of fashion. But state planning cannot responsibly be avoided for the banking sector when it is heavily dominated by state banks, as in the PRC, India, and Sri Lanka. Their governments should set forth and implement clearly articulated plans for the future of the sector, say for the coming decade.[48] For both the PRC and India, the state banking sector has a reputation of misdirecting credit, largely to favored state firm clients (see appendix 3C). Even the main offsetting benefit, broad absence of bank panics because of assurance of government support, could be eroded if the transition to a less state-dominated banking sector were not handled properly.

Where the state banking sector is predominant, governments should clearly articulate their 5- and 10-year targets for the share of banking sector assets held by the state banks. Ideological imperatives might well compel such targets to be close to current high levels. Otherwise it would seem desirable to

---

48. For the PRC, Lardy (2014, 137) notes several official commentaries in 2013–14 calling for a greater role for private banks, in part to help finance small and microenterprises. However, the steps actually taken so far have been limited.

make commitments to reduce the long-term shares of state banks to no more than 50 percent of bank assets. This process would probably involve some form of privatization. As the second main component of multiyear plans for strengthening the state banking sector (regardless of the target share), lines of action to ensure improved efficiency should be set forth. For example, in countries where the management of state banks is less experienced, requirements could be established for the presence of recognized outside managers (perhaps including from major international banks) on boards of directors.

In the transition toward lower state bank shares, governments would need to be sophisticated in designing mechanisms for handling bank failures. A sudden switch to an aggressive hands-off posture as part of the move to a larger private sector share in banking could undermine public confidence as a consequence of a jarring shift from presumed state support to presumed nonsupport, inviting bank panics. Clear rules for bank resolution, likely applied to weak, small institutions, could help achieve a more gradual and stable evolution of public expectations about banking support by the government.

Other questions posed by the state banking sector include the following: What are the appropriate capital requirements for state banks, and do they differ from those for private banks? Should the answer depend on the relative solvency of the sovereign? How would persistently state-dominated banking systems interact with the international trading regime, in an environment in which new initiatives such as the Trans-Pacific Partnership as well as bilateral economic agreements are likely to call for greater scope for US and other Western financial institutions to increase their access to the region's market in financial services? Comparative advantage would seem to recommend such access, although some might view foreign institutions as having lost their claim to excellence as a consequence of the recent US and European banking crises.

Eliminate Interest Rate Controls. As emphasized by Lardy (2014, 135–36), the PRC's practice of limiting bank deposit rates, especially to low levels that are negative in real terms, creates many distortions. It encourages excesses in wealth management products not subject to control as well as real estate speculation. By curbing household interest earnings it likely inhibits consumption and thus the desired shift from external- to internal-led growth. It is an anachronism four decades after McKinnon's analysis of counterproductive financial repression in Asia. But the PRC will also need to move further toward market determination of the exchange rate (and possibly toward looser capital controls) in parallel with lifting deposit rate ceilings, because otherwise its mechanism for sterilization of reserve buildups would be in jeopardy.[49] Another structural change that would need to accompany interest liberalization would be the development of clear rules for resolution of failed banks and the phasing down of the assumed blanket government guarantee of banks. Other-

49. Sterilization involves requiring the banks to hold more idle reserves so that yuan issued in exchange for exporter surpluses do not expand the money supply. Without deposit rate ceilings, banks would be forced to take losses on additional reserves.

wise individual banks could offer irresponsibly high interest rates and depositors would shift deposits to the banks in question without fear of potential loss, reflecting moral hazard from implicit government guarantee of all banks.

Develop Nonbank Financial Institutions but Regulate Shadow Banking. Development of nonbank financial institutions would seem desirable as part of the process of diversifying the financial sector. However, the recent US experience suggests that the sector should be developed on a basis of careful regulation and attention to adequate capitalization and in particular that its expansion should not be primarily the consequence of efforts to avoid capital and supervisory requirements of the banking sector. In the PRC in particular the large and rapidly growing shadow banking system needs closer regulation, with appropriate capital requirements and perhaps with such measures as minimum down payments for mortgages as well.

Set Bank Capital Requirements at Least at Basel III Levels and Include Meaningful Leverage Ratios. The financial crisis and Great Recession showed the need for higher bank capitalization, and as discussed above, Basel III may not go far enough in considering total assets rather than RWAs.

Provide Legal Immunity So Bank Regulators Can Do Their Job. The fact that the FSAP and Article IV reports explicitly cite the inadequacy of such legal protection in three economies (Indonesia, the Philippines, and Viet Nam) speaks volumes, in view of the strong incentive for such reports to be diplomatic, and makes one worry that this issue may be present elsewhere as well.

Develop Domestic Equity and Bond Markets. A more diversified financial sector is likely to be more resilient, as illustrated by the recent experience of the United States (more diversified) versus the euro area (heavily bank-dominated). The bond market appears relatively highly developed in the Republic of Korea and Malaysia but is tiny in Indonesia and the Philippines (if the BIS data provide an accurate portrayal; table 3.3). A fruitful area for research could be an examination of the reasons for the contrast, as well as analyzing this sector in several other regional economies for which the BIS data appear to be incomplete (including India). Measures to foster development of equity markets include ensuring shareholder rights and opening the economy to international portfolio investors. Clear creditor legal rights in case of default are important for bond markets. Governments might also consider programs designed to increase coverage of domestic firms by major international credit rating agencies.

Renew Gradual Progress toward Financial Opening. The recent trends reversing previous opening, discussed above, are not healthy for long-term development. Policies toward capital controls would seem to have much scope for liberalization without excessive risk of external shocks. Rigid controls on private capital outflows in particular are a symptom of either financial sector underdevelopment or government policy distortions or both, and even the

IMF's new flexibility on prudential capital controls does not extend to approval of persistent controls on capital outflows.

Get Macro Policies Right. The core set of government macroeconomic policies—fiscal, monetary, and exchange rate—should be managed in a coherent fashion that favors long-term growth but avoids financial crises. Sovereign debt solvency is perhaps the foremost prerequisite, because the banking system is typically heavily exposed to the sovereign (as shown by the crises in Greece recently and Argentina more than a decade ago). Monetary policy needs to weigh against credit booms that become so excessive that Minsky's dynamics seize hold and eventually result in a panic. Exchange rate policies need to move in the direction of greater flexibility in some important cases, and growth strategies correspondingly need to be consistent with trade outcomes that do not depend on high and ever-increasing trade surpluses.

Conclusion

This review suggests that the financial sectors in the main Asian emerging-market economies seem to be performing adequately their most important responsibility: the avoidance of financial crises. A likely reason is that reforms and restructuring after the East Asian financial crisis of the late 1990s left the systems in better shape than before in the five economies directly involved (Thailand, Indonesia, Malaysia, the Republic of Korea, and the Philippines). On an alternative track, the tradition of strong state involvement in the financial sector in countries with more socialist traditions has meant a low risk of collapse of public confidence in banks and thus bank runs (the PRC, India, Sri Lanka, and Viet Nam). The strong growth performance of the region in 2000–2013 further suggests that the financial sector is also managing to perform the task of mobilizing savings for investment. Investment and growth have been especially high in the PRC, India, and Viet Nam. Nonetheless, clear plans should be articulated for either reducing the share of state-owned banks in the banking sector over time or implementing mechanisms designed to increase their efficiency.

Financial sector depth is especially great in the PRC, the Republic of Korea, Malaysia, and Thailand, where credit to the private sector from banks, nonbanks, and portfolio debt securities, plus stock market capitalization, exceeds 250 to 300 percent of GDP (table 3.3). Although there is an empirical literature relating growth to financial depth, a recent study at the BIS (Cecchetti and Kharroubi 2012) finds that at some point further deepening begins to act as a drag on growth. By implication, with perhaps the exception of Indonesia and Sri Lanka, where financial depth remains relatively shallow, it might at least be said that further financial deepening is not among the highest priorities for spurring growth in the region.

Instead, a higher priority for policy is probably to ensure the robustness and quality of the financial systems. Stronger legal protections for regulatory authorities appear to be needed in some countries. In others, new needs for capital requirements and regulatory supervision seem to be emerging in the rapidly growing nonbank sectors. Clearer resolution plans would also seem prudent considering the potential too-big-to-fail problems (on average, each of the five largest banks has assets of 32 percent of GDP in Malaysia, 20 percent in the Republic of Korea, and 19 percent in Thailand).

The cases of the Republic of Korea and Mexico suggest that entry of foreign banks can help ensure banking sector stability. In economies with a strong state bank tradition, increased foreign presence might also help apply competitive discipline.[50] It is perhaps a cause for concern that recent trends in the region seem to be more in the direction of narrowing financial openness to external capital. Notwithstanding the recent IMF endorsement of capital restrictions under certain circumstances, in my view the broad empirical experience is that greater financial openness benefits rather than threatens growth, even after taking account of the potentially greater risk of sudden stops.

---

50. It is conceivable that a bilateral trade and investment agreement between the United States and the PRC could lead to greater foreign presence of banks even in the PRC, although a long phase-in period would seem likely.

Appendix 3A Financial Sector Evaluations in the FSAP and Article IV Reports

The FSAP was established in 1999 and conducts periodic reviews of financial sectors in emerging-market and developing countries (by the IMF and World Bank) and in advanced economies (by the IMF). The IMF also conducts surveillance reviews of member economies, usually annually, under Article IV of the Articles of Agreement. This appendix conveys key findings of the most recent published FSAP and (with respect to the financial sector) Article IV reports for each of the nine Asian emerging-market economies considered in this paper.

The People's Republic of China

The June 2011 FSAP report for the PRC (IMF 2011) identified several areas of risk: the impact of rapid crisis-related credit expansion on credit quality; rising off–balance sheet exposures; a reversal in rapidly rising real estate prices; and the buildup of contingent liabilities as a consequence of the government's role in credit allocation at the central and provincial levels. It did find that stress tests showed most of the large banks to be resilient to shocks. The report judged that existing financial policies fostered (overly) high savings, high liquidity, and high risk of capital misallocation and asset bubbles, especially in real estate. It noted that absorption of associated costs through the implicit tax on households through low remuneration on deposits could not be presumed to continue. The report noted that high levels of foreign exchange intervention and strong incentives for capital inflows hampered control of liquidity. It called for a shift from administrative limits on bank lending to interest rates as the instrument to govern credit expansion. It warned that banks' large exposure to SOEs and guaranteed margins from interest rate regulation undermined effective credit risk management. It called for an improved legal, regulatory, supervisory, and crisis management framework and better corporate governance in banks as preconditions to acceleration of financial deepening, liberalization of interest rates, and liberalization of the capital account.

The July 2013 Article IV report (IMF 2013a) warned that heavy reliance on credit and investment to sustain activity was raising vulnerabilities, leading to a steady buildup of leverage that was eroding the strength of the financial sector, local government, and corporate balance sheets. It found that rapid expansion of nontraditional finance, including trust companies, corporate bonds as well as alternative wealth management products, raised questions about the adequacy of supervision and regulation. The report called for liberalizing interest rates and allowing market pricing of deposits and introducing explicit deposit insurance while removing the moral hazard stemming from the perception that all interest-bearing assets are implicitly guaranteed. It correspondingly called for tolerance for occasional losses or haircuts on such instruments as corporate bonds or wealth management products. The report did not address the potentially greater resilience of the PRC's banking system to bank runs because of its predominant state ownership and instead suggested that fiscal space was narrower than believed because of larger debt (amounting to 45 percent of GDP) and deficits (10 percent) when an augmented measure including local government finance vehicles and other off-budget funds is applied. The report contained an appendix reporting progress on 29 prior recommendations of the FSAP. At the top of the list was advancing the process of interest rate and exchange rate reform; the reported progress amounted to small changes.[51]

India

The most recent FSAP report for India (IMF 2013b) makes the surprisingly frank critique that "[t]he prominent role of the state in the financial sector contributes to a build-up of fiscal contingent liabilities and creates a risk of capital misallocation that may constrain economic growth" (p. 3). "In light of its commitment to retain the public sector character of state-owned banks, the government needs to consider how to manage its ownership in ways that are compatible with the public banks prudently financing a rapidly growing economy" (p. 7). The report calls for gradually reducing mandatory holdings of government securities by financial institutions and allowing greater access to private domestic and foreign sources of capital. It commends remarkable progress toward a stable financial system but notes a worsening of bank asset quality. Nonetheless, stress tests find banks' buffers of high-quality assets robust to pressures. The report finds the regulatory and supervisory regime to be well developed and largely in compliance with international standards. Recommendations for improvement include consolidated supervision of financial conglomerates, reductions in large exposures and related-party lending limits, and stronger solvency requirements in insurance. The report notes potential conflict of interest from the inclusion of Reserve Bank of India (RBI) officers on the boards of public banks supervised by the RBI.

The Article IV report of February 2014 (IMF 2014d) expressed concern that despite the apparently strong capital adequacy ratio (at 13.8 percent in March 2013), nonperforming (4.2 percent) or restructured (5.7 percent) loans were rising, and the weakest corporations were at much more risk of default than in 2009. The review reiterated the FSAP's call for limits on loans to inter-related companies. It called for a more rigorous treatment of asset valuation in restructured loans and improvements in the insolvency framework. For their part, the authorities included better access to finance for SMEs and underserved parts of the population. The report found that India's banks are likely to require significant new capital injections over the next few years, in part

---

51. For example, deposit rates could be 1.1 times the benchmark rate instead of strictly limited; and the trading band for the renminbi against the dollar had been widened from 0.5 to 1 percent.

because of the new Basel III capital requirements. In a severe stress scenario additional capital costs for public sector banks could amount to 5 percent of 2013 GDP.

Indonesia

The FSAP report published in 2010 (IMF 2010a, 1) found the "banking system is generally healthy" and had improved significantly in the past decade. But it noted "lingering concerns over weak enforcement of the rule of law, transparency, and governance issues." It found that gaps remained in dealing with problem banks, and welcomed plans for creating an integrated supervisory agency. The report judged that the financial sector "lags behind comparable countries in terms of depth and contribution to the economy," that securities trade at a discount relative to regional peers, and wealthy Indonesian citizens still prefer to place savings offshore (p. 7). It cited "the absence of legal protection for the financial sector regulator and supervisor" and consequential "public questioning of and political interference in supervisory actions" (p. 8). Stress tests showed banks vulnerable to credit risk and some mid-sized banks to liquidity risk. The report urged the government to desist "from using moral suasion and prudential regulations to promote credit growth" to avoid weakening bank balance sheets and system stability (p. 8). It noted that the non-bank financial sector is small, and that much more should be done to develop capital markets, including the small insurance industry. The report listed 44 FSAP recommendations, beginning with bringing risk weights to at least Basel I levels and tightening the accounting definition of tier 1 capital.

The December 2013 Article IV review (IMF 2013c) found the banking system "sound as a whole, with systemic risk remaining low" (p. 18). It viewed the banks as well capitalized at a capital adequacy ratio of 17.5 percent, but noted that quality of capital remains an issue. It considered shadow banking activity to be limited, mainly through finance companies with less than 10 percent of financial system assets. The review noted that financial markets are less developed than in emerging-market peers, with stock market capitalization at 49 percent of GDP at end-2012 and domestic debt securities only 15 percent of GDP (of which 85 percent were issued by the government). It judged that "[d]eepening financial markets in Indonesia is vital for mobilizing savings to fund investment" (2013c, 21). It called for increasing the availability and liquidity of short-term treasury bills to bolster the relatively thin and volatile money market. The report urged heightened monitoring of banks with large restructured loans or heavy exposure to export-related and property sectors, as well as corporate leverage ratios in light of depreciation of the rupiah. It urged the development of crisis management protocols, especially regarding emergency liquidity and interventions in systemically important financial institutions. The report called for a more investor-friendly negative list for foreign investment and less rigidity in labor regulations, particularly severance pay.

The Republic of Korea

The May 2014 FSAP report for the Republic of Korea (IMF 2014f) finds that since the 2008 crisis, banking sector capitalization has improved, foreign currency liquidity profiles have strengthened markedly, and nonperforming loans (NPLs) have been reduced to low levels. The report calls for a more robust regulatory framework for the growing nonbank financial sector, however. In light of the high degree of capital account openness and financial integration, the report advocates more formal arrangements for macroprudential policy. It also calls for improvements toward international best practice in the resolution framework for conglomerates and systemically important financial institutions, greater independence of the supervisory system from political influence, and more meaningful fines and penalties. The overall tone of the report was that an already good financial sector could be made better and safer.

The April 2014 Article IV review (IMF 2014e) notes that although banking sector soundness remains robust, low interest rates and high credit costs have reduced banks' return on assets from over 1 percent in 2005–07 to just 0.5 percent (compared with 1 percent in 35 countries followed by the IMF's periodic *Global Financial Stability Report*). Lower profitability has contributed to retrenchment of foreign banks' operations in the Republic of Korea. The report estimates corporate debt at 127 percent of equity at end-2012 and notes a marked duality, with improved profitability of large export-driven corporations but concentration of liquidity risks and leverage in a few sectors (construction, shipbuilding, transportation) and outside the most profitable chaebols. The report finds that the Republic of Korea had emerged as a safe haven in the course of the 2013 international market turmoil.

Just as the FSAP and Article IV reports for the PRC do not mention the stability accorded to the financial sector by state ownership, the reports for the Republic of Korea are tacit about the stability provided by the high participation of foreign banks.

Malaysia

The most recent FSAP report for Malaysia (IMF 2013d) gave the financial system a sound bill of health, citing successful reforms in the 10-year financial and capital markets master plans undertaken by the central bank and the securities commission after the late 1990s financial crisis. The report noted resilience to the recent global financial crisis, helped by limited reliance of financial intermediaries on cross-border funding, a supervisory and regulatory regime highly compliant with international standards, and a well-capitalized banking system. The report did note high reliance on demand deposits, rapid loan growth, rising home prices, and high household leverage but had only nine relatively general recommendations (e.g., enhanced monitoring of household leverage), the shortest list among the FSAPs reviewed in this appendix. The report noted the extensive government ownership in the financial sector, direct and indirect, and noted that the authorities' development plans recognized the need for transition to more reliance on the private sector.

The early 2014 Article IV review (IMF 2014g) reaffirmed the favorable assessment of the financial sector, noting that deep financial markets (and a flexible exchange rate) had helped Malaysia weather the taper turmoil of mid-2013. It noted, however, that large foreign holdings of domestic bonds and equities make the economy vulnerable to capital outflows in periods of global stress. It identified high house prices, rising household debt, and banks' large exposure to real estate as areas of concern. The review found the banking sector well capitalized, with a tier 1 capital ratio of 13.9 percent at end-2012, compared to the Basel III target of 8.5 percent by 2019. The 2019 liquidity target could be more challenging.

The Philippines

The most recent FSAP report for the Philippines (IMF 2010b) found that the banking sector had been strengthened substantially since the Asian crisis of the late 1990s, had become generally resilient to macroeconomic risks, and had withstood the global financial crisis better than had been feared. It noted progress in banking supervision but called for further strengthening of the bank resolution authority. It cited bank secrecy provisions as an obstacle to supervisors' access to depositor and investment information and called for improved legal protection of supervisors. The report urged further development of nonbank financial sectors, harmonization of tax treatment of various financial products, and rationalization of overlapping state entities financing housing.

In the April 2013 Article IV review (IMF 2013e), the Fund noted strong capital adequacy and declining NPLs in the banking sector. It welcomed rapid growth of nonbank financial intermediation (new equity financing through initial public offerings raised almost half as much as new bank lending for private credit in 2012) but urged greater supervisory oversight of the growing nonbank sector. The report emphasized the need to avoid excessive bank exposure to consolidated conglomerate groups and increase attention to observing the single borrower limit. The review also expressed concern about less stringent lending standards of real estate developers, calling for macroprudential measures to contain risks in the sector. It reiterated concern about the need for legal protections of central bank supervisors.

Sri Lanka

The most recent available FSAP for Sri Lanka was issued in 2007, too long ago to be of much help. The Article IV report of May 2013 (IMF 2013f) is sparse in analysis of the financial sector. It warns about rapid credit growth (with credit about 30 percent higher in 2011 than a year before) but also reports that the base for the credit ratio was low (only 30 percent of GDP in 2010) and the pace of expansion had moderated by late 2012. Similarly, equity prices rose about fourfold from 2009 to 2011 but then eased by about 40 percent in 2012. The report indicates that a severe stress test raising NPLs to 23 percent would leave 7 of the 12 largest banks undercapitalized but also finds that the fresh capital required would amount to only ½ percent of GDP, apparently reflecting the financial shallowness of the economy.

Thailand

The most recent available FSAP report for Thailand was issued in 2008, also out of date. The Article IV report of November 2013 (IMF 2013g) noted that profitability of commercial banks has been strong. NPLs have fallen from 12 percent in 2004 to 6 percent in 2008 and 2.5 percent in 2012; the capital adequacy ratio was around 15 to 16 percent in 2010–12, and banks are expected to meet Basel III capital and liquidity requirements on time. The report noted that Thailand's private sector credit-to-GDP ratio is relatively high in Thailand, at 115 percent in early 2013. It noted that the specialized financial institutions (public banks that carry out government lending programs) reached 27 percent of total bank credit in 2012 and that their assets tend to be of lower quality. Rising household debt (reaching 78 percent of GDP in 2012) was another source of concern. The report called for expansion of central bank supervision of the special financial institutions and credit cooperatives but did not see a pressing need for tighter macroprudential policies.

Viet Nam

No FSAP has been published for Viet Nam. The July 2012 Article IV review (IMF 2012b) reported that after years of rapid credit growth, the tightening of monetary conditions and a decline in asset prices had caused intense liquidity pressure for a number of small joint stock banks accounting for about 7 percent of deposits. The government adopted a bank restructuring plan, although the report noted a reluctance to close insolvent banks. For the state-owned banks, the plan envisions continued equitization, with the state remaining a dominant shareholder. Capital is to be increased to meet Basel II requirements by 2015. For commercial banks, healthy banks are to be encouraged to consolidate and expected to support weak banks with liquidity or through mergers. Banks with temporary liquidity shortages are to be refinanced by the central bank, while weak banks will be subject to special control, including limits on dividends and suspension of managers. The report judged that "the regulatory and supervisory framework needs to be strengthened at every stage including bank resolution" (p. 14) and that supervisory authorities' staff should be protected from personal liability (and staff capacity improved).

Appendix 3B The Financial Sector in Low-Income Economies: Bangladesh, Myanmar, Nepal, and Pakistan[52]

Bangladesh and Pakistan

As with the PRC, India, Sri Lanka, and Viet Nam (as discussed in the main text), the government plays a major role in the banking sectors of Bangladesh, Myanmar, Nepal, and Pakistan. International official sector reviews tend to find that poor governance and political interference in the lending activities of state-owned banks have restricted the potential of the financial systems in Bangladesh and Pakistan. In Bangladesh, the nonperforming loan (NPL) to total loan ratio was 30 percent for state-owned commercial banks at the end of 2013, compared with 12 percent for the banking sector as a whole (IMF 2014h, 10).

Nonetheless, private commercial banks now account for the majority of bank assets in both Bangladesh and Pakistan. Their performance has improved—in terms of better asset quality, higher levels of lending stock, declining NPLs, and stronger capital adequacy ratios—even as the performance of the state-owned banks has declined. While private banks have eroded the market share of state banks, the latter still play a systemically important role in the sector (in Bangladesh, private commercial banks hold more than 50 percent of total deposits compared with 30 percent for state-owned commercial banks; IMF 2010c, 36). The state-owned banks are mandated to direct lending at targeted industries and SOEs to fulfill government social policies but private banks earn higher rates of return on their assets and have healthier loan portfolios.

While the growth of private commercial bank assets in many of the other Asian emerging-market economies has been correlated to a rapid growth in private credit, in particular to households (largely to finance purchases in the real estate sector), the growth of private commercial bank assets in Bangladesh and Pakistan has coincided with a moderation in private credit. Commercial banks in fact have a high concentration of holdings in public debt since the two sovereigns have sought to finance their large fiscal deficits by selling government securities to commercial banks. The underdeveloped housing finance and insurance institutional frameworks in Bangladesh and Pakistan could explain why there is a divergence in credit patterns compared with the previously surveyed Asian emerging-market economies.

Banks have increased their exposure to the capital markets through equity financing and transactions in the primary market for government bonds. In equity markets, from January 2011 through June 2013 the Karachi Stock Exchange far outperformed other major emerging stock markets (IMF 2013i,

---

52. This appendix was prepared by Abir Varma. It is based on IMF (2010c, 2013h, 2014h) for Bangladesh; IMF (2004, 2013i, 2014i) for Pakistan; IMF (2013j, 2014j) for Myanmar; and IMF (2014k) for Nepal.

46). There are negligible corporate bond markets in the two countries, however, and activity in the secondary market for government bonds is low.

There is significant overlap in the key IMF recommendations for strengthening the banking systems of Bangladesh and Pakistan since the financial systems in both countries largely experience the same chronic symptoms. First, both governments should strengthen the balance sheets of state commercial banks through further capital injections, formulating stronger credit risk management and compliance policies and limiting lending activities of state banks to other SOEs. Second, both governments must improve the industrywide legal and regulatory framework. Specifically, both countries should adopt clear deposit insurance schemes and develop sound loan classification and bankruptcy/liquidation laws. Finally, the governments should keep their fiscal deficits in check to prevent the possibility of financial crowding out.

Myanmar

Since Myanmar has only recently begun the process of implementing economic and financial reforms to modernize its economy, its financial system remains underdeveloped compared with those of other Asian countries. There are no foreign banks, and governance and supervision of local banks lag behind those of other countries in the region.

State banks dominate the financial system. The two biggest banks, Myanma Foreign Trade Bank (MFTB) and Myanma Economic Bank (MEB), carry out commercial operations and perform several government functions: The MFTB holds the government's foreign reserves and performs all the foreign exchange transactions for both the private and public sectors while the MEB acts as the treasury.

Nonetheless, authorities are taking many steps to reform the sector. While only land was previously accepted as collateral on loans, certain agricultural exports have now been made eligible as collateral. The Myanma Agricultural Development Bank has raised credit limits for farmers, and licenses have been issued to the Microfinance Bank and the Housing and Construction Bank (both new joint ventures between the government and the private sector). A ban on interbank trading has been lifted and a payment union for interbank settlements has been established. In addition, credit cards and ATMs have recently been introduced.

The Central Bank of Myanmar's (CBM) budget is currently set by the parliament and further reforms in the financial sector should include steps to increase the autonomy of the central bank and the monetary policy tools at its disposal. The IMF recommends that the CBM bring reserve requirements in line with international standards and establish deposit/credit and treasury securities auctions as first steps toward setting market-based interest rates. The Fund suggests that state banks be brought under the CBM's supervision, while their roles are redefined as the CBM takes over foreign exchange and monetary policy functions. For instance, the MFTB will have to be absorbed into the CBM, merged with another state bank, or liquidated.

To strengthen the regulatory framework underpinning the sector, the Fund suggests aligning bank capital and NPL definitions with accepted international standards. The Banking and Financial Institutions Law, which is currently being drafted, should include provisions to enhance data reporting and supervision of both banks and nondepository financial institutions such as microfinance and insurance institutions. The IMF endorses the government's intention to open the financial sector to foreign banks as a means of helping transfer technology and increase integration with financial markets. However, it suggests that initially only three to five licenses be awarded because of limited central bank supervisory capacity (IMF 2014j, 9).

Nepal

Like Viet Nam, Nepal's financial sector is large relative to peer countries (domestic bank deposits are 68 percent of GDP). Lax licensing rules have given rise to an excessively large number of financial institutions: As of April 2014 there were 30 commercial banks, 86 development banks, 56 finance companies, and 35 microfinance institutions (not to mention the number of credit cooperatives—totaling 17,000—that are growing rapidly and are not supervised by the Nepal Rastra Bank [NRB]). As in Bangladesh and Pakistan, NPLs are likely underreported, credit information is weak, and debt enforcement and insolvency systems are rarely enforced.

The Fund recommends a number of steps to improve the stability of the financial system. Most importantly, the NRB could undertake a thorough asset quality review of banks' balance sheets and actively guide a bank consolidation process to avoid the formation of large weak banks from small weak ones. The NRB should also strengthen bank licensing regulations and "be given special resolution powers to close insolvent banks" (IMF 2014k, 11) while debt enforcement and insolvency systems should be improved more generally. The number of state-owned banks should be reduced, and the Employment Provident Fund and Citizens Investment Trust should be brought under the joint purview of the NRB and the Insurance Board. The supervisory mandate of the Department of Cooperatives must be strengthened for greater oversight of the cooperatives sector. Lastly, the Fund recommends the creation of a collateral agency and the elimination of the Credit Information Bureau's minimum reporting threshold to make credit information more transparent.

Appendix 3C Inefficiencies in the State Banking Sectors in the People's Republic of China and India

People's Republic of China

As indicated in the main text, the PRC's banking system is heavily dominated by the state. Based on summary data from 129 banks with annual data for the period from 2003 to 2010, Xiaoxi Zhang and Kevin Daly (2011) find that the traditional "big four" state-owned banks performed worse in terms of return on assets, return on equity, and net interest margins compared with other banks during this period. Although only three wholly government-owned banks remain—each with a distinct function (agriculture, infrastructure, and export promotion)—the government has a majority stake in most banks, and private banks held only 15 percent of bank assets in 2012 (Lardy 2014, 20). The PRC's banks generally share the same governance system involving senior bank officers, a board of directors, and a board of supervisors. Senior bank officers are members of the Chinese Communist Party (CCP), and the top three positions are appointed by the Organization Department of the Party. Except for the three wholly owned state banks, in the large state-owned banks the boards of directors consist of a mix of senior bank officers, persons appointed by major shareholders (the state), and "independent directors"; the board of supervisors includes individuals appointed by the CCP, the major shareholders, the bank's labor union, and "external supervisors" (CRS 2012, 26).[53] Concomitantly, there is a regular exchange of personnel between commercial banks, the People's Bank of China (the central bank), and the China Banking Regulatory Commission (Lardy 2014, 21). Thus, the governance structure is frequently seen by commentators as evidence of excessive government influence in the financial sector.

Chinese state-owned banks are widely, albeit possibly misleadingly, perceived as providing subsidized loans to selected enterprises, generally other SOEs.[54] Even though the PRC does not officially report information on interest rates on loans by type of enterprise, many contend that SOEs are provided loans at lower interest rates. A survey-based study conducted by the Hong Kong Institute for Monetary Research in 2009 found that in 2004–05, SOEs were charged 188 basis points less than private enterprises after controlling statistically for sector and province (Ferri and Liu 2009, 10, 21).[55] In contrast,

---

53. However, there is a large number of city commercial banks, many of which are not listed, for which the role of the party in choosing senior officers is not clear. Nicholas Lardy, personal communication, October 14, 2014.

54. Lardy (2014, 94) cites—and disputes—examples from the *Economist*, *Financial Times*, and a leading international investment bank.

55. A possible critique of this result could be that the measure of interest cost is misleading because it is calculated on the basis of interest paid compared with debt, but debt includes noninterest-bearing liabilities such as accounts payable. Lardy (2014, 164) criticizes a similar

a survey of 100 Chinese financial institutions conducted by the People's Bank of China and the International Finance Corporation found that in 2004–05 average interest rates charged to state-owned companies were only slightly lower (5.67 percent) than interest rates charged to privately owned companies (5.96 percent) (IFC 2007, 57). Lardy (2014, 108) cites these results to challenge the popular image of state bank distortions favoring state firms. He also cites recent data on loan volumes to show that in 2010–12 the flow of new loans to privately owned firms substantially exceeded the flow to state-owned firms. Nonetheless, he notes that private firms still account for only one-third of the stock of loans outstanding, only one-half their estimated share of two-thirds in economic output (Lardy 2014, 109). Moreover, even if state banks charge interest rates to private firms that are broadly comparable to those they charge to state firms, to the extent that private firms can obtain loans from state banks only when their projects are politically connected (including especially private firms that are effectively owned by local political leaders), the question of misallocation remains. The rapid rise of the shadow banking system appears to be a symptom of the fact that private firms not politically connected rely heavily on borrowing from institutions outside the formal state-dominated banking system.

In chapter 9 of this volume, Nicholas Borst and Nicholas Lardy provide data showing significant improvements in the Chinese banking sector from 1999 to 2011 (for example, an increase in return on assets from 0.7 to 1.1 percent), as well as data suggesting that by 2011 Chinese banks performed well compared with the G-20 average. They cite the PRC's success in reforming state-owned financial institutions as experience that might be useful for policymakers in other Asian countries. Even so, it would seem desirable for the PRC to articulate the medium-term goal for the role of the state-owned banks and to specify mechanisms designed to ensure efficiency and market-oriented allocation, as suggested more generally for state-owned banks in the main text.

India

In India, public sector banks (PbSBs) (those with at least 51 percent government ownership) have lower profitability than private sector banks (PSBs), with lower profits per branch and per employee than PSBs (RBI 2013a, 61). PbSBs also faced a lower return on assets for almost all years from 2000 to 2012, and the latest estimates place their return on assets at 0.9 percent compared with 1.5 percent for PSBs (RBI 2013a, 62).

State-run banks account for around three-quarters of total lending in the banking sector, but their asset quality has deteriorated in recent times. In fact, there is a concern that they face a bigger bad debt problem than their nonper-

---

finding by other authors on this basis. It is unclear, however, why SOEs would have relatively larger noninterest-bearing debt, or whether that source of finance might itself be a manifestation of preferential access to credit.

forming loans ratio suggests due to the classification of many bad loans as "restructured" loans. Estimates by the *Economist* suggest that public lenders hold 93 percent of restructured loans. If the largest state bank—State Bank of India—is excluded, 80 percent of restructured loans sit with smaller state banks that hold 50 percent of the banking sector's tier 1 capital.[56] The poorer asset quality of PbSBs might be explained by what observers deem political meddling in how state banks are run. PbSBs are regulated by both the central bank and the Ministry of Finance and frequently receive directives to push the social agenda of the government; from October 2012 to January 2014, the Ministry of Finance issued 82 circulars to PbSBs.[57] It is telling that iron and steel and infrastructure (which includes power and telecommunications), sectors with many government-business partnerships, account for the highest proportions of total restructured debt (23 and 22.7 percent, respectively) (RBI 2013b, 67). Additionally, even though the statutory liquidity requirement (SLR) is set at 22 percent, the proportion of banks' liabilities that must be backed by their holdings of government bonds, most state banks hold a much greater amount of government bonds and have played a major role in funding the government's persistent fiscal deficits.[58]

---

56. "Hold Your Nose; Indian Banks," *Economist*, August 18, 2012.

57. Nupur Acharya, "Is India Ready to Relinquish Control of its State-Owned Banks?" *Wall Street Journal*, May 15, 2014. The author does not clarify, however, the extent to which the directives to state-owned banks exceed the government's more general programs of priority lending applicable to all banks.

58. Acharya, "Is India Ready."

Appendix 3D Financial Sector Indicators

Figure 3D.1   Bank loans outstanding, 2000–2013

percent of GDP

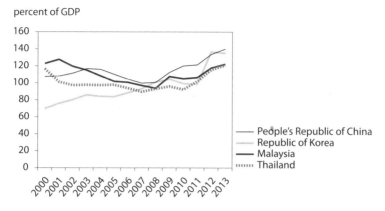

percent of GDP

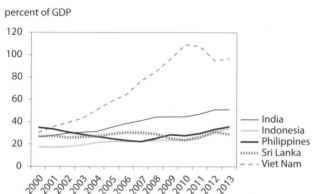

Sources: IMF (2014b); World Bank (2013, 2014).

Figure 3D.2   Nongovernment bonds outstanding, 2000–2013

percent of GDP

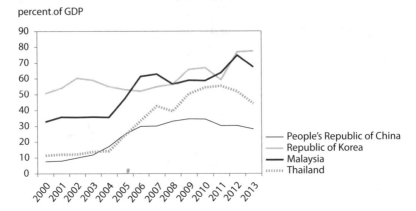

percent of GDP

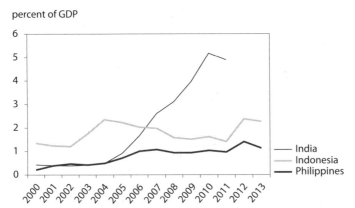

Sources: BIS (2014); World Bank (2013).

Figure 3D.3   Stock market capitalization, 2000–2012

percent of GDP

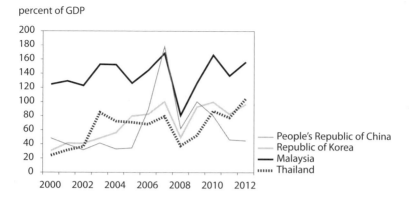

percent of GDP

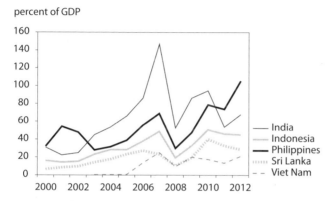

Source: World Bank (2014).

Figure 3D.4   Real stock market indices, 2006–14

index (January 2006 = 100)

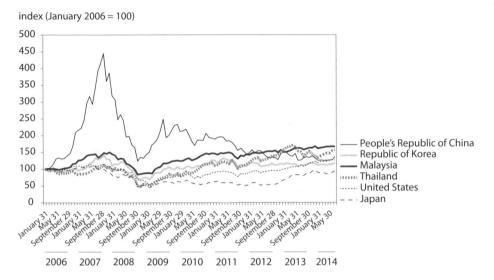

index (January 2006 = 100)

Sources: Bloomberg; IMF (2014b).

References*

Ahearne, Alan. 2012. Political-Economic Context in Ireland. In *Resolving the European Debt Crisis*, eds. William R. Cline and Guntram B. Wolff. Washington: Peterson Institute for International Economics.

Arcand, Jean-Louis, Enrico Berkes, and Ugo Panizza. 2012. *Too Much Finance?* IMF Working Paper 12/161. Washington: International Monetary Fund.

Banco Central do Brasil. 2014. *Top 50 Banks in Brazil* (June). Brasilia.

Barth, James R., Gerard Caprio, Jr., and Ross Levine. 2013. *Bank Regulation and Supervision in 180 Countries from 1999 to 2011*. NBER Working Paper 18733. Cambridge, MA: National Bureau of Economic Research.

Beck, Thorsten, Asli Demirgüç-Kunt, and Ross Levine. 2010. Financial Institutions and Markets across Countries and over Time: The Updated Financial Development and Structure Database. *World Bank Economic Review* 24, no. 1: 77–92.

Bekaert, Geert, and Campbell R. Harvey. 2005. Does Financial Liberalization Spur Growth? *Journal of Financial Economics* 77, no. 1 (July): 3–55.

Bertocco, Giancarlo. 2006. *Finance and Development: Is Schumpeter's Analysis Still Relevant?* Working Paper 2006/13. Varese, Italy: University of Insubria, Faculty of Economics.

BIS (Bank for International Settlements). 2010. *Basel III: A Global Regulatory Framework for More Resilient Banks and Banking Systems*. Basel.

BIS (Bank for International Settlements). 2014. *Debt Securities Statistics*. Basel.

Bonfiglioli, Alessandra, and Caterina Mendicino. 2004. *Financial Liberalization, Banking Crises, and Growth: Assessing the Links*. Working Paper Series in Economics and Finance 567. Stockholm: Stockholm School of Economics.

Calvo, Guillermo A. 1998. Capital Flows and Capital-Market Crises: The Simple Economics of Sudden Stops. *Journal of Applied Economics* 1, no. 1 (November): 35–54.

Cecchetti, Stephen G., and Enisse Kharroubi. 2012. *Reassessing the Impact of Finance on Growth*. BIS Working Paper 381. Basel: Bank for International Settlements.

Claessens, Stijn, and Neeltje van Horen. 2010. *Foreign Banks: Trends, Impact, and Financial Stability*. IMF Working Paper 12/10. Washington: International Monetary Fund.

Cline, William R. 2010. *Financial Globalization, Economic Growth, and the Crisis of 2007–09*. Washington: Peterson Institute for International Economics.

Cline, William R. 2013a. Sovereign Debt and Asia: International Lessons and Emerging Issues. In *Responding to Financial Crisis: Lessons from Asia Then, the United States and Europe Now*, eds. Changyong Rhee and Adam S. Posen. Washington: Asian Development Bank and Peterson Institute for International Economics.

Cline, William R. 2013b. Capital Market Integration. In *The Evidence and Impact of Financial Globalization, Volume 3*, ed. Gerard Caprio. Oxford: Elsevier.

Cline, William R. 2013c. *Estimates of Fundamental Equilibrium Exchange Rates, November 2013*. PIIE Policy Brief 13-29. Washington: Peterson Institute for International Economics.

Cline, William R. 2014. *Managing the Euro Area Debt Crisis*. Washington: Peterson Institute for International Economics.

Cline, William R., and Joseph E. Gagnon. 2013. *Lehman Died, Bagehot Lives: Why Did the Fed and Treasury Let a Major Wall Street Bank Fail?* PIIE Policy Brief 13-21. Washington: Peterson Institute for International Economics.

---

*The Asian Development Bank recognizes "China" by the name the People's Republic of China.

Coremberg, Ariel. 2014. Measuring Argentina's GDP: Myths and Facts. *World Economics* 15, no. 1 (March).

CRS (Congressional Research Service). 2012. *China's Banking System: Issues for Congress.* Washington.

Das, Mitali, and Papa N'Diaye. 2013. *Chronicle of a Decline Foretold: Has China Reached the Lewis Turning Point?* IMF Working Paper 13/36. Washington: International Monetary Fund.

Dell'Ariccia, Giovanni, Deniz Igan, Luc Laeven, Hui Tong, Bas Bakker, and Jérôme Vandenbussche. 2012. *Policies for Macrofinancial Stability: How to Deal with Credit Booms.* IMF Staff Discussion Note SDN/12/06 (June). Washington: International Monetary Fund.

Demirgüç-Kunt, Asli, and Enrica Detragiache. 1998. *The Determinants of Banking Crises in Developing and Developed Countries.* IMF Staff Papers 45: 81–109. Washington: International Monetary Fund.

Detragiache, Enrica, Thierry Tressel, and Poonam Gupta. 2008. Foreign Banks in Poor Countries: Theory and Evidence. *Journal of Financial Economics* 63, issue 5 (October): 2123–160.

Didier, Tatiana, Ross Levine, and Sergio L. Schmukler. 2014. *Capital Market Financing, Firm Growth, Firm Size Distribution.* NBER Working Paper 20336. Cambridge, MA: National Bureau of Economic Research.

Domar, Evsey D. 1946. Capital Expansion, Rate of Growth, and Employment. *Econometrica* 14, no. 2 (April): 137–47.

Drehmann, Mathias, Claudio Borio, and Kostas Tsatsaronis. 2012. *Characterising the Financial Cycle: Don't Lose Sight of the Medium Term!* BIS Working Paper 380. Basel: Bank for International Settlements.

Edison, Hali J., Ross Levine, Luca Ricci, and Torsten Slok. 2002. *International Financial Integration and Economic Growth.* NBER Working Paper 9164. Cambridge, MA: National Bureau of Economic Research.

Edison, Hali J., Michael W. Klein, Luca Antonio Ricci, and Torsten Slok. 2004. Capital Account Liberalization and Economic Performance: Survey and Synthesis. *IMF Staff Papers* 51, no. 2: 22–56.

EY (Ernst and Young). 2014. *Future Directions for Foreign Banks in China.* Beijing.

Ferri, Giovanni, and Li-Gang Liu. 2009. *Honor Thy Creditors Before Thy Shareholders: Are the Profits of Chinese State-Owned Enterprises Real?* HKIMR Working Paper 16/2009. Hong Kong: Hong Kong Institute for Monetary Research.

FRBSF (Federal Reserve Bank of San Francisco). 2011. *Asia Focus: Banking Reform in Viet Nam.* San Francisco.

Geithner, Timothy F. 2014. *Stress Test: Reflections on a Financial Crisis.* New York: Crown Publishers.

Goldsmith, Raymond W. 1969. *Financial Structure and Development.* New Haven, CT: Yale University Press.

Haber, Stephen, and Aldo Musacchio. 2013. *These Are the Good Old Days: Foreign Entry and the Mexican Banking System.* Working Paper 13-062. Boston: Harvard Business School.

Harrod, R. F. Henry. 1939. An Essay in Dynamic Theory. *Economic Journal* 49, no. 193 (March): 14–33.

Hedges, Larry V., and Ingram Olkin. 1985. *Statistical Methods for Meta-Analysis.* New York: Academic Press.

Henry, Peter B. 2000. Stock Market Liberalization, Economic Reform, and Emerging Market Equity Prices. *Journal of Finance* 55, no. 2 (April): 529–64.

Hoenig, Thomas. 2013. Basel III Capital: A Well-Intentioned Illusion. Speech presented at the International Association of Deposit Insurers, Basel, Switzerland, April 9.

Hutchison, Michael M., and Ilan Noy. 2005. How Bad Are Twins? Output Costs of Currency and Banking Crises. *Journal of Money, Credit and Banking* 37, no. 4: 725–52.

IFC (International Finance Corporation). 2007. *Reforming Collateral Laws and Registries: International Best Practices and the Case of China.* Washington.

IMF (International Monetary Fund). 2004. *Pakistan: Financial System Stability Assessment.* IMF Country Report 04/215 (July). Washington.

IMF (International Monetary Fund). 2009. *Thailand: Financial System Stability Assessment.* IMF Country Report 09/147 (May). Washington.

IMF (International Monetary Fund). 2010a. *Indonesia: Financial System Stability Assessment.* IMF Country Report 10/288 (September). Washington.

IMF (International Monetary Fund). 2010b. *Philippines: Financial System Stability Assessment—Update.* IMF Country Report 10/90 (April). Washington.

IMF (International Monetary Fund). 2010c. *Bangladesh: Financial System Stability Assessment.* IMF Country Report 10/38 (February). Washington.

IMF (International Monetary Fund). 2011. *People's Republic of China: Financial System Stability Assessment.* IMF Country Report 11/321 (November). Washington.

IMF (International Monetary Fund). 2012a. *The Liberalization and Management of Capital Flows: An Institutional View.* Washington.

IMF (International Monetary Fund). 2012b. *Viet Nam: 2012 Article IV Consultation.* IMF Country Report 12/165 (July). Washington.

IMF (International Monetary Fund). 2013a. *People's Republic of China: 2013 Article IV Consultation.* IMF Country Report 13/211 (July). Washington.

IMF (International Monetary Fund). 2013b. *India: Financial System Stability Assessment—Update.* IMF Country Report 13/8 (January). Washington.

IMF (International Monetary Fund). 2013c. *Indonesia: Staff Report for the 2013 Article IV Consultation.* IMF Country Report 13/362 (December). Washington.

IMF (International Monetary Fund). 2013d. *Malaysia: Financial System Stability Assessment.* IMF Country Report 13/52 (February). Washington.

IMF (International Monetary Fund). 2013e. *Philippines: 2013 Article IV Consultation.* IMF Country Report 13/102 (April). Washington.

IMF (International Monetary Fund). 2013f. *Sri Lanka: 2013 Article IV Consultation.* IMF Country Report 13/120 (May). Washington.

IMF (International Monetary Fund). 2013g. *Thailand: 2013 Article IV Consultation.* IMF Country Report 13/323 (November). Washington.

IMF (International Monetary Fund). 2013h. *Bangladesh: Staff Report for the 2013 Article IV Consultation.* IMF Country Report 13/357 (December). Washington.

IMF (International Monetary Fund). 2013i. *Pakistan: 2013 Article IV Consultation.* IMF Country Report 13/287 (September). Washington.

IMF (International Monetary Fund). 2013j. *Myanmar: 2013 Article IV Consultation.* IMF Country Report 13/250 (August). Washington.

IMF (International Monetary Fund). 2013k. *Brazil: Staff Report for the 2013 Article IV Consultation.* Country Report 13/312 (October). Washington.

IMF (International Monetary Fund). 2014a. *World Economic Outlook Database, April 2014.* Washington.

IMF (International Monetary Fund). 2014b. *International Financial Statistics.* Washington.

IMF (International Monetary Fund). 2014c. *Global Financial Stability Report, April 2014.* Washington.

IMF (International Monetary Fund). 2014d. *India: 2014 Article IV Consultation*. IMF Country Report 14/57 (February). Washington.

IMF (International Monetary Fund). 2014e. *Republic of Korea: 2013 Article IV Consultation*. IMF Country Report 14/101 (April). Washington.

IMF (International Monetary Fund). 2014f. *Republic of Korea: Financial System Stability Assessment*. IMF Country Report 14/126 (May). Washington.

IMF (International Monetary Fund). 2014g. *Malaysia: 2013 Article IV Consultation*. IMF Country Report 14/80 (March). Washington.

IMF (International Monetary Fund). 2014h. *Bangladesh: Fourth Review Under the Three-Year Arrangement*. IMF Country Report 14/149 (June). Washington.

IMF (International Monetary Fund). 2014i. *Pakistan: Third Review Under the Extended Arrangement*. IMF Country Report 14/184 (July). Washington.

IMF (International Monetary Fund). 2014j. *Myanmar: Second Review Under the Staff-Monitored Program*. IMF Country Report 14/91 (March). Washington.

IMF (International Monetary Fund). 2014k. *Nepal: 2014 Article IV Consultation*. IMF Country Report 14/214 (July). Washington.

IMF (International Monetary Fund). 2014l. *People's Republic of China: 2014 Article IV Consultation*. IMF Country Report 14/235 (July). Washington.

Ito, Hiro, and Menzie Chinn. 2013. Notes on the Chinn-Ito Financial Openness Index: 2011 Update (April). Portland State University. Available at web.pdx.edu/~ito/Readme_kaopen2011.pdf (accessed on January 19, 2015).

Kindleberger, Charles P. 1978. *Manias, Panics, and Crashes: A History of Financial Crises*. New York: Macmillan.

Kindleberger, Charles P., and Robert Z. Aliber. 2005. *Manias, Panics, and Crashes: A History of Financial Crises*, 5th ed. New York: John Wiley & Sons (original 1978).

King, Robert G., and Ross Levine. 1993. Finance and Growth: Schumpeter Might Be Right. *Quarterly Journal of Economics* 108, no. 3 (August): 717–37.

Laeven, Luc, and Fabián Valencia. 2013. Systemic Banking Crises Database. *IMF Economic Review* 61, no. 2: 226–70.

Lardy, Nicholas R. 2013. All about Interest Rates. *China Economic Quarterly* (March).

Lardy, Nicholas R. 2014. *Markets over Mao: The Rise of Private Business in China*. Washington: Peterson Institute for International Economics.

Levine, Ross. 2001. International Financial Liberalization and Economic Growth. *Review of International Economics* 9, no. 4: 688–702.

Levine, Ross. 2004. *Finance and Growth: Theory and Evidence*. NBER Working Paper 10766 (September). Cambridge, MA: National Bureau of Economic Research.

Levine, Ross, Norman Loayza, and Thorsten Beck. 2000. Financial Intermediation and Growth: Causality and Causes. *Journal of Monetary Economics* 46: 31–77.

Lewis, W. Arthur. 1954. Economic Development with Unlimited Supplies of Labour. *The Manchester School* 22, no. 2 (May): 139–91.

Mankiw, Gregory N., David Romer, and David N. Weil. 1992. A Contribution to the Empirics of Economic Growth. *Quarterly Journal of Economics* 197, no. 2 (May): 407–37.

McKinnon, Ronald I. 1973. *Money and Capital in Economic Development*. Washington: Brookings Institution.

Mendoza, Enrique G., and Marco E. Terrones. 2008. *An Anatomy of Credit Booms: Evidence from Macro Aggregates and Micro Data*. NBER Working Paper 14049 (May). Cambridge, MA: National Bureau of Economic Research.

Minsky, Hyman P. 1986. *Stabilizing an Unstable Economy*. New Haven, CT: Yale University Press.

Minsky, Hyman P. 1992. *The Financial Instability Hypothesis*. Working Paper 74 (May). New York: Jerome Levy Economics Institute, Bard College.

Quinn, Dennis, and A. Maria Toyoda. 2008. Does Capital Account Liberalization Lead to Growth? *Review of Financial Studies* 21, no. 3: 1403–49.

Rajan, Raghuram G., and Luigi Zingales. 2003. The Great Reversals: The Politics of Financial Development in the Twentieth Century. *Journal of Financial Economics* 69: 5–50.

RBI (Reserve Bank of India). 2013a. *Banking Structure in India—The Way Forward*. Discussion Paper (August). Mumbai.

RBI (Reserve Bank of India). 2013b. *Report on Trend and Progress of Banking in India 2012–13* (November). Mumbai.

Schumpeter, Joseph A. 1934. *The Theory of Economic Development*. Cambridge, MA: Harvard University Press (original 1911).

Solow, Robert M. 1956. A Contribution to the Theory of Economic Growth. *Quarterly Journal of Economics* 70, no. 1 (February): 65–94.

Standard and Poor's. 2014. *S&P 500 Earnings and Estimate Report*. New York.

UN (United Nations), Department of Economic and Social Affairs, Population Division. 2012. *World Population Prospects: The 2012 Revision*. New York. Available at http://econ.worldbank.org/WBSITE/EXTERNAL/EXTDEC/EXTRESEARCH/0,,print:Y~isCURL:Y~contentMDK:20696167~pagePK:64214825~piPK:64214943~theSitePK:469382,00.html.

US Census Bureau. 2014. *International Data Base: World Population by Age and Sex*. Washington. Available at http://data.worldbank.org/data-catalog/world-development-indicators.

Vanassche, Ellen. 2004. The Impact of International Financial Integration on Industry Growth. Katholieke Universiteit Leuven, Belgium. Photocopy.

World Bank. 2013. *Financial Development and Structure Dataset* (November). Washington.

World Bank. 2014. *World Development Indicators*. Washington.

Yi, Insill, Stephen M. Miller, and Yongil Jeon. 2009. The Effects of Increased Foreign Ownership on Korean Domestic Banks. *Journal of the Korean Economy* 10, no. 1 (April): 127–50.

Zhang, Xiaoxi, and Kevin Daly. 2011. *China's Bank Ownership and Performance* (August). University of Western Sydney.

4

Financial Development and Output Growth in Developing Asia and Latin America:
A Comparative Sectoral Analysis

JOSHUA AIZENMAN, YOTHIN JINJARAK, and DONGHYUN PARK

A lingering challenge in applied economics is measuring and controlling the quality of services, such as health care, education, and finance. Since services are measured at cost, their GDP share is correlated with per capita GDP. But short of controlling for the quality of services, it is not clear if the growing share of services in GDP adds to welfare. To illustrate, in 2012, the GDP share of medical services was 17.9 percent in the United States, 10.9 percent in Canada, 11.7 percent in France, and 9.4 percent in the United Kingdom. Yet there is no evidence that the United States delivers better quality health services on average. On the contrary, for most conventional measures of average quality of health, life expectancy at birth, and the like, the United States lags many other OECD countries by wide margins (OECD 2013).[1] Similar observations apply to education and other services. Even after adjusting for purchasing power parity (PPP), the links between expenditure on services and the quality of these services in the OECD countries remain tenuous at best.

For financial services, the global financial crisis underlines the relevance of such concerns. It paralyzed global financial systems and almost brought the world economy to its knees. According to conventional wisdom, financial depth contributes to the growth of the real sector, but the evidence remains

Joshua Aizenman is professor in the Department of Economics, University of Southern California, Los Angeles. Yothin Jinjarak is associate professor in the School of Economics and Finance, Victoria University of Wellington, Wellington, New Zealand. Donghyun Park is principal economist at the Asian Development Bank. The authors gratefully acknowledge useful comments by Marcus Noland, Shang-Jin Wei, and other participants at a workshop at Asian Development Bank in Manila, Philippines, on November 4, 2014.

1. Share data from the World Bank, http://data.worldbank.org/indicator/SH.XPD.TOTL.ZS (accessed on September 10, 2014).

mixed at best. The global financial crisis put to the fore the possibility that the relationship between financial depth and output growth may be nonlinear and unstable over time. That is, the development of the financial sector may benefit the real sector, but only up to a point. Beyond that point, further financial development may have no effect or even a negative effect on growth. For example, the global financial crisis was preceded by a wave of financial innovation that produced many complex high-tech financial products but entailed little obvious benefit for growth. Excessive financial innovation that overwhelms the capacity of regulatory authorities can culminate in financial crisis, which sets back growth for some time.

Concerns about too much finance are more relevant for advanced economies that already have mature, sophisticated financial sectors with a good mix of banks and capital markets than for developing economies with backward financial sectors. Diminishing marginal returns to financial development are more likely at higher levels of financial development. However, fundamental measurement issues affect both advanced and developing economies. The crux of the problem is that the standard measures of financial development are quantitative, such as the ratio of private credit to GDP. Quantitative measures are highly imperfect measures of financial development, which refers to the quality of the financial system, or its ability to allocate resources to the most productive uses. For example, it is conceivable that even as the financial system expands in size, its capacity to channel resources efficiently stagnates or even recedes. Perhaps no country epitomizes such risks better than today's People's Republic of China (PRC).

East Asian countries generally have large financial sectors relative to their income levels. Yet they remain well inside the global finance frontier, as evident in their recycling of much of their abundant savings through the financial markets of advanced economies. Even within the context of East Asia, the PRC has an exceptionally large financial sector, yet few would mistake the large size as evidence of financial development. To the contrary, there are widespread concerns that an unsustainable expansion of credit—i.e., unsustainable expansion of the financial sector—is jeopardizing financial stability and eroding the quality of investments. A specific major concern is that state-owned banks may be channeling credit to state-owned firms at the expense of credit to the dynamic private sector. Latin America and East Asia are at similar income levels but one key difference is the relative abundance of savings in the latter. As such, a comparative analysis of the finance-growth nexus in the two regions is worthwhile.

This chapter marks a preliminary attempt to explore some of the above issues by delving into the relationship between financial depth and sectoral output growth. The sectoral data encompass 10 sectors: agriculture, mining, manufacturing, construction, public utilities, retail and wholesale trade, transport and communication, financial and business services, other market services, and government services. Our analysis covers 41 economies, including 11 East Asian and 9 Latin American economies, which we compare.[2] We use data from international financial institutions for measures of financial depth, financial spreads, and several proxies for quality and availability of finance. While the financial data are far from satisfactory, this chapter provides preliminary insights about the key issues at hand and raises some questions that need further investigation. We review the literature, describe the data and empirical framework, report and discuss the preliminary results, and conclude with some final observations.

Literature Review

The importance of the quality of financial intermediation has been well recognized in the literature, though identifying its effect remains a work in progress (see Levine [2005] for a comprehensive review). John H. Boyd and Bruce D. Smith (1992) show that the quality of financial intermediation has first-order effects on capital flows and economic growth. In a model with adverse selection and costly state verification in which both debt contracts and credit rationing are observed, capital may flow from capital-scarce countries to capital-abundant countries if the capital-abundant countries have financial intermediaries that are sufficiently more effective at exerting corporate control than the capital-scarce countries. This insightful paper provides a nice interpretation to the Lucas paradox (1990) of capital flowing uphill, a topic that gained even more attention in the context of the global imbalances in the 2000s (see Alfaro, Kalemli-Ozcan, and Volosovych 2003; Ju and Wei 2011, and the references therein). Thus, even though the physical marginal product of capital is higher in capital-scarce countries, investors recognize that their expected returns depend on the monitoring quality of financial intermediaries.

Followup papers showed that the quality of financial intermediation is impacted by factors beyond the cost of monitoring. John H. Boyd, Ross E. Levine, and Bruce D. Smith (2001) showed that the quality of financial intermediation is hampered by inflation. For economies with inflation rates exceeding 15 percent, there is a discrete drop in financial sector performance. Rafael La Porta et al. (2000) highlighted the role of a well-functioning legal system in facilitating efficient financial intermediaries—greater protection of creditors' rights and more efficient courts enable more efficient intermediation. The degree of competition and market contestability also matter. The relaxation of states' regulations on interstate branching in the United States

---

2. Our analysis gives sectoral detail to the historical macrodata in Maddison (2003) from 1950 onward. The data for Asia and Latin America are based on Marcel P. Timmer and Gaaitzen J. de Vries, *A Cross-Country Database For Sectoral Employment And Productivity In Asia And Latin America, 1950–2005*, GGDC Research memorandum GD-98, Groningen Growth and Development Centre, August 2007. Data for Europe and the United States are based on an update of Bart van Ark (1996). See GGDC 10-Sector Database, www.rug.nl/research/ggdc/data/10-sector-database (accessed on January 22, 2015).

during the 1970s provided "a natural experiment" used to uncover the gains of quantity versus quality of finance. Jith Jayaratne and Philip E. Strahan (1996) found that branch reform boosted bank lending quality and accelerated real per capita growth rates. The channels at work were mostly the quality, and not the quantity, of finance. Rajeev Dehejia and Adriana Lleras-Muney (2003) found that branch reform accelerated economic growth by improving the quality of bank loans and the efficiency of capital allocation, with little evidence that branch reform boosted quantity of lending.

The importance of financial dependence heterogeneity across sectors has been highlighted by the pioneering study of Raghuram G. Rajan and Luigi Zingales (1998). Since lower costs of external finance facilitate firm growth and new firm formation, industries that are heavier users of external finance should benefit disproportionately from financial development. Rajan and Zingales's study validated this conjecture, finding that financial development has a bigger effect on the growth of industries that are more dependent on external finance, both through the expansion of existing firms and through the formation of new firms. Extending Rajan and Zingales (1998), Stijn Claessens and Luc Laeven (2003) found evidence that better property rights promote higher growth through improved asset allocation. Quantitatively, this growth effect is as large as that of improved access to financing due to financial development.

The global financial crisis renewed attention on the interplay between the quantity and quality of finance. Stephen G. Cecchetti and Enisse Kharroubi (2012) studied how financial development affects growth at both the country and industry level. Based on a sample of developed and emerging economies, they found that the level of financial development is good only up to a point, after which it becomes a drag on growth. For private sector credit extended by banks, the turning point is close to 90 percent of GDP. For advanced economies, a fast-growing financial sector can be detrimental to aggregate productivity growth. Looking at industry-level data, they found that financial sector growth disproportionately harms industries that are either financially dependent or R&D intensive. Jean-Louis Arcand, Enrico Berkes, and Ugo Panizza (2012) reported similar findings. Finance starts having a negative effect on output growth when credit to the private sector reaches 100 percent of GDP. Intriguingly, these results are not driven by output volatility, banking crises, low institutional quality, or differences in bank regulation and supervision. Instead, they appear to be in line with Peter L. Rousseau and Paul Wachtel's (2011) "vanishing effect"—i.e., credit had no statistically significant impact on GDP growth over the 1965–2004 period.

Joshua Aizenman, Brian Pinto, and Vladyslav Sushko (2013) examined how financial cycles affect the broader economy through their impact on real economic sectors in 1960–2005. Periods of accelerated growth of the financial sector are more likely to be followed by abrupt financial contractions than are periods of slower financial sector growth. While the majority of real sectors are adversely affected by financial contractions, they are not helped by expansions.

Though these studies do not identify the mechanisms associated with the "vanishing effect" of finance, they are consistent with Hyman P. Minsky (1974)'s hypothesis that over time financial deepening may eventually divert financial resources from financing real activities into speculative and ultimately destabilizing risky and bubbly yield-seeking financial investments. Rajan's (2005) seminal paper outlined the ways in which deregulation and distorted incentives induce financial managers to overlook tail risks, causing financial deepening to culminate in larger financial crises.

Recent empirical literature has validated the key role of credit cycles. Moritz Schularick and Alan M. Taylor (2009) presented long-run historical data showing that financial instability was often the result of "credit booms gone wrong" (p. 3). Their analysis lends support to the Minsky-Kindleberger view of financial crises (Eichengreen and Mitchener 2003). The credit system seems all too capable of creating its very own shocks, judging by how well past credit growth predicts future financial crises. The dynamic role of credit overhang is further validated by Òscar Jordà, Moritz Schularick, and Alan Taylor (2011). Analyzing over 200 recessions in 14 advanced countries between 1870 and 2008, they found that financial crisis recessions are more costly than normal recessions in terms of lost output. For both types of recessions, credit-intensive expansions tend to be followed by deeper recessions and slower recoveries. Credit growth also affects the behavior of other key macroeconomic variables such as investment, lending, interest rates, and inflation.

Taking stock of the literature, one may conjecture that credit boom and bust cycles associated with financial deepening would disproportionately affect activities and sectors that rely on stable external finance and are subject to larger sunk costs. The tenuous link between financial depth and growth may reflect a host of factors, including the damaging and uneven effects of credit cycles, as well as the rent seeking associated with distorted incentives in the financial sector, where excessive risk taking and financial innovation may precipitate instability that penalizes credit-dependent sectors. This is all the more likely if the greater short- and medium-run profits associated with financial innovations divert credit from the real economy to further deepening of speculative financial intermediation.

Data

Data are derived from several sources subject to data availability. Data on sectoral value-added per worker, which are used to calculate sectoral output growth (percent) for 1996–2011, are from Groningen Growth and Development Centre (GGDC) 10-Sector Database. Controls for quality of financial intermediation are available at various years and more recently. Bank private credit to GDP (percent) and lending-deposit interest spread (percent) for 1996–2011 are from Global Financial Development Database (2013)[3]; getting

---

3. World Bank, Global Financial Development Database, http://data.worldbank.org/data-catalog/global-financial-development (accessed on January 23, 2015).

credit index and resolving insolvency index for 2005–11 are from Doing Business database;[4] data on depositors with commercial bank's per 1,000 adults and SME loans from commercial banks (percent GDP) for 2005–11 are from the Financial Access Survey Database.[5]

Figure 4.1 plots average value added per worker for 1996–2011. Across the ten sectors the level of value added per worker in East Asia and the Pacific is higher than the level in Latin America and the Caribbean. The differences can be quite large, ranging from 1.1 times in the public utilities sector, 2.3 times in the manufacturing sector, all the way to 2.6 times in the financial and business services sector. In the following we examine to what extent these differences could be attributable to quality of financial intermediation between the two regions.

Table 4.1 provides the 2005–11 average quality of financial intermediation for all the 212 countries for which data are available. Figure 4.2 then summarizes regional differences in the quality of financial intermediation. Note that only countries in East Asia and Pacific, Latin America and the Caribbean, and a few other areas have sectoral output data from the GGDC, while measures of quality of financial intermediation are missing altogether for some countries. Data are available for sectoral output growth, financial depth (bank private credit to GDP), and financial efficiency (lending-deposit interest spread) for 1996–2004, and for all other measures of the quality of finance for 2005–13. As a result, we perform descriptive data analysis for 2005–11 and more formal empirical analysis for 1996–2011 on selected variables subject to data availability.

Table 4.2 reports the correlation among financial variables in East Asia and the Pacific vis-à-vis Latin America and the Caribbean. The level of financial depth as measured by bank private credit to GDP is correlated with the level of de facto financial efficiency as measured by lending-deposit interest spread in both regions, though with the opposite signs. This spread reflects the complex interaction of many factors, including the competitiveness of the banking industry, the riskiness of banks' portfolio, macropolicies (higher inflation and higher reserve ratios are positively associated with the spreads), the efficiency of the judicial system, and the protection of creditors' rights. The data further indicate that lending-deposit interest spread is negatively correlated with resolving insolvency index. In East Asia, bank private credit to GDP is also positively correlated with the getting credit index, resolving insolvency index, and small and medium-sized enterprise (SME) loans from commercial banks as percentage of GDP. In Latin America, the number of depositors with commercial banks per 1,000 adults is positively correlated with financial depth but negatively with financial efficiency.

---

4. World Bank Group, Doing Business database, www.doingbusiness.org (accessed on January 23, 2015).

5. International Monetary Fund, Financial Access Survey Database, http://fas.imf.org/Default.aspx (accessed on February 11, 2015).

Figure 4.1   Average value added (constant 2005 prices) per worker in 10 sectors in East Asia and the Pacific and Latin America and the Caribbean, 1996–2011

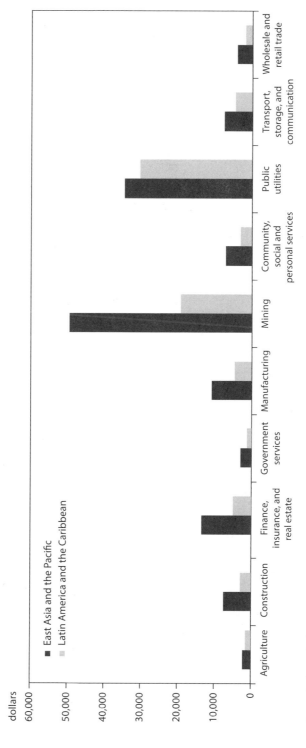

■ East Asia and the Pacific

□ Latin America and the Caribbean

Source: Authors' calculations based on Groningen Growth and Development Centre (GGDC)10-Sector Database.

Table 4.1 Financial depth, efficiency, and access, 2005–11

Economy	BCRY	SPRD	GTCR	REIN	DCBA	LSME
Afghanistan	7.1	..	16.7	17.6	96.0	..
Albania	27.5	7.0	71.9	41.0	..	..
Algeria	12.6	6.2	30.2	44.1	326.0	..
American Samoa	..	..	..	..	..	..
Andorra	..	..	..	..	..	..
Andorra	..	..	..	..	..	..
Angola	11.8	16.7	37.5	0.0	52.2	15.3
Anguilla	..	..	..	..	..	..
Antigua and Barbuda	68.3	7.2	43.8	36.9	..	..
Argentina	11.9	3.6	62.5	35.3	635.9	..
Armenia	16.7	10.5	63.5	38.4	..	..
Aruba	55.0	7.6	..	..	..	..
Australia	113.7	4.0	87.5	84.4	..	..
Austria	115.8	..	81.3	76.9	..	..
Azerbaijan	13.1	8.0	65.6	32.8	246.5	..
Bahamas	75.3	2.0	56.3	65.8	..	..
Bahrain	53.9	5.3	37.5	67.2	..	..
Bangladesh	36.9	5.9	56.3	25.5	304.9	5.2
Barbados	71.8	5.9	..	..	..	..
Belarus	24.4	0.7	39.6	34.9	..	..
Belgium	86.3	..	62.5	91.5	..	17.2
Belize	58.8	6.1	43.8	67.2	947.6	..
Benin	19.4	..	25.0	18.6	86.1	..
Bermuda	..	..	..	..	..	..
Bhutan	27.5	10.5	18.8	0.0	..	..
Bolivia	33.7	9.3	42.7	40.1	..	..
Bosnia and Herzegovina	48.9	4.5	62.5	36.9	..	24.9
Botswana	22.4	6.8	62.5	60.4	412.9	..
Brazil	40.4	34.7	50.0	13.8	500.5	..
Brunei Darussalam	37.6	4.7	43.8	49.2	1389.0	..
Bulgaria	47.3	6.2	90.6	34.5	..	..
Burkina Faso	18.0	..	25.0	22.7	..	..
Burundi	14.4	..	25.0	7.4	20.0	6.2
Cambodia	18.5	..	25.0	9.8	..	..
Cameroon	9.9	11.5	30.2	13.8	49.1	..
Canada	126.7	3.2	81.3	94.7	..	..
Cape Verde	52.4	7.2	35.4	0.0	1204.1	..
Cayman Islands	..	..	..	..	..	..
Central African Republic	6.9	11.5	31.3	0.0	27.6	..
Chad	3.8	11.5	25.0	0.0	..	..
Chile	64.6	3.8	56.3	30.9	..	7.8
China, People's Republic of	109.9	3.2	49.0	36.3	8.8	29.6
Colombia	29.2	6.9	62.5	56.3	1061.8	0.6
Comoros	11.3	6.8	18.8	0.0	61.5	2.7
Congo, Democratic Republic of	2.9	37.5	18.8	3.4	..	..
Congo, Republic of	3.5	11.5	31.3	18.5	42.8	..
Costa Rica	40.8	11.7	50.0	23.1	937.5	..
Cote d'Ivoire	15.8	..	25.0	32.2	105.2	..

(continued on next page)

Table 4.1 Financial depth, efficiency, and access, 2005–11 *(continued)*

Economy	BCRY	SPRD	GTCR	REIN	DCBA	LSME
Croatia	61.8	8.1	55.2	31.3	1440.3	..
Cuba	..	..	..	..	..	..
Cyprus	220.8	3.3	60.4	74.8	..	..
Czech Republic	40.3	4.6	71.9	27.4	..	10.0
Democratic People's Republic of Korea	..	..	..	..	..	..
Denmark	183.8	..	80.2	86.0	..	..
Djibouti	21.6	9.3	12.5	16.8	64.6	..
Dominica	49.9	6.2	56.3	29.6	..	..
Dominican Republic	19.6	9.1	55.2	8.5	569.6	..
Ecuador	24.4	7.1	51.0	17.5	437.9	..
Egypt	40.3	5.6	44.8	17.7	353.7	1.7
El Salvador	4.7	..	67.7	31.2	..	17.7
Equatorial Guinea	4.7	11.5	31.3	0.0	148.4	..
Eritrea	..	..	12.5	0.0	..	..
Estonia	86.7	3.7	69.8	40.3	1958.6	..
Ethiopia	17.3	3.4	35.4	43.5	87.4	..
Faeroe Islands	..	..	..	..	..	..
Federated States of Micronesia	..	13.4	39.6	3.5	..	8.5
Fiji	44.3	3.2	68.8	47.6	..	1.8
Finland	83.7	..	75.0	93.6	..	..
France	103.7	..	64.6	49.0	..	..
French Guiana	..	..	..	..	..	..
French Polynesia	..	..	..	..	..	..
Gabon	8.7	11.5	31.3	15.6	159.7	..
Gambia	12.0	14.9	31.3	29.1	..	..
Georgia	24.4	12.8	61.5	28.9	476.8	8.3
Germany	108.0	..	84.4	85.7	..	..
Ghana	12.9	..	46.9	25.4	250.6	..
Greece	93.5	..	52.1	47.4	..	19.8
Greenland	..	..	..	..	..	..
Grenada	69.0	7.1	43.8	0.0	..	..
Guam	..	..	..	..	..	..
Guatemala	24.6	8.2	69.8	29.6	..	..
Guinea	4.4	..	18.8	22.0	..	4.1
Guinea-Bissau	4.1	..	25.0	0.0	40.3	..
Guyana	38.1	12.2	25.0	18.6	..	..
Haiti	12.6	18.6	27.1	0.0	..	..
Honduras	45.1	8.8	71.9	21.2	..	..
Hong Kong, China	148.5	5.1	93.8	84.7	..	..
Hungary	55.6	2.4	75.0	40.4	..	13.9
Iceland	179.1	..	75.0	83.6	..	..
India	42.3	..	74.0	25.7	..	3.6
Indonesia	23.5	5.5	51.0	16.0	..	6.2
Iran	27.6	1.8	44.8	22.5	..	..
Iraq	4.2	..	18.8	0.0	..	0.2
Ireland	197.9	2.6	87.5	92.4	..	34.9
Isle of Man	..	..	..	..	..	..

(continued on next page)

Table 4.1 Financial depth, efficiency, and access, 2005–11 *(continued)*

Economy	BCRY	SPRD	GTCR	REIN	DCBA	LSME
Israel	90.7	2.9	87.5	54.9	1042.0	..
Italy	102.8	..	51.0	63.4	788.1	..
Jamaica	24.7	11.3	50.0	68.3	..	..
Japan	102.0	1.2	81.3	98.1	..	..
Jordan	76.6	4.3	25.0	29.0	..	..
Kazakhstan	41.0	..	42.7	42.3	915.9	..
Kenya	28.1	8.8	83.3	33.3	..	0.1
Kiribati	..	..	31.3	0.0	161.0	11.8
Kosovo	25.6	..	81.3	36.3	..	..
Kuwait	57.0	3.2	41.7	30.6	..	..
Kyrgyz Republic	9.1	22.1	69.8	15.3	109.6	..
Lao People's Democratic Republic	9.9	21.8	24.0	0.0	..	..
Latvia	73.2	5.6	88.5	34.1	1142.1	33.9
Lebanon	67.9	2.2	49.0	31.8	825.6	..
Lesotho	10.3	7.9	37.5	28.2	282.9	..
Liberia	11.5	11.3	28.8	8.6	..	..
Libya	6.6	3.6	..	..	675.6	..
Liechtenstein	..	..	..	..	..	..
Lithuania	46.0	2.5	68.8	52.1	..	..
Luxembourg	165.0	..	25.0	44.6	..	..
Macau, China	46.7	5.2	..	..	..	11.7
Macedonia	34.8	4.4	65.6	42.9	..	16.9
Madagascar	10.1	27.3	15.6	17.4	27.0	2.1
Malawi	9.7	21.3	43.8	15.7	163.5	2.0
Malaysia	101.8	2.9	100.0	41.1	..	16.5
Maldives	67.7	6.4	50.0	51.6	1048.9	..
Mali	17.4	..	25.0	20.8	84.9	..
Malta	117.7	2.7	..	..	934.9	35.0
Marshall Islands	..	..	35.4	18.9	..	..
Martinique	..	..	..	..	..	..
Mauritania	23.5	12.6	25.0	0.0	46.4	..
Mauritius	76.7	5.7	51.0	36.2	..	..
Mexico	16.5	4.8	68.8	68.6	267.1	4.1
Moldova	29.8	5.8	50.0	30.2	1053.2	..
Monaco	..	..	..	..	..	..
Mongolia	34.3	10.3	56.3	21.0	..	3.6
Montenegro	61.9	..	77.5	45.6	..	..
Morocco	64.0	8.0	34.4	37.8	..	8.3
Mozambique	16.6	7.7	40.6	15.9	..	..
Myanmar	..	5.0	..	..	121.7	1.6
Namibia	47.1	4.9	68.8	34.6	254.6	0.8
Nepal	38.6	5.5	64.6	25.9	316.7	..
Netherlands	185.5	0.5	68.8	90.0	..	..
Netherlands Antilles	..	..	..	..	..	..
New Caledonia	..	..	..	..	..	..
New Zealand	134.1	1.5	93.8	82.0	..	..

(continued on next page)

Table 4.1 Financial depth, efficiency, and access, 2005–11 *(continued)*

Economy	BCRY	SPRD	GTCR	REIN	DCBA	LSME
Nicaragua	31.9	7.9	49.0	36.2	..	..
Niger	9.7	..	25.0	13.3	..	..
Nigeria	22.8	7.3	59.4	29.1	406.6	0.0
Norway	77.3	1.9	62.5	95.6	1153.0	..
Oman	34.4	3.3	37.5	37.2	..	..
Pakistan	24.6	6.2	61.5	42.0	201.8	..
Palau	..	..	6.3	33.5	..	..
Panama	78.1	4.7	68.8	28.1	915.5	..
Papua New Guinea	20.4	9.1	34.4	25.3	..	..
Paraguay	23.9	24.5	56.3	17.8	91.8	..
Peru	20.4	19.4	77.1	28.0	349.8	6.4
Philippines	26.1	4.6	43.8	4.5	394.1	..
Poland	33.9	3.7	84.4	36.0	..	..
Portugal	166.1	..	50.0	76.8	..	..
Qatar	36.2	3.5	31.3	55.9	674.8	..
Republic of Korea	95.5	1.6	84.4	86.0	..	38.9
Réunion	..	..	..	..	..	..
Romania	30.5	7.5	85.4	26.5	..	..
Russian Federation	34.6	5.7	37.5	43.7	..	6.7
Rwanda	10.2	8.9	37.5	3.4	126.2	2.5
Samoa	40.7	7.1	39.6	18.9	650.1	25.1
San Marino	336.7	..	..	..	..	..
Sao Tome and Principe	27.5	18.3	12.5	4.6	349.8	..
Saudi Arabia	39.0	..	56.3	30.4	628.1	..
Senegal	22.7	..	25.0	21.5	..	..
Serbia	36.8	8.7	69.8	25.8	..	..
Seychelles	23.1	7.7	25.0	41.9	608.5	..
Sierra Leone	6.9	13.4	35.4	9.1	109.6	..
Singapore	92.4	5.0	82.3	94.7	2075.2	..
Slovak Republic	41.5	3.7	72.9	49.2	..	..
Slovenia	76.4	3.7	49.0	49.0	..	..
Solomon Islands	19.3	12.4	30.2	24.8	..	..
Somalia	..	..	..	..	..	..
South Africa	71.8	3.7	79.2	35.4	..	..
Spain	182.1	..	68.8	75.3	..	..
Sri Lanka	27.9	5.5	49.0	44.7	..	..
St. Kitts and Nevis	58.5	4.6	43.8	0.0	..	..
St. Lucia	96.8	7.3	43.8	44.8	..	..
St. Vincent and the Grenadines	48.1	6.5	43.8	0.0	..	..
Sudan	9.2	..	25.0	34.0	..	..
Suriname	19.0	6.9	25.0	8.1	..	..
Swaziland	21.6	6.2	68.8	38.5	456.8	..
Sweden	111.9	2.5	70.8	80.0	..	..
Switzerland	161.1	2.3	81.3	49.8	..	43.2
Syria	15.3	2.8	8.3	30.9	192.7	..
Tajikistan	15.4	13.0	17.7	38.9	333.8	..
Tanzania	12.9	8.1	43.8	22.8	..	..

(continued on next page)

Table 4.1 Financial depth, efficiency, and access, 2005–11 *(continued)*

Economy	BCRY	SPRD	GTCR	REIN	DCBA	LSME
Thailand	94.9	4.3	61.5	45.3	1051.1	26.3
Timor-Leste	17.0	12.7	12.5	0.0	..	..
Togo	19.3	..	25.0	27.0	118.0	..
Tonga	46.4	6.3	43.8	26.8	..	19.6
Trinidad and Tobago	28.7	6.7	79.2	26.7	..	..
Tunisia	56.6	..	41.7	54.8	693.0	..
Turkey	30.3	..	56.3	19.7	1236.4	8.8
Turkmenistan	..	..	47.9	42.9	..	..
Tuvalu	..	..	..	..	..	..
Uganda	10.0	10.4	..	..	141.1	..
Ukraine	51.1	7.0	66.7	9.2	3063.9	..
United Arab Emirates	67.5	..	46.9	29.0	..	..
United Kingdom	183.9	..	100.0	90.4	..	12.5
United States	58.4	..	93.8	82.6	..	..
Uruguay	22.5	8.0	61.5	43.1	495.3	4.6
Uzbekistan	..	..	21.9	19.0	860.7	3.5
Vanuatu	51.7	5.1	42.7	43.3	..	..
Venezuela	18.8	4.7	19.8	6.6	728.2	0.6
Viet Nam	85.3	3.0	67.7	19.4	..	..
Virgin Islands (US)	..	..	..	..	..	..
West Bank and Gaza	6.7	..	20.8	0.0	..	..
Yemen	5.9	5.4	16.7	30.2	83.0	..
Zambia	10.2	13.2	64.6	29.0	24.1	0.4
Zimbabwe	8.1	..	50.0	0.2	244.5	..
Average	50.6	7.8	50.5	35.1	510.8	11.5
Standard deviation	49.9	5.9	22.3	25.6	530.6	11.4

.. = not available

Note: This table shows measures of financial depth (bank private credit to GDP, BCRY); efficiency (lending-deposit interest spread, SPRD); governance (getting credit index, GTCR; resolving insolvency index, REIN); and access (depositors with commercial banks per 1,000 adults, DCBA; outstanding SME loans from commercial banks, LSME).

Sources: Authors' calculations based on World Bank, Global Financial Development Database (BCRY, SPRD) and Doing Business Database (GTCR, REIN); and IMF, Financial Access Survey (DCBA, LSME).

Empirical Framework and Results

To estimate the association between sectoral output growth and quality of financial intermediation, the benchmark regression is specified as the following:

$$Sectoral\ Output\ Growth = \alpha + \lambda(Lagged\ Sectoral\ Output\ Growth) +$$
$$\beta(Bank\ Private\ Credit\ /\ GDP) + \gamma(Lending\text{-}Deposit\ Interest\ Spread) + \varepsilon \quad (4.1)$$

using annual data from 1996–2011 for East Asia and the Pacific, and Latin America and the Caribbean.

Table 4.3 reports estimation results based on ordinary least squares (OLS) regressions, done across the entire sample of 41 economies, and subsamples of 11 East Asia and Pacific economies and 9 Latin American and Caribbean

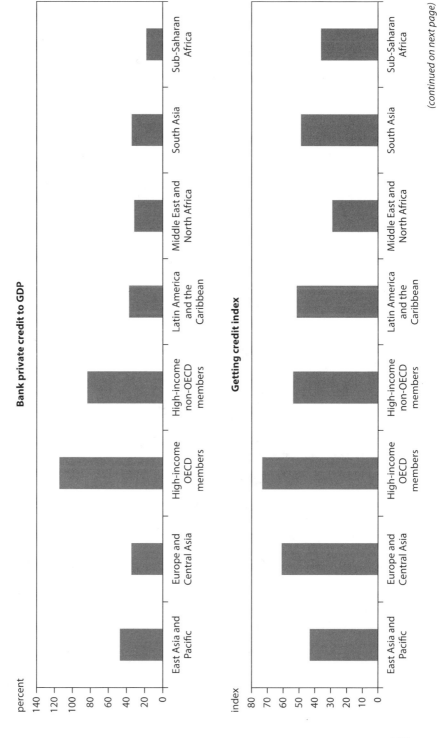

Figure 4.2   Regional differences in quality of finance, 2005–11

Bank private credit to GDP

Getting credit index

(continued on next page)

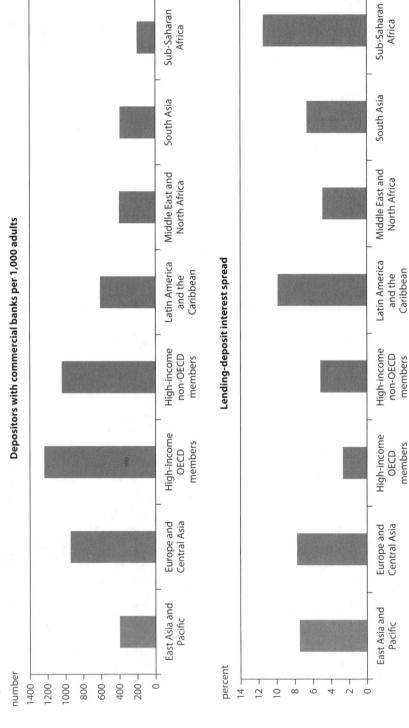

Figure 4.2 Regional differences in quality of finance, 2005–11 *(continued)*

Depositors with commercial banks per 1,000 adults

Lending-deposit interest spread

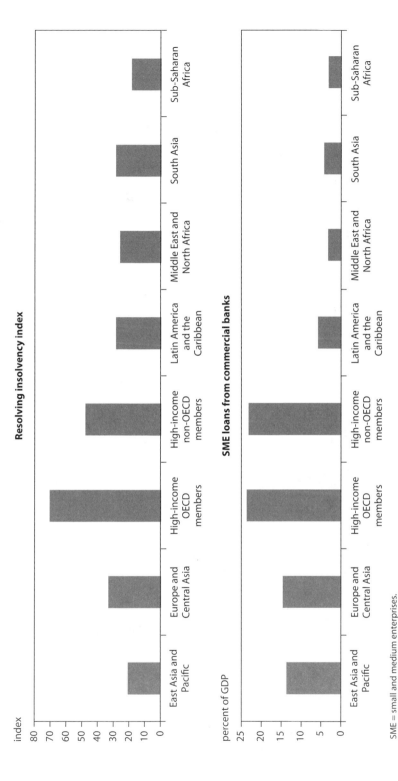

Resolving insolvency index

index

SME loans from commercial banks

percent of GDP

SME = small and medium enterprises.

Note: This figure shows an average for each region of the following measures: financial depth (bank private credit to GDP, BCRY); efficiency (lending-deposit interest spread, SPRD); governance (getting credit index, GTCR; resolving insolvency index, REIN); and access (depositors with commercial banks per 1,000 adults, DCBA; outstanding SME loans from commercial banks, LSME).

Sources: Authors' calculations based on World Bank, Global Financial Development Database (BCRY, SPRD) and Doing Business Database (GTCR, REIN); and IMF, Financial Access Survey (DCBA, LSME).

Table 4.2 Correlation between quality of finance measures, 2005–11

Measure	East Asia and Pacific					Latin America and the Caribbean				
	Bank private credit to GDP (percent)	Lending-deposit interest spread (percent)	Getting credit index	Resolving insolvency index	Depositors with commercial banks per 1,000 adults	Bank private credit to GDP (percent)	Lending-deposit interest spread (percent)	Getting credit index	Resolving insolvency index	Depositors with commercial banks per 1,000 adults
Lending-deposit interest spread (percent)	−0.7					0.3	1.0			
Getting credit index	0.5	−0.5				−0.3	0.1	1.0		
Resolving insolvency index	0.9	−0.5	0.6			−0.3	−0.4	0.6	1.0	
Depositors with commercial banks per 1,000 adults	−0.1	0.5	0.6	0.4		0.3	−0.4	−0.4	0.1	1.0
SME loans from commercial banks (percent of GDP)	0.7	−0.1	−0.6	0.5	−0.6	0.5	0.0	0.4	0.0	−0.6

SME = small and medium enterprises

Note: This table provides correlations of financial depth (bank private credit to GDP, BCRY); efficiency (lending-deposit interest spread, SPRD); governance (getting credit index, GTCR; and resolving insolvency index, REIN); and access (depositors with commercial banks per 1,000 adults, DCBA; and outstanding SME loans from commercial banks, LSME). Shaded cell signifies statistical significance at the 1 percent level.

Sources: Authors' calculations based on World Bank, Global Financial Development Database (BCRY, SPRD) and Doing Business Database (GTCR, REIN); and IMF, Financial Access Survey (DCBA, LSME).

economies. Overall, the estimation explains about half of the variation in the sectoral output growth data. Coefficient estimates on lagged sectoral output growth are negative and statistically significant, suggesting mean reversion in the output growth across sectors.

In the whole sample and both subsamples, bank private credit to GDP (financial depth) is negatively associated with the growth of the construction sector. Bank private credit growth is also negatively associated with the growth of the manufacturing sector in East Asia, whereas it is positively associated with the growth of the finance, insurance, and real estate sector in Latin America.

For the East Asian economies, lending-deposit interest spread (financial efficiency) is positively associated with the growth of the finance, insurance, and real estate sector. The growth of the construction sector is negatively associated with lending-deposit interest spread in East Asia, whereas it has a positive association in Latin America. The growth of the wholesale and retail trade sector is positively associated with financial efficiency in East Asia, whereas the association is negative in Latin America. The results seem to suggest garden variety associations between finance and sectoral growth.

While the baseline results suggest that higher bank private credit to GDP tends to reduce sectoral growth of construction and manufacturing, the results also suggest the need to experiment with nonlinear specification of bank private credit to GDP, and to possibly control for lagged bank private credit to GDP, to verify whether higher bank private credit to GDP reduces growth in construction and manufacturing. As the recent literature suggests, there is a possibility that bank private credit has a positive effect on GDP growth up to a point, but too much of it would lead to a financial crisis or declining productivity, possibly due to lower quality of debt, and thus harm growth.

Table 4.4 provides an alternative specification using the following equation:

$$Sectoral\ Output\ Growth = \alpha + \lambda(Lagged\ Sectoral\ Output\ Growth) +$$
$$\beta_1(Lagged\ Bank\ Private\ Credit\ /\ GDP) + \beta_2(Bank\ Private\ Credit\ /\ GDP) +$$
$$\beta_3(Bank\ Private\ Credit\ /\ GDP)^2 + \gamma(Lending\text{-}Deposit\ Interest\ Spread) + \varepsilon \quad (4.2)$$

The additional estimation results do not suggest nonlinear effects of bank private credit on output growth across all sectors. The coefficient estimates of the nonlinear term—i.e., the square of bank private credit to GDP—on sectoral growth are not statistically significant for manufacturing and finance in East Asia and Latin America. The coefficients on bank private credit to GDP, both lagged and current, are mostly insignificant, suggesting that the estimation of the financial depth–sectoral growth link is not robust. On the other hand, the association between interest spread and sectoral growth is consistent with the baseline specification.

Table 4.3 Baseline estimation results

Sector	Lagged sectoral growth (percent)		Bank private credit to GDP (percent)		Lending-deposit interest spread (percent)		R-squared	Observations
	Coefficient	(Standard error)	Coefficient	(Standard error)	Coefficient	(Standard error)		
Dependent variable: Sectoral output growth (percent)								
Whole sample (41 economies)								
Agriculture	–.52	(.03)***	.19	(.11)*	–1.59	(.60)***	.44	454
Mining	–.41	(.06)***	–.48	(.19)**	–1.35	(1.04)	.11	452
Manufacturing	–.50	(.02)***	.03	(.10)	–.53	(.51)	.47	455
Public utilities	–.50	(.03)***	.54	(.12)***	2.31	(.62)***	.41	456
Construction	–.50	(.02)***	–.55	(.11)***	–.70	(.57)	.50	456
Wholesale and retail trade	–.52	(.02)***	.08	(.10)	–.65	(.54)	.51	454
Transport, storage, and communication	–.47	(.02)***	–.11	(.09)	.05	(.49)	.45	454
Finance, insurance, and real estate	–.49	(.03)***	–.54	(.14)***	.96	(.72)	.34	459
Government services	–.42	(.03)***	–.00	(.13)	2.11	(.68)***	.34	343
Community, social and personal services	–.56	(.04)***	.78	(.13)***	–1.01	(.68)	.40	444
East Asia and Pacific (11 economies)								
Agriculture	–.52	(.05)***	–.09	(.16)	–8.62	(4.96)*	.49	141
Mining	–.46	(.10)***	–.34	(.32)	–5.30	(10.02)	.14	137
Manufacturing	–.52	(.04)***	–.46	(.15)***	–4.46	(4.67)	.52	139
Public utilities	–.51	(.04)***	.01	(.15)	6.06	(4.71)	.49	140
Construction	–.50	(.04)***	–.56	(.15)***	–14.20	(4.76)***	.53	139

Wholesale and retail trade	−.48	(.05)***	.64	(.17)***	10.31	(5.13)**	.52	139
Transport, storage, and communication	−.52	(.04)***	.27	(.16)*	2.00	(4.94)	.53	138
Finance, insurance, and real estate	−.43	(.05)***	−.18	(.19)	18.83	(5.86)***	.38	140
Government services	−.45	(.07)***	−.54	(.28)*	−28.88	(9.51)***	.37	92
Community, social and personal services	−.52	(.06)***	.70	(.22)***	8.58	(6.72)	.37	140
Latin America and the Caribbean (9 economies)								
Agriculture	−.44	(.06)***	1.28	(.65)*	−2.51	(.67)***	.42	111
Mining	−.62	(.08)***	−2.47	(.82)***	.18	(.83)	.37	112
Manufacturing	−.42	(.05)***	−.59	(.61)	−.77	(.63)	.42	113
Public utilities	−.47	(.07)***	.16	(.76)	2.78	(.78)***	.40	114
Construction	−.60	(.05)***	−1.90	(.59)***	.85	(.61)	.61	114
Wholesale and retail trade	−.53	(.05)***	−1.31	(.60)**	−.18	(.62)	.55	112
Transport, storage, and communication	−.49	(.05)***	1.45	(.57)**	−1.01	(.59)*	.51	112
Finance, insurance, and real estate	−.54	(.05)***	1.56	(.66)**	.30	(.69)	.52	113
Government services	−.43	(.07)***	−.23	(1.06)	2.65	(.78)***	.42	62
Community, social and personal services	−.57	(.05)***	1.40	(.62)**	−2.06	(.64)***	.53	114

SME = small and medium enterprises

Note: This table reports ordinary least squares (OLS) regression of sectoral output growth on its lagged term, bank private credit to GDP (BCRY), and lending-deposit interest spread (SPRD). The sample is from 1996 to 2011, covering 41 economies, of which 11 are in East Asia and the Pacific (People's Republic of China; Hong Kong, China; Indonesia; India; Japan; Republic of Korea; Malaysia; the Philippines; Singapore; Thailand; and Taipei,China), and 9 are in Latin America and the Caribbean (Argentina, Bolivia, Brazil, Chile, Colombia, Costa Rica, Mexico, Peru, and Venezuela). Standard errors are in parentheses; ***(**, *) denotes statistical significance at the 1 (5, 10) percent level.

Sources: Authors' calculations based on Groningen Growth and Development Centre (GGDC) 10-Sector Database and World Bank, Global Financial Development Database (BCRY, SPRD).

Table 4.4 Alternative specification I

Dependent variable: Sectoral output growth (percent)

Sector	Lagged sectoral growth (percent) Coefficient	(Standard error)	Lagged bank private credit to GDP (percent) Coefficient	(Standard error)	Bank private credit to GDP (percent) Coefficient	(Standard error)	[Bank private credit to GDP (percent)] squared Coefficient	(Standard error)	Lending-deposit interest spread (percent) Coefficient	(Standard error)	R-squared	Observations
Whole sample (41 economies)												
Agriculture	-.51	(.03)***	-1.46	(2.19)	2.90	(2.22)	-.01	(.00)***	-1.34	(.60)**	.45	454
Mining	-.41	(.06)***	-1.17	(2.95)	-.16	(3.03)	.01	(.00)	-1.52	(1.04)	.11	451
Manufacturing	-.50	(.02)***	-3.08	(2.87)	3.39	(2.92)	-.00	(.00)	-.50	(.51)	.47	455
Public utilities	-.51	(.03)***	-2.62	(2.77)	3.82	(2.80)	-.00	(.00)*	2.43	(.62)***	.42	456
Construction	-.51	(.02)***	-6.27	(3.67)*	4.34	(3.69)	.01	(.00)***	-.90	(.56)	.53	456
Wholesale and retail trade	-.52	(.02)***	-1.72	(1.59)	1.16	(1.59)	.00	(.00)**	-.76	(.54)	.51	453
Transport, storage, and communication	-.47	(.02)***	-.37	(1.07)	.49	(1.12)	-.00	(.00)	.09	(.49)	.45	454
Finance, insurance, and real estate	-.49	(.03)***	.11	(4.20)	-1.79	(4.21)	.01	(.00)***	.74	(.72)	.35	459
Government services	-.42	(.03)***	-2.54	(1.80)	2.81	(1.85)	-.00	(.00)	2.12	(.68)***	.34	343
Community, social and personal services	-.56	(.04)***	-2.98	(3.93)	4.76	(3.96)	-.01	(.00)***	-.81	(.68)	.41	442

East Asia and Pacific (11 economies)

										R²	N
Agriculture	-.52	(.05)***	-.60	(1.92)	.24	(2.02)	.00	(.00)	-9.07	(5.15)*	.49	141
Mining	-.45	(.10)***	.32	(3.03)	-.56	(3.28)	-.00	(.01)	-5.05	(10.42)	.14	137
Manufacturing	-.52	(.04)***	-3.86	(3.09)	3.55	(3.24)	-.00	(.00)	-3.47	(4.87)	.53	139
Public utilities	-.50	(.04)***	-3.99	(2.36)*	4.46	(2.45)*	-.00	(.00)	7.38	(4.82)	.51	140
Construction	-.52	(.04)***	-4.64	(3.68)	1.80	(3.74)	.01	(.00)***	-19.15	(4.56)***	.60	139
Wholesale and retail trade	-.48	(.05)***	.23	(2.44)	.78	(2.44)	-.00	(.00)	11.11	(5.31)**	.52	139
Transport, storage, and communication	-.53	(.04)***	-.69	(1.51)	2.35	(1.65)	-.01	(.00)**	4.41	(4.98)	.55	138
Finance, insurance, and real estate	-.43	(.05)***	-1.05	(3.96)	1.75	(4.00)	-.00	(.00)	20.70	(6.03)***	.39	140
Government services	-.46	(.07)***	-20.65	(21.89)	18.17	(21.82)	.01	(.00)**	-33.93	(9.51)***	.41	92
Community, social and personal services	-.52	(.06)***	-8.28	(5.13)	9.22	(5.22)*	-.00	(.00)	9.28	(6.90)	.38	140

Latin America and the Caribbean (9 economies)

										R²	N
Agriculture	-.46	(.06)***	4.29	(10.10)	-6.41	(10.95)	.05	(.04)	-2.22	(.72)***	.43	111
Mining	-.60	(.08)***	15.84	(13.89)	-26.60	(14.52)*	.12	(.05)**	.78	(.86)	.40	112
Manufacturing	-.43	(.05)***	-3.92	(9.09)	1.59	(9.47)	.02	(.04)	-.68	(.67)	.42	113

(continued on next page)

Table 4.4 Alternative specification I (continued)

Sector	Lagged sectoral growth (percent)		Lagged bank private credit to GDP (percent)		Bank private credit to GDP (percent)		[Bank private credit to GDP (percent)] squared		Lending-deposit interest spread (percent)		R-squared	Observations
	Coefficient	(Standard error)	Coefficient	(Standard error)	Coefficient	(Standard error)	Coeffi-cient	(Standard error)	Coefficient	(Standard error)		
					Latin America and the Caribbean (9 economies)							
Public utilities	-.47	(.07)***	-30.72	(19.30)	38.79	(19.62)*	-.11	(.05)**	2.21	(.80)***	.44	114
Construction	-.61	(.05)***	2.15	(6.14)	-4.28	(6.74)	.00	(.04)	.85	(.65)	.61	114
Wholesale and retail trade	-.54	(.05)***	-8.23	(8.21)	3.40	(8.77)	.05	(.04)	.11	(.65)	.56	112
Transport, storage, and communication	-.48	(.05)***	10.58	(5.26)**	-9.38	(6.03)	.00	(.04)	-.90	(.61)	.53	112
Finance, insurance, and real estate	-.55	(.05)***	7.30	(8.83)	-6.36	(8.68)	.01	(.04)	.36	(.73)	.52	113
Government services	-.43	(.07)***	-31.89	(34.41)	28.90	(33.60)	.04	(.08)	2.90	(.85)***	.43	62
Community, social and personal services	-.58	(.05)***	-8.34	(7.77)	18.03	(8.07)**	-.12	(.04)***	-2.75	(.65)***	.58	112

Note: This table reports OLS regression of sectoral output growth on its lagged term, lending-deposit interest spread (SPRD), and bank private credit to GDP (BCRY), including lagged and squared terms. The sample is from 1996 to 2011, covering 41 economies, of which 11 are in East Asia and the Pacific (People's Republic of China; Hong Kong, China; Indonesia; India; Japan; Republic of Korea; Malaysia; the Philippines; Singapore; Thailand; and Taipei,China), and 9 are in Latin America and the Caribbean (Argentina, Bolivia, Brazil, Chile, Colombia, Costa Rica, Mexico, Peru, and Venezuela). Standard errors are in parentheses; *** (**, *) denotes statistical significance at the 1 (5, 10) percent level.

Sources: Authors' calculations on Groningen Growth and Development Centre (GGDC) 10-Sector Database and World Bank Global Financial Development Database (BCRY, SPRD).

Discussion and Policy Implications

The preliminary results reported above should be taken with a grain of salt—more data and work are needed to control better for the quality of credit, and other macrocontrols are needed to reflect the stage of the business and the credit cycles. Yet our results are consistent with the conjectures outlined in the literature review. Financial deepening may lead to uneven growth patterns, where sectors more dependent on stable external finance and with limited collateral may be adversely affected by financial deepening associated with credit reallocations and instability of credit conditions.

Our empirical analysis uses data on sectoral composition of the economy with controls for the quality of financial intermediation. The quality of financial intermediation is impacted by prices (i.e., financial intermediation spreads) and quantities (e.g., financial depth and SMEs' ease of getting credit). Financial spreads are, in turn, affected by access to credit, and quality of institutions (e.g., rights of creditors and efficacy of the judicial system), and the risk level of loans.

Figure 4.3 shows the economic significance of the controls. The economic significance of bank private credit to GDP for East Asia is a product of its coefficient estimates (including lagged, current, and squared terms) from the regression in table 4.4 multiplied by its standard deviation. The calculation for Latin America and for lending-deposit interest spread is done similarly.

Intriguingly, for several sectors the control variables for our proxy of de facto *quality* of financial intermediation tend to have levels of economic significance that are larger in Latin America and the Caribbean than they are in East Asia and the Pacific. The economic significance tends to be larger for nontradable sectors—public utilities, wholesale and retail trade, community and social services, and finance, insurance, and real estate—than for other sectors. In addition, bank private credit to GDP tends to have smaller economic significance than lending-deposit interest spread. The results may reflect the greater scarcity of finance in Latin America, and possibly the smaller share of state-owned firms enjoying preferential access to credit. Since credit may be scarcer in Latin America, the marginal importance of the quantity of finance is larger than in East Asia. The larger credit base of East Asia implies that the region has reached the stage where quality may be at least as important as the quantity.

Figure 4.4 plots the average and variation of bank private credit to GDP, comparing East Asia and the Pacific vis-à-vis Latin America and the Caribbean. Over the past two decades, the level of financial depth has always been larger in East Asia. Prior to the Asian financial crisis, bank private credit to GDP was 10 percent higher in East Asia than in Latin America. From 1999 to 2003, the difference fell to about 5 percent, but has rebounded to 10 percent recently. East Asia also hosts several financial centers—Tokyo; Hong Kong, China; and Singapore—that may improve the overall quality and quantity of financial

Figure 4.3 Economic significance on sectoral output growth

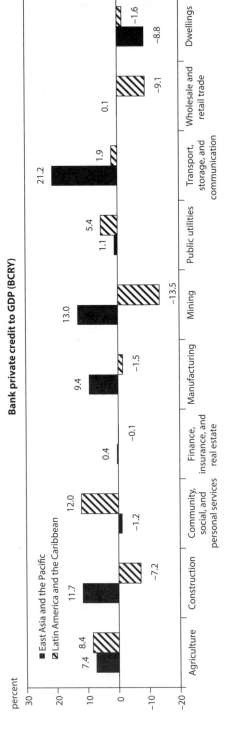

(continued on next page)

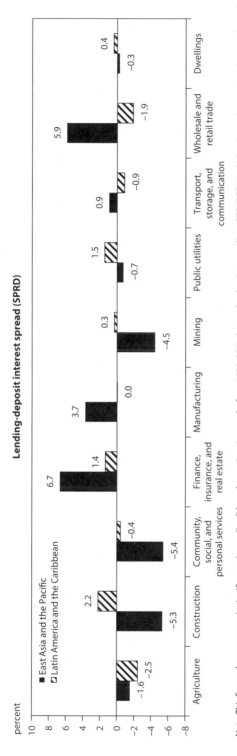

Lending-deposit interest spread (SPRD)

percent

■ East Asia and the Pacific
◫ Latin America and the Caribbean

| | Agriculture | Construction | Community, social, and personal services | Finance, insurance, and real estate | Manufacturing | Mining | Public utilities | Transport, storage, and communication | Wholesale and retail trade | Dwellings |

Agriculture: -1.6, -2.5
Construction: 2.2, -5.3
Community, social, and personal services: -0.4, -5.4
Finance, insurance, and real estate: 6.7, 1.4
Manufacturing: 3.7, 0.0
Mining: 0.3, -4.5
Public utilities: 1.5, -0.7
Transport, storage, and communication: 0.9, -0.9
Wholesale and retail trade: 5.9, -1.9
Dwellings: 0.4, -0.3

Note: This figure shows economic significance (annualized) based on estimation results from 1996–2011 data on bank private credit to GDP (BCRY; including lagged, current, and squared terms) and lending-deposit interest spread (SPRD) on sectoral output growth. The economic significance is calculated as a product of coefficient estimate and sample standard deviation of variable.

Sources: Authors' calculations based on Groningen Growth and Development Centre (GGDC) 10-Sector Database and World Bank, Global Financial Development Database (BCRY, SPRD).

Figure 4.4   Financial depth in East Asia and the Pacific vis-à-vis Latin America and the Caribbean, 1991–2011

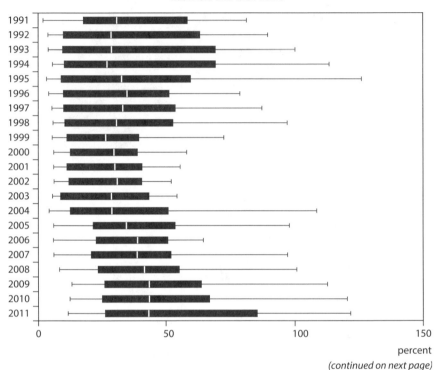

East Asia and the Pacific

percent

(continued on next page)

intermediation, although identifying the impact of financial centers remains a challenge.

Over the long run, the quality of financial intermediation should be positively correlated with the quality of macroeconomic policies and quality of institutions. We measure the quality of macroeconomic policies by the average inflation and volatility of inflation in the preceding five years. For 1976–2012, table 4.5 provides the correlation between quality of macroeconomic policies and quality of financial intermediation.

For East Asia, bank private credit to GDP is negatively correlated with average inflation, but positively correlated with risk premium on lending (measured as lending rate minus treasury bill rate). Average inflation is highly correlated with inflation volatility. For Latin America, the lending-deposit interest spread is correlated with the average and volatility of inflation, and with risk premium on lending. The volatility of inflation is also highly correlated with risk premium on lending. We have yet to formally confirm via regression analysis the association of sectoral output growth, quality of macroeconomic policies, and their interaction with the quality of financial intermediation and institutions. Furthermore, some of the financial quality measures are highly

Figure 4.4   Financial depth in East Asia and the Pacific vis-à-vis Latin America and the Caribbean, 1991–2011 *(continued)*

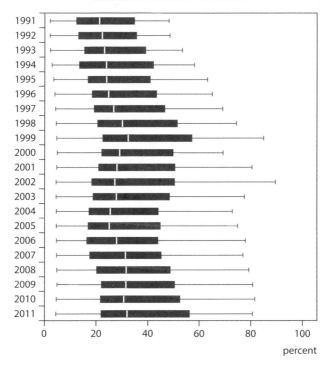

Latin America and the Caribbean

percent

Note: This figure shows box plots of bank private credit to GDP for East Asia and the Pacific vis-à-vis the ratio for Latin America and the Caribbean.

Source: Authors' calculations using World Bank, Global Financial Development Database.

correlated with each other, potentially posing multicolinearity issues. However, based on the correlation analysis, it is highly plausible that over the long run, sectoral output growth rates are driven by financial quality factors.

To capture the role of financial sector service flows in sectoral growth, we provide additional estimation results in table 4.6. Instead of bank private credit/GDP, we use bank private credit/financial and business services value added (percent), in level and nonlinear squared terms, as an alternative proxy for quality of finance. This new variable is constructed from bank private credit/GDP and financial&business services value added/GDP, both of which are available from the *World Development Indicators*.[6] Consistent with our conjecture, there is some evidence, notably for the public utilities sector and for the community and social services sector, in both the whole sample

6. World Bank, *World Development Indicators*, http://data.worldbank.org/data-catalog/world-development-indicators (accessed on January 23, 2015).

Table 4.5 Financial stability and quality of finance measures, 1976–2012 (percent)

Measure	East Asia and the Pacific				Latin America and the Caribbean			
	Bank private credit to GDP	Lending-deposit interest spread	Average inflation over the past 5 years relative to the OECD level	Inflation volatility over the past 5 years relative to the OECD level	Bank private credit to GDP	Lending-deposit interest spread	Average inflation over the past 5 years relative to the OECD level	Inflation volatility over the past 5 years relative to the OECD level
Lending-deposit interest spread	−0.05				−0.12			
Average inflation over the past 5 years relative to the OECD level	−0.22	0.12			0.07	0.20		
Inflation volatility over the past 5 years relative to the OECD level	−0.13	0.17	0.93		−0.01	0.23	0.90	
Risk premium on lending	0.25	−0.04	−0.41	−0.21	0.50	0.99	0.50	0.52

OECD = Organization for Economic Cooperation and Development

Note: This table provides for countries in estimation sample the correlations of financial depth (bank private credit to GDP, BCRY); efficiency (lending-deposit interest spread, SPRD); and financial stability (average inflation over the past 5 years above the OECD level, INFA; inflation volatility over the past 5 years above the OECD level, INFV; and risk premium on lending, RPLN). Shaded cell signifies statistical significance at 1 percent level. East Asia and the Pacific includes People's Republic of China; Hong Kong, China; Indonesia; India; Japan; Republic of Korea; Malaysia; the Philippines; Singapore; Thailand; and Taipei,China; Latin America and the Caribbean includes Argentina, Bolivia, Brazil, Chile, Colombia, Costa Rica, Mexico, Peru, and Venezuela.

Sources: Authors' calculations based on World Bank, Global Financial Development Database (BCRY, SPRD), and *World Development Indicators* (INFA, INFV, RPLN).

Table 4.6 Alternative specification II

Sector	Lagged sectoral growth (percent)		Lagged bank private credit to finance & business services		Lagged [bank private credit to finance & business services] squared		Lending-deposit interest spread (percent)		R-squared	Observations
	Coefficient	(Standard error)	Coefficient	(Standard error)	Coefficient	(Standard error)	Coefficient	(Standard error)		
Dependent variable: Sectoral output growth (percent)										
Whole sample (41 economies)										
Agriculture	−.51	(.03)***	1.08	(.21)***	−.04	(.01)***	−1.26	(.60)**	.47	449
Mining	−.40	(.06)***	−.72	(.38)*	.03	(.01)**	−.68	(1.07)	.11	446
Manufacturing	−.50	(.02)***	.00	(.19)	.00	(.01)	−.49	(.53)	.47	450
Public utilities	−.51	(.03)***	.75	(.23)***	−.02	(.01)**	2.31	(.64)***	.41	451
Construction	−.50	(.02)***	−1.25	(.20)***	.03	(.01)***	−1.26	(.57)**	.52	452
Wholesale and retail trade	−.52	(.02)***	−.21	(.20)	.01	(.01)	−.98	(.55)*	.50	450
Transport, storage, and communication	−.46	(.02)***	−.13	(.18)	.00	(.01)	−.13	(.50)	.45	450
Finance, insurance, and real estate	−.48	(.03)***	−1.18	(.27)***	.04	(.01)***	1.01	(.74)	.34	454
Government services	−.42	(.03)***	.03	(.25)	−.01	(.01)	1.76	(.69)**	.34	343
Community, social and personal services	−.55	(.04)***	1.30	(.25)***	−.03	(.01)***	−.83	(.70)	.40	437
East Asia and the Pacific (11 economies)										
Agriculture	−.52	(.05)***	−.08	(.38)	−.00	(.01)	−10.16	(5.08)**	.52	137
Mining	−.44	(.10)***	−1.35	(.77)*	.05	(.02)**	−1.24	(9.90)	.23	133
Manufacturing	−.52	(.05)***	−.40	(.40)	.01	(.01)	−3.88	(4.95)	.51	135
Public utilities	−.52	(.04)***	.69	(.38)*	−.02	(.01)**	7.21	(4.79)	.53	136
Construction	−.51	(.04)***	−2.02	(.35)***	.05	(.01)***	−19.77	(4.60)***	.59	136
Wholesale and retail trade	−.50	(.05)***	.88	(.42)**	−.02	(.01)*	11.22	(5.61)**	.49	134
Transport, storage, and communication	−.53	(.04)***	.84	(.39)**	−.02	(.01)*	3.57	(5.06)	.54	135

(continued on next page)

163

Table 4.6 Alternative specification II (continued)

Sector	Lagged sectoral growth (percent)		Lagged bank private credit to finance & business services		Lagged [bank private credit to finance & business services] squared		Lending-deposit interest spread (percent)		R-squared	Observations
	Coefficient	(Standard error)	Coefficient	(Standard error)	Coefficient	(Standard error)	Coefficient	(Standard error)		
Finance, insurance, and real estate	-.43	(.05)***	-.03	(.48)	.00	(.01)	20.48	(6.16)***	.38	136
Government services	-.48	(.07)***	-2.16	(.62)***	.05	(.02)***	-36.50	(9.00)***	.44	92
Community, social and personal services	-.50	(.06)***	1.61	(.54)***	-.04	(.01)***	9.52	(7.08)	.36	136
Latin America and the Caribbean (9 economies)										
Agriculture	-.46	(.06)***	-1.39	(1.67)	.16	(.13)	-2.05	(.70)***	.42	110
Mining	-.59	(.08)***	-6.88	(1.94)***	.46	(.16)***	.73	(.83)	.41	111
Manufacturing	-.43	(.05)***	-.74	(1.52)	.02	(.12)	-.76	(.65)	.42	112
Public utilities	-.49	(.07)***	4.31	(1.82)**	-.32	(.14)**	2.14	(.79)***	.43	113
Construction	-.60	(.05)***	-.86	(1.45)	-.03	(.11)	.75	(.62)	.62	113
Wholesale and retail trade	-.54	(.05)***	-2.77	(1.45)*	.15	(.12)	.01	(.62)	.57	112
Transport, storage, and communication	-.47	(.05)***	.36	(1.36)	.04	(.11)	-.92	(.59)	.50	111
Finance, insurance, and real estate	-.55	(.05)***	.15	(1.67)	.06	(.13)	.54	(.71)	.52	112
Government services	-.43	(.07)***	-.60	(3.87)	.06	(.41)	2.63	(.84)***	.42	62
Community, social and personal services	-.57	(.05)***	5.26	(1.48)***	-.35	(.12)***	-2.53	(.63)***	.58	111

Note: This table reports ordinary least squares (OLS) regression of sectoral output growth on its lagged term, lending-deposit interest spread (SPRD), and bank private credit to financial&business services (FSER), including lagged and squared terms. The sample is from 1996 to 2011, covering 41 economies, of which 11 are in East Asia and the Pacific (People's Republic of China; Hong Kong, China; Indonesia; India; Japan; Republic of Korea; Malaysia; the Philippines; Singapore; Thailand; and Taipei,China), and 9 are in Latin America and the Caribbean (Argentina, Bolivia, Brazil, Chile, Colombia, Costa Rica, Mexico, Peru, and Venezuela). Standard errors are in parentheses; *** (**, *) denotes statistical significance at the 1 (5, 10) percent level.

Sources: Authors' calculations based on Groningen Growth and Development Centre (GGDC) 10-Sector Database and World Bank, Global Financial Development Database (BCRY, FSER, SPRD).

and subsamples, that the effect of service flow of financial sector to sector growth is nonlinear. The coefficient estimate of lagged bank private credit/ financial&business services is positive, while the estimate of lagged [bank private credit/financial&business services] squared is negative in manufacturing and financial sectors.

The evidence suggests that the level of service flow of financial sector is good only up to a point, after which it becomes a drag on sectoral growth in the sample countries. However, we also found an opposite pattern, namely the coefficient estimate of lagged bank private credit/financial&business services is negative, while the estimate of lagged [bank private credit/financial&business services] squared is positive in construction and mining. The association of interest spread and sectoral growth remains largely the same.

Finally, we offer another alternative specification in table 4.7. To verify the possibility of "financial Dutch disease"—i.e., booming financial service flows reduce the supply of long-term funding to manufacturing and other sectors that rely on stable external finance—we add a lagged growth of financial and business services, and control for the interest spread and its interaction with the growth of financial and business services. We find some support of this hypothesis in the whole sample since the coefficient estimate on the interaction term is negative and statistically significant for the growth of the manufacturing sector.

Concluding Observations

At a broader level, this chapter was motivated by the observation that what matters for economic growth is the quality of finance rather than the quantity of finance. Yet standard measures of financial development are quantitative indicators of size rather than measures of financial efficiency that determine the capacity of a financial system to allocate financial resources to their most productive uses. The global financial crisis, which wrought havoc on the financial systems of the United States and the European Union, underlines the possibility that expansion of the financial sector may be beneficial for growth but only up to a point. Even in developing countries, quantity of finance may be a poor measure of quality of finance. For example, in the PRC, the relentless expansion of credit in recent years, much of it to state-owned firms, has given rise to concerns about deterioration in the quality of investment. A key dimension of financial efficiency is the extent to which the financial system channels resources to productive sectors of the real economy.

Overall, our evidence is consistent with the hypotheses we set forth at the outset, in particular concerning the nonlinear effect of financial development on growth and its uneven effect across sectors. For one measure of the quality of finance, we find that the level has a positive, significant effect but the squared term has a negative, significant effect for a few sectors. Therefore, our evidence lends some support to the conjecture that financial development has a nonlinear effect on output growth. In addition, we find that the effect

Table 4.7 Alternative specification III

Dependent variable: Sectoral output growth (percent)

Sector	Lagged sectoral growth (percent)		Growth of bank private credit to financial&business services		Lending-deposit interest spread (percent)		Interaction of [growth of bank private credit/financial&business services] and interest spread		R-squared	Observations
	Coefficient	(Standard error)	Coefficient	(Standard error)	Coefficient	(Standard error)	Coefficient	(Standard error)		
Whole sample (41 economies)										
Agriculture	-.52	(.03)***	-.31	(2.26)	-1.96	(.55)***	.20	(.15)	.44	449
Mining	-.40	(.06)***	3.41	(1.96)*	-.44	(.97)	-.12	(.15)	.10	445
Manufacturing	-.50	(.02)***	1.37	(1.34)	-.58	(.48)	-.09	(.10)	.47	449
Public utilities	-.51	(.03)***	-.53	(1.01)	1.17	(.60)**	.04	(.13)	.38	451
Construction	-.51	(.03)***	2.35	(1.11)**	.43	(.54)	-.08	(.09)	.48	451
Wholesale and retail trade	-.52	(.02)***	.96	(.84)	-.82	(.50)*	.03	(.08)	.51	447
Transport, storage, and communication	-.46	(.02)***	.38	(.74)	.33	(.46)	-.10	(.09)	.45	449
Finance, insurance, and real estate	-.49	(.04)***	1.53	(2.52)	2.16	(.69)***	-.10	(.17)	.31	454
Government services	-.42	(.03)***	2.25	(1.39)	2.07	(.63)***	-.07	(.12)	.34	343
Community, social and personal services	-.56	(.04)***	-2.03	(1.73)	-2.70	(.65)***	.31	(.20)	.35	436

East Asia and the Pacific (11 economies)

Agriculture	−.52	(.05)***	5.69	(7.25)	−7.12	(4.96)	−1.45	(1.57)	.50	137
Mining	−.45	(.10)***	4.06	(6.21)	−3.96	(10.01)	−1.20	(1.30)	.14	133
Manufacturing	−.53	(.05)***	−1.10	(3.41)	−2.07	(4.86)	.84	(1.25)	.50	134
Public utilities	−.51	(.04)***	−11.00	(9.55)	5.53	(4.66)	3.02	(2.17)	.51	136
Construction	−.50	(.05)***	4.90	(7.87)	−10.16	(4.93)**	−.84	(2.25)	.48	136
Wholesale and retail trade	−.50	(.05)***	−2.92	(3.21)	6.79	(5.34)	.92	(.67)	.47	134
Transport, storage, and communication	−.52	(.04)***	−1.87	(4.15)	1.18	(4.99)	−.39	(.98)	.53	135
Finance, insurance, and real estate	−.45	(.05)***	6.61	(11.78)	19.40	(5.83)***	−.46	(2.82)	.39	136
Government services	−.47	(.07)***	−11.32	(30.93)	−18.99	(8.50)**	3.25	(7.36)	.35	92
Community, social and personal services	−.49	(.06)***	−.06	(7.14)	4.14	(6.80)	1.52	(2.02)	.34	136

Latin America and the Caribbean (9 economies)

Agriculture	−.45	(.06)***	−3.80	(3.92)	−2.20	(.66)***	.31	(.25)	.41	110
Mining	−.60	(.08)***	−5.50	(3.96)	−.75	(.85)	.03	(.16)	.34	110
Manufacturing	−.43	(.05)***	.38	(3.02)	−1.01	(.61)	−.00	(.20)	.41	112
Public utilities	−.47	(.07)***	3.78	(6.43)	2.89	(.75)***	−.14	(.24)	.40	113
Construction	−.61	(.05)***	2.41	(2.56)	.22	(.62)	−.11	(.11)	.58	112
Wholesale and retail trade	−.53	(.05)***	2.64	(4.06)	−.63	(.60)	.00	(.14)	.54	111
Transport, storage, and communication	−.46	(.05)***	−.23	(2.24)	−.47	(.58)	−.14	(.20)	.47	111

(continued on next page)

Table 4.7 Alternative specification III (continued)

Sector	Lagged sectoral growth (percent)		Growth of bank private credit to financial&business services		Lending-deposit interest spread (percent)		Interaction of [growth of bank private credit/financial&business services] and interest spread		R-squared	Observations
	Coefficient	(Standard error)	Coefficient	(Standard error)	Coefficient	(Standard error)	Coefficient	(Standard error)		
Finance, insurance, and real estate	-.55	(.06)***	1.48	(2.93)	.96	(.69)	-.14	(.17)	.49	112
Government services	-.49	(.08)***	6.82	(6.73)	3.17	(.71)***	.08	(.19)	.46	62
Community, social and personal services	-.57	(.05)***	-2.99	(3.07)	-1.66	(.61)***	.52	(.27)*	.54	111

Note: This table reports ordinary least squares (OLS) regression of sectoral output growth on its lagged term, lending-deposit interest spread (SPRD), and bank private credit to financial & business services (FSER), including lagged and squared terms. The sample is from 1996 to 2011, covering 41 economies, of which 11 are in East Asia and the Pacific (People's Republic of China; Hong Kong, China; Indonesia; India; Japan; Republic of Korea; Malaysia; the Philippines; Singapore; Thailand; and Taipei,China), and 9 are in Latin America and the Caribbean (Argentina, Bolivia, Brazil, Chile, Colombia, Costa Rica, Mexico, Peru, and Venezuela). Standard errors are in parentheses; *** (**, *) denotes statistical significance at the 1 (5, 10) percent level.

Sources: Authors' calculations based on Groningen Growth and Development Centre (GGDC) 10-Sector Database and World Bank, Global Financial Development Database (BCRY, FSER, SPRD).

of financial depth on output growth varies across sectors. More specifically, we find that financial depth has a negative effect on manufacturing in East Asia and a positive effect on the finance, insurance, and real estate sector in Latin America. Financial efficiency, as measured by lending-deposit interest spread, is positively associated with the growth of the finance, insurance, and real estate sector. Construction sector growth is negatively associated with the spread in East Asia, but positively in Latin America.

More generally, several of the differences between the regions may reflect the greater scarcity of finance in Latin America in comparison to East Asia. This may explain why the marginal importance of the quantity of finance is higher in Latin America than in East Asia. It may be that the expansion of East Asia's financial sector has reached the stage where the quality of finance may be at least as important as its quantity. We also find some evidence of a financial Dutch disease. Specifically, the faster the growth of financial services and the larger the lending-deposit interest spread, the slower the growth of the manufacturing sector. It should be emphasized that our empirical analysis is preliminary and marks a first step toward more indepth analysis of an important issue. Future research would benefit greatly from better measurement—subject to data availability—of the quality of finance by controlling for, for example, the degree of financial repression and the role of directed credit and state-owned banks.

Data Appendix

Variable	Source and Definition
Sectoral output growth per worker (percent); VAK	Groningen Growth and Development Centre 10-Sector Database. Provides a long-run internationally comparable dataset on sectoral productivity performance in Asia, Europe, Latin America, and the United States. Variables covered are annual series of value added, output deflators, and persons employed for 10 broad sectors. The Database gives sectoral detail to the historical macrodata in Maddison (2003) from 1950 onward. It consists of series for 10 countries in Asia, 9 in Latin America, and 9 in Europe and the United States. The present data differentiate among 10 sectors of the economy: agriculture, mining, manufacturing, construction, public utilities, retail and wholesale trade, transport and communication, financial and business services, other market services, and government services. (Estimates for the total economy are aggregated across sectors, and given several adjustments at sectoral level, the aggregate results are not fully consistent with the national accounts aggregates. Value-added data in this database are at constant prices.)
Bank private credit to GDP (percent); BCRY	World Bank, Global Financial Development Database (GFDD); GFDD.DI.01. The financial resources provided to the private sector by domestic money banks as a share of GDP. Domestic money banks comprise commercial banks and other financial institutions that accept transferable deposits, such as demand deposits. (International Monetary Fund, *International Financial Statistics*, and World Bank GDP estimates)
Lending-deposit interest spread (percent); SPRD	GFDD; GFDD.EI.02. Difference between lending rate and deposit rate. Lending rate is the rate charged by banks on loans to the private sector, and deposit interest rate is the rate offered by commercial banks on three-month deposits. (International Monetary Fund, *International Financial Statistics*)

Getting credit index (score); GTCR	World Bank, Doing Business index: Measuring Business Regulations database. Measure of the legal rights of borrowers and lenders with respect to secured transactions through one set of indicators and the sharing of credit information through another. The first set of indicators measures whether certain features that facilitate lending exist within the applicable collateral and bankruptcy laws. The second set measures the coverage, scope, and accessibility of credit information available through public credit registries and private credit bureaus. The ranking on the ease of getting credit is based on the percentile rankings on the sum of its component indicators: the depth of credit information index and the strength of legal rights index. This measure shows the distance of each economy to the "frontier." The frontier represents the highest performance observed for each of the indicators across all economies measured in Doing Business since the inclusion of the indicator. An economy's distance to the frontier is reflected on a scale from 0 to 100, where 0 represents the lowest performance and 100 represents the frontier.
Resolving insolvency index (score); REIN	Measure of the time, cost, and outcome of insolvency proceedings involving domestic entities. The data are derived from questionnaire responses by local insolvency practitioners and verified through a study of laws and regulations and public information on bankruptcy systems. The ranking on the ease of resolving insolvency is based on the recovery rate. This measure shows the distance of each economy to the frontier. The frontier represents the highest performance observed for each of the indicators across all economies measured in Doing Business since the inclusion of the indicator. An economy's distance to the frontier is reflected on a scale from 0 to 100, where 0 represents the lowest performance and 100 represents the frontier.
Depositors with commercial banks per 1,000 adults; DCBA	International Monetary Fund, Financial Access Survey. Number of depositors with commercial banks per 1,000 adults. The data are from commercial banks-bank survey.

SME loans from commercial banks (percent GDP); LSME	Financial Access Survey. Outstanding small and medium enterprise (SME) loans from commercial banks relative to the size of GDP.
Inflation (percent); INF	World Bank, *World Development Indicators*. (FP.CPI.TOTL.ZG) Inflation, consumer prices (annual percent), as measured by the consumer price index, reflects the annual percentage change in the cost to the average consumer of acquiring a basket of goods and services that may be fixed or changed at specified intervals, such as yearly. The Laspeyres formula is generally used. Data for Argentina are from the Economist Intelligence Unit,[1] of which prior to 2007, data are from the Instituto Nacional de Estadística y Censos; from 2007 the source for consumer price inflation data is PriceStats.
Risk premium on lending (percent); RPLN	*World Development Indicators*. (FR.INR.RISK) Risk premium on lending (lending rate minus treasury bill rate, percent). Risk premium on lending is the interest rate charged by banks on loans to private sector customers minus the "risk-free" treasury bill interest rate at which short-term government securities are issued or traded in the market. In some countries this spread may be negative, indicating that the market considers its best corporate clients to be lower risk than the government. The terms and conditions attached to lending rates differ by country, however, limiting their comparability.
Bank private credit/ financial&business services (percent); FSER	*World Development Indicators*. Bank private credit/GDP divided by financial&business services/GDP. Financial&business services/GDP (NV.SRV.TETC.ZS) corresponds to ISIC (International Standard Industrial Classification) divisions 50–99 and includes value added in financial professional services, wholesale and retail trade (including hotels and restaurants), transport, government, and personal services such as education, health care, and real estate services. Also included are imputed bank service charges.

1. Economist Intelligence Unit, www.eiu.com/home.aspx (accessed on January 23, 2015).

Economies and Regions

Note: * included in the estimation sample in East Asia and the Pacific; ** in Latin America and the Caribbean; *** economies in other regions included in the estimation.

East Asia and Pacific

Cambodia, People's Republic of China, Fiji, Indonesia*, Kiribati, Democratic People's Republic of Korea, Lao People's Democratic Republic, Malaysia*, Marshall Islands, Federated States of Micronesia, Mongolia, Myanmar, Palau, Papua New Guinea, Philippines*, Samoa, Solomon Islands, St. Kitts and Nevis, Thailand*, Timor-Leste, Tonga, Tuvalu, Vanuatu, Viet Nam

Latin America and the Caribbean

Antigua and Barbuda, Argentina**, Belize, Bolivia**, Brazil**, Chile, Colombia**, Costa Rica**, Cuba, Dominica, Dominican Republic, Ecuador, El Salvador, Grenada, Guatemala, Guyana, Haiti, Honduras, Jamaica, Mexico**, Nicaragua, Panama, Paraguay, Peru**, St. Lucia, St. Vincent and the Grenadines, Suriname, Uruguay, Venezuela

Europe and Central Asia

Albania, Armenia, Azerbaijan, Belarus, Bosnia and Herzegovina, Bulgaria, Georgia, Kazakhstan, Kosovo, Kyrgyz Republic, Latvia, Lithuania, Macedonia, FYR, Moldova, Montenegro, Romania, Russian Federation, Serbia, Tajikistan, Turkey, Turkmenistan, Ukraine, Uzbekistan

High-Income OECD Members

Australia, Austria, Belgium, Canada, Czech Republic, Denmark***, Estonia, Finland, France***, Germany, Greece, Hungary, Iceland, Ireland, Israel, Italy***, Japan, Republic of Korea*, Luxembourg Netherlands***, New Zealand, Norway, Poland, Portugal, Slovak Republic, Slovenia, Spain***, Sweden***, Switzerland, United Kingdom***, United States***

High-Income Non-OECD Members

Andorra; Aruba; Bahamas, The; Bahrain; Barbados; Bermuda; Brunei Darussalam; Cayman Islands; Croatia; Cyprus; Equatorial Guinea; Faeroe Islands; French Polynesia; Hong Kong, China*; Isle of Man; Kuwait; Liechtenstein; Macau, China; Malta; Monaco; New Caledonia; Oman; Qatar; San Marino; Saudi Arabia; Singapore; Trinidad and Tobago; United Arab Emirates; Virgin Islands

Middle East and North Africa

Algeria, Djibouti, Egypt, Arab Republic of***, Islamic Republic of Iran, Iraq, Jordan, Lebanon, Libya, Morocco, Syria, Tunisia, West Bank and Gaza, Yemen

South Asia

Afghanistan, Bangladesh, Bhutan, India, Maldives, Nepal, Pakistan, Sri Lanka

Sub-Saharan Africa

Angola, Benin, Botswana***, Burkina Faso, Burundi, Cameroon, Cape Verde, Central African Republic, Chad, Comoros, Democratic Republic of Congo, Republic of Congo, Côte d'Ivoire, Eritrea, Ethiopia***, Gabon, The Gambia, Ghana, Guinea, Guinea-Bissau, Kenya***, Lesotho, Liberia, Madagascar, Malawi***, Mali, Mauritania, Mauritius***, Mozambique, Namibia, Niger, Nigeria***, Rwanda, Sao Tome and Principe, Senegal, Seychelles, Sierra Leone, Somalia, South Africa, Sudan, Swaziland, Tanzania***, Togo, Uganda, Zambia***, Zimbabwe***

References

Aizenman, Joshua, Brian Pinto, and Vladyslav Sushko. 2013. Financial Sector Ups and Downs and the Real Sector in the Open Economy: Up by the Stairs, Down by the Parachute. *Emerging Markets Review* 16: 1–30.

Alfaro, Laura, Sebnem Kalemli-Ozcan, and Vadym Volosovych. 2003. Why Doesn't Capital Flow from Rich to Poor Countries? An Empirical Investigation (December). Houston: University of Houston.

Arcand, Jean-Louis, Enrico Berkes, and Ugo Panizza. 2012. *Too Much Finance?* IMF Working Paper 12/161. Washington: International Monetary Fund.

Boyd, John H., and Bruce D. Smith. 1992. Intermediation and the Equilibrium Allocation of Investment Capital: Implications for Economic Development. *Journal of Monetary Economics* 30: 409–32.

Boyd, John H., Ross E. Levine, and Bruce D. Smith. 2001. The Impact of Inflation on Financial Sector Performance. *Journal of Monetary Economics* 47: 221–48.

Cecchetti, Stephen G., and Enisse Kharroubi. 2012. Reassessing the Impact of Finance on Growth. Presented at the Second International Research Conference of the Reserve Bank of India, Mumbai, February 1–2.

Claessens, Stijn, and Luc Laeven. 2003. Financial Development, Property Rights, and Growth. *Journal of Finance* 58: 2401–36.

Dehejia, Rajeev, and Adriana Lleras-Muney. 2003. *Why Does Financial Development Matter? The United States from 1900 to 1940.* NBER Working Paper 9551. Cambridge, MA: National Bureau of Economic Research.

Eichengreen, Barry, and Kris J. Mitchener. 2003. *The Great Depression as a Credit Boom Gone Wrong.* BIS Working Paper 137. Basel: Bank for International Settlements.

Jayaratne, Jith, and Philip E Strahan. 1996. The Finance-Growth Nexus: Evidence from Bank Branch Deregulation. *Quarterly Journal of Economics* 111: 639–70.

Jordà, Òscar, Moritz Schularick, and Alan Taylor. 2011. *When Credit Bites Back: Leverage, Business Cycles, and Crises.* NBER Working Paper 17621. Cambridge, MA: National Bureau of Economic Research.

Ju, Jiandong, and Shang-Jin Wei. 2011. When Is Quality of Financial System a Source of Comparative Advantage? *Journal of International Economics* 84, no. 2 (July): 178–87.

La Porta, Rafael, Florencio López-de-Silanes, Andrei Shleifer, and Robert Vishny. 2000. Investor Protection and Corporate Governance. *Journal of Financial Economics* 58: 3–27.

Levine, Ross. 2005. Finance and Growth: Theory and Evidence. *Handbook of Economic Growth* 1, part A: 865–934.

Lucas, Robert. 1990. Why Doesn't Capital Flow from Rich to Poor Countries? *American Economic Review* 80, no. 2: 92–6.

Maddison, Angus. 2003. *The World Economy: Historical Statistics.* Development Centre Studies Paris: OECD Publishing.

Minsky, Hyman P. 1974. The Modeling of Financial Instability: An Introduction. In *Modeling and Simulation* 5: 267–72. Paper prepared for the Fifth Annual Pittsburgh Conference on Modeling and Simulation, sponsored by the University of Pittsburgh, April 24–26. Available at http://digitalcommons.bard.edu/hm_archive/467/ (accessed on January 24, 2015).

OECD (Organization for Economic Cooperation and Development). 2013. *Health at a Glance 2013: OECD Indicators* (November). Paris. Available at www.oecd.org/els/health-systems/Health-at-a-Glance-2013.pdf (accessed on January 19, 2015).

Rajan, Raghuram G. 2005. Has Financial Development Made the World Riskier? Presented at a symposium sponsored by the Federal Reserve Bank of Kansas City, Jackson Hole, WY, August 27. Available at www.nber.org/papers/w11728 (accessed on January 19, 2015).

Rajan, Raghuram G., and Luigi Zingales. 1998. Financial Dependence and Growth. *American Economic Review* 88: 559–86.

Rousseau, Peter L., and Paul Wachtel. 2011. What Is Happening to the Impact of Financial Deepening on Economic Growth? *Economic Inquiry* 49: 276–88.

Schularick, Moritz, and Alan M. Taylor. 2009. *Credit Booms Gone Bust: Monetary Policy, Leverage Cycles and Financial Crises, 1870–2008.* NBER Working Paper 15512. Cambridge, MA: National Bureau of Economic Research.

van Ark, Bart. 1996. Sectoral Growth Accounting and Structural Change in Post-War Europe. In *Quantitative Aspects of Post-War European Economic Growth,* eds. Bart van Ark and Nicholas F. R. Crafts. Cambridge, UK: CEPR/Cambridge University Press.

5

Financing Productivity- and Innovation-Led Growth in Developing Asia:
International Lessons and Policy Issues

AJAI CHOPRA

Developing Asia's strong growth record over the last three decades has been the envy of the world. The region's growth was dented during the 1997–98 Asian financial crisis and the 2008–09 global crisis but rebounded quickly from both episodes. The impressive growth record, which has been largely dependent on investment and factor accumulation, not only raised income and reduced poverty but also expanded the region's global influence. In the future, however, growth in much of developing Asia will need to rely progressively more on higher productivity growth and less on capital deepening. Richer countries in developing Asia will also need to shift from a development model based on technology absorption to one that fosters innovation.

It will therefore be important for developing Asia to implement productivity-enhancing reforms to facilitate structural transformation into higher productivity sectors, improve the allocation of resources, and spur technological catchup. There is, however, no single reform path to spur productivity growth. Rather, higher productivity growth has been associated with more and better infrastructure and human capital, open trade, efficient and well-developed financial systems, and economic institutions that promote competition and encourage entrepreneurship and innovation. This makes it vital to implement

Ajai Chopra is visiting fellow at the Peterson Institute for International Economics. Before joining the Institute, he worked for three decades at the International Monetary Fund (IMF), where his career focused on country surveillance and IMF lending programs primarily in Europe and Asia but also in Latin America and Africa. He is grateful to Abir Varma for valuable research assistance and to William Cline, Morris Goldstein, and Marc Noland for comments.

a set of targeted and interlocking reforms to achieve the necessary structural change, reduction in resource misallocation, and technology transfer.

Furthermore, the reform priorities to spur productivity- and innovation-led growth will vary across income groups and the degree of technological advancement attained relative to advanced countries. Empirical studies suggest the following calibration of reform priorities to the stage of development (Dabla-Norris et al. 2013):

- In low-income countries, reforms should focus on strengthening economic institutions needed for market-based economic activity, reducing trade barriers, reforming agricultural and banking sectors, and improving basic education and infrastructure.

- In lower-middle-income countries, the focus should be on reforms in banking and agriculture, reducing barriers to foreign direct investment (FDI), and increasing competition in product markets to spur a more dynamic service sector, improving secondary and tertiary education, and alleviating infrastructure bottlenecks.

- And in upper-middle-income countries, deepening capital markets, developing more competitive and flexible product and labor markets, fostering a more skilled labor force, and investing in research and development of new technologies will be paramount.

Regardless of the stage of development, this is a wide-ranging reform agenda. A common element for all income groups, however, is the importance of building strong domestic financial systems to sustain high growth. Although the precise needs vary across income groups, financial system deepening is central to a more efficient allocation of capital across sectors and can facilitate innovation and technology transfer.

This chapter focuses on the policies required for Asia's financial systems to better support growth that is led by productivity and innovation. The next section reviews studies on developing Asia's historical growth record and long-term prospects to establish that future growth will need to rely progressively more on improvements in productivity growth and less on capital deepening. The risk of falling into a "middle-income trap" is also discussed. The third section discusses the policy implications of empirical research that has emerged in the aftermath of the 2008–09 global financial crisis, which highlights non-linearities in the relationship between financial development and economic growth and the danger that malfunctioning financial systems can result in the misallocation of resources. An important implication is that policymakers, especially in countries at the higher end of the income scale, should focus less on increasing the size of the financial sector and more on improving its intermediation function.

The fourth section outlines the general policy priorities for further financial development in developing Asia based on existing financial sector realities in the region and the level of country income. In view of the link to productivity, focus is put on mobilizing Asia's ample private savings for long-term financing, especially to tackle the region's infrastructure deficit, and on improving access to financing for small and medium enterprises (SMEs). As many countries in Asia shift from a development model based on technology absorption to one that promotes innovation, the fifth section discusses the critical role of specialized finance and investors in allowing innovative firms to conduct research, adopt technologies necessary for inventions, and ultimately commercialize innovations. Concluding remarks are offered in the last section.

Long-Term Growth Prospects and Role of Productivity

Asia's admirable economic growth and transformation has been the subject of numerous empirical studies. Jong-Wha Lee and Kiseok Hong (2010) and Donghyun Park and Jungsoo Park (2010) of the Asian Development Bank (ADB) use a growth accounting framework and find that growth in capital accumulation was a key factor behind developing Asia's remarkable economic expansion, especially in the 1980s and 1990s.[1] By contrast, their results show that the contribution of labor input, education, and total factor productivity (TFP) to real GDP growth was more moderate. Park and Park, however, found an important structural shift in the pattern of developing Asia's economic growth around 2002, with TFP beginning to play a larger role in the region's growth.

Lee and Hong (2010) also address the central question of whether developing Asia's rapid growth can continue in the next two decades. Their baseline projections (without significant reforms) suggest that future growth will tend to be lower than historical performance in most of the Asian economies they analyze. In particular, as these economies have already registered high rates of capital accumulation in the last three decades, the marginal productivity of capital is set to decline. Furthermore, for many economies the demographic dividend is projected to wane, constraining the contribution to growth from labor. Park and Park (2010) reach a similar conclusion and highlight the importance of policymakers pursuing supply-side policies that foster productivity growth to sustain developing Asia's future growth.

In a more recent study, David Roland-Holst and Guntur Sugiyarto (2014) use a calibrated general equilibrium (CGE) model, rather than a growth accounting framework, to capture detailed trade and domestic market interactions between and within Asia and in its relationship to the rest of the world to generate long-term forecasts for Asian economies. Their long-term forecasts also suggest that TFP growth will be essential to improve livelihoods

---

1. The analyses in Lee and Hong (2010) and Park and Park (2010) cover the People's Republic of China; Hong Kong, China; India; Indonesia; Malaysia; Pakistan; the Philippines; the Republic of Korea; Singapore; Taipei,China; Thailand; and Viet Nam, which together account for 95 percent of developing Asia's GDP, thus making this group representative of regional trends.

generally and promote regional convergence in particular. Looking at a variety of policies that facilitate productivity growth, they also find that deeper Asian financial integration results in the biggest growth dividend.

Estimates in Luis Cubeddu et al. (2014) confirm that the contribution of TFP to real GDP growth in emerging-market Asia picked up markedly in the period 2000–12.[2] But notwithstanding the improvement in TFP, factor accumulation remained an important driver of growth, with strong terms of trade growth and easy financing conditions facilitating higher investment. Furthermore, they suggest that the increase in productivity growth likely reflects gains from reforms in earlier decades (e.g., increased trade and financial liberalization); the reallocation of factors to higher-productivity sectors (e.g., employment shifts out of agriculture to higher-productivity manufacturing); and spillovers from increased foreign direct investment. But they also warn that such productivity gains could be partly temporary because productivity measures tend to be procyclical and are often overestimated in boom years, and that without additional reforms TFP growth may be lower over the medium term.

Fear of a sustained growth slowdown in middle-income economies after a period of sustained rapid growth has prompted a literature on the so-called middle-income trap.[3] Unless they move up the value chain, countries that get caught in this trap find it difficult to compete with either low-income countries that have the advantage of lower labor costs or high-income countries that rely more on high-tech products and services. Barry Eichengreen, Donghyun Park, and Kwanho Shin (2013) analyze the historical experience with growth slowdowns to shed light on future prospects. Their analysis indicates that slowdowns are more likely when old age dependency ratios are high, investment rates are elevated (as this may translate into low future returns on capital), and real exchange rates are undervalued (as this provides a disincentive to move up the technology ladder). They also point out that these patterns are consistent with conditions and policies in the People's Republic of China (PRC). Eichengreen, Park, and Shin also find that slowdowns are less likely in countries with high levels of secondary and tertiary education and where high-tech products account for a large share of exports, underscoring the importance of moving up the technology ladder to avoid the middle-income trap.

Similarly, Shekhar Aiyar et al. (2013) find that a number of emerging Asian economies run the risk of falling into a middle-income trap.[4] They emphasize that whether a country will experience a sustained growth slowdown

2. The emerging-market Asia group analyzed in Cubeddu et al. (2014) includes the same countries as in Lee and Hong (2010) and Park and Park (2010), except that it does not include Pakistan and it adds Brunei Darussalam and Sri Lanka.

3. In Asia, only the Republic of Korea; Taipei,China; Hong Kong, China; and Singapore have moved up from middle income to high income, classified by the World Bank as economies with a gross national income per capita of $12,476 or more.

4. See also Tho (2013) and Felipe (2012) for an analysis of the middle-income trap in Asia.

depends on the quality of its policies and institutions and also a range of structural features such as trade structure, infrastructure, demographics, and macroeconomics (e.g., investment and capital inflows). Lant Pritchett and Lawrence Summers (2013), however, take a different approach, arguing that regression to the mean is the empirically most salient feature of economic growth, a feature that shows greater robustness in the data than the middle-income trap. But even they highlight the importance of the quality of policies and institutions, noting that the risk of an abrupt end to episodes of growth well above the mean is much higher with weak institutions and organizations for policy implementation.

The common conclusion of various studies of Asia's historical growth record and future prospects is that economic growth will need to rely progressively more on improvements in productivity growth and less on capital deepening. This is not to say that investment and factor accumulation will not be important drivers of growth, especially in low- and middle-income countries with large infrastructure gaps, but rather that productivity will need to become a more important driver of growth in developing Asia.

Although there is no single reform path to spur productivity growth and policy needs vary across income groups, financial system deepening is central to a more efficient allocation of capital across sectors and can facilitate innovation and technology transfer. Before turning to the central issue of the policies required for Asia's financial systems to better support growth that is led by productivity and innovation, it is worthwhile to review some of the recent developments in the literature on the nexus between finance and growth, prompted in part by the 2008–09 global financial crisis and its aftermath.

Financial Development and Growth: Implications of the Evolving Literature

The theoretical and empirical literature on the role of the financial system in influencing economic growth is vast and continues to evolve. A classic survey by Ross Levine (2005) concluded that the predominant evidence suggests that both financial intermediaries and markets matter for growth and that this relationship is not driven solely by reverse causality.[5] An important insight of this literature is that financial development and deepening affect growth primarily by fostering more efficient allocation of capital across firms and industries and spurring productivity growth, not by raising the rate of aggregate

---

5. The issue of causality, however, is not settled and Joan Robinson's (1952) dictum that "where enterprise leads, finance follows" also has resonance. Recent skeptics include Rodrik and Subramanian (2009), whose focus is on financial globalization. In addition, whether finance matters for steady-state growth or for convergence has also been questioned, with Aghion, Howitt, and Mayer-Foulkes (2005) suggesting that financial development speeds up convergence but does not affect long-run growth.

saving or capital accumulation (Beck, Levine, and Loayza 2000; Rajan and Zingales 2001; Tressel 2008).

The financial system's impact on growth depends on how well it performs its critical functions of mobilizing savings, allocating those savings, monitoring the use of those funds by firms and individuals, pooling and diversifying risk, and easing the exchange of goods and services. Levine (2011, 276–77) summarizes the channels through which a well-performing financial system tends to promote growth and expand economic opportunities:

> Financial systems that perform these functions well promote growth. For example, when banks screen borrowers effectively and identify firms with the most promising prospects, this is a first step in boosting productivity growth. When financial markets and institutions mobilize savings from disparate households to invest in these promising projects, this represents a second crucial step in fostering growth. When financial institutions monitor the use of investments and scrutinize their managerial performance, this is an additional, essential ingredient in boosting the operational efficiency of corporations, reducing waste and fraud, and spurring economic growth. When securities markets ease the diversification of risk, this encourages investment in higher-return projects that might be shunned without effective risk management vehicles. And, when financial systems lower transactions costs, this facilitates trade and specialization, which are fundamental inputs into technological innovation and economic growth.

But Levine (2011) also emphasizes that growth is hindered when financial systems perform poorly. Examples he highlights include when financial systems simply collect funds and pass them along to cronies, the wealthy, and politically connected, the result is a misallocation of resources and slower economic growth. Or when financial institutions fail to exert sound corporate governance, managers find it easier to pursue projects that benefit themselves rather than the firm and the overall economy.

Similar concerns have given rise to a new strand of empirical research that raises new doubts about the relationship between financial development and economic growth.[6] The origins of this literature are related in part to questions raised by academics and policymakers in the aftermath of the 2008–09 global financial crisis about the possibility that malfunctioning financial systems can discourage saving and encourage speculation, resulting in underinvestment and a misallocation of resources (Law and Singh 2014).[7] Using a variety of methodologies, a number of papers in this new literature find troubling results about the relationship between financial development and economic growth.

---

6. Panizza (2013) provides a selective summary of this new literature, which qualifies the results of what he calls the "traditional" literature covered in the Levine (2005) survey. Beck (2012) and Sawyer (2014) also review some of this new literature.

7. Such concerns are not new. For example, José De Gregorio and Pablo Guidotti (1995) find that higher financial intermediation when the financial system is liberalized but allowed to operate in a poor regulatory environment may have negative effects on growth performance. An important point made in much of the new literature, however, is that the correlation between financial depth and growth may dissipate even for countries with good policies and institutions.

A key conclusion of the new literature is that there are nonlinearities in the relationship between finance and growth—namely, the level of financial development is good only up to a point, after which it can inhibit growth (Arcand, Berkes, and Panizza 2012; Beck et al. 2012; Cecchetti and Kharroubi 2012, 2013; Gambacorta, Yang, and Tsatsaronis 2014; Law and Singh 2014).[8] At low levels, a larger financial system does go hand-in-hand with higher productivity growth, but at what point does increased financial activity become associated with lower growth? The studies examining this question suggest that finance starts to have a negative effect on output growth when credit to the private sector reaches a threshold of between 90 and 120 percent depending on the country sample and estimation methodology used.

The data samples in these studies have typically included both advanced and emerging-market economies, with the negative relationship more relevant for high-income countries. Focusing only on a sample of 21 advanced economies, Stephen G. Cecchetti and Enisse Kharroubi (2012) also find that a fast-growing financial sector is detrimental to aggregate productivity growth, suggesting that financial booms are bad for trend growth. But by the same token, there is evidence that the effect of financial deepening is stronger for low- and middle-income countries; for financial development below the credit-to-GDP threshold, increased financial depth will exert a positive effect on growth.

Various explanations, which are not mutually exclusive, have been offered for the nonlinear relationship between finance and growth. A partial list includes, first, that financial development helps countries catch up to the productivity frontier, but it has limited or no growth effect for countries that are close to the frontier (Aghion, Howitt, and Mayer-Foulkes 2005). Second, who gets the credit matters. The growth effect of financial deepening comes through credit to firms rather than credit to households (Beck et al. 2012). To the extent that financial deepening in high-income countries comes through additional household lending, it might explain the insignificant finance-growth relationship across high-income countries. Thus, the issue might not be "too much finance" but rather "too much household finance" (Panizza 2013). Third, as financial systems grow too large relative to the real economy, they compete for resources with the rest of the economy, requiring not only physical capital but also highly skilled workers (Philippon 2010). As put by Cecchetti and Kharroubi (2012, pp. 1–2): "Finance literally bids rocket scientists away from the satellite industry. The result is that people who might have become scientists, who in another age dreamt of curing cancer or flying to Mars, today dream of becoming hedge fund managers." Finally, although the empirical literature focuses on financial depth as measured by credit to the private sector as a share of GDP, this might be too crude to capture quality improvements at higher levels of financial development as banks move toward "nonintermediation" financial activities (Demirgüç-Kunt and Huizinga 2010).

8. Other notable cautionary studies on the efficiency of modern finance include Barajas et al. (2013), Greenwood and Scharfstein (2013), Philippon (2012), Rousseau and Wachtel (2011), and Demirgüç-Kunt and Huizinga (2010).

More generally, the 2008–09 global financial crisis has been a stark reminder that the way in which finance helps the real economy and growth—namely, through maturity and liquidity transformation from short-term savings and deposit facilities into long-term investments—also makes the system fragile and susceptible to shocks, the so-called dark side of finance (de la Torre, Ize, and Schmukler 2012; Beck 2012). Furthermore, financial crises are costly, in terms of both output loss and fiscal costs, although Luc Laeven and Fabian Valencia (2012) find that emerging-market and developing countries tend to experience smaller output losses and increases in public debt than advanced countries, which to some extent is because advanced countries have deeper banking systems, making crises more disruptive.[9] However, Jean-Louis Arcand, Enrico Berkes, and Ugo Panizza (2012) point out that their result showing that financial deepening has a negative effect on growth after reaching a threshold is robust to controlling for growth-reducing financial crises. Thus, they conclude that the explanation for their result is not financial crises and volatility, but misallocation of resources. Regardless, the dark side of finance has critical implications for financial regulation.

Since the empirical findings of the new literature on the finance-growth nexus suggest that more finance is not always better and that it can harm growth after a point, what are the policy implications for developing Asia? First, it is important to emphasize that the level of income and financial development matters. The evidence suggests that the positive effect of financial deepening on growth is stronger for lower-income countries than higher-income countries. Similarly, for financial development below the threshold, the empirical results indicate that finance will exert a positive effect on economic growth, which implies that growth will increase when financial development improves. Furthermore, it is important to keep in mind that although high-income countries have greater credit depth, they also have slower growth because of convergence, suggesting that the empirical threshold results need to be treated with caution.[10] Therefore, it does not necessarily follow that countries where credit depth is above the threshold should aim to reduce total credit relative to GDP, although if the ratio has been boosted because of an unsustainable credit boom greater caution is warranted.[11]

---

9. Specifically, Laeven and Valencia (2012) calculate that for banking crises from 1970 to 2011, the average cost, measured as a percent of GDP, for advanced countries was 32.9 percent for output loss and 21.4 percent for the increase in public debt. The corresponding figures for emerging-market countries was 26 and 9.1 percent, respectively, and for developing countries 1.6 and 10.9 percent, respectively. See the paper for details of how these figures were calculated.

10. In chapter 3 of this volume, William Cline presents a skeptical assessment of the empirical threshold results. For example, he points out that the Cecchetti and Kharroubi (2012) results indicate that Canada would grow faster by 1.3 percent annually, and Switzerland by 0.7 percent, if they were to shrink the size of their financial sectors back to the growth-maximizing point.

11. See Dell'Ariccia et al. (2012) for a discussion of the consequences of credit booms and how to deal with them.

Second, policymakers should focus less on increasing the size of the financial sector and more on improving its intermediating function. In other words, the quality of financial intermediation matters more than the quantity of intermediation.[12] The advice of Siong Hook Law and Nirvikar Singh (2014, 43) is worth echoing: "Measures to strengthen quality and moderate finance need to be undertaken, rather than just promoting more finance, in fostering economic development." In the same vein, Thorsten Beck (2013) notes that because the relationship between financial deepening and economic growth goes through enterprise credit (as opposed to the insignificant relationship between household credit and growth), policies that refocus the financial system on intermediation, and especially enterprise credit, can be helpful. Another implication noted by Beck (2013) is that policies aimed at creating a financial center do not necessarily bring long-term growth benefits.

Third, Leonardo Gambacorta, Jing Yang, and Kostas Tsatsaronis (2014) focus on whether the structure of finance—that is, bank-based versus market-based intermediation—matters in the nonlinear relationship between financial activity and growth.[13] Their results confirm the widely accepted view that both banks and markets are important for economic growth, although they also find that there is a point after which further growth in financial activity no longer contributes to growth and may even slow it down. But again, the level of income and development matters. Banks provide intermediation services that differ from those provided by financial markets and that are particularly beneficial for countries at an earlier stage of development. Notably, banks are especially beneficial in lower-income countries because they provide inexpensive risk management for standardized risks and can compensate for weaker institutions. But as countries mature and become richer and their financial products become more elaborate, markets are better able to provide products tailored to specific users. Gambacorta, Yang, and Tsatsaronis also point out that as the demand for a broader set of risk management and capital-raising tools increases with economic maturity, countries would benefit from a legal and regulatory structure that supports market-based activities.[14]

---

12. See Iftekhar Hasan, Michael Koetter, and Michael Wedow (2009) for an empirical confirmation of this point using data from 11 advanced European Union countries. They highlight the importance of specifying three distinct channels through which banks may foster productivity growth: more credit, more efficient intermediaries, and the interaction of the two. They find that the efficiency effect is approximately three times as large as that of the quantity channel.

13. The conclusion of the traditional literature surveyed in Levine (2005) was that financial structure per se does not matter because it is the overall provision of financial services by banks and financial markets taken together that is important for growth. For a more recent analysis, see also Demirgüç-Kunt, Feyen, and Levine (2011).

14. Gambacorta, Yang, and Tsatsaronis (2014) also study the implications of financial structure on output volatility. They find that when it comes to moderating business cycle fluctuations, banks and markets differ considerably in their effects. In normal downturns, healthy banks help cushion the shock, but when recessions coincide with financial crises, they find that the impact on GDP can be three times more severe for bank-oriented economies than for market-oriented ones.

Finally, prudential regulation and supervision are indispensable to make finance safer for taxpayers and society while promoting growth-enhancing financial sector development. Strong micro- and macroprudential measures will need to be deployed to defend against the region's internal and external financial vulnerabilities.

Productivity-Enhancing Policy Priorities for Financial Development

The design of policies to improve productivity and growth performance is context specific and depends on a country's distance to the global technology frontier (Aghion and Howitt 2006, 2009). An empirical study by Era Dabla-Norris, Giang Ho, and Annette Kyobe (2013) uses the conceptual framework of distance to frontier to examine the association between productivity growth and a variety of reform measures. The reform and institutional measures they include in the analysis reflect recent theoretical and empirical findings on productivity and growth determinants, and they rely on indices of de jure reforms and liberalization in domestic financial systems, trade, liberalization of agriculture, and FDI. These measures were supplemented by variables that capture institutional quality (for example, the strength of property rights and protection and legal frameworks) and regulatory restrictiveness (for example, the extent of business and labor regulations), which previous studies have shown to influence economic outcomes. Their empirical framework also allows the authors to examine the role of policy and reform for both aggregate productivity (TFP and average labor productivity) and productivity growth in the services and manufacturing sectors.

The empirical results in Dabla-Norris, Ho, and Kyobe (2013) confirm that the reform drivers of productivity growth operate with differing force across country groups depending on their distance to the technology frontier, as approximated by a country's real per capita GDP or productivity gap with the United States, a proxy for the frontier. In the area of financial sector reforms to increase productivity growth, the general policy priorities they highlight are as follows for different income groups.[15]

- *Low-income and lower-middle-income countries.* Countries in this group tend to have more bank-based financial systems, and the empirical results suggest that they could benefit most from further banking system reforms.[16] Banking sector reforms in these countries should aim to mobilize domestic saving, lower the cost of and improve access to credit, and promote the allocation of financial resources to the most productive sectors. In addition,

---

15. See also Dabla-Norris et al. (2013).

16. Lone Christensen, Martin Schindler, and Thierry Tressel (2013) also provide empirical evidence that banking system reforms are positively and significantly associated with TFP growth in low- and middle-income countries.

where financial repression—such as restrictions on the price or quantity of credit—is still present, reducing it can also help induce resources to move to their more productive uses across and within sectors. Recent firm-level evidence from ten Eastern European countries in Larrain and Stumpner (2013) confirms the positive outcomes of financial market liberalization. They found that reforms focused on reducing financial repression raised aggregate manufacturing productivity by 17 percent, with the main channel being through an improvement in the within-industry allocation of capital across firms. To prevent excessive risk taking and promote the quality rather than quantity of intermediation, reform measures will need to be complemented by strong prudential policies.

- *Upper-middle-income countries.* The empirical results in Dabla-Norris, Ho, and Kyobe (2013) suggest that upper-middle-income countries can reap significant productivity gains by further deepening their capital markets.[17] They note that policies that encourage the formation and development of equity, bond (particularly local currency bonds), and securities markets can be particularly effective to increase TFP and labor productivity by lowering the cost of capital and facilitating the financing of new capital and innovation. Although there has been significant capital market development in many large emerging-market countries (for example, a larger menu of available financial instruments, improved market infrastructure, and a more diversified investor base), capital markets in upper-middle-income countries still lag those in advanced economies in size, turnover, liquidity, and development of institutional investors.

The financial sector realities in Asia, as comprehensively documented by Tatiana Didier and Sergio L. Schmukler (2014), confirm that the broad agenda for productivity-enhancing financial sector reform outlined above is relevant for the region. Notably, their main finding is that although financial sector development in developing Asia has made significant strides in the last two decades, becoming deeper and more complex, the overall depth of financial systems in Asia remains less developed than in advanced countries (but more developed than in Eastern Europe and Latin America).[18] They document

---

17. For firm-level evidence of a positive relationship between the use of external finance (both debt and equity) and future productivity growth within firms, see Oliver Levine and Missaka Warusawitharana (2014), whose analysis is based on data from advanced European countries. The authors provide evidence against a reverse-causality explanation, and for one country in their sample (the United Kingdom) they find direct evidence that the firms use financing to invest in productivity-enhancing projects.

18. Didier and Schmukler (2014) focus on the seven largest countries in developing Asia, namely the PRC, India, Indonesia, the Republic of Korea, Malaysia, the Philippines, and Thailand. Based on World Bank country classifications, India, Indonesia, and the Philippines fall in the group of lower-middle-income countries; Malaysia, the PRC, and Thailand in the group of upper-middle-income countries; and the Republic of Korea is a high-income country. See also Goyal et al. (2011) for a broader discussion of financial deepening in emerging-market countries.

that bond and equity markets in Asia have increased in absolute and relative size and that the private sector is issuing longer maturity bonds in domestic markets, indicating a moderate transition from a mostly bank-based model to one that is more complete and interconnected.[19] But they also report that a few large companies continue to capture most capital market issuance and that, with a few exceptions, secondary markets remain relatively illiquid. Furthermore, the public sector captures a significant share of the bond market. Thus, their fundamental conclusion is that Asia's financial systems remain less developed than aggregate measures suggest.

Didier and Schmukler (2014) also point to the paradox that financial underdevelopment in Asia seems to coexist with a large pool of domestic and foreign funds in the economy. They observe that the availability of funds will naturally provide a continuing deepening of some markets, but that for some reason the financial system does not seem to intermediate those funds and service a broad and growing range of firms. They ascribe part of the problem to the financial intermediation process because many assets available for investment are not purchased by banks and institutional investors. Rather, consumer and mortgage lending have grown relative to corporate financing and banks seem to have moved to financing standardized retail products that are easy to commoditize and involve relatively low risk (for example, leasing and collateral lending). Similarly, they note that capital markets seem to prefer to finance large firms over small ones and institutional investors seem to shy away from risk.

It is beyond the scope of this chapter to conduct an indepth analysis of financial sector developments in a broader range of developing Asian countries. But a glimpse can be obtained by grouping countries by income level and examining simple metrics such as credit to the private sector (figure 5.1); banking system assets (figure 5.2); private domestic debt securities (figure 5.3); stock market capitalization (figure 5.4); and debt financing (loans, bonds, and securitized loans) obtained by nonfinancial corporations (figure 5.5). The following points stand out:

- For low-income and lower-middle-income countries, the ratio of private credit to GDP has risen somewhat since 2007 and was about 50 percent in 2012 (figure 5.1). Viet Nam is an exception, with a ratio of just under 100 percent in 2012. But Viet Nam, where unbridled credit growth resulted in the credit-to-GDP ratio soaring from 64 to 109 percent between 2006 and 2010, also illustrates that a credit boom can be distinct from financial deepening. The credit binge led to a hangover with weak banks facing liquidity problems and worsening asset quality, forcing abrupt deleveraging.

---

19. In chapter 3 of this volume, Cline also documents the transition from bank-dominated systems to more diversified systems in emerging-market Asian countries. In particular, he points out that there is a strong presence of bond, equity, and to a lesser extent nonbank loan financing in most Asian emerging-market economies, rather than exclusive reliance on the traditional banking sector. He attributes this phenomenon in part to the process of globalization. Countries that continue to be bank-dominated in finance to the private sector are the PRC and Viet Nam.

Figure 5.1   Private credit to GDP ratio, 2007 and 2012

a. Low-income countries

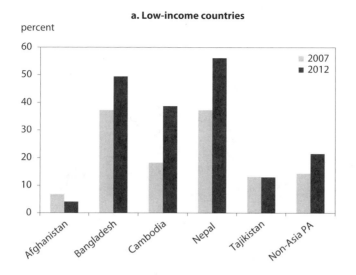

b. Lower-middle-income countries

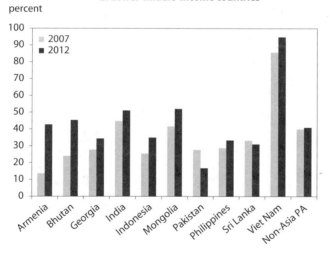

(continued on next page)

Figure 5.1 Private credit to GDP ratio, 2007 and 2012
(continued)

c. Upper-middle-income countries

percent

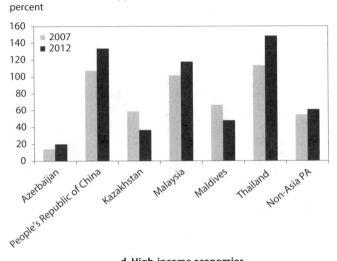

d. High-income economies

percent

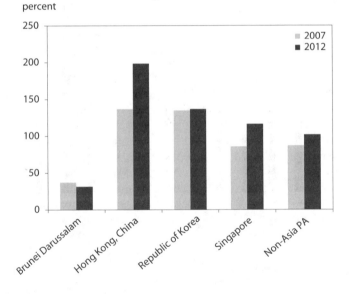

Note: Non-Asia PA is non-Asia peer average. For country income levels, the World Bank's 2014 country classifications are used. Low-income non-Asia peers are Kenya, Madagascar, Malawi, Mozambique, Tanzania, and Uganda. Lower-middle-income non-Asia peers are Bolivia, Côte d'Ivoire, Egypt, Morocco, Nigeria, and Ukraine. Upper-middle-income non-Asia peers are Bulgaria, Colombia, Hungary, Mexico, Peru, Romania, South Africa, and Turkey. High-income non-Asia peers are Chile, Croatia, Poland, and Portugal.

Source: World Bank, World Development Indicators database.

Figure 5.2   Banking sector assets to GDP ratio, 2007 and 2013

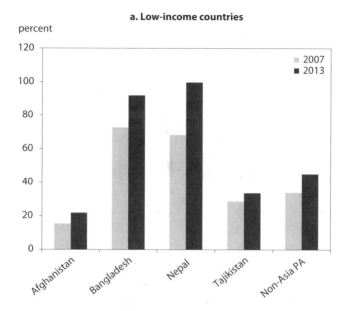

a. Low-income countries

percent

Legend: 2007, 2013

Categories: Afghanistan, Bangladesh, Nepal, Tajikistan, Non-Asia PA

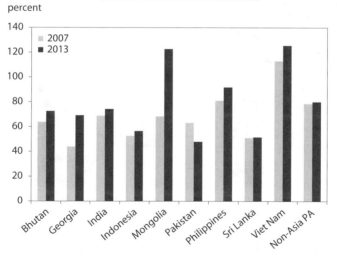

b. Lower-middle-income countries

percent

Legend: 2007, 2013

Categories: Bhutan, Georgia, India, Indonesia, Mongolia, Pakistan, Philippines, Sri Lanka, Viet Nam, Non-Asia PA

(continued on next page)

Figure 5.2　Banking sector assets to GDP ratio, 2007 and 2013 *(continued)*

c. Upper-middle-income countries

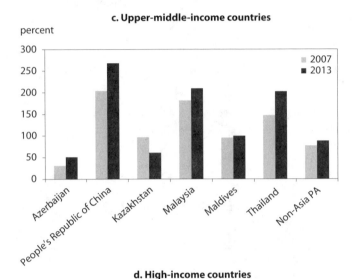

percent

Legend: 2007, 2013

(Categories: Azerbaijan, People's Republic of China, Kazakhstan, Malaysia, Maldives, Thailand, Non-Asia PA)

d. High-income countries

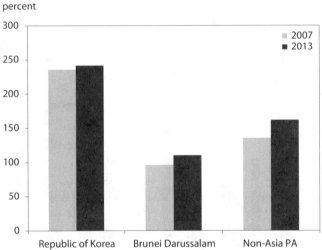

percent

Legend: 2007, 2013

(Categories: Republic of Korea, Brunei Darussalam, Non-Asia PA)

Note: Non-Asia PA is non-Asia peer average. For country income levels, the World Bank's 2014 country classifications are used. Low-income non-Asia peers are Kenya, Madagascar Malawi, Mozambique, Tanzania, and Uganda. Lower-middle-income non-Asia peers are Bolivia, Côte d'Ivoire, Egypt, Morocco, Nigeria, and Ukraine. Upper-middle-income non-Asia peers are Bulgaria, Colombia, Hungary, Mexico, Peru, Romania, South Africa, and Turkey. High-income non-Asia peers are Chile, Croatia, Poland, and Portugal.

Sources: IMF, *International Financial Statistics*; IMF, *World Economic Outlook* database.

Figure 5.3   Domestic debt securities to GDP ratio, 2007 and 2013

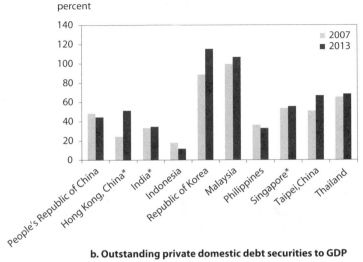

a. Outstanding total domestic debt securities to GDP

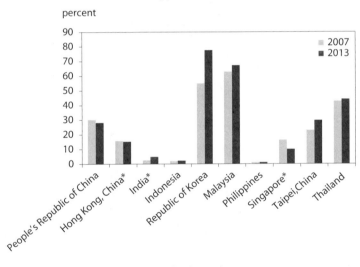

b. Outstanding private domestic debt securities to GDP

* = data unavailable for 2013, so replaced with 2011 data.
Sources: Bank for International Settlements; IMF, *World Economic Outlook* database; World Bank, *World Development Indicators* database.

Figure 5.4   Stock market capitalization to GDP ratio, 2007 and 2012

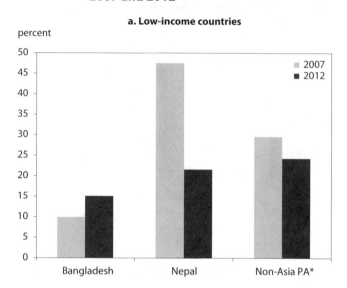

a. Low-income countries

b. Lower-middle-income countries

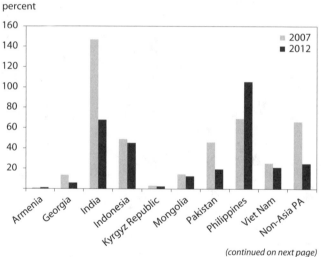

(continued on next page)

Figure 5.4 Stock market capitalization to GDP ratio, 2007 and 2012 (continued)

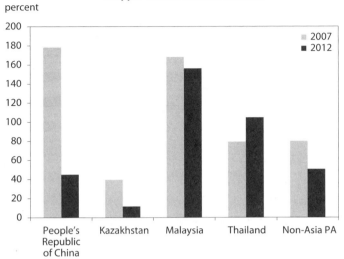

c. Upper-middle-income countries

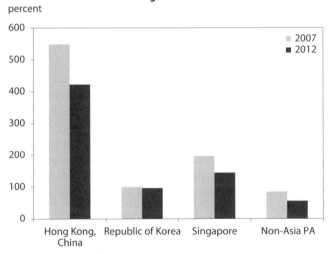

d. High-income economies

* = 2007 data unavailable for Malawi, Tanzania, and Uganda so 2008 data are used for these three countries.

Note: Non-Asia PA is non-Asia peer average. For country income levels, the World Bank's 2014 country classifications are used. Low-income non-Asia peers are Kenya, Malawi, Tanzania, and Uganda. Lower-middle-income non-Asia peers are Bolivia, Côte d'Ivoire, Egypt, Morocco, Nigeria, and Ukraine. Upper-middle-income non-Asia peers are Bulgaria Colombia, Hungary, Mexico, Peru, Romania, South Africa, and Turkey. High-income non-Asia peers are Chile, Croatia, Poland, and Portugal.

Source: World Bank, *World Development Indicators* database.

Figure 5.5 Debt financing obtained by nonfinancial corporations, 2011

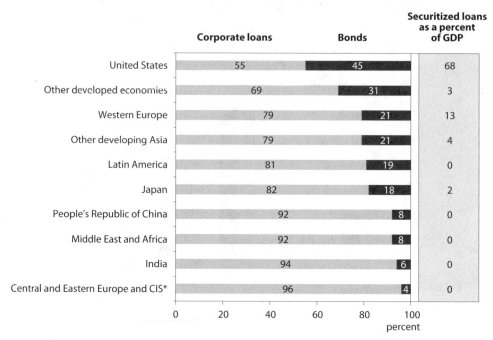

	Corporate loans	Bonds	Securitized loans as a percent of GDP
United States	55	45	68
Other developed economies	69	31	3
Western Europe	79	21	13
Other developing Asia	79	21	4
Latin America	81	19	0
Japan	82	18	2
People's Republic of China	92	8	0
Middle East and Africa	92	8	0
India	94	6	0
Central and Eastern Europe and CIS*	96	4	0

CIS = Commonwealth of Independent States
Sources: Group of Thirty (2013); McKinsey Global Institute.

- Upper-middle-income countries in Southeast and East Asia show substantial credit depth, with a ratio of private credit to GDP above 100 percent. For those countries in this region where global liquidity and domestic policies have contributed to rapid credit growth in recent years, it will be important to ensure that credit standards are sufficiently tight to contain risks, especially if both credit growth and real property prices are well above norms.[20] In Central Asia, by contrast, the credit ratio for upper-middle-income countries is much lower and comparable to that in lower-income groups.

- The ratio of banking assets to GDP (figure 5.2) yields similar qualitative results for each income group as outlined above for the ratio of private credit to GDP.

---

20. Early warning models of financial strain flash red when both credit growth and real property prices are significantly above trend (Borio 2012, BIS 2014). BIS (2014) points out that early warning indicators should be robust to changes in the equilibrium levels of debt due to financial deepening, but the banks' ability to screen potential borrowers and manage risks puts a limit on how fast this process can take place. Nicholas Borst (2013) documents the PRC's credit boom over the 2009–13 period, noting that because much of the credit growth came from the less regulated areas of the financial system, overall risk increased.

- Outstanding private domestic debt securities as a proportion of GDP is highest in the Republic of Korea and Malaysia (about 70 to 80 percent), followed by Thailand and the PRC (around 30 to 40 percent) (figure 5.3). For other countries, this ratio is very small.

- For most countries across all income groups, the share of stock market capitalization as a percentage of GDP is a small fraction (about one-fifth) of their total banking sector assets (figures 5.2 and 5.4). By contrast, these two ratios are close for India, Indonesia, and the Philippines, and to a lesser extent for Malaysia and Thailand, where stock market capitalization is about half of total banking sector assets.[21]

- Corporate bond markets and securitized loans remain small outside the United States (figure 5.5), indicating that long-term finance depends on a narrow range of instruments in many countries, including those in Asia.

Overall, the data for financial development in Asia support the general policy reform priorities for different income groups outlined above. The specific reform priorities for productivity-enhancing financial sector reform will vary from country to country depending on their distinct features and institutional context. Nevertheless, despite the diversity of developing Asia and the need to adapt reform policies to take advantage of individual country circumstances, some common themes for financial sector development and policies have the potential to enhance productivity-driven growth.

The focus in the rest of this section is on two such themes. First, channeling long-term finance into long-term investment in the assets that expand the productive capacity of a modern economy is essential. Because developing Asia has an infrastructure deficit that hampers productivity, particular attention is put on financing infrastructure needs. Second, improving SMEs' access to finance is vital because it can promote competition and dynamic efficiency. A separate section is devoted to a third theme, specialized financing for innovation, which is particularly relevant for countries facing the danger of falling into the middle-income trap.

Promoting Long-Term Finance

Long-term finance and investment enhance the productive capacity of an economy. They cover a wide range of tangible assets (such as energy, transport and communication infrastructure, factories, commercial buildings, hospitals, and new housing) and intangible assets (such as education and R&D) that increase future prospects for innovation and competitiveness (European

---

21. Data for 2012 show that the two ratios are also fairly close in the United States, at 118 percent of GDP for banking sector assets and 115 percent of GDP for stock market capitalization. For a small group of other advanced countries (Australia, Canada, France, Germany, Japan, and the United Kingdom), the median stock market capitalization is about one-fourth the median of banking system assets (77 percent of GDP versus 319 percent of GDP).

Commission 2013, Group of Thirty 2013). Many of these investments have an element of being a public good because they eventually generate greater returns for society. Furthermore, long-term finance is less procyclical than short-term finance and may hence be more supportive of sustained long-term growth, and it exerts a stabilizing influence on the financial system.[22] This focus on long-term finance is also consistent with the emphasis on improving the quality rather than just the quantity of intermediation.

Long-maturity instruments and investors with long time horizons are needed to finance long-term investment. Figure 5.6 from a report by the Group of Thirty (2013) depicts the flow of long-term finance from providers through the intermediation process to end users. Providers of long-term finance include domestic and foreign households, corporations, and governments. In the case of self-financing (corporate earnings, government revenue, or household income and wealth), a portion may go directly to end users without being intermediated. Otherwise, long-term finance flows through intermediaries such as banks, insurance companies, and pension funds, or alternatively capital markets may undertake the intermediation. The balance of intermediation by financial institutions versus markets varies across the globe.

However, despite a large pool of savings, the range of instruments for long-term financing in developing Asia remains narrow (Didier and Schmukler 2014). Banks still dominate the financial sector in Asia, as they do in Europe, in contrast to the United States, where equity and bond markets have a larger role. But commercial bank loan maturities average only 2.8 years in emerging economies and 4.2 years in developed economies, much shorter than bond maturities (Group of Thirty 2013). Moreover, as documented in various issues of ADB's *Asia Bond Monitor*, although many countries in developing Asia have improved the size and liquidity of their bond markets in recent years, these markets remain dominated by low-risk issues, especially those of governments. In addition to a lagging corporate bond market, securitization and equity markets remain underdeveloped in developing Asia despite the fact that the region accounts for a rising share of the world's wealth (see figure 5.5). And long-term institutional investors such as pension funds and insurance companies, which have long-dated liabilities, have not contributed sufficiently to the development of local markets, preferring to put the bulk of their portfolios in government bonds and deposits.[23]

Didier and Schmukler (2014) refer to this situation in Asia as a "trap" where investors avoid local capital markets and the markets remain underdeveloped, which suggests that there is considerable scope for policy actions to

---

22. By contrast, short time horizons and procyclical investment strategies, such as bank lending that relies on imprudent short-term funding and excessive maturity transformation, are more prone to instability, as demonstrated by the 2008–09 global financial crisis.

23. On average in East Asian countries, insurance companies are usually the largest institutional investors (26 percent of GDP), while mutual funds average 17 percent and pension funds, 15 percent (Didier and Schmukler 2014).

Figure 5.6 Framework for the provision of finance for long-term investment

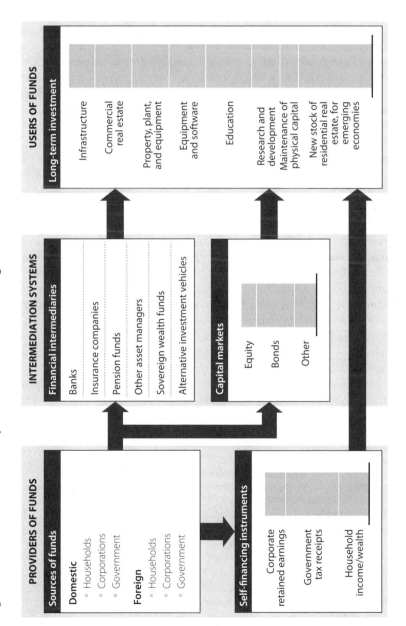

Sources: Group of Thirty (2013); McKinsey Global Institute.

help channel available funds to foster local long-term financing markets. The policy requirements to address the barriers to long-term finance are inevitably multifaceted, but the following are worth highlighting in the Asian context.[24]

- First, policy should be designed to ensure that investors are better able to take a long-term horizon in their investment decisions. This will require action by national and international regulatory bodies to remove biases in asset allocation of investors who might otherwise invest for the long term. For example, at the national level, regulatory and accounting treatments that favor short-term horizons should be reconsidered, and the pros and cons of gradually phasing out the preferential treatment of sovereign debt in insurance and bank regulation over a period of time should be weighed (Group of Thirty 2013). Such steps would remove the distortion that favors "safe" assets such as government bonds and increase insurers' incentives to invest in corporate bonds, equity, and other long-term instruments. And at the international level, standard-setting bodies should review the regulatory and accounting treatment of assets held with long-term horizons to avoid excessive focus on short-term market volatility.

- Second, further efforts are needed to develop debt and equity capital markets to promote a broader spectrum of financing instruments. Although local currency bond markets in Asia have grown over the last decade, continued heavy reliance on bank financing tends to make long-term investment decisions dependent on risky and volatile maturity transformation. Policies should therefore continue to aim to build deeper and more liquid bond markets, especially for corporate bonds, as this could reduce risk premiums and lower the cost of capital in addition to enhancing financial stability.[25] Generating turnover and improving liquidity will require a more active role for market makers, the development of hedging instruments including derivatives, and repo and securities lending (Zhu 2014). Furthermore, opaque bankruptcy law and procedures in many Asian countries will need to be addressed to lower risks for investors and speed development of corporate bond markets (Walsh 2014).[26] And for equity markets, improvements in the regulation of securities markets could enhance their role as a

---

24. For a more comprehensive list of policy proposals in an international context for advanced and emerging-market economies see Group of Thirty (2013). For policy proposals in the European context, which like Asia is largely bank-based, see European Commission (2013). For policy proposals more specific to the Asian context see, among others, Ding, Lam, and Peiris (2014), Felman et al. (2014), Walsh (2014), and Zhu (2014).

25. A number of initiatives are already under way on this front, including the ASEAN+3 Bond Market Initiative and the Asian Bond Fund. See various issues of the Asian Development Bank's *Asia Bond Monitor* for details. These periodic monitors also cover country-specific topics. For example the June 2014 issue (ADB 2014b) includes a detailed analysis of developments and challenges in Kazakhstan's bond markets.

26. Walsh (2014) points out that the small budget deficits in many Asian countries have affected the evolution of a government yield curve, making it more difficult for investors to price corporate bonds, thus slowing development of the market.

stable and reliable source of financing. Further, if the tax system creates a bias against equity investment, such biases should be removed or at least substantially reduced. Other impediments that will need to be addressed include the embryonic legal and regulatory framework for nonbank financial institutions—shadow banks—and a lack of information provision, including pricing transparency (Zhu 2014).

- Third, encouraging a broader and more diverse long-term investor base and promoting institutional investors and foreign participation will be important to build a stable source of finance. For example, the development of long-term pension- and insurance-based savings could be fostered by setting up compulsory auto-enrollment saving programs (Group of Thirty 2013). Such institutions would aggregate more savings into funds with long investment horizons, especially where household wealth is concentrated in bank deposits and other short-term instruments. The low penetration of institutional investors also hampers the development of debt and equity capital markets. The growth of traditional domestic investors such as contractual saving schemes can, however, be slow. Overseas firms can help expand the investor base, compensating for this slow growth, and because global bond funds are large compared to local bond markets, even a modest increase in the weight of emerging markets in their portfolio could lead to a significant increase in demand (Felman et al. 2014). Furthermore, greater participation by foreign investors will improve liquidity because they are more likely to trade the securities than domestic institutional investors, whose strategy is more likely to be to buy and hold. Joshua Felman et al. (2014) also point to a potential virtuous circle—as interest rates fall and liquidity improves, more firms will find it attractive to issue bonds, thereby expanding the size of the market and attracting more investors.

- Finally, in view of the importance of cross-border capital flows to support the efficient global allocation of capital to long-term investment, enhanced regional and global perspectives will be essential to address increasing regulatory and supervisory challenges as financial systems deepen and become more integrated and complex (Group of Thirty 2013, Zhu 2014). In particular, as regulators and supervisors encourage prudent financial innovation, they will need to ensure that they have good cross-border cooperation and adequate regulatory powers to act and stay alert to risks.

Issues concerning the long-term financing of Asia's infrastructure needs are worth examining for two reasons. First, building infrastructure can improve productivity growth, including by reducing travel times and the cost of freight, power, and communications. Better infrastructure thus increases the potential growth rate of an economy.[27] Second, emerging Asia generally scores

---

27. For empirical evidence see David Canning and Peter Pedroni (2008), who use cross-country data to show that infrastructure positively contributes to long-run economic growth despite substantial variations across countries.

lower on the adequacy of infrastructure than its industrialized peers in the region and elsewhere.[28] In a comprehensive study, the ADB (2009) put Asia's total infrastructure investment needs at $8 trillion over ten years, or about 4 percent of the region's GDP per year.

Apart from public infrastructure investment, mobilizing financial resources for infrastructure investment has been difficult in many countries. Although commercial banks are a source of infrastructure funding through project finance, bank liabilities are short-term while infrastructure projects have payback periods of 20 to 30 years, which exacerbates maturity mismatches and impedes long-term infrastructure finance.[29] Furthermore, the problem has not been the lack of funds because Asia is a region with a savings surplus. Rather, the problem is that Asia as a whole is a net capital exporter— instead of investing in Asia, the savings are invested in low-yield treasury bonds or other securities in Europe and the United States (Groff 2014; Ding, Lam, and Peiris 2014). The challenge, therefore, is to better direct Asia's large pool of savings into long-term financing that will help close the infrastructure deficit and raise productivity.

The policy agenda to meet this goal is similar to the one outlined above, namely fostering long-term horizons in investment decisions, further developing local currency bond markets, and promoting a long-term investor base. However, more specialized approaches are necessary for infrastructure assets because they are complex to evaluate and heterogeneous in nature, making it more difficult for traditional long-term institutional investors such as pension funds and insurance companies to invest. Ding Ding, W. Raphael Lam, and Shanaka J. Peiris (2014) have a detailed discussion of the issues specific to infrastructure financing, three of which are highlighted here. First, unlisted funds set up by management companies on behalf of institutional investors would provide them with exposure to infrastructure projects without having to develop in-house expertise.[30] Second, it will be important to develop an infrastructure bond market to help draw nontraditional investors into

---

28. This assessment is based on the World Competitiveness database published by the International Institute for Management Development (IMD). The assessment is made more vivid in metrics cited by Groff (2014), who notes that ASEAN has barely 10 kilometers of roads and 0.25 kilometers of rail per 1,000 people, compared to more than 200 kilometers of roads and five kilometers of rail in Organisation for Economic Co-operation and Development (OECD) countries. Furthermore, the electrification rate in ASEAN is 72 percent, versus 99.8 percent in OECD countries, and only 86 percent of ASEAN's population has access to clean water, compared to 99.6 percent in the case of the OECD.

29. Basel III capital requirements mandate banks to hold more capital against long-term finance typical in public-private partnerships. In addition, the large size of investments could run up against banks' single borrower limits even with syndication (Ding, Lam, and Peiris 2014).

30. Drawing on data from the *Asia Bond Monitor* of November 2013, Ding, Lam, and Peiris (2014) point out that there are 88 unlisted infrastructure funds that invest in Asia, with a growing total of $22 billion committed. Although this is a start, it is important to keep this figure in perspective—it is tiny relative to the $8 trillion needed for infrastructure over ten years.

financing infrastructure projects. Packaging long-term bonds that can be sold to investors tends to be more feasible once the construction phase of an infrastructure project is over and it is generating a steady stream of revenue over a long horizon.[31] Third, in addition to further financial deepening, greater regional financial integration would facilitate intraregional financial flows and mobilize resources from the aging savers in industrialized Asia to finance infrastructure investment in emerging Asia. The degree of financial integration within Asia is currently low, in part because of capital account restrictions in a number of countries in the region. Thus, strengthening financial ties within the region and globally, together with strong prudential frameworks, would help diversify sources of financing and reduce the cost of funding in emerging Asia.[32]

Expanding Financial Access for SMEs

There is evidence that financial development is especially helpful for smaller firms. Beck et al. (2008) find that underdeveloped financial systems are particularly detrimental to the growth of firms with fewer than 20 employees, and that financial development boosts the growth of small-firm industries more than large-firm industries. Going beyond finance and looking also at legal constraints to firm growth, Thorsten Beck, Asli Demirgüç-Kunt, and Vojislav Maksimovic (2005) provide evidence that SMEs face greater financial, legal, and corruption obstacles compared to large firms, and that small firms stand to benefit the most from improvements in financial development and a reduction in corruption. And in one of the first cross-country studies on the links between SMEs and economic growth and poverty alleviation, Beck, Demirgüç-Kunt, and Levine (2005) find a strong positive relationship between the relative size of the SME sector and economic growth. The data, however, do not support the conclusion that SMEs exert a *causal* impact on long-run growth. Furthermore, the authors did not find evidence that the size of the SME sector alleviates poverty or decreases income inequality.

These studies, all of which use cross-country data, do not shed much light on the channels through which finance helps firm or productivity growth. Moreover, they do not rule out that firm size is endogenous. A more recent study by Karthik Krishnan, Debarshi Nandy, and Manju Puri (2014), however, analyzes how increased access to financing by small firms affects their TFP

---

31. Ding, Lam, and Peiris (2014) note that in some Asian markets, bonds issued by infrastructure-related companies already represent a substantial share of total bonds outstanding. Notably, in Malaysia, 40 percent of bonds outstanding are issued by infrastructure-related firms. Nevertheless, given the small size of debt markets in Asia, the magnitude of financing from this source remains small.

32. This conclusion about the benefits of greater financial integration is supported by the model simulations presented in Ding, Lam, and Peiris (2014). Roland-Holst and Sugiyarto (2014) reach similar conclusions about the important benefits of deeper Asian financial integration for more efficient regional capital allocation.

by exploiting a natural experiment in the United States following interstate banking deregulation that increased access to bank financing. Using the Small Business Administration's funding eligibility criteria the authors show that TFP increases following the deregulations are significantly greater for financially constrained firms. Their results suggest that greater access to financing allows financially constrained small firms to invest in productive projects that may otherwise not be taken up.

Although they do not explicitly focus on firm size, Virgiliu Midrigan and Daniel Yi Xu (2014) use producer-level data from the Republic of Korea, the PRC, and Colombia to evaluate the role of financial frictions in reducing aggregate productivity. They show that financial frictions can have a large negative effect on productivity because they prevent credit-constrained entrepreneurs from entering the modern sector and decisions about technology adoption. In contrast, the misallocation of capital among modern-sector producers due to borrowing constraints has only small productivity effects for those already in this sector because financial frictions can be mitigated by self-financing.

Overall, the evidence confirms that expanding access to finance for SMEs and aspiring entrepreneurs can promote dynamic efficiency, including through the adoption of new technologies that could result in new industries, products, and services. In addition, ensuring the availability of credit and financing for all types of firms, including new entrants rather than just established ones, could stimulate competition that is favorable for productivity growth.

The policy issues associated with expanding SMEs' access to finance are covered well in a number of ADB studies. ADB (2014a), produced jointly with the Organization for Economic Cooperation and Development (OECD), is a comprehensive study on expanding SMEs' access to finance, drawing lessons from international experience and the recent crisis that resulted in a sharp credit crunch for SMEs. In addition, an SME finance monitor has been launched (ADB 2014c) to support efforts by developing Asian countries to design a comprehensive range of policy options to promote SMEs by providing timely and comprehensive data and analysis. Shigehiro Shinozaki (2014) focuses on the diversification of financing modalities beyond conventional bank lending and the steps that will be needed to develop capital market financing for SMEs in emerging Asia. In particular, equity instruments, hybrid debt-equity instruments, and asset-based finance all have underexploited potential.

Other recent studies on this topic include Beck et al. (2014), which, based on data from 21 countries in Central and Eastern Europe, concludes that although the literature has pointed to the benefits of having diverse lending techniques within a banking system, "relationship lending" can be particularly helpful in alleviating credit constraints for SMEs during a cyclical downturn.

A key policy message based on these findings is to support the collection of the necessary "hard" information about SMEs through credit registries and thus improve incentives for banks to invest more in generating "soft" information themselves. And focusing on alleviating a credit crunch, which can have a disproportionate adverse effect on smaller firms, Gert Wehinger (2014) provides a review of government programs (e.g., government loan guarantee programs, strengthening the capital base of support institutions, direct credit, export facilitation, and credit mediation and monitoring) adopted by OECD countries to facilitate SMEs access to financing.

Financing for Innovation

As discussed in the previous section, the reforms required to enhance productivity-driven growth depend on the distance to the global technology frontier. As a country gets near it, innovation instead of imitation becomes more important to sustain productivity and output growth (Acemoglu, Aghion, and Zilibotti 2006). A considerable body of research now shows that the capacity to innovate and bring innovation successfully to market is crucial to increase productivity and global competitiveness and thus contributes to job creation and economic growth (OECD 2007). In addition, a major study by the ADB (2014d), *Innovative Asia: Advancing the Knowledge-Based Economy,* makes a persuasive case that knowledge and innovation will become increasingly important as a source of the productivity and output growth necessary for middle-income Asian countries to avoid getting stuck in the middle-income trap and converge more quickly to per capita incomes in OECD economies. The ADB report also points out that although investing in knowledge-based economies has major advantages for middle-income countries, it can also benefit low-income countries because it can promote higher productivity and efficiency and thus help transform low-income economies. The nature of knowledge-based investment in the two cases, however, tends to differ.

An effective innovation system that creates and diffuses new knowledge is integral to knowledge-based economies, but it is not the only pillar on which such economies are built.[33] The ADB (2014d) report also discusses the other three pillars—education and skills, the information and communications infrastructure, and the economic and institutional regime. For the Asia and Pacific region, the average "knowledge economy index" for all four pillars is 4.4, compared to an average of 8.25 for OECD countries. And, as shown in figure 5.7, for the innovation pillar alone, the result is similar—the Asia and Pacific average index of 4.5 is still well below the average index of 8.5 for OECD countries, despite the impressive improvements made by some Asian

---

33. Drawing on work by the World Bank, ADB (2014d) defines *innovation* as the scope of activities that lead to the creation and diffusion of new and better products and processes, and the concomitant accumulation of intellectual assets to capture returns from the value they create. An effective "innovation system" is composed of firms, research centers, universities, and other intermediaries that engage in these knowledge-intensive activities: monitor and accrue technologies and processes from the growing stock of global innovation, assimilate and adapt them to local needs, and create new knowledge-based innovations.

Figure 5.7   Innovation index

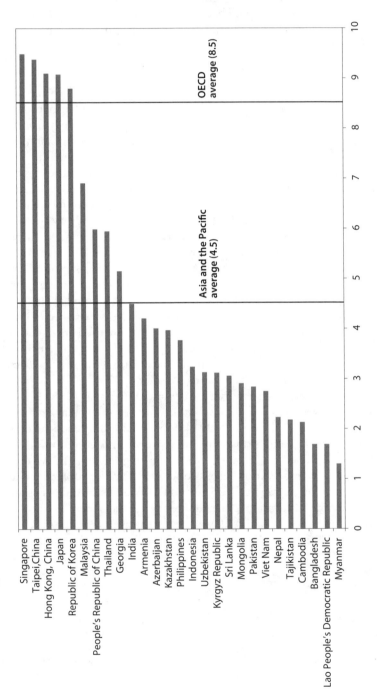

Note: Three variables are used to construct this index: royalty and license fee payments and receipts; patent applications granted by the US Patent and Trademark Office; and scientific and technical journal articles. Countries are ranked in order from "best" to "worst" using their actual scores on each variable and then their scores are normalized from 0 to 10 against all the countries in the comparison group. For a full explanation of the methodology, see http://web.worldbank.org/WBSITE/EXTERNAL/WBI/WBIPROGRAMS/KFDLP/EXTUNIKAM/0,,contentMDK:20584281~menuPK:1433234~pagePK:641-6844S~piPK:64168309~theSitePK:1414721,00.html.

Source: World Bank Innovation Sub-index from the World Bank Knowledge Economy Index, 2012.

countries (for example, the PRC, India, and Indonesia) over the last decade.[34] ADB (2014d) also documents that although some emerging economies in Asia have substantially increased their expenditure on R&D, a key ingredient for innovation, they still significantly lag behind advanced countries in the OECD and there is still substantial catching up to do for many countries.[35]

As Asia shifts from a development model based on technology absorption to one that fosters more productivity-enhancing innovation, strengthening the financing available for such innovation becomes increasingly important. In view of the risk of falling into the middle-income trap, enhancing financing for innovation is an immediate issue, and one where policymakers should start making headway now. The remainder of this section therefore deals with a number of related questions, drawing on the "financing innovation" module of the *Innovation Policy Platform* developed by the OECD and World Bank.[36] The questions are, Why is finance important for innovation? Why does innovation often require specialized finance and what are the sources of finance for innovation? What supporting framework is needed to finance innovation? What policy interventions are needed to encourage finance for innovation? And what are the implications for policymakers in Asia based on the experience in high-income Asia and OECD countries?

Why Is Finance Important for Innovation?

Innovation requires resources, which makes access to finance an essential ingredient for many forms of innovation activity. Finance allows firms and organizations to conduct research, adopt technologies needed for inventions, and commercialize and market these inventions. If appropriate finance is not available, it may prevent firms from investing in innovative projects, improving their productivity, funding their growth, covering working capital requirements, or meeting market demand. Furthermore, there is evidence that access to finance is a key determinant of entrepreneurship (Kerr and Nanda 2009).

---

34. These relative indices for Asia and the OECD are based on World Bank's Knowledge Economy Index. The qualitative conclusions from the World Bank's indices are broadly comparable to the Global Innovation Index 2014, available at www.globalinnovationindex.org/ (accessed on January 21, 2015).

35. The PRC is an important exception. It is now the second largest spender on R&D in the world in purchasing power parity (PPP) terms and has emerged as a leader in registering patents (ADB 2014d).

36. See *Innovation Policy Platform*, https://innovationpolicyplatform.org (accessed on January 21, 2015), for the main platform, and *Financing Innovation*, https://innovationpolicyplatform.org/content/financing-innovation?topic-filters=11384 (accessed on January 21, 2015), for the "financing innovation" module. The web-based platform aims to provide policy practitioners in advanced and developing countries with a simple, easy-to-use tool to support them in the innovation policymaking process. In addition, see UNECE (2009) for a comprehensive discussion of the policy options and instruments for financing innovation based on international experience. Hall (2009) also provides a valuable review of the theoretical and empirical research related to the financing of innovative firms.

Access to finance is thus an important driver in the creation, survival, and growth of innovative firms.

Why Does Innovation Often Require Specialized Finance?

Innovation typically requires investment of patient capital (with incentives that reward everyone who contributes to the process), while financial systems instead often promote impatient capital that avoids long connections with investment projects that might be inherently risky (FINNOV 2012). But by nature, innovative firms are involved in processes whose outcome is uncertain, and they own assets (e.g., patents) that are intangible and difficult to evaluate. Innovative firms may therefore face considerable barriers for accessing financing. This "finance mismatch," where the supply of finance does not meet demand, undermines their ability to undertake innovative projects.

A key reason for such a capital market imperfection is information asymmetries because firms may have relevant information that is not available to lenders and investors. In addition, monitoring difficulties, such as principal-agent problems related to the shareholder-manager relationship, may leave potential borrowers unable to obtain finance at any price. Liquidity constrained small and new ventures are particularly affected by these capital market imperfections. The smaller and younger the business, the less likely it is to have a sufficient track record or collateral, and the more opaque the information on its business performance and financial solidity.

It should be emphasized that although credit rationing and difficulty in accessing finance also affect traditional SMEs and traditional entrepreneurs, for many of the reasons mentioned here, they have a disproportionately severe effect for new innovative SMEs and innovative entrepreneurs (Hall 2009, Auerswald 2007). This is confirmed by OECD data suggesting that innovative small and new enterprises are at a particular disadvantage in receiving debt financing compared to traditional businesses (OECD 2010).[37]

The stages of development of a firm and its innovation projects have major implications for its funding needs and funding availability. The innovative firm's upfront feasibility and product development costs, and the length of its market development and entry process, will affect its financing needs. The "funding escalator" metaphor is often used to describe how the sources of funding available evolve as a firm's innovation project develops. As figure 5.8 shows, the cash flow follows a J-curve pattern over time, with an initial drop at the seed stage (the so-called valley of death) because of the financial resources innovative young firms need to spend on the proof of a business concept.

In this initial seed and startup phase, when inventions are developed and research is conducted, there is considerable uncertainty about the innovation

---

37. The OECD data are for European countries and take fast enterprise growth as a proxy for innovation. The data show that the success rate for bank loans in European countries is consistently higher for average enterprises than for enterprises with fast growth.

Figure 5.8 Development stages, cash flow, and sources of finance

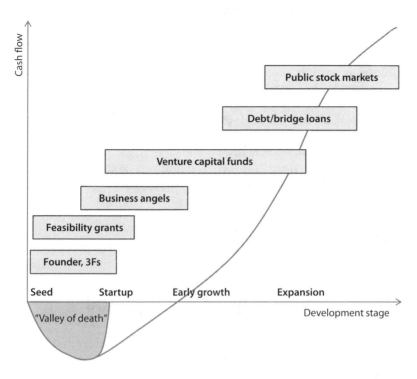

3Fs = friends, family, and fools
Source: UNECE (2009).

that will emerge, if any, which makes it difficult to obtain funding. In this initial phase, self-financing is particularly important for technology-driven SMEs because innovative entrepreneurs cannot overcome information asymmetry and therefore rarely find any lenders or investors, even for projects that are potentially profitable. Consequently, in addition to resources from the founder and other entrepreneurs, the main sources of funding are family and friends.[38] As discussed further below, these financial constraints are a key reason why public policy often plays an important role in funding the early stages of technological development.

In due course, as firms advance up the escalator and prototypes and the commercialization of inventions is developed, specialized investors who are skilled in assessing new technologies and can handle risk become more willing to provide funding. In particular, financing may be provided by capital invest-

---

38. As pointed out in UNECE (2009) there is sometimes another potential funding source, namely "fools." Friends, family, and fools make up the "3Fs" in figure 8. In some funding escalator diagrams, there is a reference to 4Fs—founders, family, friends, and fools.

ment from informal private investors (e.g., business angels) and in some cases by financing funds and venture capitalists. Subsequently, in the final stages, once technological and market uncertainty have been largely addressed and technology adoption and diffusion come to the fore, more traditional suppliers can provide the required funding to scale up operations and to finance purchasers interested in adopting new innovations. In this expansion stage, innovative young firms generally require increasing amounts of equity to maintain R&D and to expand marketing and sales activities, amounts that are typically available only through sources such as initial public offerings on stock exchanges.

The innovation process may involve the same stages in large established firms and small startup firms, but there is significant variation in the sources of finance that they may have available. Established firms, especially those at the larger end of the size spectrum, can finance their R&D activities more easily by using internal resources, such as retained earnings. These firms often prefer to use internal financing rather than external financing, which can be more costly. Thus, if they have sufficient internal resources, they may choose to undertake projects that would not be undertaken if they needed access to external finance to develop the project. In some cases, they may not even have access to external financing. External financing, when available, includes getting a loan from a bank using tangible assets as collateral if required, issuing bonds, or raising equity finance in stock markets. A review of empirical research by Bronwyn H. Hall and Josh Lerner (2009) concludes that (1) debt tends to be a disfavored source of financing R&D investment compared with other sources, and (2) established firms prefer internal funds to finance R&D investments and manage their cash flow to ensure this.

By contrast, startups do not have sufficient assets to use as collateral and they lack a track record. In addition, for startups that focus on innovative activities, their innovation investment tends to be less diversified and may represent a larger share of their overall activities. Therefore, the traditional sources of financing are not fully available for such enterprises. As the United Nations Economic Commission for Europe (UNECE 2009) pointed out, because of the negative cash flow and high risk of failure at their early stages of development, traditional sources of finance are not suitable for such young enterprises, and they ideally need forms of financing that do not seek guaranteed repayment. Thus, the main distinguishing characteristic of developing innovative firms lies in the need to overcome early-stage uncertainty to reveal or create their commercial potential.

Data limitations make it difficult to get a clear picture of the availability of specialized risk capital in developing Asia and other emerging markets. However, based on regional (as opposed to country-level) information, Didier and Schmukler (2014) note that private equity and venture capital funds are better developed in Asia than in Latin America. And of the two sources, private equity has a significantly larger presence than venture capital, raising on average $46 billion per year in Asia between 2003 and 2009.[39] Therefore, although nascent and small, a risk capital industry does exist in Asia.

What Supporting Framework Is Needed to Finance Innovation?

Before discussing the rationale and objectives of public policy interventions to encourage finance for innovation, it is important to outline the underlying supporting framework for possible policy interventions to succeed. Specifically, markets require a set of well-functioning institutions to work well, and hence institutional shortcomings can thwart access to finance for innovators. The *Innovation Policy Platform* highlights three important institutional priorities.

First, bankruptcy regulation affects innovative businesses by shaping the perceived risk of innovating and the conditions for access to finance. Evidence shows that countries with poorer investor protection tend to have smaller and narrower capital markets, which may make access to finance more difficult. Public policy can support innovative businesses by achieving the right balance in bankruptcy legislation to fit both firms' and creditors' interests. An efficient judicial system is also important to ensure that the objectives of bankruptcy law are met. The World Bank's Doing Business indicator for resolving insolvency suggests that the 2008–09 global financial crisis has helped spur improvements in bankruptcy legislation in many economies, including the following in Asia: Armenia; Cambodia; Georgia; Hong Kong, China; India; Japan; Kazakhstan; Kyrgyz Republic; Malaysia; the Philippines; the PRC; the Republic of Korea; Samoa; Solomon Islands; Tajikistan; and Uzbekistan. Nevertheless, Asia still lags high-income OECD countries in terms of the time taken (which is longer) and the recovery rate (which is smaller), making this an important area of policy that will need to be addressed (see figure 5.9).[40]

Second, adequate intellectual property rights can facilitate access to finance for innovative firms because they help turn knowledge into a commodity that can be used as collateral to obtain funding, and as an asset that can be salvaged by equity investors if the firm fails.

And third, developed bank-based and market-based financial institutions are indispensable for firms that need external funding to invest in innovation. The reform priorities on this front were covered in a previous section. Additionally, banking sector reforms that promote competition and reduce concentration can help fight discrimination in credit markets, especially toward

---

39. Didier and Schmukler (2014) do not provide a corresponding figure for venture capital funds raised by Asia, but they note that an average of $12 billion of venture capital was raised per year outside the United States and Europe during the 2003–09 period, representing 25 percent of the total raised.

40. See World Bank, Doing Business (2014). It should be emphasized that comparing bankruptcy legislation across countries is not straightforward, and the indicators in the reports should be viewed as proxies for the overall efficiency of the insolvency regulatory framework.

Figure 5.9 Recovery rate in case of insolvency

cents on a dollar

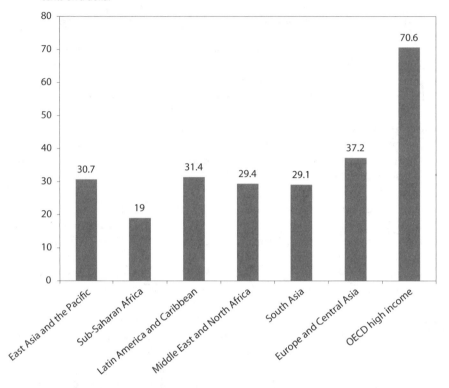

OECD = Organization for Economic Cooperation and Development
Source: World Bank (2014).

innovative entrepreneurs (OECD 2013a). Such reforms help prevent banks from engaging in discriminating behavior, while providing greater choice for borrowers. Financial market development needs to be complemented with appropriate financial market regulation. Such regulation can shape how intermediaries evolve and the resulting structure of financial institutions in a country, which in turn can have an impact on the types and sources of financing available for innovation activity.

UNECE (2009) also stresses that policy initiatives aimed at improving the environment for early-stage financing of innovative enterprises need to establish an appropriate framework by addressing the problem of simultaneity of (1) capital, (2) specialized financial intermediaries, and (3) entrepreneurs. In order to create a vibrant risk capital market, each of these elements will emerge and develop only if the other two are present and active. For the three components—capital, specialized intermediaries, and entrepreneurs—to simultaneously engage and operate in a self-propelling process, several elements need to interact. First, intermediaries need to be able to access sufficient amounts of capital (fundraising). Second, they need to be able to allocate the capital to promising entrepreneurs (investing). Third, they need to provide appropriate additional value to these enterprises to enhance their potential for success (value-adding). And fourth, they need to be able to liquidate their investments and redeploy their capital to a new wave of enterprises (exiting). The complementary character of these components of the private financing cycle needs to be kept in mind when designing policies.

What Policy Interventions Can Encourage Finance for Innovation?

The rationale for public policy intervention in finance for innovation is to correct for market failures that negatively affect the performance of innovative businesses. Without public intervention, markets generally provide less finance for innovation than would be socially desirable. One market failure relates to the issue of capital market imperfections because of information asymmetries and principal-agent problems, which is discussed above (under the question "Why does innovation often require specialized finance?"). Another market failure relates to the positive externalities of knowledge creation. The nonrival nature of many knowledge creations (that is, the use of a piece of knowledge does not prevent its simultaneous use by another party) means that knowledge can create spillovers: The innovator benefits but so do others, including competitors and follow-on innovators. Thus, unless there is compensation through monopoly rights created by the intellectual property system or grants for conducting innovation, the social rate of return for knowledge creation may exceed the private rate of return, resulting in investment in the production of new knowledge that is below the socially optimal level. Such risks might reduce the financial resources firms will mobilize internally to fund innovative activities and might also reduce external financial resources available.

In view of such market imperfections, public policies play an important role in facilitating finance through a wide range of instruments. The *Innovation Policy Platform* categorizes these instruments to increase the availability of finance for innovation as follows.

Direct Funding of Firms' R&D. Governments frequently use direct funding to stimulate firms' R&D through various instruments, including grants of various types (for example, matching grants, proof-of-concept grants, and patent application grants), subsidized loans, and venture capital and seed funds. In addition to basic research and product development, eligible activities for funding could include training, process innovation, technology commercialization, and early-stage funding for technology startups. A key objective of direct funding programs is to induce an "additionality" effect in firms so that they invest more of their own resources in R&D than originally planned. Public funding may produce a signal effect that facilitates firms' access to external sources of finance in addition to providing much-needed funding to complement internal resources. The most common practice in providing direct funding is to run a competitive merit-based selection process that targets specific areas and types of firms. This allows R&D grants to be aligned with strategic priority areas and to contribute to other policy goals such as promoting innovation in SMEs, entrepreneurship, collaboration among firms, or university-industry collaboration.

Direct funding, however, requires relatively higher bureaucracy and administrative costs and often raises concerns about the prospect of governments "picking winners." If the private sector has sufficient entrepreneurial knowledge, the selection process can be outsourced. But when private expertise is scarce, government agencies may choose to rely on the advice of scientists and public research organizations. UNECE (2009) suggests that to produce positive effects such government schemes should support large numbers of new enterprises instead of focusing on a few potentially best business ideas, although budget constraints will need to be observed.

Debt and Risk-Sharing Schemes. The aim of such schemes is to reduce the risk for lenders and investors to facilitate access to external finance for innovative firms. Credit guarantee schemes are a common tool to facilitate access to finance for firms with a higher risk profile since they limit the loss that a bank faces if the firm defaults. They can help address lack of access to finance for young innovative firms that have insufficient collateral or credit histories. Typically, bank losses on the loans covered by the guarantee are only partially insured by the government, and banks are left to decide which loans to give to take advantage of their credit assessment expertise (or to build such expertise). Alternative types of debt financing, such as convertible and subordinated loans, can also be supported by public policy through fiscal incentives to lenders or partial coverage of losses in case of bankruptcy or liquidation. Business training and coaching to minimize the risk of business failure can increase the success of such a program and make it less costly.

But credit guarantee schemes also have potential pitfalls that put a premium on designing them with care. The design needs to minimize potential misalignments of incentives because they can otherwise make banks less careful when screening what companies to fund. Although funding higher-risk loans is usually the intended aim of the policy, governments sometimes have little control on whether the "wrong type" of risky company is being selected and whether banks are putting sufficient effort into monitoring loans. Furthermore, a higher share of the loan guaranteed by public institutions might allow more constrained borrowers to get access to external financing, but it could also result in greater adverse selection and moral hazard as lenders become more complacent about screening and monitoring. Credit guarantee programs should be designed to ensure that reliable borrowers are progressively phased out of the scheme because they should be expected to receive loans through traditional channels.

An alternative to credit guarantee schemes is direct lending through a specialized government-owned bank. Although this provides greater control than credit guarantee schemes, it requires expertise and attention to ensure that soft budget constraints and political objectives do not lead to poor credit cultures and insufficient discipline.

Government Support for Private Finance for Innovation. Increasing the availability of equity finance is a common goal of government intervention. Instruments include public fund-of-funds and public-private coinvestment funds. A fund-of-funds is a holding of other investment funds rather than investing directly in startup firms. These public funds invest in private venture capital firms often with the requirement that other private institutional investors also invest. Coinvestment funds use public money to match private investment. These programs usually match public funds with those of approved private investors on the same terms. Coinvestment schemes not only leverage private money but also are seen as drivers in building, growing, and professionalizing the seed and early stage investment market by providing a more structured investment process.

These two hybrid public-private approaches have become increasingly prevalent in the last five years (OECD 2013b). Despite the growth of these programs, however, there is little evidence of the impact of these instruments and whether or not they crowd out private investors. This makes it important to consider various types of risks when designing such public interventions to support equity finance for innovation. For example, large interventions can be counterproductive, not only crowding out current investment—that is, replacing innovative activities that firms would undertake even in the absence of public support—but also damaging the future development of the risk capital industry.

In addition to stimulating the venture capital industry, public policy can play a role in setting framework conditions for new sources of private capital such as crowdfunding, which refers to money raised from society at large through the use of online platforms. In addition to raising funds for innovative projects by tapping a large number of people for small contributions, crowdfunding can improve attitudes toward entrepreneurship.

Fiscal Measures. Tax incentives based on expenditure or income are a common instrument. Typical expenditure-based tax incentives include R&D tax credits. In addition, business angels can be supported by providing tax incentives to private individuals investing in specific investments and businesses. Income-based tax incentives include preferential rates on royalty income and other income from knowledge capital.

What Are the Implications for Policymakers in Asia?

Although there is a clear rationale for policy intervention in the area of finance for innovation, the limitations of the various interventions outlined above need to be recognized. There is no guarantee that government policy can address market failure in a way that effectively improves the outcome. In addition, the policy may fail to achieve its goals because of inadequate policy design, implementation issues, and governance failure. Furthermore, evidence on the effectiveness of many programs tends to be scarce or mixed, in part because only a small proportion of programs in OECD countries have been formally evaluated, and empirical analysis is constrained by data on firms at the seed or early stage.

But these difficulties do not negate the need for policy action. In her book *The Entrepreneurial State: Debunking Public vs. Private Sector Myths*, Mariana Mazzucato (2013) documents that countries that today lead in terms of smart innovation-led growth have had state support. The ADB (2014d) emphasized that it will be important for developing Asia to cultivate new forms of innovation financing that go beyond just R&D funding and "there is a need for public sector funding to bridge the so-called valley of death, which prevents new technologies and knowledge from being commercialized by local start-ups and SMEs" (p. 49). The potential pitfalls of public intervention should therefore be viewed as challenges that need to be overcome, and international experience shows that it is possible to design programs with positive outcomes. In particular, the decision to intervene needs to weigh benefits and risks, and the achievements of government intervention need to be scrutinized not only ex ante but also ex post. Furthermore, different countries face different problems, requiring adjustments in policy instrument and design. For example, merit-based research grants require a more knowledge-based approach by governments than some other types of support, affecting the choice of instrument that should be used.

Examples of policies and institutions that have been found to be effective in advanced countries include the Small Business Innovation Research (SBIR) program in the United States.[41] The evidence shows that recipients of SBIR grants were able to obtain more funding elsewhere and that such firms grew faster afterwards when compared with a matched sample of firms that did not receive SBIR funds (Hall 2009). An important strength of the program contributing to its success is the decentralization of funding decisions spread across 11 federal agencies (UNECE 2009). SITRA, a Finnish innovation fund, invested equity in Nokia early, when its mobile phone venture was viewed as an odd aberration by a paper company; when Nokia blossomed, SITRA made a direct return, which it used to fund new companies (Mazzucato 2013). In Israel, the Yozma program has been successful in kick-starting the venture

---

41. For a more comprehensive list of diverse programs and their operational details, see UNECE (2009), which features 34 programs in a range of countries (the United States, the European Union, Germany, France, the United Kingdom, Canada, the Netherlands, Denmark, Finland, Spain, Norway, Israel, the Czech Republic, Slovakia, and the Russian Federation). In addition, Mazzucato (2013) describes a variety of programs, and ADB (2014d) contains some relevant examples. However, there is little systematic and rigorous analysis of whether these programs have succeeded or failed.

capital industry, although not on the first try (Hall 2009). And in Latin America, Bronwyn H. Hall and Alessandro Maffioli (2008) found that the effectiveness of technology development funds they analyzed depends on the financing mechanism used, the presence of nonfinancial constraints, firm-university interaction, and the characteristics of the target beneficiaries. In addition, they found that the funds do not crowd out private investment; instead, they positively affect R&D intensity, and participation in the funds induces a more proactive attitude of beneficiary firms toward innovation activities. In general, programs have been more successful when there has been a critical mass of growth-oriented entrepreneurs and private investors.

State investment banks offer a more direct tool for funding innovation. In addition to the example of Germany's KfW, Mazzucato (2013) highlights two emerging-market state banks that have been successful in meeting their innovation objectives. The Brazilian state development bank, BNDES, has been actively investing in innovation in clean technology and biotechnology. In 2010, the bank's return on equity was 21 percent, much of which was reinvested in new sectors focusing on the valley of death stage of biotechnology (in which private venture capital tends to be absent). The author points out that the role of state investment banks goes further, as in the case of the China Development Bank (CBD), which is not only a substitute for private finance that is too risk averse to invest in Chinese high-tech manufacturers but also a means of creating opportunities for these and other manufacturers by providing financing to foreign purchasers of their products (for example, for wind farms using wind turbines manufactured in the PRC).

Patarapong Intarakumnerd and Juruhee Wonglimpiyart (2012) do a comparative study of Singapore and Taipei,China, economies with strong national innovation systems, and Malaysia and Thailand, whose innovation systems are less strong, with the result that they have been less successful in technological catching up and industrial development.[42] The authors depict the stages of catching-up industrialization in figure 5.10. To gain insight into how countries can move from stage two to stage three or four, the authors do (1) a macro-level analysis of the national innovation systems in the four economies, and (2) an operating-level analysis of the content, efficiency, and effectiveness of the economies' schemes in taxation, grants, loans, direct equity financing, and capital market financing.

Intarakumnerd and Wonglimpiyart (2012) summarize the factors underlying successful government innovation financing programs as follows.

- First, in the more successful cases of Singapore and Taipei,China policy instruments to finance innovation and levels of technological and innovative capabilities of firms have evolved together. Thus it is important to adopt a dynamic rather than static approach, requiring the ability to initiate and

---

42. The study is summarized in a detailed presentation by Intarakumnerd (2012).

Figure 5.10   Stages of catching-up industrialization

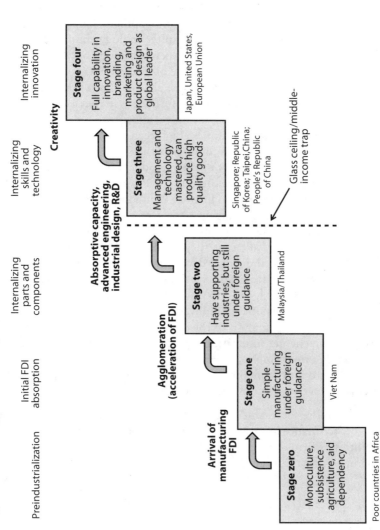

FDI = foreign direct investment; R&D = research and development

Sources: Intarakumnerd and Wonglimpiyart (2012), adapting Ohno (2011), www3.grips.ac.jp/~gist/en/events/document/gistseminar_35.pdf.

implement new policy instruments to fit the changing needs of firms at different levels of capability.

- Second, the key success factors, generally present in Singapore and Taipei,China and to a lesser extent in Malaysia, were (1) a higher level of flexibility and policy coordination and learning and (2) the use of a greater variety of policy instruments and catering them selectively to the particular needs of industrial sectors, clusters, technologies, types of firms, or even individual firm demands.

- Third, developing technological and innovative capabilities takes a long time, which makes the amount, duration, and continuity of government support schemes crucial.

- Fourth, policymakers need to develop a deep understanding of what constitutes innovation systems and how they evolve over time. For example, Thailand narrowly focused on R&D-led innovation, while Singapore and Taipei,China broadened their activities to other innovation processes.

- Fifth, financing innovation policies require other corresponding policy initiatives to make them work successfully, for example: improving the quality of human resources, attracting foreign talent, and helping organizations such as research institutes work together with financing innovation schemes.

- Finally, institutional factors—namely, laws and regulations, unity and capability of government bureaucracy, trust, entrepreneurship, attitudes toward corruption and the role of government in supporting private firms—shape the choice and effective implementation of policies. But institutional shortcomings can be corrected, at least to some extent.

Three misconceptions about access to finance for innovation have implications for the design of public policy in Asia. First, there is a misconception that private venture capitalist funds are essential to drive innovation. However, as pointed out in OECD (2010), venture capital is a niche phenomenon that touches a tiny share of entrepreneurs and moves a relatively small share of capital at the global level. In addition, it typically addresses the expansion stage of business rather than the startup phase and is highly sensitive to the economic cycle. Hall and Lerner (2009) also provide evidence of the limits to venture capital as a solution to the funding gap faced by innovative firms, especially in countries where public equity markets for venture capital exit are not fully developed. Furthermore, Mazzucato (2012 and 2013) reports that because of venture capital's emphasis on returns that are high but quick and low risk, it has had a detrimental effect on the ability of venture capital-backed companies to produce real value for the economy, that is, new products and jobs. In a similar vein, FINNOV (2012) notes that over half of early stage venture capital investment in Europe is provided by "hybrid" funds that are supported with public money. The hybrid approach has been important because private venture capital funds have performed poorly and have trouble raising enough money to reach the size needed to be commercially viable. Finally, Laura Bottazzi (2009) concludes that although venture capital has been effective in helping innovative firms overcome credit constraints, it has had a limited effect on their ability to grow and create jobs.[43] Therefore, the role of venture capital should be considered within the architecture of financing for innovation, which includes complementary and alternative instruments.

Second, there is a misconception that most growth is driven by new innovations brought by new entrants and creative destruction, as described in Joseph Schumpeter's endogenous growth models. Concomitantly, it is sometimes argued that more entrepreneurs and SMEs are needed to drive economic growth and innovation because they engage in more "radical" innovations to replace incumbents. However, Daron Acemoglu and Dan Vu Cao (2010) point out that a large fraction—but not all—of US industry-level productivity is accounted for by existing firms and continuing establishments because they have access to technology for incremental innovations and can improve their existing machines and products. Daniel Garcia-Macia, Chang-Tai Hsieh, and Peter J. Klenow (2014) reach similar conclusions based on data on US manufacturing firms. And based on data from Europe, FINNOV (2012, 6) concludes, "While some SMEs and entrepreneurs contribute to innovation and growth, most do not and the ones that do are atypical. The majority of start-ups end up as marginal, undersized, poor performance enterprises that can drive down profits, increase factor prices for high-potential firms, confuse investors, and fail to generate benefits commensurate with the amount of public support they receive." Accordingly, as emphasized by Mazzucato (2012), what matters for policy is finding ways to target the high-growth innovative companies, regardless of their size and whether they are incumbents or new entrants. That is, the point of finance for innovation should be to allow new things to happen and to create better SMEs rather than more SMEs.

Third, there tends to be a misconception that the state is incapable of "picking winners" because it is clumsy, bureaucratic, and not suited for entrepreneurial risk taking, and therefore losers end up picking the state. But Mazzucato (2013, chapter 1) argues that operating in difficult territory makes the probability of failure higher. As she puts it, "Public venture capital, for example, is very different from private venture capital. It is willing to invest in areas of much higher risk, while providing greater patience and lower expectations of future returns. By definition this is a more difficult situation. Yet the returns to public versus private venture capital are compared without taking this difference into account." She asserts, therefore, that the policy debate needs to go beyond the worry about picking winners and that more thought should be given to how to reward the successes when they happen. As a result, returns would be available to cover losses from inevitable failures and to fund future wins. Instruments that meet these goals are income-contingent loans,

---

43. Bottazzi (2009), however, points out that her result clashes with the evidence on the role of venture capital for US companies.

equity, and returns earned by state investment banks. In addition, it will be important to design programs and processes in a way that reduces the likelihood of political capture, which previous experience with industrial policy in East Asia suggests could be a greater drawback than one of government bureaucrats picking winners (Noland and Pack 2005).[44]

Concluding Remarks

Much of developing Asia will need to rely more on improvements in productivity growth and less on capital accumulation to drive growth in the future. Middle-income countries in the region will need to move up the technology ladder and improve the quality of infrastructure to avoid falling into the middle-income trap. Enhancing productivity-led growth is, however, a complex and multidimensional task, with reform priorities that vary across income groups and distance to the global technology frontier.

This chapter has focused on the role of the financial sector in facilitating developing Asia's transformation to productivity- and innovation-led growth. Financial development and deepening affect growth primarily by fostering more efficient allocation of capital across firms and industries and spurring productivity growth, not by raising the rate of aggregate saving or capital accumulation. Moreover, policymakers should focus less on increasing the size of the financial sector and more on improving its intermediating function. Micro- and macroprudential regulatory policies will be indispensable to make finance safer for taxpayers and society while promoting growth-enhancing financial sector development.

Low-income and lower-middle-income countries in Asia tend to have more bank-based financial systems and could benefit most from further banking system reforms. Such reforms should aim to mobilize domestic savings, lower the cost of and improve access to credit, and promote the allocation of credit to the most productive sectors. Where financial repression is present, reducing it would help induce resources to move to their most productive uses. Upper-middle-income Asian countries can reap significant productivity gains by further deepening their capital markets. Policies that encourage the further development of equity, bond, and securities markets can contribute to better TFP and labor productivity by lowering the cost of capital and facilitating the financing of new capital and innovation.

Developing Asia must also build and continually replenish the tangible and intangible capital that induces productivity growth and innovation. Such

---

44. In a study of industrial policy in East Asia, Noland and Pack (2005) argue that although Japan, the Republic of Korea, and Taipei,China pursued intervention policies to promote preferred high-technology sectors, the actual pattern of interventions observed were largely determined by political, not analytical, considerations. The political capture by special interests, which also affected bureaucrats who might be thought of as being less susceptible, resulted in resource transfers via direct and indirect subsidies going to declining natural resource sectors (e.g., agriculture, forestry, fisheries, mining), with the manufacturing sector being a net taxpayer.

investments require long-term finance. However, despite Asia's large pool of savings, the range of instruments for long-term financing in the region remains narrow. Addressing the barriers to long-term finance in Asia should therefore be a priority. In view of the infrastructure deficit in much of developing Asia, particular attention will need to be devoted to the long-term financing of infrastructure projects. Greater access to loans allows financially constrained SMEs to invest in productive projects that may otherwise not be taken up. The emphasis by policymakers in developing Asia on improving SMEs' access to finance, supported by analysis and advice from the Asian Development Bank, is therefore appropriate.

As a country approaches the global technology frontier, innovation instead of imitation becomes more important to sustain productivity and output growth. For middle-income Asian countries, knowledge and innovation are becoming increasingly important as a source of productivity growth necessary for them to avoid the middle-income trap and converge more quickly to per capita incomes in OECD countries. Promoting the specialized financing needed for innovation is hence an immediate issue for policymakers in the region. In view of capital market imperfections and positive externalities from knowledge creation, there is an important role for public policy interventions to promote such specialized finance for innovation. Successful government innovation programs in more advanced countries in Asia and elsewhere provide valuable lessons.

References*

Acemoglu, Daron, Philippe Aghion, and Fabrizio Zilibotti. 2006. Distance to Frontier, Selection, and Economic Growth. *Journal of the European Economic Association* 4, no. 1: 37–74.

Acemoglu, Daron, and Dan Vu Cao. 2010. *Innovation by Entrants and Incumbents*. NBER Working Paper 16411 (September). Cambridge, MA: National Bureau of Economic Research.

Aghion, Philippe, and Peter Howitt. 2006. Joseph Schumpeter Lecture—Appropriate Growth Policy: A Unifying Framework. *Journal of the European Economic Association* 4, no. 2–3: 269–314.

Aghion, Philippe, and Peter Howitt. 2009. *The Economics of Growth*. Cambridge, MA: MIT Press.

Aghion, Philippe, Peter Howitt, and David Mayer-Foulkes. 2005. The Effects of Financial Development on Convergence: Theory and Evidence. *Quarterly Journal of Economics* 120: 173–222.

Aiyar, Shekhar, Romain Duval, Damien Puy, Yiqun Wu, and Longmei Zhang. 2013. Is Middle-Income Asia at Risk of a Sustained Growth Slowdown? Chapter 3 in *Regional Economic Outlook: Asia and Pacific*, International Monetary Fund, April. Washington.

Arcand, Jean-Louis, Enrico Berkes, and Ugo Panizza. 2012. *Too Much Finance?* IMF Working Paper WP/12/161 (June). Washington: International Monetary Fund.

ADB (Asian Development Bank). 2009. *Infrastructure for a Seamless Asia*. Manila.

ADB (Asian Development Bank). 2014a. *ADB-OECD Study on Enhancing Financial Accessibility for SMEs: Lessons from Recent Crises*. Manila.

ADB (Asian Development Bank). 2014b. *Asia Bond Monitor: June 2014*. Manila.

*The Asian Development Bank recognizes "China" by the name the People's Republic of China and "Vietnam" by the name Viet Nam.

ADB (Asian Development Bank). 2014c. *Asia Small and Medium-sized Enterprise (SME) Finance Monitor 2013*. Manila.

ADB (Asian Development Bank). 2014d. *Innovative Asia: Advancing the Knowledge-Based Economy*. Manila.

Aueswald, Philip. 2007. The Simple Economics of Technology Entrepreneurship: Market Failure Reconsidered. In *Handbook of Research on Entrepreneurship Policy*, ed. David B. Audretsch, Isabel Grilo, and A. Roy Thurik. Cheltenham, UK: Edward Elgar.

Barajas, Adolfo, Thorsten Beck, Era Dabla-Norris, and Reza Yousefi. 2013. *Too Cold, Too Hot, or Just Right? Assessing Financial Sector Development Across the Globe*. IMF Working Paper WP/13/81. Washington: International Monetary Fund.

Beck, Thorsten. 2012. Finance and Growth: Lessons from the Literature and the Recent Crisis. Paper prepared for the LSE Growth Commission. London. Available at www.lse.ac.uk/researchAndExpertise/units/growthCommission/documents/pdf/contributions/lseGC_beck_Finance.pdf (accessed on January 15, 2015).

Beck, Thorsten. 2013. Finance and Growth: Too Much of a Good Thing? VoxEU, October 27. Available at www.voxeu.org/article/finance-and-growth (accessed on February 24, 2015).

Beck, Thorsten, Asli Demirgüç-Kunt, and Ross Levine. 2005. SMEs, Growth, and Poverty: Cross-Country Evidence. *Journal of Economic Growth* 10, no. 3: 199–229.

Beck, Thorsten, Ross Levine, and Norman Loayza. 2000. Finance and the Sources of Growth. *Journal of Financial Economics* 58: 261–300.

Beck, Thorsten, Asli Demirgüç-Kunt, and Vojislav Maksimovic. 2005. Finance and Legal Constraints to Firm Growth: Does Size Matter? *Journal of Finance* 60, no. 1: 137–77.

Beck, Thorsten, Asli Demirgüç-Kunt, Luc Laeven, and Ross Levine. 2008. Finance, Firm Size, and Growth. *Journal of Money, Credit and Banking* 40, no. 7: 1379–1405.

Beck, Thorsten, Berrak Buyukkarabacak, Felix Rioja, and Neven Valev. 2012. Who Gets the Credit? and Does It Matter? Household vs. Firm Lending Across Countries. *B.E. Journal of Macroeconomics* 12: Issue 1 (Contributions), Article 2.

Beck, Thorsten, Hans Degryse, Ralph de Haas, and Neeltje van Horen. 2014. *When Arm's Length Is Too Far: Relationship Banking over the Business Cycle*. EBRD Working Paper 169. London: European Bank for Reconstruction and Development.

BIS (Bank for International Settlements). 2014. *84th BIS Annual Report, 2013/2014* (June). Basel. Available at www.bis.org/publ/arpdf/ar2014e.htm (accessed on January 20, 2015).

Borio, Claudio. 2012. *The Financial Cycle and Macroeconomics: What Have We Learnt?* BIS Working Paper 395. Basel: Bank for International Settlements.

Borst, Nicholas. 2013. *China's Credit Boom: New Risks Require New Reforms*. PIIE Policy Brief 13-24 (October). Washington: Peterson Institute for International Economics.

Bottazzi, Laura. 2009. The Role of Venture Capital in Alleviating Financial Constraints of Innovative Firms. *EIB Papers* 14, no. 2: 30–53.

Canning, David, and Peter Pedroni. 2008. Infrastructure, Long-Run Economic Growth and Causality Tests for Cointegrated Panels. *The Manchester School* 76, no. 5: 504–27.

Cecchetti, Stephen G., and Enisse Kharroubi. 2012. *Reassessing the Impact of Finance on Growth*. BIS Working Papers 381 (July). Basel: Bank for International Settlements.

Cecchetti, Stephen G., and Enisse Kharroubi. 2013. Why Does Financial Sector Growth Crowd Out Real Economic Growth? In *Finance and the Wealth of Nations Workshop*. San Francisco: Federal Reserve Bank of San Francisco and Institute of New Economic Thinking.

Christensen, Lone, Martin Schindler, and Thierry Tressel. 2013. Growth and Structural Reforms: A New Assessment. *Journal of International Economics* 89: 165–80.

Cubeddu, Luis, Alex Culiuc, Ghada Fayad, Yuan Gao, Kalpana Kochhar, Annette Kyobe, Ceyda Oner, Roberto Perrelli, Sarah Sanya, Evridiki Tsounta, and Zhongxia Zhang. 2014. *Emerging Markets in Transition: Growth Prospects and Challenges.* IMF Staff Discussion Note 14/06 (June). Washington: International Monetary Fund.

Dabla-Norris, Era, Giang Ho, Kalpana Kochhar, Annette Kyobe, and Robert Tchaidze. 2013. *Anchoring Growth: The Importance of Productivity-Enhancing Reforms in Emerging Market and Developing Economies.* IMF Staff Discussion Note 13/08 (December). Washington: International Monetary Fund.

Dabla-Norris, Era, Giang Ho, and Annette Kyobe. 2013. *Reforms and Distance to Frontier.* IMF Technical Note to Staff Discussion Note 13/08. Washington: International Monetary Fund.

De Gregorio, José, and Pablo Guidotti. 1995. Financial Development and Economic Growth. *World Development* 23, no. 3: 433–48.

de la Torre, Augusto, Alain Ize, and Sergio L. Schmukler. 2012. *Financial Development in Latin America and the Caribbean: The Road Ahead.* Washington: World Bank.

Dell'Ariccia, Giovanni, Deniz Igan, Luc Laeven, and Hui Tong. 2012. *Policies for Macrofinancial Stability: How to Deal with Credit Booms.* IMF Staff Discussion Note 12/06 (June). Washington: International Monetary Fund.

Demirgüç-Kunt, Asli, Erik Feyen, and Ross Levine. 2011. *The Evolving Importance of Banks and Securities Markets.* World Bank Policy Research Working Paper 5805. Washington: World Bank.

Demirgüç-Kunt, Asli, and Harry Huizinga. 2010. Bank Activity and Funding Strategies: The Impact on Risk and Returns. *Journal of Financial Economics* 98, no. 3: 626–50.

Didier, Tatiana, and Sergio L. Schmukler. 2014. *Financial Development in Asia: Beyond Aggregate Indicators.* World Bank Policy Research Working Paper 6761 (January). Washington: World Bank.

Ding, Ding, W. Raphael Lam, and Shanaka J. Peiris. 2014. *Future of Asia's Finance: How Can It Meet Challenges of Demographic Change and Infrastructure Needs?* IMF Working Paper WP/14/126. Washington: International Monetary Fund.

Eichengreen, Barry, Donghyun Park, and Kwanho Shin. 2013. *Growth Slowdowns Redux: New Evidence on the Middle-Income Trap.* NBER Working Paper 18673 (January). Cambridge, MA: National Bureau of Economic Research.

European Commission. 2013. *Green Paper: Long-Term Financing of the European Economy* (March 25). Brussels.

Felipe, Jesus. 2012. *Tracking the Middle-Income Trap: What is It, Who is in It, and Why?* ADB Economics Working Paper Series 306 (March). Manila: Asian Development Bank.

Groff, Stephen P. 2014. ASEAN's Infrastructure Crisis. *Wall Street Journal,* July 28.

Joshua Felman, Simon Gray, Mangal Goswami, Andreas A. Jobst, Mahmood Pradhan, Shanaka Peiris, and Dulani Seneviratne. 2014. ASEAN-5 Bond Market Development: Where Does It Stand? Where Is It Going? *Asia-Pacific Economic Literature* 28, no. 1: 60–75.

FINNOV. 2012. Financing Innovation and Growth: Reforming a Dysfunctional System. *European Policy Brief* (February). Brussels: European Commission. Available at http://ec.europa.eu/research/social-sciences/pdf/policy-briefs-finnov-022012_en.pdf (accessed on August 18, 2014).

Gambacorta, Leonardo, Jing Yang, and Kostas Tsatsaronis. 2014. Financial Structure and Growth. *BIS Quarterly Review* (March): 21–35.

Garcia-Macia, Daniel, Chang-Tai Hsieh, and Peter J. Klenow. 2014. How Destructive Is Innovation? Paper presented at the Cowles Foundation Summer 2014 Conference, May 27. Available at http://cowles.econ.yale.edu/conferences/2014/summer/macro_klenow.pdf (accessed on January 21, 2015).

Goyal, Rishi, Chris Marsh, Narayanan Raman, Shengzu Wang, and Swarnali Ahmed. 2011. *Financial Deepening and International Monetary Stability*. IMF Staff Discussion Note 11/16. Washington: International Monetary Fund.

Greenwood, Robin, and David Scharfstein. 2013. The Growth of Finance. *Journal of Economic Perspectives* 27, no. 2 (spring): 3–28.

Group of Thirty. 2013. *Long-term Finance and Economic Growth*. Washington.

Hall, Bronwyn H. 2009. The Financing of Innovative Firms. *EIB Papers* 14, no. 2: 8–29.

Hall, Bronwyn H., and Josh Lerner. 2009. *Financing of R&D and Innovation*. NBER Working Paper 15325 (September). Cambridge, MA: National Bureau of Economic Research.

Hall, Bronwyn H., and Alessandro Maffioli. 2008. Evaluating the Impact of Technology Development Funds in Emerging Economies: Evidence from Latin America. *European Journal of Development Research* 20, no. 2: 172–98.

Hasan, Iftekhar, Michael Koetter, and Michael Wedow. 2009. Regional Growth and Finance in Europe: Is There a Quality Effect of Bank Efficiency? *Journal of Banking and Finance* 33: 1446–53.

Intarakumnerd, Patarapong. 2012. How to Effectively Finance Innovations? Available at www3.grips.ac.jp/˜gist/en/events/document/gistseminar_35.pdf (accessed on January 22, 2015).

Intarakumnerd, Patarapong, and Juruhee Wonglimpiyart, eds. 2012. *Towards Effective Policies for Innovation Financing in Asia*. Bangkok: International Development Research Center.

Kerr, William R., and Ramana Nanda. 2009. *Financing Constraints and Entrepreneurship*. Harvard Business School Working Paper 10-013. Cambridge, MA: Harvard University.

Krishnan, Karthik, Debarshi Nandy, and Manju Puri. 2014. *Does Financing Spur Small Business Productivity? Evidence from a Natural Experiment*. NBER Working Paper 20149. Cambridge, MA: National Bureau of Economic Research.

Laeven, Luc, and Fabian Valencia. 2012. *Systemic Banking Crises Database: An Update*. IMF Working Paper WP/12/163 (June). Washington: International Monetary Fund.

Larrain, Mauricio, and Sebastian Stumpner. 2013. *Financial Reforms and Aggregate Productivity: The Microeconomic Channels*. Working Paper available at Social Science Research Network, http://papers.ssrn.com/sol3/papers.cfm?abstract_id=2172349 (accessed on January 21, 2015).

Law, Siong Hook, and Nirvikar Singh. 2014. Does Too Much Finance Harm Growth? *Journal of Banking and Finance* 41: 36–44.

Lee, Jong-Wha, and Kiseok Hong. 2010. *Economic Growth in Asia: Determinants and Prospects*. ADB Economics Working Paper Series 220 (September). Manila: Asian Development Bank.

Levine, Oliver, and Missaka Warusawitharana. 2014. *Finance and Productivity Growth: Firm-Level Evidence*. Finance and Economics Discussion Series 2014-17. Washington: Division of Research & Statistics and Monetary Affairs, Federal Reserve Board.

Levine, Ross. 2005. Finance and Growth: Theory and Evidence. In *Handbook of Economic Growth*, ed. Philippe Aghion and Steven N. Darlauf, 865–943. Amsterdam: Elsevier.

Levine, Ross. 2011. Regulating Finance and Regulators to Promote Growth. In *Achieving Maximum Long-Run Growth*, 271–311. Proceedings of the Federal Reserve Bank of Kansas City Symposium, Jackson Hole, WY, August 25–27.

Mazzucato, Mariana. 2012. *Rebalancing What? Reforming Finance for Creative Destruction not Destructive Creation*. London: Policy Network.

Mazzucato, Mariana. 2013. *The Entrepreneurial State: Debunking Public vs. Private Sector Myths*. London and New York: Anthem Press.

Midrigan, Virgiliu, and Daniel Yi Xu. 2014. Finance and Misallocation: Evidence from Plant-Level Data. *American Economic Review* 104, no. 2: 422–58.

Noland, Marcus, and Howard Pack. 2005. *The East Asian Industrial Policy Experience: Implications for the Middle East*. PIIE Working Paper 05-14. December. Washington: Institute for International Economics.

OECD (Organization for Economic Cooperation and Development). 2007. *Innovation and Growth*. Paris.

OECD (Organization for Economic Cooperation and Development). 2010. *Measuring Innovation: A New Perspective*. Paris.

OECD (Organization for Economic Cooperation and Development). 2013a. The Missing Entrepreneurs. In *Policies for Financing*. Paris.

OECD (Organization for Economic Cooperation and Development). 2013b. *Policies for Seed and Early Stage Finance: Findings from the 2012 OECD Financing Questionnaire*. Paris.

Ohno, Kenichi. 2011. Avoiding the Middle-Income Trap: Renovating Industrial Policy Formulation in Vietnam. Paper presented at the Development Policy Lecture, sponsored by the Asian Development Bank, Manila, January. Available at www.grips.ac.jp/vietnam/KOarchives/doc/EP32_ADB_HQ_MIT.pdf (accessed on August 25, 2014).

Panizza, Ugo. 2013. Financial Development and Economic Growth: Known Knowns, Known Unknowns, and Unknown Unknowns. Paper prepared for the 2013 AFD-BMZ-EUDN annual conference on Development, Berlin, December 11. Available at www.afd.fr/jahia/webdav/site/afd/shared/PRESSE/Evenements/eudn/EUDN2013_Session%203_Ugo%20Panizza%20(speaker).pdf (accessed on July 23, 2014).

Park, Donghyun, and Jungsoo Park. 2010. *Drivers of Developing Asia's Growth: Past and Future*. ADB Economics Working Paper Series 235 (November). Manila: Asian Development Bank.

Philippon, Thomas. 2010. Financiers vs. Engineers: Should the Financial Sector Be Taxed or Subsidized? *American Economic Journal Macroeconomics* 2, no. 3: 158–82.

Philippon, Thomas. 2012. *Has the U.S. Finance Industry Become Less Efficient? On the Theory and Measurement of Financial Intermediation*. NBER Working Paper 18077. Cambridge, MA: National Bureau of Economic Research.

Pritchett, Lant, and Lawrence Summers. 2013. Asiaphoria Meets Regression to the Mean. Paper presented at the Federal Reserve Bank of San Francisco conference on Prospects for Asia and the Global Economy, San Francisco, November 3–5. Available at www.frbsf.org/economic-research/events/2013/november/asia-economic-policy-conference/ (accessed on January 21, 2015).

Rajan, Raghuram G., and Luigi Zingales. 2001. Financial Systems, Industrial Structure, and Growth. *Oxford Review of Economic Policy* 17, no. 4: 467–82.

Robinson, Joan. 1952. The Generalization of the General Theory. In *The Rate of Interest and Other Essays,* 67–142. London: Macmillan.

Rodrik, Dani, and Arvind Subramanian. 2009. *Why Did Financial Globalization Disappoint?* IMF Staff Papers 56: 112–38. Washington: International Monetary Fund.

Roland-Holst, David, and Guntur Sugiyarto. 2014. *Growth Horizons for a Changing Asian Regional Economy*. ADB Economics Working Paper Series 392 (March). Manila: Asian Development Bank.

Rousseau, Peter, and Paul Wachtel. 2011. What Is Happening to the Impact of Financial Deepening on Economic Growth? *Economic Inquiry* 49: 276–88.

Sawyer, Malcolm. 2014. *Financial Development, Financialization and Economic Growth*. FESSUD Working Paper Series 21. Leeds: Financialisation, Economy, Society and Sustainable Development, Leeds University Business School.

Shinozaki, Shigehiro. 2014. *Capital Market Financing for SMEs: A Growing Need in Emerging Asia.* ADB Working Paper Series on Regional Economic Integration 121 (January). Manila: Asian Development Bank.

Tressel, Thierry. 2008. Unbundling the Effect of Reforms. Paper presented at an IMF conference on the Causes and Consequences of Structural Reforms, Washington, February 28–29. Available at www.imf.org/external/np/seminars/eng/2008/strureform/pdf/unbund.pdf (accessed on July 22, 2014).

Tho, Tran Van. 2013. *The Middle-Income Trap: Issues for Members of the Association of Southeast Asian Nations.* ADBI Working Paper Series 421 (May). Manila: Asian Development Bank.

UNECE (United Nations Economic Commission for Europe). 2009. *Policy Options and Instruments for Financing Innovation: A Practical Guide to Early-Stage Financing.* New York and Geneva: United Nations.

Walsh, James P. 2014. The Future of Asian Finance. *Finance and Development* (June): 18–21.

Wehinger, Gert. 2014. SMEs and the Credit Crunch: Current Financing Difficulties, Policy Measures and a Review of Literature. *OECD Journal: Financial Market Trends* 2013/2. Available at www.oecd-ilibrary.org/finance-and-investment/smes-and-the-credit-crunch_fmt-2013-5jz-734p6b8jg (accessed on August 3, 2015).

World Bank. 2014. Doing Business: Resolving Insolvency. Washington. Available at www.doing-business.org/data/exploretopics/resolving-insolvency (accessed on January 20, 2015).

Zhu, Min. 2014. Asia's Seismic Shift: How Can the Financial Sector Serve Better? *iMFDirect*, July 21. Available at http://blog-imfdirect.imf.org/2014/07/21/asias-seismic-shift-how-can-the-financial-sector-serve-better/ (accessed on January 21, 2015).

6

Enhancing Financial Stability in Developing Asia

ADAM S. POSEN and NICOLAS VÉRON

Developing Asia faces a much greater intellectual and policy challenge on the financial side of the economy than on the real side (i.e., the side concerned with producing goods and services). There is pretty clear consensus and even a roadmap for the trade and investment side of the spectacular East Asian development stories over the last 60 years. These were largely based on integration with global markets and value chains under rules that have been framed mostly by the United States and Western Europe. In the financial area, however, there is no such clear consensus.

A number of Asian countries, including Japan, the Republic of Korea, and Singapore, succeeded while pursuing a different path than the United States and United Kingdom on the treatment of household savings and maintaining limits on financial development. The excesses of Anglo-American financial liberalization being the apparent cause of the North Atlantic financial crisis of 2008–11 only deepened their caution. Major failures in risk management were identified in the rich Western countries, in both the public and private sectors. The understanding of financial linkages and of the system as a whole by relevant public authorities was inadequate (Gorton 2009), as was their prudential supervision of many individual financial firms. Financial innovation was associated with opacity, instability, and a potentially nefarious "shadow

Adam S. Posen is the president of the Peterson Institute for International Economics. Nicolas Véron, visiting fellow since October 2009, is also a senior fellow at Bruegel, a Brussels-based economic policy think tank he cofounded in 2002–04. Posen's research in this area is partially supported by a major grant from the Alfred P. Sloan Foundation. The authors are grateful to Marcus Noland and Douglas Rediker for helpful suggestions. The views expressed here are solely those of the authors, and not necessarily those of the Peterson Institute, the Asian Development Bank, the Sloan Foundation, Bruegel, or any members of their Boards.

banking system" (Pozsar et al. 2010). These failures were an echo of those that caused the Asian financial crisis of 1997–98, though in both crises the message was exaggerated and oversimplified (Rhee and Posen 2013).

Yet, a number of Asian countries have wanted to create internationally competitive financial centers within their borders, which also require high levels of liberalization and financial innovation. Key elements of this effort included the development of market-based finance in the form of tradable equities, bonds, and even instruments of risk transfer such as derivatives and securitization; a deepening of international financial integration, associated with the elimination of cross-border capital controls and the adoption of common financial standards; and the creation of strong, competent, and independent institutions for financial sector oversight, within existing central banks or as autonomous agencies. Furthermore, the recent crisis notwithstanding, there is substantial evidence that financial repression imposes direct costs, if not outright limits, on broader economic development (Cline 2010), and, as demonstrated by the summer 2015 equity market developments in the People's Republic of China (PRC), can itself contribute to financial instability.[1]

Simultaneously, the elevation of the Group of Twenty (G-20) to its new status as "premier forum for international economic cooperation" among its member constituencies,[2] with an initial strong emphasis on financial regulatory matters (Rottier and Véron 2010), was intended to send a message that a new policy consensus was being defined. This new policy consensus, like the G-20 itself, was supposed to involve developing and emerging-market economies on an equal footing with advanced ones. The G-20 reform program has recorded a few successes, notably the rapid finalization of the Basel III accord on capital, leverage, and liquidity for traditional banks, whose key elements were agreed by the end of 2010. The message, however, promised more than the G-20 could realistically deliver. As a result, the policy guidance for enhancing financial stability remains unsettled—and arguably deficient in terms of addressing the specific needs of emerging markets and nonbank activities.

In particular, the new G-20-centered framework's goal of providing more balance among developing, emerging-market, and advanced economies in shaping common global financial policies has not yet been fully realized. On the positive side, the membership of key bodies such as the Financial Stability Board (FSB), Basel Committee on Banking Supervision (BCBS), or Committee on the Global Financial System (CGFS) has been significantly rebalanced to better represent Asian jurisdictions (as described below in the section on Cross-Border Integration). For reasons that involve both emerging-market and incumbent advanced economies, though, the influence of non-Western members of such bodies in their workings and outcomes is often less than the

---

1. Mikitani and Posen (2001) sets out how financial repression and partial protection of certain banking sectors in the United States and Japan led to the savings and loan crisis of the 1980s and the Japanese banking crisis of the 1990s, respectively.

2. Group of Twenty, Pittsburgh Summit Declaration, September 2009.

weight of those members' formal representation—and that is the case at the FSB (Véron 2014, Walter 2015).

In the absence of a generally accepted framework for financial stability, policymakers in developing Asia need to exercise judgment while determining which choices are best suited to their specific situation. The most important point is that there is no simple linear relationship between financial repression and stability—postponing or avoiding financial liberalization not only has costs but so doing can itself undermine systemic stability in developing economies. That fact holds, even though it is undeniable that Anglo-American light-touch financial regulation and supervision were destabilizing and warn us to avoid extreme deregulation. We offer the following guidelines for policymakers pursuing financial stability in developing Asia:

- Bank-based or bank-centric financial systems are not inherently safer than systems that include meaningful roles for securities and capital markets.

- Domestic financial systems should be steadily diversified in terms of both number of domestic competitors and types of saving and lending instruments available (and thus probably types of institutions).

- Financial repression should be focused on regulating the activities of financial intermediaries and investment managers/funds, not on compressing interest rates and returns for domestic savers.

- Cross-border lending from regional financial centers in foreign currency should be in limited quantities only for top companies, but creation of multinational banks' subsidiaries in the local economy—and local currency lending and bond issuance—should be encouraged.

- Macroprudential tools can be useful and, if anything, are more effective in less open or less financially deep economies than in more advanced financial entrepots, but they must be used aggressively when needed and are particularly suited for dealing with real estate booms/busts.

The next four sections develop these ideas in more detail for banking, nonbank finance, macroprudential policy, and cross-border issues. This chapter aims at supporting Asian policymakers' judgment by providing policy views and recommendations that are based on our analysis of the recent sequence of events in the United States and Europe and of earlier crisis episodes, including those in Asia (including Japan) during the 1990s. The last section synthesizes the commonalities between developing Asia and some of these advanced-economy crises.

Banking Policy

Banks are the backbone of the financial system in most developing Asian countries and will remain so for the foreseeable future. Thus, banking policy will remain fundamental to shaping the financial system and ensuring financial stability.

In almost all cases, this policy should aim at fostering market mechanisms in the functioning of the banking system, especially the setting of interest rates for saving and borrowing and competition among banks. It is natural for governments everywhere to be tempted to distort the functioning of the financial system to facilitate the financing of their own operations or of specific economic activities or agents that they favor, a stance that the economic jargon loosely refers to as "financial repression." But this temptation of financial repression should be resisted in most circumstances, except during wars or other acute and temporary national emergencies. Specifically, the compression of interest rates offered to savers through a combination of capital controls and constraints on domestic banks—a common form of financial repression—is typically destabilizing, because it encourages savers to find their way around the interest rate caps with harmful unintended consequences. The PRC over the past decade offers a relevant illustration of this mechanism, in which the repression of savings has encouraged both unproductive overinvestment and the buildup of financial risk in the "shadow banking" sector (Lardy 2014).

Financial repression also exists under different forms in advanced countries, and its track record there is no more compelling than in less wealthy countries. The experience of the European Union offers a cautionary tale. Many EU member states entered the crisis of the late 2000s with a legacy of policies that included

- significant levels of public ownership of banks (at the national or local government level);
- other levers of government influence to direct lending, such as tax loopholes and tweaks in regulatory requirements, e.g., the now notorious practice of assigning a zero risk-weight to all EU sovereign debt;
- sector-specific accounting, auditing, and disclosure frameworks and practices;
- curbs on nonbank finance, e.g., the prohibition of activities such as leasing and factoring without a banking license, which enhanced the dominance of banking intermediation; and
- selective or complacent enforcement of competition policy in the banking sector.

The detail of these cases of "financial repression with European characteristics" varied across EU countries. Overall, they significantly contributed to the systemic banking fragility that has been plaguing European growth since the initial shock of 2007–08.

The need for competition and market-based price setting and credit allocation, however, should not offset the equally important need for proper bank regulation. Banks are inherently leveraged institutions, and, because they collect deposits, are repositories of trust in society. In addition, the services they provide are rife with asymmetries of information, which no amount of public

Figure 6.1 Share of state-owned banks in selected Asian economies

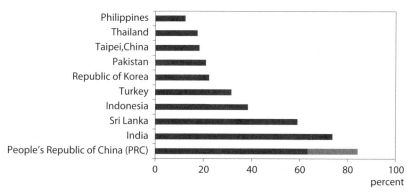

Notes: Ratio of aggregate assets of state-owned banks to total banking assets, as of 2011 (PRC) and 2010 (other countries). The light-shaded section on the PRC bar refers to banks in which a government entity holds a controlling minority stake.

Sources: Opper, Andersson, and Burzynska (2013) and authors' calculations for the PRC; World Bank Banking Regulation and Supervision Survey, 2013, for other economies.

financial education can adequately check. As a consequence, the regulation and supervision of banks by public authorities is a vital condition for financial stability and efficient financing of the economy.

The public-interest nature of depository institutions is one of the reasons why many countries have brought significant swaths of their banking system under public ownership. This is by no means unique to Asia. As mentioned above, Europe is a case in point. To give only a few examples among advanced economies, Italy nationalized many banks in the 1930s, and France in the 1940s, even though most of these were privatized in the 1990s. At present, more than a third of Germany's banking system is still in public hands. Even in the United States, the federal government guaranteed the two large US mortgage companies, Fannie Mae and Freddie Mac, before the crisis and now owns them as well. More often than not, however, the benefits of public bank ownership in terms of anchoring trust are offset by the challenges it creates in terms of poor corporate governance, politicized lending, interference of trade unions in management (in some countries), and other flaws that typically result in inferior risk management. Thus, those developing Asian economies that have reached a level of development that supports functioning large-scale private sector organizations should favor private over public ownership of their banking system (figure 6.1).

Nevertheless, again because of the same public-interest aspect of deposit taking and other features of banking, the operations of private sector banks should be ring-fenced from other forms of private sector activity. The principle known in the United States as "separation of banking and commerce," according to which banking and nonfinancial activities should not coexist within the same commercial entity, has gradually emerged as a response to the frequent abuses of bank-industry links, typically in the form of preferential financing by banks of related business operations against the interest of their other claimants, including depositors.

In developing and emerging-market economies, however, the separation between banking and commerce is often porous to nonexistent. In many such countries, established families or groups with multiple business interests are the only nonstate stakeholders that can provide the necessary financial and reputational capital to establish successful banks. This arguably justifies the recent initiatives in both the PRC and India to grant new bank licenses to existing corporate groups to check state-owned banking behemoths.

Even in advanced economies, the separation is seldom absolute. For example, several European automotive manufacturers have large credit-financing arms that are considered banks under EU legislation (even though they do not collect deposits), and in the United States, automakers and industrial equipment suppliers like GE had long maintained a sizeable quasi-bank financial arm. Policymakers in developing Asia, however, should remain acutely aware of the vast potential for conflicts of interest that exists when a bank is part of a broader commercial or industrial group. This is also true in the context of new internet-based financial services, which are often "bundled" with nonfinancial commercial offerings. While such bundling may represent an attractive and efficient proposition for consumers, it should be subject to adequate supervision.

A separate policy debate refers to the possible separation, within financial groups, of different types of financial activities and particularly of commercial and investment banking. In the United States, the Glass-Steagall Act of 1934 introduced such a stark separation, which was repealed in 1999, arguably to ill effect. Similarly in the United Kingdom, merchant banks were kept separate from commercial banks until the deregulation of the 1980s and 1990s. Similar provisions have existed or still exist in several Asian countries such as the PRC, India, Japan, and the Republic of Korea. For example, in the PRC, banks are prohibited from equities brokerage, which is the sole preserve of securities firms under a separate regulator. Following the recent financial crisis, the public anger against bailouts of large banks has led to the introduction or reintroduction of legal constraints on the structure of banking groups in the United States and Europe. These include the Volcker rule, which aims at prohibiting proprietary trading by banks in the United States; the Vickers reform in the United Kingdom, which mandates the ring-fencing of retail and commercial banking operations from other financial services; and EU legislation on banking structural reform, which, however, is still under discussion at the time of writing.

While mantras such as "banks should not be allowed to speculate with household deposits" resonate with politicians and the general public, however, a more in-depth analysis suggests caution against simplistic solutions of separation. The legal definition of "speculation" as opposed to hedging or market-making has proved elusive, and the highly complex implementation of the Volcker rule does not appear to satisfy its initial promoters more than its critics. Similarly, the spread of credit-transfer techniques such as derivatives has irreversibly blurred the boundary between commercial and wholesale banking, and it is not evident that the distinction has much substance from a systemic risk perspective.

That said, some principles of separation appear necessary and healthy. Insurance operations in a broader financial group should be conducted in a separate subsidiary with its own capital. Asset management activities also require separation, in order to ensure that funds under a bank's custody are not confused with those under the bank's direct ownership. Furthermore, some structural measures may be necessary to ensure or facilitate a bank's resolution in the event of failure (see below on resolution). But these may be better left to the judgment of supervisors, and thus tailored to the specific situation of each banking group, than defined uniformly in legislation.

For bank capital regulation, the Basel III capital accord, first defined in 2010 and continuously refined since, provides a global framework of reference. The BCBS has initiated reviews of individual jurisdictions' compliance with Basel III in terms of laws and regulations (leaving aside the question of how these are implemented and enforced), dubbed the Regulatory Consistency Assessment Program (RCAP). Asian jurisdictions whose RCAP reviews have been published so far—Japan in October 2012, Singapore in March 2013, the PRC in September 2013, Hong Kong, China in March 2015, and India in June 2015—have all been deemed "compliant," the best grading in the RCAP process. This is in contrast with both the United States and European Union, which have been found, respectively, "largely compliant" and "materially noncompliant" in their RCAP reports, both published in December 2014. Other Asian jurisdictions that will be reviewed under RCAP in the near future include the Republic of Korea (June 2016) and Indonesia (September 2016).[3] No equivalent assessment is available at this point for developing Asian jurisdictions that are not BCBS members.

The Basel III framework has occasionally been criticized for being ill suited for developing or emerging-market economies and for excessively constraining, for example, bank lending to small and medium-sized enterprises (SMEs). The Basel calibrations, however, have taken into account observations from across the BCBS membership, including emerging-market economies. The critique of the impact on SME lending has been acute in Europe as well, leading to deviations from Basel III in setting capital charges for loans to SMEs in the legislation that transposes Basel III into EU law, known as the Capital Requirements Regulation (CRR). This is a significant reason for the low grading of the European Union under RCAP as materially noncompliant. In reality, lending to SMEs is inherently risky and the artificial reduction of the corresponding capital charges, as in CRR, represents a questionable distortion of the prudential framework.

---

3. BCBS website, www.bis.org/bcbs (accessed on August 6, 2015).

In any case, the Basel framework is intended only for larger internationally active banks. In general, developing Asian countries should aim at such large banks' compliance with Basel III while engaging actively with the BCBS standard-setting process in order to ensure that it fairly takes into account the realities of all jurisdictions. The Basel III standards on bank capital and leverage, and the complementary standards from the FSB on additional requirements on systemically important financial institutions (SIFIs) and total loss-absorbing capacity (TLAC) requirements currently under discussion, are based on long-standing experience with capital requirements. Many aspects remain hotly debated, including the principle of measuring capital ratios against risk-weighted assets; nevertheless, the framework can in general terms be considered tried and tested, and broadly balanced.

By contrast, the parts of Basel III that deal with liquidity issues are more experimental in nature and subject to more uncertainty as to their possible unintended consequences. These include the liquidity coverage ratio (LCR), aimed at ensuring resilience against a temporary liquidity shock, and the net stable funding ratio (NSFR), aimed at ensuring ongoing sustainability of a bank's funding structure. The LCR is still in a period of phasing-in that will be completed only in early 2019 (BCBS 2013). The definition of the NSFR was finalized only in October 2014, and its introduction is planned for early 2018 (BCBS 2014). Countries in developing Asia, especially those that are not BCBS members, have no need to rush into implementation of these measures and may gain from observing their early implementation in other jurisdictions.

For all its importance, regulation is only one part of the banking policy framework and must be complemented with effective arrangements for supervision and crisis management. In spite of some improvement, bank supervision capacity remains constrained in many developing Asian countries. To be effective, supervision must be based on an in-depth analysis of risk in the banks' balance sheets and their environment and not just on the formulaic application of prudential ratios. Capacity constraints make it particularly important to complement supervision with an effective framework for market discipline, based on strong standards for accounting, auditing, and supervisory disclosures (the so-called third pillar of the Basel framework). Similarly, stress testing has emerged as an increasingly prominent component of the supervisory toolkit (see chapter 8 by Morris Goldstein in this volume) but also requires the buildup of adequate capacity.

Resolution frameworks are an even more challenging issue for many developing and emerging-market economies, including those in Asia. The familiar tradeoff, when a bank faces severe difficulties, is between bailing out all creditors, at the risk of a severe fiscal burden and erosion of market discipline in the rest of the banking system, and "bail-in" (the imposition of losses on creditors and, if necessary to plug the capital gap, on some depositors), at the risk of contagion to other banks and a larger eventual financial and economic cost. The case of Kazakhstan's BTA Bank in February 2009 shows that such contagion can be managed in some cases, at least in countries with a strong fiscal position.[4] Ideally, an orderly resolution system makes it possible to distribute losses to private sector stakeholders in a manner that does not undermine systemic trust. The US Federal Deposit Insurance Corporation (FDIC)'s track record of resolving small and medium-sized depository institutions offers the most prominent model for this. It is now being emulated in the European Union with the Bank Recovery and Resolution Directive (BRRD) of 2014 and in the euro area with the establishment of a Single Resolution Board to handle future bank crises.

A predictable resolution system, however, involves a lot of prerequisites in terms of the rule of law, functioning court system (because the resolution process is always defined with reference to the alternative of court-ordered insolvency), and the administrative capacity of the resolution authority itself. Even in the United States, the operation of the Dodd-Frank Act of 2010 in the case of future crises involving systemically important financial institutions remains entirely to be tested. As a consequence, developing Asian countries should put emphasis on crisis prevention rather than resolution and carefully observe developments in other jurisdictions to optimize their capacity to respond to future banking crises.

The creation of a credible system for deposit insurance is another component of bank crisis management frameworks. The specific features of deposit insurance schemes are important to ensure effectiveness, and poorly designed systems can be detrimental rather than beneficial to financial stability (Demirgüç-Kunt and Detragiache 2000). But if properly set up and funded, a deposit insurance framework can have an important stabilizing effect by reducing the disruption associated with retail bank runs. Here again, the buildup of adequate capacity and credibility is crucial to the effectiveness of the policy framework.

A proper competition policy is also important in the banking sector, which is prone to concentration of market power in a limited number of dominant banks that benefit from an implicit "too big to fail" guarantee. Local credit unions, cooperatives, and microlending institutions often play a vital role in financing small businesses and job creation in developing economies as in advanced ones. Public authorities should ensure that the environment does not prevent their development, while simultaneously refraining from giving them special competitive privileges.

In banking as in other economic sectors, new technology is disrupting the competitive landscape, fostering both new risks and new opportunities. The massive spread of computing power and mobile service accessibility, combined with increasingly large mobilization of venture capital for "fin-tech" (financial technology) startup enterprises, is likely to significantly change the way financial services are offered and delivered in the next few years. The

---

4. "Restructuring Banks: Don't Start from Here—Kazakhstan shows it is possible to make banks' creditors share the pain," *Economist,* November 25, 2010, www.economist.com/node/17583123 (accessed on August 7, 2015).

M-Pesa money transfer service, pioneered by Vodafone in Kenya and Tanzania since 2007 and now used in a growing number of other countries, and the Alipay payment platform, launched by Alibaba in the PRC in 2004 and complemented by a highly successful online savings offering (Yu'e Bao) since 2013, are illustrations of the transformative power of mobile finance. Better use of technology also holds vast potential to combat corruption, money laundering, and the financing of terrorism across borders, in spite of numerous practical and political obstacles.

Because developing countries in Asia and other regions are less encumbered with legacy systems, they can often adopt such new technologies quickly and can thus "leapfrog" services or practices that are more widespread in advanced economies but are rapidly becoming obsolete. Technology-enabled access to financial services, including on a cross-border basis, may increase the cost of financial repression and reduce its effectiveness. The disruption of finance by these technologies has barely started, and it is not possible at this early stage to predict its future intensity and the exact challenges it will entail. What is already clear, however, is that public authorities in developing Asia and elsewhere need to devote appropriate resources to monitor financial technology developments in real time and understand what these developments mean for them.

Nonbank Finance

The Asian financial crisis of 1997–98 memorably led the then chairman of the US Federal Reserve to observe: "Before the crisis broke, there was little reason to question the three decades of phenomenally solid East Asian economic growth, largely financed through the banking system. The rapidly expanding economies and bank credit growth kept the ratio of nonperforming loans to total bank assets low. The failure to have backup forms of intermediation was of little consequence. The lack of a spare tire is of no concern if you do not get a flat. East Asia had no spare tires."[5] Since then, countries in developing Asia and elsewhere have endeavored to develop bond markets and local-currency issuance (Goswani and Sharma 2011). In the PRC, some diversification away from a purely bank-dominated system has been achieved through the toleration by public authorities of the rapid development of "shadow" finance (see chapter 9 by Nicholas Borst and Nicholas Lardy in this volume). The concern to develop nonbank finance is by no means limited to Asia. In the European Union, the European Commission has similarly announced an agenda of "capital markets union," even though its exact content has not yet been determined (European Commission 2015).

---

5. Alan Greenspan, "Do efficient financial markets mitigate financial crises?" Remarks at the Financial Markets Conference of the Federal Reserve Bank of Atlanta, Sea Island, GA, October 19, 1999, www.federalreserve.gov/boarddocs/speeches/1999/19991019.htm (accessed on August 7, 2015).

The development of nonbank finance has a two-pronged rationale. First, the "spare tire" argument holds that alternative financing channels can take the baton of credit provision when banks need to deleverage and restructure themselves, which typically happens after a systemic crisis. Furthermore, capital markets, particularly their equity component, provide a powerful mechanism for risk sharing across regions (Asdrubali, Sørensen, and Yosha 1996; IMF 2013). As in natural ecosystems, diversity of the financial system is a factor of resilience and stability. Second, capital markets and the nonbank sector offer forms of financing that are better suited than bank lending to support specific patterns of development, especially service innovators and other high-growth companies that don't have tangible assets to pledge as collateral (Philippon and Véron 2008). Thus, the development of nonbank finance enhances the economy's growth potential and counts as a form of structural reform.

These arguments are generally compelling when applied to advanced economies such as the European Union (Véron and Wolff 2015, Langfield and Pagano 2015). In developing economies, their relevance has to be assessed against each country's specific context. Even well-developed local-currency bond markets primarily benefit larger companies. Corporate loan securitization is unsuited to lending to small companies, because the costs associated with the required documentation and corresponding corporate transparency are prohibitively high: Even in the world's most developed securitization market, the United States, the volumes of SME loan securitization are low. Thus, countries where SMEs carry out most of the business activity will struggle to establish vibrant national capital markets. These countries might benefit more from opening up to cross-border capital flows to favor external—but not necessarily foreign currency—financing of their highest-potential companies through foreign intermediaries rather than domestic ones (see section on Cross-Border Integration).

The development of the Chinese shadow banking sector also offers an important reference point for developing Asia. Given the sector's generally insufficient transparency, it is difficult at the time of writing to form firm opinions about its medium-term economic impact. There are widely different assessments about the risk it represents for overall systemic stability. Nevertheless, the authorities appear to have reached the conclusion that, even if it does put competitive pressure on the incumbent banks, the shadow banking system cannot be allowed to grow unchecked. The lack of data makes it difficult to evaluate the contribution of the PRC's shadow banking system to nonfinancial corporate financing at this point, but in any case, it is unlikely to grow as dynamically as it has in the last few years. Furthermore, the unique size of the PRC economy and internal market means that its experience cannot be directly replicated in other countries of developing Asia.

Dynamic capital markets and nonbank finance can be very beneficial to the economy if they function properly, as the example of the United States illustrates. But to function properly, they have to meet a number of conditions. In particular, insolvency and debt restructuring frameworks are essential components of the intangible infrastructure that supports them. In countries where insolvency processes are either inefficient or easily hijacked by special interests or both, riskier forms of nonbank credit (such as high-yield bonds, securitization, or mezzanine credit) are likely to be difficult to introduce, because of the lack of underlying trust that creditors' interests will be suitably defended in case the supported venture is not successful.

Similarly, equity markets and several segments of nonbank credit markets require a high standard of corporate governance and financial transparency to function properly. Many developing Asian economies have made progress toward accounting transparency by adopting International Financial Reporting Standards (IFRS), which generally represent an improvement on preexisting national standards in terms of the quality of financial statements. As of mid-2014 this was the case in Brunei Darussalam; Cambodia; Hong Kong, China; the Republic of Korea; Malaysia; the Maldives; Mongolia; Nepal; Singapore; and Taipei,China, among others. Furthermore Bangladesh, Myanmar, Pakistan, Sri Lanka, and Uzbekistan are using standards that differ from IFRS only on a limited number of points, while the PRC, India, Indonesia, Japan, and Thailand have for the moment retained national accounting standards even though these are partly modeled on the IFRS (Pacter 2015). In any event, accounting standards are only one part of a robust corporate financial reporting framework. Equally important are the requirements and practices that govern auditing and the enforcement of accounting standards by public authorities (generally securities markets regulators). On both these dimensions, and despite the near total absence of reliable comparative data, it appears that most developing Asian countries have significant potential for progress.

Financial ecosystems change only slowly. In their ambition to foster financial development and particularly the expansion of nonbank finance, policymakers in developing Asia should resist the temptation to artificially accelerate the financial evolutionary process by subsidizing market segments that they see as desirable or granting them special tax or regulatory privileges. This is particularly true in the area of venture capital (VC), a segment that many governments in developing, emerging-market, and advanced economies alike view as disproportionately beneficial to the economy because it is associated with innovative, high-growth firms, including disruptive technological innovators.

In Europe, for example, a number of governments have intervened directly in the VC market, by setting up public funds that either invest in private sector VC funds or invest directly in companies, alone or in coinvestment with private sector VC funds. Many such funds exist in Europe at the subnational, national, and European levels (the European Investment Fund is managed by the European Investment Bank). Generally speaking, the track record of these funds is poor, and there is even evidence that they represent a drag rather than a stimulant for the growth of a healthy VC sector (Veugelers 2011). It appears that the stringent control mechanisms that are inherent in the deployment of public money are incompatible with the high-risk, high-failure-rate, judgment-based approach that defines VC investment. Developing Asian countries should learn from the European failures in this area. Rather than throwing scarce public money at the sector, they should focus on the environment that shapes VC activity, including the quality of higher education, predictability of tax and regulatory developments, protection of intellectual property rights, openness to foreign investment, and integrity of the justice system.

All things considered, the potential for nonbank finance in developing Asia depends heavily on each country's specific context of financial, economic, and institutional development. For some, a homegrown nonbank financial sector with critical mass can provide benefits in terms of both higher growth potential and higher stability; for other countries, it is more promising to become more open to financing from outside by pursuing cross-border financial integration (see section on Cross-Border Integration). Banks will continue to play an irreplaceable role in the financing of the economy in all Asian countries.

Macroprudential Tools and Their Use

Macroprudential policy concepts have evolved gradually since the 1970s from the realization that the regulation and supervision of individual financial firms may not always be sufficient to ensure the stability of the financial system as a whole (Borio 2003, Clement 2010). The corresponding instruments include, in particular, loan-to-value (LTV) limits, countercyclical capital buffers and time-varying reserve requirements, and targeted taxes and levies on financial activities. The existence of a track record varies depending on the instrument: Some measures have been used long before being given a "macroprudential" label, the use of which has become significantly more widespread over the last decade; others are largely or entirely untested.

The dataset of past macroprudential actions assembled by Longmei Zhang and Edda Zoli (2014) suggests that Asian countries have a higher propensity to engage in such measures than jurisdictions in other regions (figure 6.2). This dataset establishes a distinction between macroprudential policies and capital flow management (CFM) measures, which are occasionally associated with a macroprudential objective. The same source identifies a marked increase in CFM measures in Asia following the peak of the financial crisis in late 2008 but at a pace that is far lower than that of the Latin American region, which leads in this category.

Macroprudential measures, of course, distort the operation of market mechanisms and in principle should be introduced only in response to a specifically identified market failure. The absence of relevant general equilibrium economic models of financial systems, however, implies that there is a strong heuristic element in the elaboration of such measures, which itself is made more challenging by the difficulty of assessing their effectiveness in terms of both benefits and costs (Claessens 2014).

The area in which macroprudential measures appear to have had the most compelling record of effectiveness is in real estate booms and busts. Such

Figure 6.2   Macroprudential actions in Asia and other regions, 2000–2012

macroprudential policy actions (index)

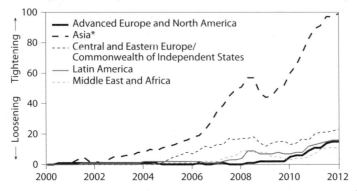

* Economies include the People's Republic of China; Hong Kong, China; India; Indonesia; Republic of Korea; Malaysia; Mongolia; Philippines; Singapore; Taipei,China; Thailand; Viet Nam.

Source: Zhang and Zoli (2014).

booms and busts are one of the major drivers of systemic financial crises, as illustrated in recent years by the United States but also by several European countries including Ireland, Spain, and the Baltic countries. Developing Asian countries should introduce macroprudential tools to dampen property booms, or maintain and refine them if they already have (Jeanne 2014). Beyond this sector-specific aspect, there is a case for being cautious—developing status and absence of a globalized financial center in this instance can be a virtue, as most asset price booms with systemic implications will be confined largely to real estate (whether commercial or residential).

In any event, it is important for all Asian countries, as in the rest of the world, to devote resources to better monitor and understand developments in their financial system beyond the banking sector. These include the timely collection and publication of statistics. For these, Asian countries should seek compliance with international standards and practices as developed by the BIS Irving Fisher Committee and the work developed since 2008 under the aegis of the G-20 to address "data gaps" (FSB and IMF 2014).

Cross-Border Integration

Financial stability frameworks are not purely domestic, since cross-border financial integration affects all countries at least to a certain extent. The impact of such integration on stability, however, is ambiguous and easy to misunderstand. Generally speaking, the judgment of national authorities is inherently skewed in this area, as they tend to view and treat homegrown risks that arise under their watch more leniently than risks coming from abroad. A quintessential example of this bias was offered by European prudential authorities in the first few years of the recent financial crisis, which they blamed on the United States without an in-depth examination of why European banks had ended up with an aggregate exposure to the US subprime market risk that was equal to if not larger than that of American banks (IMF 2009). It took an unjustifiably long time for these authorities to finally admit that faulty risk management systems and inadequate incentives, not just cross-border financial integration, had played an essential part in the corresponding buildup of risk in European banks' balance sheets and that these could and should be addressed through domestic initiatives (Posen and Véron 2009).

Depending on circumstances, cross-border financial integration can be a source of financial resilience or of financial fragility. For example, the presence of foreign banks can have a powerful stabilizing effect in a domestic crisis. A classic example of this was the housing market downturn in the three Baltic countries of the European Union (Lithuania, Latvia, and Estonia) in 2008–09. Following large-scale privatizations in the 1990s and early 2000s, most banks in these countries were owned by foreign financial institutions from Sweden and Norway. These banks were able to absorb the losses associated with the downturn without suffocating the local economies through a massive credit crunch, an outcome that would most probably not have been achieved if the banking sector had been domestically owned. This factor played a significant role in the rapid rebound of growth in these countries after a severe downturn and fiscal adjustment. More generally, in Central and Eastern Europe, the large presence of foreign (mostly Western European) banks, which in several countries of the region represent more than half of total banking assets, helped absorb the initial shock of the crisis in 2008–09. It became a potential drag, however, when several of these banks, for example, those headquartered in Spain and Italy, were forced to reduce their exposures to the region because of problems in their home countries.

In this context, developing Asian countries should take a pragmatic and open approach to cross-border lending and cross-border bank ownership. The presence of foreign banks can provide significant and welcome competitive pressure, forcing domestic banks to improve their efficiency and to offer better-quality services, even if domestically headquartered banks retain the largest share of the local banking market, as is the case in most Asian jurisdictions. Similarly, the offshoring by domestic banks of some of their activities to regional or global financial centers, especially in wholesale market activities such as derivatives trading and asset management, can be a good thing for the local economy if it enables these banks to offer better-priced services based on those financial centers' critical size and depth. Most developing Asian countries should try to leverage the strength of existing regional financial centers, primarily Singapore and Hong Kong, China, rather than trying to create international financial centers of their own—a seductive objective for many developing countries but that more often than not results in costly failure to reach critical mass and attract international market participants.

In Asia, financial integration lags compared with economic integration more broadly, and the level of financial integration is typically higher with non-Asian countries than inside the region (Kim and Lee 2008, Borensztein and Loungani 2011, Pongsaparn and Unteroberdoerster 2011). This suggests a significant scope for allowing more cross-border financial services and investment without creating a risk to financial stability. Developing Asian countries might consider measures such as the reduction of tax and regulatory distortions between domestic and foreign banks and investors as well as adopt an open-minded approach to inward mergers and acquisitions in the banking and financial sector.

Developing Asia would also gain from a common institutional framework to level the playing field and ensure convergence in financial standards and practice. Realistically, the ambition should stop short of a seamlessly integrated single market in financial services. The experience in the European Union suggests that such "deep" financial integration can lead to destabilizing incentives for national authorities when it is not accompanied by a strong supranational supervisory and regulatory function, which is eventually being created in Europe (in particular with the euro area's banking union) but is not realistic in the Asian context (Dobson 2011).

Specifically, the Association of Southeast Asian Nations (ASEAN) endorsed a regional Banking Integration Framework in 2011 and is working on implementing it at a differentiated pace among its members. Unlike the European banking union, this development is unlikely to alter the ASEAN countries' fundamental reliance on national policy frameworks for banking sector soundness and financial stability (Wihardja 2013). Rather than emulating European banking integration, Asian countries could build on the existing institutional framework at the international level. International financial institutions have markedly improved the representation of Asian jurisdictions in their membership and decision-making bodies since the start of the financial crisis, mostly through a reduction (but not elimination) of the prior overrepresentation of European countries (figure 6.3).

This recent rebalancing, however, is not yet sufficient to ensure adequate "ownership" of these global institutions by Asian policymakers and public opinions. While the membership of the global bodies has evolved, their leadership remains heavily skewed toward nationals from the United States, Europe, Canada, and Australia (Véron 2014). Furthermore, their location in Europe and the United States creates an imbalance that makes it more difficult for Asians to engage, in terms of distance and time zones. The relocation of at least some of the existing institutions to Asia, as well as the establishment in Asia of any newly formed global financial regulatory organization, would improve the prospects for a more balanced system.[6]

---

6. Nicolas Véron, "Move the Financial Stability Board's Secretariat to Asia," RealTime Economic Issues Watch, Peterson Institute for International Economics, May 10, 2012, http://blogs.piie.com/realtime/?p=2871 (accessed on August 7, 2015).

**Figure 6.3   EU and Asian (excluding Japan) representation
in global financial bodies**

percent

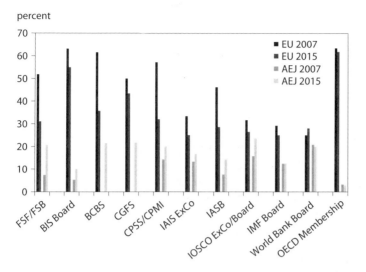

AEJ = Asia excluding Japan; EU = European Union; FSF/FSB = Financial Stability Forum/
Financial Stability Board; BIS = Bank for International Settlements; BCBS = Basel Committee
on Banking Supervision; CGFS = Committee on the Global Financial System;
CPSS/CPMI = Committee on Payment and Settlement Systems/Committee on Payments
and Market Infrastructures; IAIS ExCo = International Association of Insurance Supervisors
Executive Committee; IASB = International Accounting Standards Board; IOSCO ExCo = Inter
national Organization of Securities Commissions Executive Committee; IMF = International
Monetary Fund; OECD = Organisation for Economic Co-operation and Development
Sources: Institutional websites and authors' calculations.

Conclusion

Asian policymakers are right to put financial stability at the top of their
agendas, right to question whether Anglo-American turbo-charged financial
liberalization really serves development, and right to doubt that the measures
undertaken by the FSB and G-20 will provide their economies with adequate
or targeted buffers. The questioning, however, should not go so far as to result
in an excessive distrust of financial liberalization. The path to financial stability has more similarity across levels of development than may first appear.
Upon closer examination, it quickly becomes clear that similar sorts of crises
arise at all levels of financial development—the parallels between the Asian
crises of 1997–98 and the US/UK (2007–10) and euro area (2007–15) crises
are quite evident. If anything, the Americans and Europeans would likely have
done better in responding to their crises had they adhered to the recommendations they made to Asia a decade earlier (Rhee and Posen 2013). Of course,
financial stability and development are more than matters of crisis response,
so the common threads are a little less obvious than avoiding throwing good
money after bad and injecting capital where necessary.

We believe the most important parallel with respect to financial stability between the recent advanced economies' experience and the challenges facing Asian policymakers is the repeated failure of financial repression to provide stability. Across southern Europe even in recent years, and earlier in the American "heartland" and among the mid-sized banks in Japan, various forms of financial repression bottling up household savings in protected financial institutions were widespread—and instability still befell these economies. While the recent North Atlantic financial developments were importantly worsened by too big to fail distortions, in Europe in the 2010s, like in Japan in the 1990s and the United States in the 1980s, most of the problems were generated in and on the balance sheets of government-guaranteed smaller financial institutions (Goldstein and Véron 2011, Mikitani and Posen 2001). Similarly, cross-border capital flows also played a huge part in the buildup of unsustainable lending—be it in Greece or Nevada, Ireland or Florida—but those destabilizing inflows took place across a wide variety of exchange rate regimes, levels of development, and even domestic financial institutions.

Because there is no simple positive correlation between financial liberalization and instability, the optimal policy approach is not about achieving a lukewarm compromise between repression and liberalization. We have offered a few specific suggestions for Asian policymakers about how to implement a balanced strategy in practice. These general principles can be followed at most stages of economic and financial development and are not complicated matters of sequencing or conditionality depending upon what form development has taken to date.

This wide applicability comes from the fact that financial stability ultimately stems from having adequately varied sources of commercial credit and outlets for household savings, so that fragility—or even mismanagement or supervisory capture—of one piece of the system does not bring down the economy's whole framework. The greater depth and diversity of the US financial system versus the UK concentrated banking development meant the former contributed to a much better and more rapid recovery from crisis than was seen in the latter.[7] A similar argument could be made for Singapore versus some other smaller East Asian economies in 1997–98, or the resilience of Japan in 2008 versus 1988. Capital markets and local lenders are both good things to have.

Thus, our foremost recommendation is that Asian policymakers should promote diversity in domestic financial institutions, which is generally a factor of resilience and stability. This calls for diversification of national financial systems away from the dominance of banks and for openness to cross-border (though not necessarily foreign-currency) financial services and intermediar-

---

7. Adam Posen, "Why is their recovery better than ours? (Even though neither is good enough)," speech at the National Institute of Economic and Social Research, London, March 27, 2012, www.bankofengland.co.uk/publications/Documents/speeches/2012/speech560.pdf (accessed on August 7, 2015).

ies. This is indeed a call for continued financial liberalization where needed but not for laissez-faire supervision or the ongoing diminution of traditional banking or importation of all the latest financial innovations. The issue is one of institutional structures within the financial sector.[8]

We repeat that diversity is also a call for multiple financial institutions within any given (sub-)sector—that is, for number not just type. While the many examples cited indicate that problems can arise in protected small institutions like Spanish savings banks (*cajas*) or US savings and loans, that is simply a caution not to assume size is everything or that more players are always better. We fully endorse the idea that every developing economy should have more than one major bank or financial institution, even if a foreign-owned one, given all the political economy problems that too big to fail entails, and that there is no development advantage to promoting a financial "national champion"—what matters is the resilience of provision of financial services to the economy, which is better served by multiple players in type and number.[9]

Second, we recommend that financial repression be limited to those measures that can be equally characterized as strong prudential regulation—that put the focus on financial sector activities, the most destabilizing of which can be identified and restricted. So doing takes away the focus on restricting the location and investment vehicles of household savers. Bad financial repression of the sort focused on bottling up savings to subsidize lending is actually destabilizing for economies at all levels of development. Interest rate compression will lead to increasingly frantic efforts by savers to get around limits and even border controls, which will result in speculative bursts in limited asset classes to potentially great harm. Arguably, this is the source of the market instability and the real estate downturn in the PRC in 2015. Low interest rates or a large gap between what savers get and borrowers pay from what the market rate would be are not only an inefficient, often politicized, way to allocate resources but also contrary to financial stability goals. Again, a sensible set of policies includes strong regulatory oversight of financial activities without having to resort to either full-on liberalization or ongoing financial repression.

---

8. This statement is based solely on financial stability considerations. There is a historical and plausible economic argument that a Japan–Republic of Korea–Taipei,China bank-centric model fosters helpful industrial policy through a state-dominated banking system insulated from the outside world. While we are skeptical of the virtues of this approach, also shown to have limits in Western Europe, we recognize that policymakers in developing Asia will have to take into account the desire to follow this model in tradeoff with the financial stability benefits of a more open and diverse capital system. For a longer-term perspective on these developments, see Jeanne et al. (2014).

9. The pursuit of national champion banks even by global financial centers in an advanced economy is mistaken for the same reasons. See Adam Posen, "It's time the UK stopped 'fetish-ising' its banks," remarks at the Just Banking Conference, Edinburgh, April 19, 2012, www.ianfraser.org/boes-adam-posen-at-the-just-banking-conference (accessed on August 7, 2015).

Third, policymakers should carefully monitor the potential impact of the use of new information technology in finance in the next few years. While banks and other financial firms have not been subject to as much technology-based change as other sectors for the moment, such change is likely to become increasingly prominent as the potential of mobile services in finance is operationalized. The development of a data-centric culture, together with enhanced public transparency about financial firms and systems in compliance with international data standards, can help prepare for future disruptions. This is a situation where diversity and entry by new players can rapidly be taken too far, and some consumer protection as well as supervision is called for. In this area as well, there is room to distinguish between leapfrogging past constraints via mobile and internet in terms of payment systems, including government disbursement, which should be encouraged, and allowing a free-for-all in internet-driven trading and investment offers, which should not.

Asian policymakers need to develop an information and supervisory infrastructure that keeps pace with development—something that actually is feasible, so long as best practices can be imported and advised and so long as the presumption is "allow but only within the tent." Similar to the old saying "trust but verify," this means that policymakers concerned about financial stability can indicate that they are always open to new products and providers, but only so long as those new offers are under some form of disclosure, monitoring, and clear accountability for losses.

Less financially developed economies whose policymakers eschew financial fads and national champion banks can actually benefit from not having to be at the innovative cutting edge. There is little cost to the economy from using blunter tools than sometimes are available in the most advanced markets and from requiring all financial sector–like developments to be centrally monitored. Disputes over the cost of regulating financial innovation, and the risks that go with excessive game playing, can be left to the handful of global financial centers—so long as the policymaker of developing Asia is committed to ongoing relative innovation, that is bringing the domestic financial sector along toward the frontier of deepening markets. A similar argument is valid for the use of macroprudential tools in terms of blunt instruments to temper large sustained asset price swings: So long as the underlying and general commitment is to market-determined asset prices, financial and monetary policymakers need not worry about the occasional use of overwhelming force to stem, say, real estate bubbles fueled by foreign capital (as in fact a number of Asian authorities are rightly doing at the moment). In a less developed financial system, such tools should be more effective than in economies where financial innovation and globalization shields some financial activities from macroprudential policies' reach. That should give Asian policymakers the confidence to continue to pursue financial development, just not at breakneck speed.

References*

Asdrubali, Pierfederico, Bent Sørensen, and Oved Yosha. 1996. Channels of Interstate Risk Sharing: United States 1963–90. *Quarterly Journal of Economics* 111: 1081–110.

BCBS (Basel Committee on Banking Supervision). 2013. *Basel III: The Liquidity Coverage Ratio and Liquidity Risk Monitoring Tools* (January). Basel: Bank for International Settlements. Available at www.bis.org/publ/bcbs238.pdf (accessed on July 29, 2015).

BCBS (Basel Committee on Banking Supervision). 2014. *The Net Stable Funding Ratio* (October). Basel: Bank for International Settlements. Available at www.bis.org/bcbs/publ/d295.pdf (accessed on July 29, 2015).

Borensztein, Eduardo, and Prakash Loungani. 2011. *Asian Financial Integration: Trends and Interruptions.* IMF Working Paper WP/11/4 (January). Washington: International Monetary Fund.

Borio, Claudio. 2003. *Towards a macro-prudential framework for financial supervision and regulation?* BIS Working Paper 128 (February). Basel: Bank for International Settlements.

Claessens, Stijn. 2014. *An Overview of Macroprudential Policy Tools.* IMF Working Paper WP/14/214 (December). Washington: International Monetary Fund.

Clement, Piet. 2010. The term "macroprudential": Origins and evolution. *BIS Quarterly Review* (March). Basel: Bank for International Settlements.

Cline, William R. 2010. *Financial Globalization, Economic Growth, and the Crisis of 2007–2009.* Washington: Peterson Institute for International Economics.

Demirgüç-Kunt, Asli, and Enrica Detragiache. 2000. *Does Deposit Insurance Increase Banking System Stability?* IMF Working Paper WP/00/3 (January). Washington: International Monetary Fund.

Dobson, Wendy. 2011. Asia's evolving economic institutions: Roles and future prospects. *East Asia Forum* (August 21).

European Commission. 2015. *Green Paper: Building a Capital Markets Union.* Communication COM(2015) 63 (February). Brussels.

FSB and IMF (Financial Stability Board and International Monetary Fund). 2014. *The Financial Crisis and Information Gaps: Fifth Progress Report on the Implementation of the G-20 Data Gaps Initiative* (September). Basel and Washington.

Goldstein, Morris, and Nicolas Véron. 2011. *Too Big to Fail: The Transatlantic Debate.* PIIE Working Paper 11-2. Washington: Peterson Institute for International Economics.

Gorton, Gary. 2009. *Slapped in the Face by the Invisible Hand: Banking and the Panic of 2007* (May). Yale School of Management and National Bureau of Economic Research.

Goswani, Mangal, and Sunil Sharma. 2011. *The Development of Local Debt Markets in Asia.* IMF Working Paper WP/11/132 (June). Washington: International Monetary Fund.

IMF (International Monetary Fund). 2009. *Global Financial Stability Report: Responding to the Financial Crisis and Measuring Systemic Risks* (April). Washington.

IMF (International Monetary Fund). 2013. *Towards a Fiscal Union for the Euro Area: Technical Background Notes* (September). Washington.

Jeanne, Olivier. 2014. Capital Flow Management and Macroprudential Policies in Asia. In *Asian Capital Market Development and Integration: Challenges and Opportunities,* ed. Asian Development Bank and Korea Capital Market Institute. Oxford University Press.

---

*The Asian Development Bank recognizes "China" by the name the People's Republic of China.

Jeanne, Olivier, Marcus Noland, Arvind Subramanian, and John Williamson. 2014. Financial Globalization and Long-Run Growth: Is Asia Different? In *Asian Capital Market Development and Integration: Challenges and Opportunities,* ed. Asian Development Bank and Korea Capital Market Institute. Oxford University Press.

Kim, Soyoung, and Jong-Wha Lee. 2008. *Real and Financial Integration in East Asia.* ADB Working Paper on Regional Economic Integration no. 17 (June). Manila: Asian Development Bank. Available at www.adb.org/publications/real-and-financial-integration-east-asia Manila.

Langfield, Sam, and Marco Pagano. 2015. *Bank bias in Europe: effects on systemic risk and growth.* ECB Working Paper no. 1797 (May). Frankfurt: European Central Bank.

Lardy, Nicholas R. 2014. *Markets over Mao: The Rise of Private Business in China.* Washington: Peterson Institute for International Economics.

Mikitani, Ryoichi, and Adam S. Posen. 2001. *Japan's Financial Crisis and Its Parallels to US Experience.* Special Report 13. Washington: Institute for International Economics.

Opper, Sonja, Fredrik N. G. Andersson, and Katarzyna Burzynska. 2013. *Lending for Growth? An Analysis of State-owned Banks in China.* Department of Economics, Lund University, Working Paper Series 07/2013. Lund, Sweden.

Pacter, Paul. 2015. *IFRS as global standards: a pocket guide.* IFRS Foundation.

Philippon, Thomas, and Nicolas Véron. 2008. *Financing Europe's Fast Movers.* Bruegel Policy Brief 2008/01 (January). Brussels: Bruegel.

Pongsaparn, Runchana, and Olaf Unteroberdoerster. 2011. *Financial Integration and Rebalancing in Asia.* IMF Working Paper WP/11/243 (October). Washington: International Monetary Fund.

Posen, Adam, and Nicolas Véron. 2009. *A Solution for Europe's Banking Problem.* PIIE Policy Brief 09-13 (June). Washington: Peterson Institute for International Economics.

Pozsar, Zoltan, Tobias Adrian, Adam Ashcraft, and Hayley Boesky. 2010. *Shadow Banking* (July). New York: Federal Reserve Bank of New York.

Rhee, Changyong, and Adam S. Posen, eds. 2013. *Responding to Financial Crisis: Lessons from Asia Then, the United States and Europe Now.* Manila and Washington: Asian Development Bank and Peterson Institute for International Economics.

Rottier, Stéphane, and Nicolas Véron. 2010. *Not All Financial Regulation Is Global.* PIIE Policy Brief 10-22. Washington: Peterson Institute for International Economics.

Véron, Nicolas. 2014. Asia's Changing Position in Global Financial Reform. In *Asian Capital Market Development and Integration: Challenges and Opportunities,* ed. Asian Development Bank and Korea Capital Market Institute. Oxford University Press.

Véron, Nicolas, and Guntram Wolff. 2015. *Capital Markets Union: A Vision for the Long Term.* Bruegel Policy Contribution 2015/05 (April). Brussels: Bruegel.

Veugelers, Reinhilde. 2011. *Mind Europe's Early-Stage Equity Gap.* Bruegel Policy Contribution 2011/18 (December). Brussels: Bruegel.

Walter, Andrew. 2015. *Emerging Countries and Basel III: Why Is Engagement Still Low?* (March). Center for International Governance Innovation.

Wihardja, Maria Monica. 2013. *Financial Integration Challenges in ASEAN beyond 2015.* ERIA Discussion Paper ERIA-DP-2013-27 (November). Jakarta: Economic Research Institute for ASEAN and East Asia.

Zhang, Longmei, and Edda Zoli. 2014. *Leaning Against the Wind: Macroprudential Policy in Asia.* IMF Working Paper WP/14/22 (February). Washington: International Monetary Fund.

7

Enhancing Bank Supervision in Asia:
Lessons Learned from the Financial Crisis

MICHAEL J. ZAMORSKI and MINSOO LEE

Financial integration in emerging Asia increased over the past decade, as close linkages across economies developed. Regional initiatives to create more competitive, open, and internationalized financial sectors—such as the Association of Southeast Asian Nations (ASEAN) Banking Integration Framework—reinforced this trend.[1] A key priority is to ensure that regulatory and supervisory regimes support this changing environment by controlling the related risks to financial stability.

This chapter highlights the key attributes of effective supervision and regulation needed to enable emerging Asia's banking systems to support sound, sustainable growth and development. The analysis considers lessons learned from the 2007–08 financial crisis in the United States and Europe, insights from the International Monetary Fund (IMF)/World Bank Financial Sector Assessment Program (FSAP), the features and context of emerging Asia's banking industry, and postcrisis efforts to reform and enhance international bank regulatory and supervisory standards and practices.

Michael J. Zamorski is an advisor on financial stability and supervision for the South East Asian Central Banks (SEACEN) Research and Training Centre. Minsoo Lee is senior economist in the Macroeconomics Research Division of the Economic Research and Regional Cooperation Department at the Asian Development Bank.

1. ASEAN central bank governors endorsed the ASEAN Banking Integration Framework in April 2011 (Wihardja 2013).

Causes of the 2007–08 Crisis and the Need for Enhanced Supervision

The crisis caused central bankers and regulators around the world to reflect on several questions:

- What were the root causes of the crisis?
- Why did regulators and policymakers fail to see the crisis coming, especially given its severity and wide-ranging and systemic effects?
- With the passage of time and opportunity for reflection, what lessons were learned for national authorities and policymakers seeking to avoid future crises?

In an attempt to offset the adverse economic effects of the financial crisis and stimulate economic growth, many central banks, particularly in the advanced economies at the epicenter of the crisis, lowered policy rates to zero or near zero. They also implemented other accommodative policy measures, such as quantitative easing. The resultant ultralow interest rate environment in many markets induced a global search for yield among investors. Significant capital flowed into emerging markets, including emerging Asia, where higher returns were available and economic growth prospects more favorable.

Economies receiving sizable amounts of foreign investors' funds have to carefully manage the risks of these potentially volatile capital inflows, which can cause unsustainable asset price inflation in local markets. They also need to be prepared for the possibility of substantial capital flow reversals when investor sentiment changes and better returns become available elsewhere. In countries where capital inflows fuel rapid rises in asset prices, bank supervisors need to ensure that institutions' lending decisions, particularly for commercial and residential real estate mortgages, are based on borrowers' sustainable cash flow/repayment capacity and not on the presumption of continuing increases in the value of real estate collateral.

Effective bank regulation and supervision is critical to ensuring that stable and resilient banks are well positioned to meet the productive credit needs of their customers and allow depositors to accumulate savings, which provides a stable funding source for loan portfolio growth. A sound banking system is one in which problems are manageable. If failures do occur, they are not large or systemic, and their overall impact is small. Banks and other regulated financial intermediaries remain willing and able to meet prudent requests for credit.

A key goal of supervision is the reduction of systemic risk. A 2001 Group of Ten (G-10) report on financial sector consolidation describes systemic financial risk as "the risk that an event will trigger a loss of economic value or confidence in, and attendant increases in uncertainty about, a substantial portion of the financial system that is serious enough to quite probably have significant adverse effects on the real economy" (BIS 2001, 126).

Table 7.1   Median outcomes of banking crises, by type of economy, 1970–2011

	All	Advanced	Emerging	Developing
Output loss (percent of GDP)	23.0	32.9	26.0	1.6
Increase in debt (percent of GDP)	12.1	21.4	9.1	10.9
Monetary expansion (percent of GDP)	1.7	8.3	1.3	1.2
Fiscal costs (percent of GDP)	6.8	3.8	10.0	10.0
Fiscal costs (percent of financial system assets)	12.7	2.1	21.4	18.3
Duration (years)	2.0	3.0	2.0	1.0
Peak liquidity (percent of deposits and foreign liabilities)	20.1	11.5	22.3	22.6
Liquidity support (percent of deposits and foreign liabilities)	9.6	5.7	11.1	12.3
Peak nonperforming loans (percent of total loans)	25.0	4.0	30.0	37.5

Source: Laeven and Valencia (2012).

A joint report by the IMF, the Bank for International Settlements (BIS), and the Financial Stability Board describes systemic risk as the "risk of disruption to financial services that (a) is caused by an impairment of all or parts of the financial system and (b) has the potential to have serious negative consequences for the real economy."[2] Fundamental to this definition is the notion of negative externalities from a disruption or failure in a financial institution, market, or instrument. "All types of financial intermediaries, markets, and infrastructure can potentially be systemically important to some degree" (IMF, BIS, and FSB 2009, 2).

The regulatory and financial stability reform agendas being pursued by international standard-setters such as the Financial Stability Board and the Basel Committee on Banking Supervision are intended to both reduce the probability that banks will fail and mitigate the costs of failures and preserve public confidence in the banking system should failures occur.

The direct and indirect costs of financial crises are typically very high. Adverse impacts to the real economy include curtailment of economic output, constrained availability of credit, and declines in asset values. Luc Laeven and Fabian Valencia (2012) analyze banking, currency, and sovereign debt crises between 1970 and 2011. They identify 134 systemic banking crises during this 42-year period and quantify the economic impact (table 7.1).[3]

---

2. "The Financial Stability Board was established in April 2009 as successor to the Financial Stability Forum." Its mandate is to serve as "a mechanism for national authorities, standard setting bodies and international financial institutions to address vulnerabilities and to develop and implement strong regulatory, supervisory and other policies in the interest of financial stability" (www.financialstabilityboard.org/about/history). A comprehensive description of the FSB's various initiatives is available at www.financialstabilityboard.org.

3. They consider a banking crisis to be systemic if there are "significant signs of financial distress in the banking system (as indicated by significant bank runs, losses in the banking system,

The Basel Committee's Core Principles for Effective Supervision

The Bank for International Settlements (BIS), located in Basel, Switzerland, is owned by the world's central banks and monetary authorities.[4] It seeks to promote international cooperation among central banks and other regulators and global financial stability.

Toward those ends, it sponsors various financial sector regulatory and supervisory standard-setting committees, which identify and promulgate sound regulatory and supervisory practices and standards. These committees cover the supervision and regulation of the banking, insurance, and securities (capital markets) industries; payment and settlement systems; and cross-sectoral financial stability issues. Committee members include top regulators and policymakers from member jurisdictions. Although the committees' pronouncements do not have the force of law, as the BIS and its sponsored committees have no supranational supervisory or regulatory authority, their expert consensus pronouncements commonly form the basis of countries' financial sector laws, regulations, and policies.

The Basel Committee on Banking Supervision (BCBS or Basel Committee), founded in 1974, is the oldest of the BIS standard-setters. It provides a forum for cooperation on supervisory matters, develops international standards and sound practices for the global banking industry, and encourages convergence toward common approaches.

It is perhaps best known for its development and promulgation of international capital standards. But it has also performed ground-breaking work in identifying the preconditions for effective bank supervision programs. These conditions are embodied in the "Core Principles for Effective Supervision" (known as the Basel Core Principles, or BCP).

The BCP were first issued in 1997 and revised in 2006 and 2012. The 2012 BCP enumerate 29 Core Principles (CPs) that identify infrastructure, minimum standards, and approaches to an effective bank supervision program. The BCP provide a framework against which bank regulatory authorities can benchmark their bank supervision programs through self-assessments. The IMF and World Bank use the BCP to assess the effectiveness of jurisdictions' bank supervision regimes during their FSAP reviews.

The BCP represent important preconditions for an effective supervisory system. However, the ultimate test of supervisory effectiveness is whether a prudential supervisor's actual practices in implementing the BCP and the regulator's supervisory culture result in the detection and curtailment of

---

and/or bank liquidations)" and "significant banking policy intervention measures in response to significant losses in the banking system" (Laeven and Valencia 2012, 4). The complete dataset is available at www.imf.org/external/pubind.htm.

4. This section is adapted from Zamorski (2013a).

imprudent risk taking or other unsound practices at their incipient stages. The effectiveness of the BCP also depends on the existence of basic supportive national circumstances and infrastructure, such as political stability, the rule of law, property rights, and credible accounting and financial reporting standards.

Assessment Methodology

The BCP detail the specific criteria for assessing CP compliance, the definition of the grading system, and practical considerations in conducting assessments. Each CP is intended to apply to the prudential supervision of all banks, ranging from small deposit-taking institutions to large, complex, internationally active banks. The BCP recognize that supervisory resources should be allocated in proportion to the risk profile and systemic importance of banks (BCBS 2012a).

Assessment criteria have been specified for each CP. They are designated as either "Essential Criteria" ("minimum baseline requirements for sound supervisory practices universally applicable to all countries") or "Additional Criteria" ("supervisory practices that exceed current baseline expectations but will contribute to the robustness of individual supervisory frameworks") (BCBS 2012, 7–8). Compliance is assessed on a four-grade scale: compliant, largely compliant, materially noncompliant, and noncompliant. FSAP BCP assessments grade compliance based only on the "Essential Criteria," though a jurisdiction can voluntarily choose to be assessed against the "Additional Criteria" as well.

Rationale for 2012 Revisions

The objective of the 2012 BCP revisions was to maintain their relevance as global standards of good practice by incorporating lessons learned from the US/eurozone crisis of 2007–08 and feedback from the FSAP process.[5] Revisions of the CP assessment criteria reflect the need for

- greater supervisory intensity and adequate resources to deal effectively with systemically important banks,
- application of a systemwide, macro perspective to the microprudential supervision of banks, to assist in identifying, analyzing, and taking preemptive action to address systemic risk, and
- sharper focus on effective crisis management, recovery, and resolution measures in order to reduce the probability and impact of bank failures (BCBS 2012b).

---

5. The revised BCP are available at www.bis.org/publ/bcbs230.htm.

The revised BCP were restructured to make clearer what bank supervisors need to do and what they expect banks to do. CPs 1 through 13 address supervisory powers, responsibilities, and functions. They focus on effective risk-based supervision and the need for early intervention and timely supervisory actions. CPs 14 through 29 address the supervisory expectations of banks.[6] They emphasize the importance of good corporate governance and risk management, as well as compliance with supervisory standards (BCBS 2012).

A new CP was added for corporate governance, reflecting its importance in ensuring institutional and systemic stability. It emphasizes that corporate governance is the responsibility of banks' boards and senior management. Two other new CPs significantly expand coverage of supervisory independence, powers, transparency, and cooperation, which were previously covered in a single CP. They recommend greater public disclosure and transparency and enhanced financial reporting and external audit.

Self-Assessment

The BCBS encourages bank supervisory authorities "to move towards the adoption of updated and new international supervisory standards as they are issued" (BCBS 2012, 5). Bank supervisors should coordinate with other relevant national authorities to conduct self-assessments using the revised BCP. Some jurisdictions have publicly disclosed their BCP self-assessments in the interest of transparency and accountability.

When internal and external BCP assessments disclose less than full compliance with individual CPs, remedial action should be pursued to achieve full compliance. Such action may require changes in laws, rules, regulations, procedures, policies, and/or supervisory practices. The BCBS issued a paper in 2001 to help jurisdictions produce comprehensive, credible, and action-oriented self-assessments of their supervisory systems.

Lessons Learned from the 2007–08 Crisis

Assessments of the financial crisis identified long lists of contributing factors. The most important factors are discussed here.[7]

---

6. Early intervention refers to banking laws, such as "prompt corrective action" (PCA) statutes, that require bank supervisors to place increasingly stringent operating restrictions on undercapitalized banks as their capital declines. The general objective of PCA is to close nonviable institutions or transfer their operations to new ownership well before book capital is zero or negative, in order to minimize losses to deposit insurers, depositors, and other creditors. Restrictions can include dividend prohibitions, curtailment of nondeposit borrowings or asset growth, and executive compensation limitations.

7. This section is adapted from Zamorski (2012).

Bank Supervision Was Too Weak

Ineffective financial sector regulation and supervision contributed to both the onset and severity of the crisis. Some of the most frequently cited supervision-related causes include the following:

- laxity in allowing banks to operate with excessive leverage
- failure to curtail unsafe and unsound lending, primarily residential real estate mortgages to subprime borrowers, that was based on the "support" provided by perceived collateral values, without realistic property appraisals or verification and analysis of borrowers' repayment capacity
- failure to conduct regular on-site supervisory inspections or examinations at reasonable intervals and in sufficient depth
- improper implementation of the concept of risk-based supervision[8]
- failure to identify ineffective bank risk management methods and governance structures and shortcomings in bank risk cultures
- overemphasis on institutions' historic operating results and static financial conditions in assessing risk, without fully considering potential vulnerabilities
- overreliance on off-site surveillance systems, which rely on banks' self-reported data, to monitor bank risk
- failure to understand the risks and policy implications of new bank products and services and changing bank business models
- ineffective communications/information sharing between domestic and foreign supervisors.

Analyses by the IMF, the Financial Stability Board, and the Basel Committee identified additional causal factors:

- failure to adequately monitor and control macroprudential risks (monitoring that focused on the risks in individual institutions failed to consider that a buildup of macroeconomic risks and vulnerabilities could adversely affect multiple institutions simultaneously, posing systemic risk)
- analytical approaches that focused too narrowly on financial modeling, in some cases with unrealistic inputs and assumptions and without adequate analysis and interpretation of model outputs
- failure to conduct comprehensive stress testing of the banking system and other economic sectors, including low-probability/high-impact scenarios

---

8. Risk-based supervision refers to the allocation of finite supervisory resources to the greatest areas of banks' perceived risk. In the context of an on-site supervisory examination, it refers to preplanning and risk-scoping examinations that focus on the most important risk areas.

- insufficient attention to concentrations of risk and interdependencies, including cross-border risks
- failure to consider risks in the shadow banking industry or cross-sectoral risks posed by nonbank financial intermediaries.[9]

Bank Supervision Needs to Be Timely and Proactive

For bank supervision to be effective, it must be timely, proactive, anticipatory, and forward looking. It must detect potential problems early. There is no substitute for a regular program of on-site examinations or inspections conducted by experienced professional bank examiners who perform a reasonable level of transaction testing.

On-site interactions with bank management provide examiners with the opportunity to understand a bank's risk management capabilities and assess the quality and depth of its executive management team and the quality of oversight provided by its board of directors. Corporate governance and risk management competencies are a key part of examiners' forward-looking analyses to assess the resiliency of a bank to the onset of unfavorable business conditions. When unacceptable practices or conditions are disclosed during an examination, bank supervisors need to ensure that the bank takes timely remedial action.

Bank supervisors need to be aware of banks' changing business strategies and product offerings as close to real time as possible, in order to practice proactive supervision and prevent problems. Banks can modify their strategies and risk appetite quickly, changing their overall risk profile. These changes may not be immediately detectible through off-site monitoring techniques. Bank business strategies and product offerings may change, possibly creating excessive risks or raising other concerns that call for the issuance of timely guidance from regulators.

There are no universally accepted standards or guidelines regarding the priority, frequency, and scope of on-site examinations. Practices vary across jurisdictions, but annual full-scope on-site examinations, supplemented by interim regulatory reporting, seem to be common.

In an attempt to be more proactive, some regulators conduct "thematic reviews," which entail selecting a sample of banks and conducting on-site reviews of a particular issue or risk area. (A thematic review could be conducted for commercial real estate lending, for example.) Bank examiners review individual institutions' practices and follow up on areas of concern. Common concerns emanating from all of the reviews could form the basis for an industry alert or policy guidance from regulators to try to control these risks

---

9. The FSB describes shadow banking as parts of the financial system that extend credit but are outside the regular banking sector. FSB (2013) contains a comprehensive discussion of shadow banking and associated financial stability risks.

proactively, as some banks might not be scheduled to receive a near-term examination.

Off-Site Surveillance of Banks Helps Identify Potential Problems

Off-site surveillance of banks is based on periodic (usually at least quarterly) unaudited/unverified self-reporting of their financial positions and operating results to regulators and the public using standardized datasets. There can be significant time lags between financial reporting dates and public availability of the data (which promotes market discipline), though regulators typically have earlier access.

Off-site surveillance is not a substitute for on-site examinations, though it enables analysis of the level and trend of key financial ratios and peer group comparisons, which are important in detecting red flags and identifying outliers. This information can then be used to prioritize on-site examination activities and allocate examiner resources to the areas of greatest perceived risk. Some regulators have developed proprietary monitoring systems that attempt to predict changing bank risk profiles and ratings based on the level and trend of key financial ratios and peer group comparisons.

Macroprudential Policy Should Be Used to Control Systemic Risk

The crisis underscored the urgent need for national bank supervisory authorities to improve surveillance systems to detect, at their incipient stages, the buildup of macroeconomic risks, vulnerabilities, or threats that could jeopardize the stability of the financial system.[10] Macroprudential policies are designed to safeguard systemic financial stability. They consist of measures that can be taken, alone or in concert with other policy actions, to avert, dampen, or mitigate periods of instability or crisis. To safeguard systemic financial stability, macroprudential policy requires a rich set of instruments to prevent and mitigate financial stability risks—related to credit, liquidity, and capital risks—stemming from vulnerabilities building up in the broader financial system.[11]

The BCBS is increasingly guided by the need for a macroprudential perspective in financial regulation. Much progress has been made on the regulatory front, especially with the Basel III rules on the quantity and quality of bank capital (e.g., countercyclical capital buffers). Macroprudential policy aims to enhance the system's resilience to shocks and to limit the buildup of systemic risk. Efforts are directed toward identifying systemic risks to financial markets, strengthening the resilience of the financial system to preserve financial stability, and avoiding a recurrence of crisis.

---

10. This section is adapted from Zamorski (2013b).

11. The scope of macroprudential policy covers banking, insurance, pension funds, financial infrastructures, and shadow banking.

Macroprudential policy measures fall into three broad categories (Lim et al. 2011):

■ credit controls (caps on the loan-to-value ratio, the debt-to-income ratio, and foreign currency lending as well as ceilings on credit or credit growth),

■ regulation of liquidity (limits on net open currency positions or currency mismatches, limits on maturity mismatches, and reserve requirements), and

■ capital requirements (countercyclical capital requirements, time-varying/ dynamic positioning, and restrictions on profit distribution).

Macroprudential tools (such as minimum capital ratios and loan-to-value ratios) have been used for some time. Having dealt with previous threats to financial stability, especially from volatile capital flows, Asian countries have experience implementing a variety of macroprudential measures to prevent or address asset price bubbles or other threats to financial stability.

Emerging economies, mostly bank-dominated economies, with less developed financial systems tend to face greater challenges in managing the consequences of the procyclicality of financial system and cross-border financial linkages. The use of macroprudential measures in advanced economies and emerging markets depends on the economy's financial structure and the characteristics of the financial market (Claessens, Ghosh, and Mihet 2013).

The macroprudential approach has a time dimension and a cross-sectional dimension. In the time dimension, the source of systemwide distress can be the procyclicality of the financial system: financial institutions and markets overexpose themselves to risks in the upswing of the financial cycle and then become overly risk averse in the downswing, leaving the entire financial system and economy vulnerable to booms and busts. The cross-sectional dimension of systemic risk arises from the interconnectedness of financial institutions and markets: the actions and problems of individuals or financial institutions can have spillover effects on the overall financial system. Given their interconnectedness, the contemporary market-based financial sector should be thought of as including not only deposit-taking, loan-making commercial banks but also investment banks, money market funds, insurance companies, and potentially even hedge funds and private equity funds.

Operationalizing macroprudential policies is a challenge given that it is largely a judgmental process, albeit one informed by empirical analyses. Moreover, even if macroprudential policy measures appear to achieve desired policy objectives, it can be difficult to establish the efficacy of policy actions.

Responsibility for implementing various macroprudential measures may reside in different national authorities. Monetary, fiscal, and tax policies can affect systemic risk. Policy actions therefore require close cooperation and coordination by domestic authorities to ensure that they do not have contradictory goals or offset one another.

The BCBS (2012) notes that "the recent crisis highlighted the interface between, and the complementary nature of, the macroprudential and microprudential elements of effective supervision." Macroprudential approaches and methods do not supplant microprudential activities, especially the need to conduct on-site examinations at reasonable intervals that include an appropriate level of transaction testing. There is also a need for off-site surveillance systems that allow ongoing monitoring of industry trends and identification of outliers through peer group comparisons and other analytical methods. As Jaime Caruana (2012), the general manager of the BIS, has pointed out, macroprudential policy tools "are inadequate in the absence of effective and at times intrusive supervision: the incentives for regulatory arbitrage are simply too powerful." Indeed, a conglomerate could avoid the impact of a jurisdiction's macroprudential policy actions by moving activities to a subsidiary in a jurisdiction that has not implemented such measures. Cross-border coordination of policy actions might prevent such regulatory arbitrage, though doing so may be difficult given differing national circumstances.

Other Lessons

One of the most comprehensive and insightful sources of detailed information about the root causes of US bank failures and the performance of bank supervisors before and during the crisis is the material loss reviews (MLRs) conducted by inspectors general for US banking supervisory authorities— the Federal Reserve Board of Governors; the Department of the Treasury (the regulator for federally chartered banks, the Office of the Comptroller of the Currency [OCC], is part of Treasury); and the Federal Deposit Insurance Corporation (FDIC). The inspectors general are nominated by the president of the United States and confirmed by the US Senate; they are operationally independent of the agencies whose activities they oversee. Their mandate is to conduct performance audits of agency operations. MLRs are prepared when bank failures result in significant losses to the FDIC or failures that involve unusual circumstances.

In 2013 FDIC Inspector General Jon T. Rymer testified before the US Senate Committee on Banking, Housing, and Urban Affairs regarding the agencies' MLR findings about the financial crisis, in which more than 400 US banks failed and some of the country's largest institutions required governmental intervention. Factors for the failures cited in the MLR included the following:

- aggressive bank growth strategies,
- concentrations of asset (mostly loans) risks,
- poor loan underwriting standards,
- deficient credit administration practices, and
- precipitous declines in real estate values (commercial real estate values fell more than 42 percent).

In his testimony Rymer stated:

> In response to unprecedented circumstances, the regulators generally fulfilled their supervisory and resolution responsibilities as defined by statutes, regulations accounting standards, and interagency guidance in place at the time.... However, material loss review findings...showed that the FRB [Federal Reserve Board], OCC, and FDIC could have provided earlier and greater supervisory attention to troubled institutions that ultimately failed.[12]

The Financial Sector Assessment Program

The IMF and the World Bank conduct periodic assessments of member countries' overall financial stability through the FSAP (IMF 2014a). These reviews began in 1999, after the 1997–98 Asian financial crisis and other costly and disruptive episodes of financial instability and banking system crises, many of which involved multiple jurisdictions (IMF 2014b).

The severity of the global financial crisis caused the IMF and World Bank to evaluate whether precrisis FSAPs adequately identified risks and vulnerabilities, given lessons learned from the authorities' performance in handling the crisis. Based on this review, in 2009 they revised the FSAP to achieve "more systematic, candid, and transparent" financial stability assessments.[13]

As of August 2014, 144 member countries had requested and undergone FSAPs, most of them more than once. The IMF conducts 14 to 16 FSAPs a year, at an annual cost of $13 million to $15 million (IMF 2014a).

FSAPs are an important part of the IMF's ongoing surveillance activities, providing independent assessments of the strength and resiliency of countries' economies and financial system infrastructure.[14] They are based primarily on on-site missions and other field work performed by experienced teams of trained assessors, including subject matter experts in various aspects of financial stability.

---

12. Lessons Learned from the Financial Crisis Regarding Community Banks, statement of Jon T. Rymer, Inspector General, Federal Deposit Insurance Corporation, June 13, 2013, before the Committee on Banking, Housing, and Urban Affairs, US Senate, www.fdicig.gov/testimony%5CIG_Statement_FinCrisis061313.pdf, page 3.

13. Key revisions included closer analysis of linkages between the broader economy and the financial sector; coverage of a wider variety of sources of risk; presentation of a Risk Assessment Matrix in FSAP reports; and greater emphasis on cross-country links, spillover effects, and coordination arrangements.

14. The views expressed in FSAP reports are based on the information available at the time they were completed. The views expressed are those of the staff and do not necessarily reflect the views of the government of the jurisdiction being assessed or the Executive Board of the IMF. FSAP reports contain a qualification similar to the following: "FSAP assessments are designed to assess the stability of the financial system as a whole and not that of individual institutions. They have been developed to help countries identify and remedy weaknesses in their financial sector structure, thereby enhancing their resilience to macroeconomic shocks and cross-border contagion. FSAP assessments do not cover risks that are specific to individual institutions, such as asset quality, operational or legal risks, or fraud."

Mandatory FSAP assessments are conducted at least once every five years for the 29 jurisdictions deemed to have systemically important financial sectors (IMF 2014a). The IMF publishes the results in its Financial System Stability Assessment reports, accessible on its website.[15]

Although the coverage and scope of FSAPs are similar, they are not identical. They are tailored to a country's stage of economic development and the composition, size, and complexity of its banking system and financial markets. FSAPs typically address countries' current macroeconomic conditions, performance during the crisis, recent economic performance and future prospects, systemic resiliency to internal and external shocks, and whether financial sector supervision and regulation meet international standards.

FSAP reports contain a wide variety of findings, conclusions, and recommendations for remedial action, reflecting the diverse characteristics of the jurisdictions reviewed. The FSAP report is the core country assessment document. Multiple supporting documents provide more detailed analyses and commentary.

The FSAPs usually emphasize the following issues:

- macroeconomic and macroprudential stress testing,
- compliance with the BCP and the soundness of actual supervisory practices,
- crisis preparedness and resolution, and
- countries' financial stability self-assessments.

Many countries conduct periodic financial stability self-assessments, using criteria and approaches similar to those used in the FSAP. Self-assessments inform policymakers about potential risks and vulnerabilities to financial stability. They also consider whether a jurisdiction's infrastructure and approaches to promoting financial stability meet international standards.

The Challenge of Providing Consolidated Supervision of Financial and Banking Conglomerates

The past 20 years have seen the emergence and expansion of many large banking conglomerates throughout emerging Asia. Some of these institutions operate systemically important banks in more than one country. The structures of companies providing banking and other financial services continue to evolve as institutions seek to expand their geographic reach and achieve

---

15. A searchable index of FSAP and ancillary reports issued since 2001 is available at www.imf. org/external/np/fsap/fsap.aspx. This page also contains links to IMF documents that provide an in-depth discussion of the FSAP process and related matters. IMF surveillance and FSAP assessment activities for a jurisdiction are sometimes conveyed in multiple reports, each providing detailed assessments of a particular risk area or conformity to international standards and practices. FSAP findings may incorporate or reference the findings of these reports in an overall country assessment that is presented in a Financial System Stability Assessment report, commonly referred to as an FSSA report.

economies of scale and scope as restrictions on banks' affiliations and permissible activities are relaxed or removed in many countries.

Some banking organizations are part of large, multitiered conglomerates with complex organizational/ownership structures. Organizational structures include financial conglomerates that provide traditional banking services (focused on deposit taking and lending) as well as other financial services, such as insurance, securities brokerage, and investment banking. Banking organizations may also be affiliated with, or owned by, commercial enterprises (such organizations are known as mixed-activity conglomerates). Some of these conglomerates' subsidiaries or activities may be unregulated.

Gaps in supervisory oversight, unregulated activities, and other opacities within a financial conglomerate may inhibit the timely detection of financial weaknesses or excessive risks. Various mechanisms, such as intercompany transactions, can allow problems in one part of a conglomerate to rapidly spread and infect other parts. Such contagion risk can affect the financial soundness of bank subsidiaries.

Banking conglomerates typically identify, measure, monitor, and control risk on a consolidated group basis. Consolidated risk profiles can obscure potential weaknesses or contagion risk within a banking group, however. Although conglomerates' subsidiary banks have the same controlling owners, they have different depositors and creditors, to whom their boards of directors have legal/fiduciary responsibilities.[16] The directors of affiliated banks must determine that affiliate transactions are in the best interests of the bank they serve and do not jeopardize the safety of depositors' funds.

Affiliated banks' capital and liquidity are not fungible; funds cannot be moved around within a conglomerate at will. To prevent the transmission of problems throughout a banking group, many jurisdictions have well-defined rules governing affiliate transactions. These rules may include restrictions on the movement of capital, such as dividend limitations, and stringent requirements for loans between and among affiliated banks, including conservative limits on amounts and requirements for collateral in excess of the loan amount (for example, 120 percent of the loan), to protect against declines in collateral values.

Banking conglomerates or individual banks may move activities or risks off their balance sheets to other legal entities within a banking group or to sister banks or other affiliates in different jurisdictions, including unregulated entities, in order to evade or circumvent legal prohibitions or take advantage of less stringent (or no) legal requirements, laxer supervision, or even the ab-

---

16. Legal definitions of "control" vary across jurisdictions but typically specify a threshold percentage of ownership deemed to constitute control. In the United States, for example, 25 percent ownership of voting stock may constitute control. However, the determination of whether control exists may require the bank supervisory agency to make subjective judgments. For example, a group of individuals may have individual stockholdings below the specified control threshold, but they may be deemed to be exercising control if their combined ownership exceeds the control threshold because the supervisor has determined that they are "acting in concert."

sence of oversight of certain activities. Adoption of international standards and harmonization of regulatory practices will help prevent regulatory arbitrage.

Bank supervisors need to fully understand the risks posed by affiliate relationships in order to have a holistic and forward-looking view of potential threats and vulnerabilities to the safety and soundness of affiliated banks. The size of some of these organizations and/or their interlinkages may make them systemically important in multiple jurisdictions.

Bank supervisory authorities in jurisdictions where conglomerates operate subsidiary banks need to ensure timely and effective two-way communication and information sharing with their foreign counterparts. Coordination among supervisors enables better understanding of the risks and financial soundness of the conglomerate's parent and its bank and nonbank subsidiaries, as well as the risks posed by transactions between and among affiliated organizations.

The IMF has expressed concerns about widespread weaknesses in countries' execution of consolidated supervision identified during their FSAP country reviews. Given the significance of large banking conglomerates in emerging Asia and ongoing financial integration, national authorities should perform joint self-assessments of countries' compliance with the "Essential Criteria" of CPs 12 and 13 of the 2012 BCP.[17]

Crisis Management, Recovery, and Resolutions

The 2012 BCP consider material weaknesses in supervisory methods and vulnerabilities that came to light during the crisis. One such area is banks' and regulatory authorities' state of readiness with respect to crisis management, recovery, and resolution measures. The Basel Committee has stated that preventing bank failures should not be an objective of bank supervision, although "supervision should aim to reduce the probability and impact of a bank failure, including by working with resolution authorities, so that when failure occurs, it is handled in an orderly manner" (BCBS 2012, 6).

Banking is highly dependent on maintaining public confidence. The ability to provide accurate and timely information to the public and stakeholders during times of instability and crisis is critical to preventing an erosion of confidence that can adversely affect banks' financial conditions. Adverse publicity about a bank can spill over to other banks. If not brought under control, it can lead to a broader erosion of public confidence that could pose systemic concerns.

Communications and crisis management protocols need to be crafted and formulated in advance, as there may be intense time pressure in times of crisis. Reactive approaches to crises usually result in unnecessarily expensive solutions and may have undesirable unintended consequences that could be avoided with planning.

---

17. These assessment criteria can be found at www.bis.org/publ/bcbs230.htm.

The establishment, since 1997, of large, geographically disbursed banking organizations that operate across emerging Asia through multiple legal entities has made crisis communications particularly challenging. Some of these conglomerates operate separately organized banking companies in more than 10 countries. Domestic communication protocols must include supervisors and policymakers from each country in which the conglomerate operates. The complexity of some of these arrangements is challenging; keeping them up to date requires substantial ongoing effort.

In times of crisis, multiple governmental entities, such as central banks, finance ministries, deposit insurers, and other financial regulators, may divide or share decision making. Before a crisis, these parties should discuss how communications and decision making will occur, so that there is no uncertainty during a crisis. As players change over time, these discussions must be updated periodically.

Zamorski and Lim (2013) analyze 22 countries' FSAP assessments completed during 2012 and 2013. The countries included a diverse mix of size and developmental stages. Nine of the 22 were deemed to have systemically important financial sectors. The FSAPs identified fundamental deficiencies in many jurisdictions' crisis management and resolution arrangements and preparedness. Shortcomings were evident in the following areas:

- crisis management planning,
- specification of roles of national authorities in a crisis,
- legal powers to take various emergency actions in a crisis,
- information-sharing arrangements with relevant authorities, both domestically and internationally,
- arrangements for providing emergency liquidity to banks,
- specification of resolution strategies and options for failing or failed banks, and
- crisis simulation exercises.

Many countries, including advanced economies, still did not have sufficient legal powers or crisis management capabilities or infrastructure to deal with financial instability or systemic crises.

A range of resolution strategies and options can be formulated in advance that will cover most eventualities. National authorities should seek the legal authority to deal with a broad range of potential crises and have discretion to implement resolution strategies appropriate to the circumstances.

Countries should periodically conduct simulation exercises to assess whether their crisis contingency plans will work, testing the efficacy of such arrangements under multiple scenarios. Formal interagency agreements should clarify the roles and responsibilities of different national authorities in a crisis. Countries should also introduce explicit deposit insurance schemes.

Crisis management and resolution arrangements should consider cross-border operations. Arrangements can include participation in cross-border crisis management groups and establishment of crisis communication systems among supervisors of multinational banking conglomerates.

In addition to monitoring bank financial data, bank supervisors monitor how exogenous risk factors may affect the safety and soundness of individual banks, the banking industry, and an economy's overall financial stability. This information is useful in helping set supervisory priorities and focus resources on external risk factors that pose the greatest threats to banks' safety and soundness. Central banks typically identify significant external risk factors in their financial stability reports.

Significant external risk factors to financial stability in Asia Pacific and other regions include the following:

1. Expectations of the ending of accommodative monetary policy and the reduction or cessation of extraordinary policy actions by central banks in some advanced economies have already precipitated negative market reactions and volatility. Interest rate movements, exchange rate volatility, and capital outflows related to this risk could have negative consequences for some economies. Depending on the magnitude and velocity of changes, rising rates could adversely affect the prices of and markets for financial assets and real estate, inducing adverse knock-on effects. Unfavorable exchange rate shifts can have serious consequences for economies with substantial public and private sector debt denominated in foreign currency.

2. Sharply declining oil prices have positive and negative impacts, depending on national circumstances, the duration of lower prices, and other factors. Some economies, particularly net oil exporters, could be significantly adversely affected. Servicing their public debt levels and maintaining overall economic activity may be highly dependent on high prices.

3. A sustained period of extremely low interest rates induced sharp increases in sovereign debt, business borrowing, and consumer debt in many economies. A rise in interest rates could make it difficult to service this debt. Concerns about rapid expansion of consumer and residential mortgage debt have caused some jurisdictions to take macroprudential measures to prevent defaults and address real estate price bubbles financed by excessive borrowing.

4. Equity valuations in some markets may be out of line with economic values. Prices in these markets may be inflated by the global search for yield in the face of historically low interest rates. High levels of margin debt in some markets are an additional risk factor.

5. Significant problems in some larger economies could cause financial instability that could spread across borders.

6. Shadow banking system risks vary across jurisdictions. They have generally not been a major concern in most of emerging Asia. The Financial Stability Board and other standard-setters have expressed concern that these risks are a potential source of systemic risk and regulatory arbitrage. Activities,

primarily lending, may be moved to financial intermediaries with less stringent standards, potentially creating systemic risk (as occurred in the United States during the crisis). Countries need to define the "regulatory perimeter" appropriate to their context: What nonbank financial intermediaries and other financial services should be regulated and supervised? What is the appropriate intensity of that supervision? Getting the balance right is important because soundly operated nonbank financial intermediaries help entrepreneurs and small and medium-sized enterprises until they are able to obtain bank credit.

Conclusions and Recommendations

It has been more than 17 years since the last major episode of cross-border financial instability and banking crisis in emerging Asia. To extend this impressive record, bank supervisory authorities need to assess the effectiveness of their supervisory systems, infrastructure, and practices. This chapter highlights standards, practices, and lessons learned that may help them do so. If assessments disclose the need for changes, enhancements, or remedial actions, the relevant authorities should develop a plan to prioritize and implement them expeditiously.

The following actions are priorities for emerging Asia:

- Conduct self-assessments of compliance with the BCP, using outside experts as assessors if necessary, and promptly remedy instances of less than full compliance. Particularly important are CPs 12 and 13, which relate to consolidated supervision.

- Ensure that legal powers exist to allow examination and inspection of all banks' affiliates, including unregulated entities. Laws governing transactions with affiliates must require that they conform to safe and sound banking practice to prevent contagion effects.

- Ensure that the country's legal and regulatory frameworks support domestic and cross-border supervisory cooperation and information exchange, including the sharing of confidential supervisory information, between supervisors and other relevant authorities, such as deposit insurers. These powers are essential for ongoing consolidated supervision, crisis management, recovery, and resolution planning.

- Ensure that surveillance methods and infrastructure can detect elevated risk at individual financial institutions (microprudential supervision) as well as increases in macroeconomic risk (macroprudential risk), such as real estate and other asset bubbles.

- Ensure that supervisory authorities are properly resourced and that staff have the necessary skills to supervise banks of the relevant size, business models, and complexity.

- Ensure that the organization's supervisory culture and training approach develop examiners' ability to understand bank strategy and risk taking rather than simply assess compliance.

- Ensure that bank regulators adopt the international standards promulgated by the Basel Committee and other international standard-setters. Adoption of these standards promotes harmonization across jurisdictions and reduces opportunities for regulatory arbitrage or other efforts to circumvent regulations or forum shop.

- Ensure that well-defined crisis management and resolution plans are in place so that nonviable banks can be resolved in an orderly manner. Domestic and foreign authorities should be clear on their roles and decision-making authority. The potential for cross-border resolutions greatly increases the complexity of crisis and contingency planning. Once plans are developed, a mechanism should be in place to keep them current and periodically tested, to ensure that they will work when needed.

- Confirm that laws provide for timely interventions and resolutions for nonviable banks, in order to preserve public confidence and minimize losses to bank depositors, deposit insurers, other bank creditors, and taxpayers.

There is some intentional overlap in these recommendations. Investment of time and resources to perform the recommended assessments will provide valuable insights on ways to improve effectiveness and meet future challenges. Most important, this effort will help ensure a sound and stable banking system that supports local and regional financial stability.

References

BCBS (Basel Committee on Banking Supervision). 2012a. *Principles for the Supervision of Financial Conglomerates.* Joint Forum, September. Basel.

BCBS (Basel Committee on Banking Supervision). 2012b. *Core Principles for Effective Banking Supervision.* Basel.

BIS (Bank for International Settlements). 2001. *Group of Ten: Consolidation in the Financial Sector.* Basel.

Caruana, Jaime. 2012. *Dealing with Financial Systemic Risk: The Contribution of Macroprudential Policies.* Panel remarks at the Central Bank of Turkey/G20 Conference on "Financial Systemic Risk," Istanbul, September 27–28. Available at www.bis.org/speeches/sp121002.htm (accessed on April 26, 2015).

Claessens, Stijn, Swati R. Ghosh, and Roxana Mihet. 2013. Macro-Prudential Policies to Mitigate Financial System Vulnerabilities. *Journal of International Money and Finance* 39: 153–15.

FSB (Financial Stability Board). 2013. *An Overview of Policy Recommendations for Shadow Banking.* August 29, Basel. Available at www.financialstabilityboard.org/wp-content/uploads/r_130829a.pdf (accessed on April 26, 2015).

IMF (International Monetary Fund). 2014a. The Financial Sector Assessment Program Factsheet. Washington. Available at www.imf.org/external/np/exr/facts.htm (accessed on September 30, 2014).

IMF (International Monetary Fund). 2014b. Financial Sector Assessment Program: Frequently Asked Questions. Washington. Available at www.imf.org/external/np/fsap/faq (accessed on August 7, 2014).

IMF (International Monetary Fund), BIS (Bank for International Settlements), and FSB (Financial Stability Board). 2009. *Report to the G-20 Finance Ministers and Governors, Guidance to Assess the Systemic Importance of Financial Institutions, Markets and Instruments: Initial Considerations.* October. Washington.

Laeven, Luc, and Fabian Valencia. 2012. *Systemic Banking Database: An Update.* Working Paper WP/12/163. Washington: International Monetary Fund.

Lim, C., F. Columba, A. Costa, P. Kongsamut, A. Otani, M. Saiyid, T. Wezel, and X. Wu. 2011. *Macroprudential Policy: What Instruments and How to Use Them? Lessons from Country Experiences.* IMF Working Paper WP/11/238. Washington: International Monetary Fund.

Wihardja, Maria Monica. 2013. *Financial Integration Challenges in ASEAN beyond 2015.* Economic Research Institute for ASEAN and East Asia Discussion Paper 2013-27. Jakarta: Centre for Strategic and International Studies.

Zamorski, Michael J. 2012. Post-Crisis Strategies to Enhance Prudential Supervision and Regulation to Promote Financial Stability. Panel remarks at the Centro de Estudios Monetarios Latinoamericanos—SEACEN Conference, Punta del Esta, Uruguay, November 15. Available at http://www.cemla.org/actividades/2012/2012-11-cemla-seacen/2012-11-cemla-seacen-12.pdf (accessed on 5 August 2015).

Zamorski, Michael J. 2013a. The Basel Committee on Banking Supervision's September 2012 Revisions to Its Core Principles for Effective Banking Supervision. *SEACEN Economic Letter* No. 3. Kuala Lumpur: South East Asian Central Banks (SEACEN) Research and Training Centre. Available at www.seacen.org/products/702001-100305-PDF.pdf (January 14, 2013).

Zamorski, Michael J. 2013b. Mitigating Systemic Risks: Externalities and Monetary Policy. Remarks at the SEACEN High-Level Seminar on Integrating Monetary Policies with Macroprudential Framework, South East Asian Central Banks, Bali, Indonesia. November 7. Available at www.seacen.org/products/702003-100348-PDF.pdf (November 7, 2013).

Zamorski, Michael J., and Vincent Choon-Seng Lim. 2013. Financial Stability Insights from Recent IMF/World Bank FSAP Assessments. *SEACEN Financial Stability Journal* 1, November. Available at www.seacen.org/products/702002-100320-PDF.pdf (October 29, 2013).

8

Bank Stress Tests and Financial Stability:
Lessons from the 2009–14 US and EU-Wide Tests for Asian Emerging Economies

MORRIS GOLDSTEIN

Bank stress tests assess whether a bank or group of banks will be adequately capitalized even in a stressed economic scenario. This chapter looks at the bank stress tests conducted over the past five years by bank supervisors in the United States and the European Union, following what former chairman of the Federal Reserve Ben Bernanke declared was "the worst financial crisis in global history."[1] The purpose is to identify those lessons that would be most helpful to Asian emerging economies.

Stress tests are conducted to evaluate whether banks have sufficient self-insurance to withstand adverse economic shocks, so that a costly banking crisis can be avoided. The lost output cost to the United States, the epicenter of the 2007–09 crisis, has been estimated at $6 trillion to $14 trillion (Atkinson, Luttrell, and Rosenblum 2013). In addition to huge output and employment costs, banking crises generate large fiscal costs—mostly due to the fall in tax revenue linked to a deep recession (Reinhart and Rogoff 2009). While banks in emerging Asia suffered less in the 2007–09 crisis than banks in the

Morris Goldstein, nonresident senior fellow, has held several senior staff positions at the International Monetary Fund (1970–94), including deputy director of its Research Department (1987–94). From 1994 to 2010, he was the Dennis Weatherstone Senior Fellow at the Peterson Institute. He is indebted to Ajai Chopra, Bill Cline, Jacob Kirkegaard, Nick Lardy, Marc Noland, Adam Posen, and Steve Weisman for helpful comments on an earlier draft, and to Anish Tailor for his help with the tables and charts.

1. Pedro Nicolaci da Costa, "Bernanke: 2008 Meltdown Was Worse Than the Great Depression," *Wall Street Journal, Real Time Economics*, August 26, 2014, http://blogs.wsj.com/economics/2014/08/26/2008-meltdown-was-worse-than-great-depression-bernanke-says/ (accessed on January 26, 2015).

United States, the euro area, and the United Kingdom,[2] massive bank losses were registered by Indonesia, Thailand, and the Republic of Korea during the 1997–98 Asian financial crisis. Luc Laeven and Fabian Valencia (2013) report that the banking crises in these three countries were among the 10 largest in their multicountry sample of systemic banking crises spanning the entire 1970–2011 period.[3] More broadly, given their high degree of openness, emerging Asian economies must be concerned not only with the risk of internally generated banking crises but also with contagion from banking fragility elsewhere within the region and from the West.[4]

Six messages can be drawn from the stress tests conducted in the United States and the European Union.

First, bank stress tests are apt to become an increasingly important part of bank supervision globally because they carry advantages not shared by other supervisory tools and because they offer more flexibility than the Basel international regulatory regime. Accordingly, emerging Asian economies should invest in upgrading their stress-testing systems to approach a standard of best practice.

Second, the credibility of stress tests depends in good measure on their institutional framework and design, including (1) the coverage of systemically important banks and links between these banks and large nonbank financial institutions/sectors; (2) the resources, legal authority, and independence of the supervisor conducting the tests; (3) the relevance and severity of the adverse scenarios analyzed in the tests; (4) the quality of the suite of models used by the supervisors to assess the impact of shocks on bank capital; (5) the definition and level of the capital target that banks must meet under stressed conditions; and (6) the mechanism for linking test results to recapitalization actions. A challenge for emerging Asia is to ensure that stress tests run by national bank supervisors have the requisite degree of independence and transparency.

Third, stress tests need to be useful for crisis prevention and crisis management. It is troubling that just before the global economic and financial crisis, stress tests almost uniformly failed to provide early warning of the banking system's vulnerability. To help remedy that failing, two improvements are necessary: (1) the integration into the analysis of top-down, dual-threshold models of banking crisis[5] and (2) a fuller treatment of feedback, contagion,

---

2. The IMF (2010) estimates that emerging Asian banks incurred losses equal to roughly 1.5 percent of their total assets during the 2007–09 crisis; the corresponding losses for US, UK, and euro area banks during that crisis were about 7, 5, and 3 percent, respectively.

3. Indonesia's 1997 banking crisis had a fiscal cost of 57 percent of GDP; the corresponding fiscal costs for the Thai and Korean banking crises were 44 and 31 percent of GDP, respectively (Laeven and Valencia 2013).

4. In Goldstein and Xie (2009) I analyze various channels of spillover effects from financial crises elsewhere in emerging Asia.

5. In such models, crisis vulnerability is highest when there is both an abnormally rapid rate of growth of credit to the nonfinancial private sector and an abnormally rapid rise in real property prices; see the section titled "Criticisms of Stress Testing Methodology and the Measurement of Bank Capital."

and amplification effects into the modeling of the financial sector (so that even a moderate shock can produce real-economy effects similar to those observed during a severe banking crisis). Such criticisms of earlier stress tests are hardly academic for emerging Asia. The Bank for International Settlements (BIS 2014) has recently suggested that just such a dual-threshold model of banking crises is now signaling high vulnerability both for the People's Republic of China (PRC) and for an Asian emerging-economy aggregate composed of Hong Kong, China; Indonesia; Malaysia; the Philippines; Singapore; and Thailand. As for contagion, one only needs to recall what occurred during the Asian financial crisis of 1997–98.

Fourth, capital shortfalls revealed by stress tests should be remedied in a way that is friendly to economic growth. A higher desired capital ratio should be translated into an absolute amount of capital rather than allowing banks to achieve the higher capital ratio by cutting back on loans, by engaging in fire sales of assets, and by manipulating risk weights.

Fifth, because capital ratios that use an unweighted measure of bank assets in the denominator—called leverage ratios—do a much better job (ex ante) for large banks of distinguishing sick banks from healthy ones than risk-based measures of bank capital, a leverage ratio test should be included in all future supervisor-led bank stress tests conducted in the Asian region. Over time, a leverage ratio should become the primary metric for bank stress tests. Risk-based measures of bank capital should be relegated to a backup role. Asia is well placed to help lead the charge on leverage ratios. A recent International Monetary Fund report (IMF 2014a) indicates that emerging Asia and advanced Asia had average tangible leverage ratios (corrected for international differences in accounting standards) of 5.8 and 6.0 percent, respectively, versus 4.5 percent for North America and 3.6 percent for the euro area.

Sixth, because theory and empirical evidence indicate that the optimal level of bank capital is likely to be far above the minimum ratios set out under Basel III and the actual capital ratios prevailing around the world, bank supervisors in emerging Asia and elsewhere should consider gradually raising the capital hurdle rates in bank stress tests. Again, emerging Asia is in a good position to be part of the leading edge of reform. Its current capital ratios are above the fully phased-in Basel III minimums, and banks in the region increased their capital ratios in 2009–12 without raising the cost of credit or restricting its availability (McCauley 2014).

The US and EU-Wide Stress Tests

Bank stress tests have been conducted by the IMF since the late 1990s, by national central banks and other regulatory authorities before that, and by commercial and investment banks going even farther back.[6]

---

6. Stress tests are also sometimes conducted for nonbank financial institutions of various kinds (including insurance companies). This chapter restricts the analysis to stress tests for banks.

What put bank stress tests on the front page of major newspapers around the world, however, is of more recent origin. In February–May 2009, US authorities conducted the Supervisory Capital Assessment Program (SCAP)[7] shortly after the fall of Lehman Brothers and during high anxiety about the viability of major US financial institutions (Geithner 2014). To bolster the SCAP's credibility, bank-by-bank results were published, and a new, more stringent definition of high-quality bank capital was introduced: *tier 1 common* (T1C). The test also employed a severe loss rate on bank loans (over 9 percent—higher than even during the Great Depression) in the adverse scenario.[8] Because the US cri-

---

7. The SCAP was announced on February 10, 2009, and the test results were released on May 7, 2009.

8. Alas, in a chapter on bank stress tests, it is necessary to have some discussion of different measures of bank capital—admittedly, an arcane topic. This chapter makes reference to two types of bank capital ratios: one based on risk-weighted assets (RWA) in the denominator, called risk-based measures of capital; and the other based on unweighted assets/exposures in the denominator, called leverage ratios. Risk weights mostly (about 85 percent) reflect credit risk differences across assets, but market and operational risk are also taken into account. Risk weights typically fall between zero and 100 percent but can exceed 100 percent for some very risky assets. The other main source of differences among capital ratios derives from differences in the quality of bank capital, captured in the numerator of the capital ratio. The highest quality of capital is usually regarded to be common equity because it doesn't need to be repaid, it doesn't require payments of dividends or interest, and it stands last in line in bankruptcy or insolvency proceedings (Elliott 2010). Tangible common equity—defined as common equity minus intangible assets (goodwill, deferred tax assets, minority interest, etc.) is of even higher quality than common equity because it has greater loss absorbency. In descending order of quality, this chapter makes reference to the following risk-based measures of capital: *common equity tier 1* (CET1), the equity measure at the center of Basel III; *tier 1 common* (T1C), the equity measure relied on in the earlier US stress tests; *core tier 1* (CT1), the equity measure used in the 2011 EU-wide stress test (usually defined as common equity plus government hybrid instruments); *tier 1* (T1), the high quality capital measure used in the first two EU-wide stress tests; *tier 2* (T2), a lower quality component of bank capital; and the *total capital ratio* (CAR), the broadest measure of bank capital, consisting of tier 1 plus tier 2 capital. The Basel Committee on Banking Supervision (BCBS 2010, 13) defines common equity tier 1 capital as consisting of the following elements: (1) common shares issued by the bank that meet the criteria for classification as common shares for regulatory purposes; (2) stock surplus (share premium); (3) retained earnings; (4) accumulated other comprehensive income and other disclosed reserves; (5) minority interest that meets the criteria for inclusion in CET1; and (6) regulatory adjustments.

Douglas Elliott (2010) provides the useful intuitive explanation that the noncommon stock elements of tier 1 capital are mainly those kinds of preferred stock that are more like common stock, while the elements of tier 2 capital are mainly those kinds of preferred stock that are more like debt; tier 2 capital also includes subordinated debt. Again in descending order of quality, the three leverage ratios discussed in this chapter are: the tangible leverage ratio—defined as the ratio of adjusted tangible equity to adjusted tangible assets (see Hoenig 2015); the *leverage ratio*—defined as ratio of the book vaule of equity to the book value of total assets (see Pagano et al. 2014) ; and the Basel III *tier 1 leverage ratio*—defined as the ratio of tier 1 capital to total exposure. Total exposure includes both on-balance sheet assets and off-balance sheet expoures such as over-the-counter derivatives, cleared derivatives, repo-style transactions, and other off-balance sheet exposures. Total exposure is always larger than total assets. For a more precise definition of total exposure, see BCBS (2013) and Davis Polk (2014). Some analysts refer to the denominator of the Basel III leverage ratio as "average assets" because the calculation is the average of three month-end lever-

sis management effort had many important elements beyond bank stress tests, it is difficult to assess the impact of the stress test itself. Nevertheless, the results seemed to persuade market participants that 9 of the 19 largest US banks had sufficient capital to weather the storm and that the remaining 10 banks that fell short of the regulatory standard would be promptly recapitalized. Interbank lending spreads, credit default spreads for pressured banks, and the volatility fear index in the broader US stock market all improved dramatically immediately after the SCAP, and the 10 banks identified as needing additional capital were able to raise almost all ($66 billion of $75 billion) of the aggregate shortfall within a month (and without additional government funds).

Buoyed by this record, further rounds of US bank stress tests were conducted in 2011, 2012, 2013, and 2014.[9] Indeed, such stress tests are now a mandatory and permanent part of the US regulatory and supervisory framework.[10]

Senior US regulatory officials (Tarullo 2014b, Bernanke 2013, Fischer 2014b) argue that the 2009–14 stress tests made an important contribution to financial stability. They highlight that the 30 firms participating in the 2014 stress test had doubled their CET1 capital (ratios) since 2009,[11] and their liquidity position had improved markedly relative to precrisis levels.[12] Looking

---

age ratios over a quarter. The *supplementary leverage ratio* (SLR) and the *enhanced supplementary leverage ratio* (ESLR) are the US banking agencies' implementation of the Basel III leverage ratio. The ESLR applies to the eight largest US bank holding companies (BHCs) that are designated as global systemically important banks (G-SIBs). The SLR applies to other large US banks that meet certain size criteria (greater than or equal to $250 billion in total assets, or greater than or equal to $10 billion of on-balance sheet foreign exposures); banks that meet these criteria are classified as "advanced approach" banks.

9. All of these tests, except the 2011 one, published bank-by-bank results.

10. Large US banks are now required to participate in two distinct but related supervisory programs in which stress tests are a key component. The first is the stress testing required by the 2010 Dodd-Frank Wall Street Improvement and Consumer Protection Act. The second is the stress testing included in the wider annual capital plan assessment, called the Comprehensive Capital Analysis and Review (CCAR). The main distinctions are the following: The Dodd-Frank stress tests apply to a broader range of companies (bank holding companies [BHCs], savings and loan companies, state banks with total assets greater than $10 billion, and nonbanks designated by the Federal Stability Oversight Council for supervision by the Federal Reserve), and the focus is almost exclusively on the "quantitative" outcomes of the stress tests. In contrast, the CCAR covers only large, complex US BHCs with consolidated assets of $50 billion or more, and it includes not only stress test methodology and results but also a more "qualitative" assessment of the capital planning process, including policies covering dividends, common stock issuance, and share repurchases. The Federal Reserve coordinates these two stress test exercises, while seeking to reduce duplication and minimize burden. See Board of Governors (2014), Tarullo (2014b), and Bernanke (2013).

11. The 30 firms participating in the 2014 CCAR stress test increased their aggregate CET1 ratio from 5.5 percent in the first quarter of 2009 to 11.6 percent in the fourth quarter of 2013 (Board of Governors 2014).

12. Bernanke (2013) reports that banks' holding of cash and high-quality liquid securities more than doubled between end-2007 and April 2013.

at the large banks as a group is said to have facilitated a more "macropruden-tial" approach to supervision with greater focus on total bank lending and economic growth, while also making it easier to identify risk outliers. Publi-cation of bank-by-bank results is seen as aiding the efforts of market partici-pants to reach more informed judgments about the true condition of banks. Finally, the stress tests are regarded as having upped the ante for sound risk management, since failure either to meet the regulatory capital benchmark or to demonstrate that the capital planning process is otherwise up to snuff car-ries nontrivial reputational cost.

A second moment in the sun for bank stress tests has been their applica-tion within the European Union: first during the crisis of 2007–09, and later during the European debt crisis of 2010–13 and the recent efforts to create a banking union. The results of the first EU-wide bank stress test were released in October 2009. Additional EU-wide tests were completed in July 2010, July 2011, and October 2014, just before the European Central Bank (ECB) took over as Single Supervisor of Europe's largest banks.

EU policymakers say that these tests have helped to assess objectively the health of the European banking system and that concerns about failing the test have prompted banks to raise much more capital than they would other-wise. The median T1C capital ratio for large and complex banks in the euro area in the first quarter of 2014 was within a half percentage point of their global peers (ECB 2014). Also, the difference between price-to-book ratios for large and complex banks in the United States and those in the euro area narrowed significantly over the 2012–14 period. Yet the release of the first EU-wide stress test in 2009 was not immediately followed by a sharp improve-ment in confidence in EU or euro area banks; so, too, with the 2010, 2011, and 2014 tests.[13] Indeed, if one looks at market indicators of EU banking stress/confidence, the sharp improvements came instead after the announcement of the long-term refinancing operation (LTRO) in December 2011, and most of the all, the statement in July 2012 by ECB President Mario Draghi that the ECB would do "whatever it takes" to save the euro.

Why Did the EU-Wide Stress Tests Fare So Poorly?

The limp market reaction to the first three EU-wide stress tests appears to result from four factors.[14]

First, the organizations coordinating the EU-wide stress tests, that is, the Committee of European Banking Supervisors (CEBS) for the 2009 and 2010

---

13. David Greenlaw et al. (2012) performed an event-study comparison of the market reaction to the 2009 US stress test with that for the 2009 EU-wide test. Drawing on bank equity prices and credit default spreads, they found that the markets assessed the US test much more favorably than the EU-wide one.

14. In Goldstein (2015), I also argue that the low credibility of the EU-wide stress tests reflects in part the unsuccessful efforts of eurozone economic officials to put together a set of economic policies that make thin the catastrophic tail for banking sector outcomes.

tests, and the European Banking Authority (EBA) in 2011, were new and had little clout vis-à-vis national bank supervisors. The CEBS and EBA also lacked staffing and resources and could only recommend, not compel, recapitalization (Posen and Véron 2014). By contrast, the Federal Reserve, which oversaw stress tests in the United States, had much greater resources and authority.

Second, the EU stress tests of 2009–11 were run before a critical mass had formed on an EU banking union. Before June 2012, there was no agreement on either bank resolution or EU-wide funding of bank failures, whereas in the United States the Treasury had more than $200 billion left from the initial TARP (Troubled Asset Relief Program) legislation that could be used to recapitalize undercapitalized US banks. Also, EU banks are much larger relative to home-country GDP, compared with that of US banks,[15] and banking is more important in the European Union relative to capital markets. In other words, the "too big to fail" (TBTF) problem is worse in the European Union than in the United States. When funding for bank recapitalization is in question, it is not unreasonable for investors to worry that estimated capital shortfalls in stress tests are being low-balled because supervisors don't want to identify bank problems that don't have an immediate solution, lest they stoke market turbulence.

A third detracting factor for the EU tests is that outside estimates of the capital shortfall in the banking system have been considerably larger than the shortfalls emerging from the stress tests. Ever since IMF Managing Director Christine Lagarde (2011) put a spotlight on the need for "urgent capitalization" of Europe's banks in August 2011, a flurry of estimates have suggested that EU banks are significantly undercapitalized. Viral Acharya and Sascha Steffen (2014) conclude that euro area banks have been "severely undercapitalized" since the 2007–09 financial crisis. Using book values of equity and assets, they estimate an aggregate EU capital shortfall of 82 billion to 176 billion euros. If the market values of equity and assets are employed instead, this estimated capital shortfall rises to between 230 billion and 620 billion euros. And when the estimate of the capital shortfall is applied to a hypothetical systemic financial crisis (with a 40 percent decline in a market equity index), the shortfall is about 580 billion euros.[16] The IMF (2011a) and the OECD (2013) also published estimates suggesting that the aggregate capital shortfall for euro area banks was in the neighborhood of 200 billion to 300 billion euros and

---

15. Goldstein and Véron (2011) give the ratio of the banking assets of the five largest banks relative to GDP (in 2009): for the United States, the ratio is 43 percent. For the larger EU economies, the ratios are as follows: the Netherlands (406), United Kingdom (336), France (250), Spain (189), Italy (121), and Germany (118). If one looks instead at total bank assets relative to GDP in 2013, the conclusion is similar: the US ratio is 87 percent versus 350 percent for the euro area; see IMF (2014a). Goldstein and Véron (2011) also report that the share of total credit intermediation undertaken by banks is about three times higher in the euro area than in the United States.

16. Acharya, Schoenmaker, and Steffen (2011) reached similar results on undercapitalization in EU banks.

400 billion euros, respectively. These shortfall estimates are much larger than those in the adverse scenarios of the EU stress tests.[17] They also loom large relative to the 55 billion euro common resolution fund agreed by EU finance ministers in December 2013.

Investors who were underwhelmed by the euro area stress tests no doubt were also influenced by the weak macroeconomic environment in which EU-wide stress tests had been conducted. But it merits emphasis that the design of the EU stress tests also contributed to their poor reception.

The methodology and results of the initial October 2009 test were described solely in a three-page press release that summarized the presentation made by CEBS to Ecofin ministers and governors. No individual bank results were published (thereby making it impossible to distinguish weak from strong banks). The capital benchmark used in the 2009 test was the T1 ratio rather than the more demanding T1C or CT1 ratios, and since no bank among the 22 major cross-border banks in the sample saw its T1 capital ratio fall below 6 percent—even in the more adverse scenario—there were no capital actions taken (beyond the government support measures previously announced during the crisis).

The second stress test, with results released in July 2010, was an improvement: A 55-page report detailed its objectives, methodology, and results for 91 banks representing 65 percent of total European banking assets. Individual bank results were published. Amid mounting market concerns over sovereign debt sustainability, the report provided data on banks' exposures to European Union/European Economic Area (EU/EEA) central and local government debt, and included an adverse sovereign debt scenario, resulting in losses to banks' trading books. This time, seven banks saw their T1 capital ratios fall below 6 percent in the adverse scenario, leading to an aggregate shortfall of 3.5 billion euros. Still, as emphasized by Adrian Blundell-Wignall and Patrick Slovik (2010), the sovereign debt scenario was widely viewed as inadequate, since 83 percent of sovereign debt exposures were held in the banking book—not the trading book—and no haircuts were assumed for the former.[18] Another blow to credibility came in October 2010 when the Irish banking system melted down at enormous cost to Ireland's public debt position and to the Irish taxpayer, only several months after Ireland's two largest banks had passed the July 2010 test.

The third EU-wide stress test (July 2011) was coordinated by the European Banking Authority (EBA), with some more improvements, including

---

17. The official estimates of the aggregate shortfalls in the four EU-wide stress tests were as follows: 2009 test, no shortfall published; 2010 test, aggregate shortfall of 3.5 billion euros; 2011 test, aggregate shortfall of 26.8 billion euros; 2014 test, aggregate shortfall of 24.6 billion euros. In the 2011 EU-wide capital exercise, the aggregate shortfall was estimated to be 115 billion euros (CEBS 2009, 2010; EBA 2011, 2012, 2014a).

18. Blundell-Wignall and Slovik (2010) calculate that if the same losses assumed for the trading book were also extended to the banking book, losses on sovereign debt exposures would have been 165 billion euros instead of 26 billion euros.

additional data from banks.[19] The bank capital measure used in the test, CT1 capital, was more restrictive (tougher) than the T1 measure used in the two earlier tests, although this was offset by the lowering of the stressed capital target from 6 percent (in the July 2010 test) to 5 percent (in the July 2011 test). Haircuts on sovereign debt exposures of banks in the trading book were updated and an increase in provisions was implemented for sovereign debt held in the banking book. Also, market concerns about sovereign debt exposures were allowed to affect the cost of funding in the adverse scenario. The difference between the baseline scenario and the adverse scenario was larger than in previous tests. Thirty of the 91 banks in the test fell below the 5 percent capital hurdle rate, with an aggregate shortfall of 27 billion euros. The EBA also issued its first formal recommendation to national supervisory authorities: Banks below the 5 percent threshold should promptly remedy their shortfall, and those with capital ratios above but close to the threshold and with sizable exposure to sovereigns under stress should strengthen their capital positions.

Despite these improvements, the Stoxx Europe 600 Banks Index fell by more than 3 percent (to a two-year low) on the first trading day after the July 2011 EU-wide stress test results were released (Ahmed et al. 2011).[20]

Stung by the poor market reaction, the EBA soon undertook its EU-Wide Capital Exercise in October 2011.[21] The results, revealed in October 2012,[22] assessed the capitalization of 70 banks against an exceptional and temporary capital benchmark of 9 percent CT1 capital. Thirty-seven banks fell below the target, with an aggregate capital shortfall of 116 billion euros. The EBA urged national banking supervisors to implement recapitalization plans for all undercapitalized banks.

Both the 2011 stress test and the follow-up EU-Wide Capital Exercise have been widely criticized. The most salient criticism comes from Jakob Vestergaard and María Retana (2013). They argue that the EBA made three major mistakes.[23]

First, the EBA employed only risk-based measures of bank capital despite the accumulating evidence that such measures have very limited ability to

---

19. Enam Ahmed et al. (2011) report that 3,200 data points per bank were supplied compared with 149 per bank in the 2010 stress test.

20. The behavior of Bloomberg's Europe 500 Bank and Financial Services Index, in the year following release of the 2011 stress tests results, provided a similar market verdict on that test.

21. In October 2011, the EBA also conducted the Basel III monitoring exercise on a sample of 158 European banks. Its main finding was that more than half the banks did not meet the Basel III targets for either equity to risk-weighted assets (7 percent) or the leverage ratio of equity to total assets (3 percent) (Vestergaard and Retana 2013).

22. This is well described in Vestergaard and Retana (2013). I provide a summary of their account.

23. Some others have offered additional criticisms, including that the 2011 stress test did not contain a sovereign default scenario (Ahmed et al. 2011).

discriminate between healthy and sick (large) banks.[24] A leverage ratio of 4.5 percent would have identified all the banks that failed over the subsequent two years; in contrast, there was no value of the risk-based CT1 measure that would have identified the failing banks while still allowing some banks to pass the test.

A second charge made by Vestergaard and Retana (2013) is that the EBA selected the CT1 capital measure as the pass-fail metric because it wanted the test to generate two results: that there would be relatively few failures and that these failures would occur primarily in relatively small banks on the periphery of the euro area. If a leverage ratio of 3 percent had been chosen instead, 26 banks would have failed (instead of 3 with the CT1 ratio), and among the failures would have been quite a few large German and French banks, including Deutsche Bank, Commerzbank, BNP Paribas, and Société Générale.[25]

The third major mistake, according to Vestergaard and Retana (2013), was to specify the bank capital target as a *ratio* rather than as absolute amounts of bank capital,[26] thereby opening the door for banks to meet much of the target by cutting back on loans, engaging in fire sales of assets, and manipulating risk weights (by decreasing the denominator of the capital ratio). Verstergaard and Retana (2013) were therefore not surprised that only 38 percent of the reported recapitalization occurred through the raising of new equity capital.

Yet a further blow to credibility came when Dexia—the large ($700 billion) Belgian-French bank that got an easy pass (from the CT1 measure) in the adverse scenario of the July 2011 test—plunged into crisis later that year, requiring a bailout by Belgian and French authorities at considerable expense to taxpayers.[27] Viral Acharya, Dirk Schoenmaker, and Sascha Steffen (2011) report that Dexia's leverage ratio—using unweighted assets in the denominator and either the market or book value of equity in the numerator—was only between 0.49 percent and 1.34 percent.

Despite the poor market reception to the first three EU-wide stress tests, some analysts were cautiously optimistic that the 2014 stress test would earn higher marks because at least some of the handicaps and flaws outlined above were expected to be corrected or at least diminished (Posen and Véron 2014).

---

24. Vestergaard and Retana (2013) point to the empirical work of Blundell-Wignall and Roulet (2012), who looked at a sample of 94 US and European banks during 2004–11 and found that (risk-based) T1 capital ratios had no support as a predictor of default, whereas a simple (unweighted) leverage ratio found strong support in the data.

25. If the hurdle rate for the leverage ratio had instead been set at 4.5 percent, 50 of the 70 banks would have failed the 2011 test. Vestergaard and Retana (2013) also show that German and French banks have much lower ratios of risk-weighted assets to total assets and lower leverage ratios than Spanish and Italian banks, and these differences almost guarantee that the largest German and French banks will look much better under risk-based capital measures than under unweighted capital measures.

26. This argument was also made by, among others, IMF (2011a) and Greenlaw et al. (2012).

27. "How Did Europe's Bank Stress Test Give Dexia a Clean Bill of Health?" *Guardian*, October 5, 2011.

The 2014 results for the EU-wide stress test and accompanying asset quality review (AQR) were published on October 26, 2014. There were three key findings[28]: (1) the aggregate capital shortfall for the 123 participating banks was 24.6 billion euros, (2) 14 banks in Italy, Greece, and Cyprus failed to meet the capital hurdle rates in the baseline and/or adverse scenarios, and (3) the largest banks in France and Germany had ample capital.

Despite extensive documentation, choice of a higher quality of capital in the numerator of the capital ratio, and a larger decline (than in previous tests) for the capital ratio under the adverse scenario, the 2014 results have drawn, at best, a mixed response. Some critics emphasized that (as in earlier tests) the exclusion of a leverage ratio test biased the results in the direction of few failures and in favor of large French, German, and Dutch banks (Goldstein 2014). Other critics focused on the failure to include a deflation scenario and on the artificial boosting of capital ratios due to the ECB's permissive attitude toward deferred tax assets. In contrast, more positive assessments of the results highlighted the considerable resources devoted to the AQR and the ECB's rigorous methodology (Heim 2014).

Thus far, the market verdict on the test has been negative. The Stoxx Europe 600 Banks Index is marginally lower at the time of writing than it was on the last workday immediately preceding the test (October 24, 2014). Moreover, Benn Steil and Dinah Walker (2014) show that 28 of the 31 banks in the Stoxx Euro 600 Banks Index that were tested now trade at lower price-to-book ratios than they did before the test results were released.

Although the US and EU-wide tests have captured most of the attention, bank stress tests are now widespread. All 27 members of the Basel Committee on Banking Supervision (BCBS) use them, including Hong Kong, China; India; Indonesia; the PRC; the Republic of Korea; and Singapore (Bernanke 2013). The IMF also includes stress tests of banks as an element of its wider Financial Sector Assessment Program (FSAP), and makes an FSAP assessment mandatory at least once every five years for 25 jurisdictions with systemically important financial sectors (in emerging Asia, this list includes Hong Kong, China; the PRC; the Republic of Korea; and Singapore).

Operational Features of the US and EU-Wide Tests

Tables 8.1 and 8.2 illustrate operational features of the US and EU-wide tests, along the following lines.

Coverage. The focus is on the largest and most interconnected banks. The US CCAR tests employ a simple asset size cutoff, whereas the EU tests cover at least 50 percent of banking assets in each country.[29]

---

28. In addition to these findings, it was reported that the AQR resulted in a decrease in the weighted-average core CET1 capital ratio of only 40 basis points.

29. Nonbanks are typically not included, presumably because bank supervisors do not have the same authorization to recommend/mandate corrective action if their banks should fail the test,

Table 8.1   US bank stress tests, 2009–14

Stress test	Date	Supervisors	Coverage	Time horizon	Scenarios	Scenarios	Models
SCAP	October 2009	Fed, FDIC, OCC	19 largest domestic BHCs; 66% of banking system assets	2009–10	Baseline (supervisor led) More adverse (supervisor led)	Macroeconomic: real GDP, unemployment rate, house prices. Market Stress Scenario: firms with trading assets greater than or equal to $100 billion	Supervisor models
CCAR	March 2011	Fed, FDIC, OCC	19 BHCs (same as SCAP)	2011–12	Baseline (supervisor led) More adverse (supervisor led) Company-run equivalents of above	Macroeconomic: Real GDP, unemployment rate, asset prices. Severe Global Market Shock[a]	Bank models checked by supervisors
CCAR	March 2012	Fed, FDIC, OCC	19 BHCs (same as SCAP)	2012–13	Baseline (supervisor led) More adverse (supervisor led) Company-led equivalents of above.	Macroeconomic and Financial Market: deep recession in US, asset price declines, increase in risk premia, slowdown in global economic activity Severe Global Market Shock[a]	Supervisor models and bank models
CCAR	March 2013	Fed, FDIC, OCC	18 BHCs; 70% of banking assets	2013–15	Baseline (supervisor led). Adverse (supervisor led). Severely adverse (supervisor led). Company-led equivalents of above.	Macroeconomic and Financial Market Interest Rate Scenarios Severe Global Market Shock[a]	Supervisor models and bank models
CCAR	March 2014	Fed, FDIC, OCC	30 BHCs; 80% of assets of all BHCs (including 12 BHCs that did not participate in previous CCARs)	2014–15	Baseline (supervisor led). Adverse (supervisor led). Severely adverse (supervisor led). Company-led equivalents of above.	Macroeconomic and Financial Market Interest Rate Scenarios Severe Global Market Shock[a] Counterparty Default[b]	Supervisor models and bank models

Bank capital

Stress test	Hurdle rate	Average change in capital ratio (stressed minus starting)	Failures	Disclosure	Remedial actions
SCAP	Tier 1 (stressed) 6% Tier 1 common (stressed) 4%	Median loss is −7.5% of risk-weighted assets under more adverse scenario.	10 of 19 banks needed additional capital	Bank-by-bank results	Firms that didn't meet hurdle rate were required to raise dollar amounts of capital within 6 months; government backup in place if a firm couldn't raise enough private capital.
CCAR	Tier 1 common (stressed) 5% Tier 1 leverage (stressed) 3% Also must maintain four capital ratios above minimum regulatory requirements.	Not available	Not available	No bank-by-bank results	One month after CCAR report, firms receive detailed assessment of their capital plans—including areas where plans and processes need to be strengthened.
CCAR	Tier 1 common (stressed) 5% Tier 1 leverage (stressed) 3% Also must maintain four capital ratios above minimum regulatory requirements.	Tier 1 common: −3.8% (6.3% vs 10.1%) Tier 1 leverage: −2.7% (4.7% vs 7.4%)	4 of 19 firms had one or more stressed capital ratios that fell below hurdle rates	Bank-by-bank results	Federal Reserve notifies BHCs if it has any objections to its capital plan; if Fed objects, no capital distributions permitted until Fed gives written approval.
CCAR	Tier 1 common (stressed) 5% Tier 1 leverage 3–4% Also must maintain four capital ratios above minimum regulatory requirements.	Tier 1 common: −4.5% (6.6% vs 11.1%) Tier 1 leverage: −2.7% (5.3% vs 8.0%)	2 of 18 received objection to capital plan. Two other firms received conditional non-objection to plans	Bank-by-bank results	Federal Reserve notifies BHCs if it has any objections to its capital plan; if Fed objects, no capital distributions permitted until Fed gives written approval.
CCAR	Tier 1 common (stressed) 5% Tier 1 leveraged (stressed) 3–4% Also must maintain four capital ratios above minimum regulatory requirements.	Tier 1 common: −5.0% (6.6% vs 11.6%) Tier 1 leverage: −3.0% (5.4% vs 8.4%)	5 of 30 received objection to capital plans (of which 4 of 30 had objection on qualitative grounds, and one on quantitative grounds)	Bank-by-bank results	Federal Reserve notifies BHCs if it has any objections to its capital plan; if Fed objects, no capital distributions permitted until Fed gives written approval.

SCAP = Supervisory Capital Assessment Program; BHCs = bank holding companies; CCAR = Comprehensive Capital Analysis and Review; OCC = Office of the Comptroller of the Currency; FDIC = Federal Deposit Insurance Corporation

a. Applies to six largest firms with significant trading activities.
b. Applies to eight firms with significant trading activity and/or important custodial operations.

Source: Board of Governors (2009a, 2009b, 2011, 2012, 2013, 2014).

Table 8.2 EU-wide bank stress tests, 2009–14

Stress test	Date	Supervisors	Coverage	Time horizon	Scenarios		Models
First EU-wide stress test	October 2009	CEBS, EC, ECB, national supervisors	22 major cross-border banking groups, 60% of total EU banking assets	2009–10	Baseline (supervisor led) More adverse (supervisor led)	Macroeconomic: EU real GDP, unemployment rate, property prices (same variables in US).	Supervisor models
Second EU-wide stress test	July 2010	CEBS, EC, ECB, national supervisors	91 European banks, 20 EU member states, covers 65% of EU total banking assets	2010–11	Baseline (supervisor led) More adverse (supervisor led)	Macroeconomic: EU real GDP, unemployment rate, property prices, foreign economic activity. Sovereign debt shock to trading book.	Banks' own models, supervisor models
Third EU-wide stress test	July 2011	EBA, ECB, ESRB, EC, national supervisors	90 European banks, 21 EU members	2011–14	Baseline (supervisor led) More adverse (supervisor led)	Macroeconomic: Sovereign debt shock to trading book; increased provisions for sovereign debt in banking book.	Banks' own models, supervisor models
Fourth EU-wide stress test	October 2014	EBA, ECB, ESRB, EC, national supervisors	123 European banks, covers more than 70% of total EU banking assets	2014–15	Baseline (supervisor led) More adverse (supervisor led)	Macroeconomic: adverse scenario to include (1) increase in global bond yields; (2) further deterioration in credit quality in EU countries with feeble demand; (3) stalled policy reforms; (4) lack of progress on bank balance sheet repair.	Banks' own models, supervisor models

Bank capital

Stress test	Hurdle rate	Average change in capital ratio (stressed minus starting)	Failures	Disclosure	Remedial action
First EU-wide stress test	Tier 1 (stressed): 6.0%	Tier 1: −0.1% (7.8% versus 7.9%)	None announced	No bank-by-bank results published	None
Second EU-wide stress test	Tier 1 (stressed): 6.0%	Tier 1: −1.1% (9.2% versus 10.3%)	7 banks	Bank-by-bank results; sovereign debt exposures	Remedial actions to be decided by national supervisory authorities
Third EU-wide stress test	Core tier 1 (stressed): 5%	Core tier 1: −1.5% (7.4% versus 8.9%)	20 banks	Bank-by-bank results; sovereign debt exposures	EBA recommends that national supervisors request all banks failing stress tests to promptly eliminate their capital shortfalls. Also, EBA launches EU-Wide Capital Exercise in October 2011.
Fourth EU-wide stress test	Common equity tier 1: 8% baseline, 5.5% (stressed) adverse scenario	Common equity tier 1: −2.6% (8.5% versus 11.1%); also, decline of 0.4% due to asset quality review	24 banks (14 banks, after 2014 capital raising)	Bank-by-bank results	Banks failing test have two weeks to submit new capital plan. Banks below baseline (adverse) hurdle rate have six (nine) months to achieve hurdle rate.

EC = European Commission; ECB = European Central Bank; CEBS = Committee of European Banking Supervisors; EBA = European Banking Authority; ESRB = European Systemic Risk Board

Sources: CEBS (2009, 2010); EBA (2010, 2011, 2012, 2013, 2014a, 2014b).

Frequency. Since 2011, US supervisors have been required by legislation to conduct supervisor-led stress tests annually.[30] No such requirement exists in the European Union. An annual requirement prevents authorities from delaying a test out of concern over exposing the banking system's fragility. More frequent (supervisor-led) stress tests are seen as impractical because of the data and modeling requirements.[31]

Scenario horizons. The US and EU tests generally cover two calendar years in a row, a time frame that fits two-year baseline forecasts for the home economy and for its main trading partners (such as in the IMF's *World Economic Outlook*). A two-year horizon is long enough to allow shocks to take effect but not so long as to invite large forecast errors.

Types of scenarios. Bank stress tests include a baseline scenario and at least one "adverse" scenario.[32] The most popular variables are real GDP growth, inflation, the unemployment rate, housing prices, and equity prices. Bank solvency is deemed threatened when a recession is paired with a collapse of property and equity prices. Over time, more variables have been added, including a wider array of interest rates and asset prices and a fuller characterization of foreign economic conditions. The 2014 CCAR scenarios (Board of Governors 2014) contained a block of 48 variables. "Bespoke" scenarios have also become more common, reflecting either market concerns at a point in time or structural vulnerabilities of some banks in the test. For example, the EU-wide tests have included a sovereign debt scenario since 2010, while the US tests have always included—for the six largest banks with significant trading activity—an adverse global market scenario (meant to capture a severe deterioration in market conditions, like that prevailing between June and December of 2008).

Models used to estimate the effects of the scenarios on bank capital. Stress test managers now rely on a multiplicity or "suite" of models.[33] In ad-

---

and perhaps because stress tests for nonbanks would require different scenarios than for banks. Foreign banks with subsidiaries are increasingly included if they are thought to be important for the functioning of the financial system.

30. That same legislation requires company-run stress tests, at least twice a year.

31. See EBA (2014a) for an enumeration and explanation of the substantive data requirements for banks participating in the EU-wide stress tests. Ahmed et al. (2011) reported that data points per bank rose from about 150 in the 2010 EU-wide stress test to 3,500 per bank in the 2011 test. The 2014 EU-wide test used roughly 12,000 data points per bank. Bernanke (2013) indicates that for the 2013 CCAR, the supervisors collected and analyzed loan and account-level data on more than two-thirds of the $4.2 trillion in accrual loans and losses held by the 18 banks participating in the test. In the United States, it takes about six months after the submission of the last bank data for stress test results to be published.

32. The guideline for adverse scenarios is that they should be "severe but plausible." For the US tests, supervisors have pledged that the severely adverse scenario will reflect, at a minimum, the economic and financial conditions typical of a severe post-WWII US recession (Tarullo 2014b).

33. Bernanke (2013) acknowledged that the Federal Reserve uses more than 40 models to project how categories of bank losses and revenues would respond to hypothetical scenarios.

dressing why so many models are needed, analysts (Bank of England 2013; Borio, Drehmann, and Tsatsaronis 2012) offer the following explanations.

Stress tests involve credit risk, market risk, sovereign risk, and liquidity and funding risks. A single model will not be capable of handling all these types of risk. Although attention often centers on loan losses, models of bank earnings are no less important.[34] Standard macromodels don't capture the effect of macroconditions on the elements of bank balance sheets; to do so requires specialized auxiliary models. Since the probability of model error is high, a "consensus" approach based on the output of a group of models is warranted. So-called bottom-up approaches that rely on banks' own models to estimate the effect of shocks on bank performance are good for capturing the granularity and idiosyncratic aspects of individual banks, but those short-fall estimates need to be weighted against "top-down" estimates, in which the regulator imposes consistency and uses its own set of models. A set of models also makes it harder for the banks to "game" the tests by increasing exposure to risks that are underestimated by a particular model.

Capital hurdle rates. The capital hurdle rate indicates the minimum capital ratio that banks need to reach under the various scenarios. Falling below the hurdle rate yields a verdict of failure (as in the EU-wide tests) and/or (as in the CCAR tests) requires a new capital plan that enables the bank to pass the test.

The capital hurdle rate is meant to convey the message that banks have sufficient capital to absorb losses under adverse conditions while still meeting international, regional, and national regulatory minimums for capital adequacy. Minimum international regulatory standards for bank capital are represented by Basel III.[35] The United States and the European Union issued final Basel III implementation regulations in mid-2013. Since the BCBS decided to phase in the Basel III requirements over a six-year period ending in December 2018, and since the phase-in period is different for different measures of bank capital, meeting the Basel III minimums is a moving and differentiated target. The only relevant regional minimum capital standard for our purposes is the EU's fourth *Capital Regulation Directive* (CRD IV); it too went into effect in mid-2013. It mostly mirrors Basel III, but has been criticized both for watering down some of the excluded items in the definition of CET1 capital and for making it harder for EU countries to impose national minimum capital standards that are considerably above the Basel III minimums (Goldstein 2012, Vestergaard and Retana 2013). Outside the European Union, there

---

34. Recent studies of bank capital increases over the 2007–12 period show that retained earnings made the largest contribution to such increases (Cohen and Scatigna 2014).

35. The minimum capital adequacy levels under Basel III are 4.5 percent of risk-weighted assets for CET1 capital (exclusive of several additional buffers), 6 percent of risk-weighted assets for T1 capital, 8 percent of risk-weighted assets for total capital, and 3 percent of (unweighted) total assets for T1 leverage.

are no limits to how much national minimum capital standards may exceed Basel III.[36]

Table 8.1 shows that the 2009 SCAP used a stressed capital hurdle rate of 4 percent for T1C. When the CCAR was introduced in 2011, the stressed capital hurdle rate was raised to 5 percent. A stressed T1 leverage rate of 3 percent was also introduced into the tests. In the 2012–14 CCARs, the stressed T1C hurdle rate was maintained at 5 percent, while in 2014, the stressed hurdle rate for T1 leverage was raised to 4 percent. Table 8.1 also shows the average change in the capital ratio, defined as the difference between its stressed level in the most adverse scenario and the starting level just before the first year of the scenarios. What the calculations show is that the fall in the capital ratio under the most adverse scenario has been getting larger over the 2012–14 period, thus lending support to the claim that the CCAR scenarios cum stress test models are becoming somewhat tougher over time.[37]

Table 8.2 provides similar information on stressed bank capital hurdle rates for the first four EU-wide stress tests. The first two EU tests had a 6 percent stressed hurdle rate, but applied it to a lower-quality measure of bank capital, namely, T1. Not until the 2011 EU-wide test was the hurdle rate defined as CT1 capital, and then the rate was lowered to 5 percent. In the 2014 stress test, the hurdle rate was defined as CET1, and the stressed hurdle rate was increased to 5.5 percent. A leverage ratio was not part of the 2014 test. As in the US tests, the decline in the capital ratio during the adverse scenario has gotten larger over time.

Disclosure. The United States had no supervisor-led test in 2010, and the European Union had no EU-wide tests in either 2012 or 2013. Moreover, the first CCAR report in 2011 contained no bank-by-bank results, and this was only two years after the widely acclaimed success of such bank-by-bank disclosure in the 2009 SCAP. In the face of market skepticism, the CEBS and the EBA appeared to be dragged, kicking and screaming, into progressively greater disclosure over the 2009–11 period. During 2012–13, those concerned about

---

36. In a recent Bank of Canada study, Éric Chouinard and Graydon Paulin (2014) suggest that most large, internationally active banks should have little trouble in meeting the Basel III standards, at least under nonstressed conditions. Using a broad sample of 100 large banks, they report that the average CET1 capital ratio was 9.5 percent in mid-2013, and that only five of the 100 banks had a CET1 ratio below 7 percent (the Basel III minimum that would apply for CET1 plus the 2.5 percent capital conservation buffer). Similarly, Chouinard and Paulin (2014) indicate that the (aggregate) T1 leverage ratio for this same group of banks was 4.3 percent in mid-2013, again above the Basel III minimum.

37. Senior US regulatory officials have stated that, unlike a professional golf tournament, US stress tests are not designed with a prespecified failure rate in mind (Tarullo 2014b). The failure rate in a stress test is not necessarily a good indicator of the severity of the test because, among other things, the failure rate is so sensitive to the definition and height of the capital hurdle rate.

European banking fragility had to wait for what was advertised as a bigger and better stress test cum AQR, undertaken only in October 2014.[38]

Still, the steps toward greater disclosure in the United States and the European Union have been substantial in terms of test objectives, participating banks, recent trends in bank capital and liquidity, methodology, macroeconomic and market risk scenarios, model approach, treatment of securitizations, data templates, and individual bank loses by type of exposure. All in all, I would hardly call the process a "black box." Apparently, supervisory officials in the United States and the European Union have concluded that what they gain from greater transparency and disclosure surrounding the stress tests—in terms of market discipline, improved public confidence during crises, and fuller bank engagement in the exercise—more than compensates for any risk of market turbulence or false complacency associated with publication of the results.

Remedial policy actions in response to the test results. Without remedial action on individual banks or the system as a whole, stress tests would not be of much help. The unhappy Japanese experience with "zombie" banks in the 1990s is but one case in point. In planning the framework for its own stress tests, due in late 2014, the Bank of England (2013) has set out the measures that banks could be required to take if there was a need to strengthen their capital. These include (1) constraining dividend distributions, share buybacks, or discretionary payments on certain T1 capital instruments; (2) constraining (variable) remuneration to staff; (3) issuing equity or other capital instruments that can definitely absorb losses on a "going concern" basis (outside of resolution or liquidity); (4) engaging in liability management exercises; and (5) reducing certain risk exposures or business lines.

If the stress tests reveal that the banking system as a whole is significantly undercapitalized, there are likewise remedial policy actions that could be taken, including increasing the countercyclical capital buffer, increasing national minimum capital requirements, constraining dividend payments for all banks, requiring new equity issuance, and, in a deep crisis, using public funds to recapitalize banks unable to tap private sources.

Criticisms of Stress Testing Methodology and the Measurement of Bank Capital

Even though stress testing is now a "cornerstone of a new approach to regulation and supervision of the . . . largest banks," as Daniel Tarullo (2014b) of the Federal Reserve Board has asserted, some critics have identified serious problems in the methodology. Four such concerns merit discussion.

---

38. As noted earlier, the EBA published the results of a Basel III monitoring exercise in April and September 2012 and the results of an EU-wide capital exercise in October 2012, but neither analyzed the conditions of EU banks under an adverse scenario.

First, bank stress tests have been found seriously wanting as an early warning indicator of banking crises. Claudio Borio, Mathias Drehmann, and Kostas Tsatsaronis (2012, 7) offer the following bold charge: "To our knowledge, no macro stress test carried out ahead of the [2007–09] crisis identified the build-up of the vulnerabilities. The message was overwhelmingly: 'The system is sound.' Rather than being part of the solution, stress tests turned out to be part of the problem." For example, they point to the clean bill of health given to Iceland's banking sector in the 2008 IMF FSAP.[39]

According to Laeven and Valencia (2013), 18 countries experienced "systemic" banking crises during the 2007–11 period. Since they report that all of these systemic crises (with the exception of Nigeria) started in 2007 or 2008, I looked at the FSAPs (cum bank stress tests) published by the IMF in 2006–07 for the seven larger economies that were on the Laeven-Valencia list: Greece (2006), Denmark (2006–07), Ireland (2006), Spain (2006), the United Kingdom (2006), Belgium (2006), and Portugal (2006).[40] What I was looking for in these FSAPs (preferably in the executive summaries) was a clear published warning of a potentially serious banking crisis, along with a recommendation for strong corrective policy response.[41] I found little of it (Goldstein 2015). From an early warning perspective and taken as a group, there is not a lot here for the IMF to brag about.[42]

The BIS authors are highlighting a disconnect between the early warning literature on banking crises and the adverse scenarios typically employed in the bank stress tests. Banking crises typically occur when credit growth to the private sector and real property prices are well above their norms. These are dual-threshold models in which a crisis is indicated when credit growth and real property prices are at or near the peak (Borio and Drehmann 2009; Borio, Drehmann, and Tsatsaronis 2012; BIS 2014).[43] The intuition is that credit growth is a proxy for leverage (and lending standards), while property prices are proxy for collateral (BIS 2014). Sharp declines in real economic growth or large increases in the unemployment rate *do not* stand out as good advance indicators of banking crises, since these crises typically begin when output growth is still

---

39. "The banking system's reported financial indicators are above minimum regulatory requirements and stress tests suggest that the system is resilient" (Borio, Drehmann, and Tsatsaronis 2012, 1).

40. The United States did not have an FSAP during this period. According to the IMF's Independent Evaluation Office (IMF 2011c), the IMF repeatedly asked to do an FSAP during the 2004–07 period, but US authorities declined those requests.

41. I say "published" warning because I am told that IMF FSAP missions typically leave with country authorities a confidential memorandum that is not published; since such memoranda are not available to outside analysts, I have to base my commentary on the published reports alone.

42. My assessment is similar to that reached by the IMF's Independent Evaluation Office in 2011 (IMF 2011c) in its report on the performance of Fund surveillance in the 2004–07 run-up to the global economic and financial crisis.

43. The BIS authors also find that debt service ratios can be useful in the near term in anticipating financial strains and crises.

in the upswing. Once a banking crisis erupts, real output does show a marked fall and this output decline has a negative feedback effect on banks. But it is the banking crisis that causes output to fall, not the other way around. A major selling point of these early warning models is that they seem to have caught the bulk of the systemic banking crises over the past 40 years or so, including the 2007–09 crises in the United States and the United Kingdom, and the Asian financial crisis of 1997–98 (BIS 2014). The takeaway is that stress tests may be a good way to differentiate weak banks from stronger ones once a banking crisis is already under way, but they are not apt to see one coming, especially when many other risk indicators—like credit default spreads, interest rate spreads, and equity market volatility—are sending "all is clear" signals.

Because credit-to-GDP ratios typically fall after banking crises, US and EU supervisors might respond that it would not have been useful to include a credit boom scenario in their 2009–14 series of stress tests; indeed, during this recovery period, the concern was to get bank lending up, not down. If credit growth and property prices become elevated in the future, that would be the time—so the argument might go—to include such a scenario in the stress tests.

According to the BIS (2014), red lights are flashing for the credit-to-GDP and property-price early warning indicators for an Asian emerging-economy aggregate, composed of Hong Kong, China; Indonesia; Malaysia; the Philippines; Singapore; and Thailand. The credit-to-GDP indicator is likewise flashing red for the PRC (and for Brazil, Switzerland, and Turkey), and it is flashing yellow for the Republic of Korea.[44] In short, a prominent early warning model of banking crises is pointing to high potential vulnerability in much of emerging Asia over the next few years.

Hong Kong, China; Malaysia; the PRC; the Republic of Korea; and Singapore have had IMF FSAP missions cum bank stress tests during the 2011–14 period. My reading of those FSAP reports—sometimes supplemented by looking at the recent Article IV consultation report—is that they are better than the FSAPs done in 2004–07 in identifying and highlighting the systemic risk to the banking system caused by very rapid credit growth and highly elevated property prices.[45] But those IMF reports still place too much confidence in the usually reassuring results of the stress tests; and even more so, the reports are still too timid in recommending strong corrective and protective remedial measures.[46]

---

44. The BIS early warning indicator for credit booms refers to total credit to the private sector and hence is not affected by sharp shifts between bank and shadow bank financing.

45. Going beyond credit booms and property prices, the recent IMF FSAPs are also better than ones done earlier in dealing with liquidity risks and in evaluating various types of contagion.

46. My reasons for suspecting that too much confidence is being placed in the largely optimistic outcomes of stress tests are explained more fully in the remainder of this section. In short, the stress tests rely almost exclusively on risk-based measures of capital instead of leverage ratios, and the stress test models themselves do not include either enough adverse feedback effects from the financial sector to the real sector or large amplification effects within the bank and nonbank financial sectors. See Goldstein (2015) for quotes from these FSAP reports pertaining to Asian emerging economies.

Even when and where early warning models of banking crises and IMF-run stress tests reach a similar verdict, national bank supervisors may disagree with the findings. The People's Bank of China, referring to its own stress tests covering 17 systemically important domestic banks, concluded: "Under light, middle and heavy stress scenarios, the banking system's overall capital adequacy would remain at the relatively high level: even the most serious scenarios would not see capital adequacy fall below 10.5 percent.[47,48]

A second major criticism of bank stress tests is that they fail to capture adequately the heightened uncertainty, nonlinearity, and contagion that make the output loss deeper and the recovery slower for recessions accompanied by financial crises than for normal recessions.[49] As emphasized by Borio, Drehmann, and Tsatsaronis (2012), the feedback effects from financial sector stress to the real economy tend to be rather weak in the models underlying the tests, with the result that it takes very large shocks to generate serious capital inadequacy for banks.[50] In contrast, during a real systemic banking crisis, risks can migrate quickly from one institution, asset class, or county to others; insolvency and liquidity risks can reinforce one another, leading to severe funding strains for banks and their customers; and market participants whose claims are not guaranteed may find it logical to "run" into cash or treasuries until they get better information.[51] On top of this, delays or conflicts in formulating a muscular government response to a crisis can undermine confidence in ways that are not evident from earlier time series.

---

47. See "China Confident After Bank Stress Tests, Even As Growth Slows," Reuters, April 30, 2014.

48. There are also the views of outside analysts to consider on the risk of banking crises. Speaking in April 2014, Nicholas Lardy (2014) concluded that the risk of a financial crisis in the PRC—despite the large run-up in credit—has been somewhat exaggerated and emphasized six mitigating factors: (1) bank lending is almost entirely funded by relatively stable (and largely captive) bank deposits and not by wholesale funding sensitive to sudden stops; (2) the shadow banking sector, despite recent growth, is still smaller as a percentage of GDP than both the global average and its counterpart in the United States; (3) the PRC still has a plain vanilla financial system, with relatively limited loan securitization; (4) although external debt is on the rise, the PRC's net international investment position is very strong; (5) the rate of credit growth could well moderate in the next few quarters, as it has often done in the past after sharp increases; and (6) the effects of a credit slowdown are likely to be tolerable, since the slowdown's negative effect on growth is likely to be offset in part by improved credit allocation to the private sector (where rates of return are much higher).

49. See Reinhart and Rogoff (2009) for the differences between banking crises and normal recessions.

50. As Borio, Drehmann, and Tsatsaronis (2012, 7) state, "the very essence of financial instability is that normal-size shocks cause the system to break down."

51. Kartik Anand, Guillaume Bédard-Pagé, and Virginie Traclet (2014) indicate that when the Bank of Canada included liquidity and spillover effects, in addition to solvency risk, in the stress tests that ran for its 2013 FSAP with the IMF, it found that the capital position of Canadian banks was 20 percent lower than when these effects were omitted. I suspect that this is a lower bound to the true effects.

One example of the forces at work comes from the Asian financial crisis of 1997–98, where the initial shock was to the economy of Thailand—not one of the world's major trading or investment hubs.[52] Yet the crisis spread quickly to Indonesia, Malaysia, the Republic of Korea, and the Philippines, leaving in its wake crashes in exchange rates and equity markets, deep recessions, and banking crises. I offered the "wake-up call" hypothesis as an explanation (Goldstein 1998).[53] I posited that Thailand served as a wake-up call for international investors to reassess the credit worthiness of Asian borrowers. And when they made that reassessment, they concluded that quite a few emerging Asian economies had vulnerabilities similar to Thailand's: large external deficits, appreciating real exchange rates, sizable currency mismatches, weak financial sectors with poor prudential supervision, export slowdowns (in 1996), and declining quality of investment. As currencies and equity markets were written down to reflect this reassessment, the crisis spread. A weighted average of fundamentals that gives greater weight to those where Thailand was relatively weak is more consistent with an ordinal ranking of the Asian economies most affected by the crisis than does one predicated on either the extent of bilateral interdependence with Thailand or the strength of fundamentals irrespective of similarities with Thailand.[54]

This example suggests that it is possible to generate a systemic crisis from a relatively modest initial shock if that shock leads to a reassessment of risk in a wider class of assets or financial institutions where previously vulnerabilities were underestimated.

---

52. A second good example comes from the 2007–09 global economic and financial crisis, where an intriguing question is how a shock to the relatively small US subprime mortgage market wound up generating such a widespread and systemic crisis. Part of the answer comes from what Gary Gorton and Andrew Metrick (2010) call the "run on repo," that is, a run on the repurchase market. Here, weakness in the subprime mortgage market in early 2007 caused repo buyers of securitized bonds to become anxious about the quality of their collateral. As real estate and mortgage prices continued to slump, that anxiety continued to increase and it was reflected in large-scale selling of collateral and demands for larger "haircuts" in a widening segment of the huge repo market. Because many of the largest US investment houses and commercial banks were using the repo market to fund themselves, it wasn't long before the drying up of funds in the repo market led to fears about the liquidity of counterparties in the interbank market. The forced rescue of Bear Stearns in March 2008 stoked further fears and induced the contagion to spread to highly rated credit securities unrelated to the subprime markets. Soon the entire securitized banking model came under intense pressure. In the second half of 2008, the panic hit a wider array of asset markets, financial institutions, and the real economy, ultimately contributing to the failure of Lehman Brothers, the AIG bailout, and the government takeovers of Fannie Mae and Freddie Mac.

53. I call it a "wake-up call" because judging from most market indicators of risk, private creditors and rating agencies were "asleep" about vulnerabilities in the crisis countries prior to the outbreak of the Thai crisis.

54. Pavan Ahluwalia (2000) also finds that shared (visible) characteristics with the "ground zero" country—what he calls "discriminating contagion—were helpful in explaining the pattern of currency crises during the Mexican, Russian, and Asian crises (after controlling for trade and financial interdependence).

Efforts to get more "chaos" and feedback effects into the models employed in stress tests are making some progress, but they are still at an early stage. Adverse liquidity scenarios are now more prevalent, and the use of current market prices rather than historical book values to capture changing risk profiles is increasingly standard. And several central banks—including the Bank of England (2013) and the Bank of Canada (Anand, Bédard-Pagé, and Traclet 2014)—have systemwide stress testing models in place that incorporate some kinds of feedback loops and amplification mechanisms.

A third important criticism of stress tests is directed at the measuring rod for the whole exercise: a *risk-weighted* measure of bank capital. The last five years have witnessed a growing chorus of doubts about the reliability of RWAs, the aggregate that serves as the denominator for all risk-weighted capital metrics. This is no narrow technical disagreement, but rather an assault on what the current chairman of the BCBS has called the "cornerstone" of the Basel framework since it was introduced 25 years ago (Ingves 2014a, 2).[55]

Critics (myself included) argue that the deficiencies of these measures are so serious that the leverage ratio should instead serve as the primary measuring rod for capital adequacy. The case for downplaying the risk-based measures has been made forcefully by Andrew Haldane (2013, 2012) and by Thomas Hoenig (2013, 2012). Their main points are the following:

- Risk-based capital ratios did poorly in predicting bank failures during the 2007–09 crisis (among a sample of 100 large, complex global banks) compared with a simple leverage ratio, and this finding seems to be robust to the inclusion of macrocontrol variables.

- Risk-based capital measures misled investors and the public during the global crisis about the safety of the 10 largest US banking firms, which reported an average T1 capital ratio of above 7 percent and were regarded as well capitalized. Yet many needed official support during the crisis. Their average leverage ratio was only 2.8 percent—not enough to absorb a major shock (Hoenig 2013).[56]

---

55. Recall that when Basel I was introduced in 1988, there was only a small set of supervisor-set risk weights. Responding to criticism that Basel I did not include enough risk sensitivity and granularity, Basel II, agreed to in 2004, vastly expanded the number of risk weights by permitting banks to use internal models to calculate these weights (subject to supervisory oversight) and by increasing risk weight gradations in the standard, supervisor-set model to include credit ratings and a host of other refinements.

Major disappointment with the performance of Basel II in the run-up to the global economic and financial crisis of 2007–09 led, in turn, to agreement on Basel III in 2010. In brief, Basel III made improvements to the quantity and quality of bank capital, and introduced quantitative liquidity standards. It also included for the first time (in an international agreement) a minimum capital ratio (called the leverage ratio) that uses *unweighted* assets in the denominator. The leverage ratio is meant to serve as a backstop or safety net to guard against flaws in the risk-based capital standards.

56. Hoenig (2013) also points out that for the US banking industry as a whole, average tangible leverage ratio decreased from 5.2 percent in 1999 to 3.3 percent in 2007.

- A tangible leverage ratio (tangible equity to tangible assets) is more closely related to market measures of bank health (the price-to-book ratio, estimated default frequency, credit default swap spreads, and the market value of equity) than is the ratio of T1 capital to risk-weighted assets.

- The ratio of risk-weighted assets to total assets for 17 major international banks fell from over 70 percent in 1993 to below 40 percent at the end of 2011. Yet neither the record of bank fragility before and during the recent crisis nor the behavior of market-based measures of bank riskiness suggest that bank safety has been on a steadily declining trend (Haldane 2013). By contrast, bank leverage (the inverse of the leverage ratio) has risen over this period and is negatively correlated with bank risk weights.[57]

- Risk weights have produced an uneven playing field. Banks with the same hypothetical portfolios derive quite different risk weights from their internal models, particularly for trading book assets (Haldane 2013). Modeling choices seem to be the main drivers of the variation in risk weights (Chouinard and Paulin 2014). Banks using internal models for calculating risk weights (usually larger banks) typically exhibit much lower ratios of RWA to total assets than banks that use standardized risk weights (usually small banks) (Hoenig 2013). In some of the largest international banks, risk weight management has made it possible to drive the ratio of RWA to total assets (TA) to less than 20 percent. In the fourth quarter of 2012, Deutsche Bank reported a ratio of RWA/TA of just 17 percent.

- The superior diagnostic performance of leverage ratios suggests that "noise" is overwhelming "signal" in risk weight calculations (Haldane 2013). One reason is that risk weights are static and backward-looking, and banks may use misleading sample periods for estimating them. As Robert Engle (2009) concludes, risk weights suffer from the risk that risk will change.[58]

- For all of these reasons, at least one of the bank capital hurdle rates in stress tests should be an unweighted leverage ratio (as the Federal Reserve has done, starting with the March 2012 CCAR stress test). Mark Carney, former governor of the Bank of Canada and the sitting governor of the Bank of England, has stated: "If I had to pick one reason why Canadian banks fared as well as they did [during the 2007–09 crisis], it was because

57. Haldane (2013) states that the downward trend in risk weights is consistent with the hypothesis that banks have had the incentives and the ability to "game" the system to artificially boost their capital ratios. Stanley Fischer (2014b, 2), vice chair of the Federal Reserve, observes, "Any set of risk weights involves judgments and human nature would rarely result in choices that made for higher risk weights."

58. Some worry, of course, that if an unweighted leverage ratio replaced risk-weighted measures of bank capital, banks would shift unduly into high risk–high return assets. But Hoenig (2013) argues that with more capital at risk and without regulatory risk weights affecting choices, managers will allocate capital in accordance with market risk and returns.

we had a leverage ratio."[59] Over time, we should be moving toward making the leverage ratio the primary indicator of bank solvency.

Asian economies would be wise to take note of the evidence on risk-weighted assets. As Andrew Sheng (2013) indicates, banks in emerging Asia have made relatively little use of the internal ratings approach to estimating risk weights, instead favoring the more conservative standardized approach. Asian banks therefore tend to have relatively high ratios of RWA/total assets, particularly in comparison with European banks. Vanessa Le Leslé and Sofiya Avramova (2012) report that the average RWA/total assets for banks in the Asia-Pacific was a little over one-half (0.55) in 2011, considerably higher than the 0.35 ratio recorded by European banks.

More fundamentally, Asian emerging economies should lean on measures of bank capital that provide an accurate picture of bank solvency. There is small comfort in double-digit risk-weighted capital ratios if, when faced with an extremely adverse scenario, the banks can remain solvent only with massive public support.

Asian authorities appear to be committed to meeting the 3 percent target by the BCBS deadline at the end of 2018. Table 8.3, drawing on a recent Moody's (2014) study, shows what is announced and expected about leverage ratio implementation in the United States, Europe, the Asia-Pacific, and the Middle East and Africa. All the Asian economies listed plan to meet the BCBS deadline. The PRC opted both for early implementation (2013) and for a more ambitious level of 4 percent. India too plans to exceed the minimum by adopting a 4.5 percent standard (Moody's 2014).[60]

Figure 8.1 shows regional averages for actual T1 leverage ratios.[61] For year-end 2013, the average for the Asia-Pacific is slightly above 6 percent, which is below the averages for North America, Latin America, and the Middle East, but above that for Europe.[62]

---

59. "Mark Carney Sees Logic in Tougher Cap on Banks' Leverage," *Independent*, September 29, 2014.

60. In other regions, the economies that already have or plan to exceed the BCBS minimum include the United States, Bermuda, the United Kingdom, Switzerland, and South Africa. In 2014, the US authorities issued a leverage rule for the eight firms that are classified as global systemically important banks (G-SIBs). They face a minimum (T1) leverage ratio of 5 percent for the holding company and 6 percent for the lead bank subsidiary.

61. While the leverage ratio embodied in Basel III is defined as T1 capital relative to total exposure, many analysts (including me) would prefer a definition of the leverage ratio that would have the highest quality of capital in the numerator, so as to benefit from its superior loss absorbency both in good times and in crisis.

62. Asian economies rank higher in cross-regional comparisons of leverage ratios when "tangible" leverage ratios are the metric; see the discussion in the section on "Lessons for Emerging Asia." Comparing bank leverage ratios between US and European banks has long been complicated by the different accounting treatment accorded to derivatives in the two locations. US banks use US Generally Accepted Accounting Principles (GAAP), whereas European banks use the International Financial Reporting Standards (IFRS). The GAAP provide a more lenient treatment of "netting"

Table 8.3 Leverage ratio implementation

Americas

	BCBS	US ✓ (advanced)	US (nonadvanced)	Bermuda ✓	Canada	Mexico	Brazil
Pillar 1 requirement	2018	2018	2015	2018	2018	2018	2018
Minimum ratio	3%	3% (5% G-SIB)	4% (GAAP ratio)	7%	3%	3%	TBD

Europe

	BCBS	UK[a] ✓	France	Germany	Austria	Spain	Portugal	Netherlands	Swiss Institute of Bioinformatics ✓	Russian Federation	Denmark	Norway	Sweden
Pillar 1 requirement	2018	2014	2018	2018	2018	2018	2018	2018	2013	2018	2018	2018	2018
Minimum ratio	3%	3%	3%	3%	3%	3%	3%	3%	>4%[b]	TBD	3%	3%	3%

Asia Pacific

	BCBS	People's Republic of China ✓	Hong Kong, China	Taipei, China ✓	Australia	Singapore	Indonesia	Malaysia	Thailand	Philippines	India ✓	Republic of Korea	Japan	New Zealand
Pillar 1 requirement	2018	2013	TBD	TBD	2018	TBD	2018	TBD	2018	TBD	2018	2018	TBD	n.a.
Minimum ratio	3%	4%	3%	3%	3%[c]	TBD	3%	TBD	3%	TBD	5%	3%	TBD	n.a.

Middle East and Africa

	BCBS	South Africa ✓	Israel	Pakistan	Saudi Arabia	Kuwait	Oman	Morocco	Qatar
Pillar 1 requirement	2018	2018	TBD	TBD	2018	TBD	TBD	TBD	TBD
Minimum ratio	3%	4%	TBD	3%	3%	TBD	TBD	TBD	TBD

BCBS = Basel Committee on Banking Supervision; n.a. = not available; GAAP = Generally Accepted Accounting Principles; G-SIB = global systemically important banks; TBD = to be determined

✓ = More strict than BCBS

a. Capital numerator is fully loaded common equity tier 1 (CET1) and transitional tier 1.
b. Uses total capital in the numerator, including contingent capital instruments.
c. Fully loaded tier 1; no transitional measures.

Source: Moody's Investors Service (2014).

Figure 8.1 Leverage ratio (Tier 1/average assets): Asia-Pacific versus other regions

percent

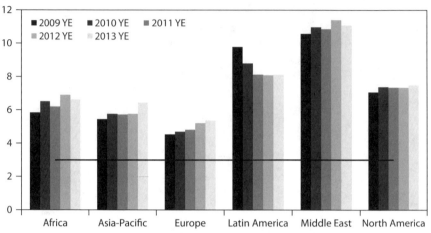

YE = year end

Note: Black line indicates 3 percent Basel Committee on Banking Supervision Tier 1 leverage.

Source: Moody's Investors Service, Banking Financial Metrics, 2014.

A fourth criticism addresses the *level* of the capital hurdle rate. Even after Basel III is fully implemented in 2019, the concern is that minimum bank capital requirements will still be far too low and that bank stress tests ought to assist the path toward a more appropriate level of bank capital by using higher hurdle rates.

Table 8.4 shows the minimum capital ratios agreed under Basel III and the transition path to full implementation. Consider the minimums for risk-weighted capital. If one takes the minimum 4.5 percent ratio for CET1 and adds to it 2.5 percent for the capital conservation buffer and, say, another 2.5 percent for the surcharge applicable to a G-SIB, the minimum CET1 ratio rises to 9.5 percent.[63] This is clearly better than the 2 percent minimum for CET1 applied under Basel II. But critics (including me) say that Basel III capital minimums are still too low, citing bank losses during a country's most serious crisis, the implications of a macroprudential approach for capital holdings, and the benefit-cost calculus for higher capital levels.

---

for derivative positions than does IFRS, with the result that total assets of US banks with large derivative positions are much smaller under the GAAP than under the IFRS. See Hoenig (2013) for the effect of these accounting differences on leverage ratios. Chouinard and Paulin (2014) indicate that for a sample of 100 large, internationally active banks, the average leverage ratio, defined as T1 capital divided by total exposure (using Basel III definitions) was 4.3 percent.

63. At the discretion of national authorities, a "countercyclical" capital buffer of another 1 to 2.5 percent could be added on during credit-boom periods to bring the total to 10.5 to 12 percent.

Table 8.4 Basel III phase-in arrangements, 2013–19 (percent)

	Basel II	2013	2014	2015	2016	2017	2018	2019
		Capital						
Leverage ratio	None	Parallel run (2013–17), disclosures start January 1, 2015					Pillar 1 (3.0)	
Minimum common equity tier 1 (CET1) ratio	2.0	3.5	4.0	4.5	4.5	4.5	4.5	4.5
Capital conservation buffer (CCB)	None	0	0	0	0.625	1.250	1.875	2.5
Min CET1 plus CCB	2.0	3.0	4.0	4.5	5.125	5.75	6.375	7.0
Phase-in of deductions from CET1	None	0	20	40	60	80	100	100
Minimum tier 1 ratio	4.0	4.5	5.5	6.0	6.0	6.0	6.0	6.0
Minimum capital adequacy ratio	8.0	8.0	8.0	8.0	8.0	8.0	8.0	8.0
Capital instruments that no longer qualify as noncore tier 1 or tier 2 capital	n.a.	Phased out over 10-year horizon, starting 2013						
Countercyclical capital buffer (voluntary)	None	0	0	0	0.625	1.250	1.875	2.5
		Liquidity						
Liquidity coverage ratio	None			60	70	80	90	100
Net stable funding ratio	None						Introduce minimum standards	

n.a. = not applicable

Source: Moody's Investors Service (2014).

In assessing bank capital levels, one can ask what capital ratio would be sufficient for banks to meet the market pressures that induce them to hold more capital than the regulatory minimums, while also keeping them solvent and able to lend after a systemic banking crisis. Samuel Hanson, Anil Kashyap, and Jeremy Stein (2010) employed just such an approach to US banking losses during the 2007–09 crisis. They observed that the four largest banks were holding a T1C capital ratio of roughly 8 percent of risk-weighted assets in the first quarter of 2010, near the lower end of the economic cycle. This was four times the regulatory minimum. The authors argued that banks were holding that excess because markets (mindful of losses in the crisis) were pressuring them to do so. Hence, they regard 8 percent as the market-induced minimum at the lower end of the cycle. They also note from IMF (2010) figures that US banks lost about 7 percent of assets during the 2007–09 crisis. They then ask the following question: If banks want to meet the market-induced minimum capital ratio at the bottom of the cycle after suffering a loss equal to 7 percent of total assets, what should the minimum capital ratio be at the top of the cycle? Their answer is 15 percent (since 15 percent minus an asset loss of 7 percent equals a market-induced minimum of 8 percent).

The T1C capital ratio of the 30 banks participating in the 2014 CCAR stress test in the fourth quarter of 2013 was 11.6 percent.[64] Applying the same methodology, again using the 7 percent asset loss from the 2007–09 crisis, yields a minimum (for the top of the cycle) of around 19 percent, and this without even accounting for the difference between total assets and risk-weighted assets (RWAs are approximately 50 percent of TAs in the United States for the largest banks under the US GAAP). Redoing the calculation using RWAs produces an answer closer to a risk-weighted capital minimum of roughly 25 percent.

Asian economies remained relatively unscathed in terms of incurred bank losses during the 2007–09 crisis.[65] But the Asian financial crisis of 1997–98 was marked by massive bank losses in Indonesia, Thailand, and the Republic of Korea. Hence, for the emerging Asian economies (and starting with a T1C capital ratio of roughly 10 percent), that same methodology would likewise yield estimates for the minimum risk-weighted capital ratio that are far above both current levels and the Basel III minimums.

If we moved from risk-based measures of bank capital to leverage ratios, then the same methodology (for example, using a current level of the T1 leverage ratio for large US banks of 8 percent) would imply that the minimum ought to be in the neighborhood of 15 percent.[66] That is far above the Basel III minimum T1 leverage ratio of 3 percent.

---

64. Using a broad sample of 100 internationally active banks, Chouinard and Paulin (2014) find that the average fully-phased-in CET1 common capital ratio in mid-2013 was 9.5 percent.

65. The IMF (2010) estimates that emerging Asian banks incurred losses equal to about 1.5 percent of total assets during the 2007–09 global crisis.

66. As noted earlier, the denominator in the Basel III leverage ratio is total exposure—a measure that is broader and larger than total assets; there are also some strong hints that the excess of total

A second route to the higher minimum capital conclusion is through the implications of the macroprudential approach to supervision. As outlined by Greenlaw et al. (2012), the macro approach focuses on (1) the balance sheet capacity of the banking system to support the economy, (2) averting runs by wholesale creditors on systemic banks, (3) avoiding fire sales and bank deleveraging during periods of stress, and (4) the links between banks and nonbanks. They argue that with substantial reliance on uninsured wholesale financing, the "run point" for a systemic bank happens at a higher capital ratio than the solvency point, so such banks need more capital to avoid runs. To support the weaker parts of the financial system during periods of stress, even solvent banks may be required to resist drawing down their capital. The bottom line of Greenlaw et al. (2012) is that if one wants to discourage runs that have costly macroeconomic effects, the banking system needs higher capital.

Two recent examples help to illustrate this macroprudential perspective. Boston Federal Reserve President Eric Rosengren (2014) lamented that US broker-dealers still obtain over half their funding from the short-term repo market. US money market mutual funds are the largest net suppliers of repurchase agreement financing. Despite some postcrisis reforms to the money market funds industry, Rosengren (2014) argues that there could again be serious interruptions in repo financing from money market funds, with cascading effects on broker-dealer liquidity. Rosengren (2014, 11) recommends that since "highly capitalized institutions are much less subject to runs," there should be an increase in capital for any (bank) holding company with significant broker-dealer operations.[67]

A second example recently highlighted by Philip Turner (2014) and summarized by the BIS (2014) concerns the shift from bank lending to market-based debt financing by nonfinancial corporations in emerging-market economies. Turner (2014) shows that financing of emerging-market nonbanks by international bonds is about twice as large as cross-border lending by international banks (to these borrowers). The availability of market funding is very procyclical and funding strains could develop when interest rates eventually go up significantly in the advanced economies. Turner (2014) also draws attention to the fact that nonfinancial corporate deposits in some emerging economies stand at more than 20 percent of the banking system's total assets.

---

exposure over total assets is biggest for G-SIBs. This means that bank losses will be smaller relative to total exposure than to total assets, thereby reducing the optimal leverage rate. The problem is that since the Basel III leverage ratio was introduced only in 2010, the time-series is very short and there is no reliable way of knowing whether the ratio of total exposure to total assets is different in crises than during normal periods. My best guess is that for large US banks, substituting total exposure for total assets would use reduce estimates of the optimal Basel III leverage rate from 15 percent to perhaps 12 to 13 percent.

67. Lest one think that Rosengren's (2014) concern about potential runs from wholesale creditors is a narrow, special case confined to the United States, Greenlaw et al. (2012), drawing on IMF (2010) research, point out that among 14 advanced economies examined, the United States had one of the lowest ratios of dependence on wholesale funding relative to bank capital.

If these firms lose access to nonbank financing, they may have to run down their bank deposits—causing, in turn, funding problems for banks.

The importance of nonbank funding looms large in emerging Asia, where the financial system exhibits considerable diversity and is not dominated by banks. In chapter 3 of this volume, William Cline examines four channels of financial intermediation: bank loans, loans by nonbanks, bonds and debt securities, and stock market capitalization. If bank loans make up 50 percent or more of the total, Cline labels the system bank dominated; if bonds plus equity market capitalization account for 60 percent or more of the total, the system is portfolio dominant; and if neither of those two thresholds are reached, the system is called diversified.

Of the nine emerging Asian economies examined, only two, the PRC and Viet Nam, are bank dominated. Malaysia, the Philippines, and Sri Lanka are portfolio-dominated; and India, Indonesia, the Republic of Korea, and Thailand are diversified. As another indicator of diversity, a recent McKinsey report (Alvarez et al. 2013) sees India, Indonesia, Malaysia, Thailand, and Viet Nam as characterized by relatively heavy reliance on retail deposits, lack of wholesale funding opportunities, relatively low banking penetration, relatively high asset growth, and relatively high interest rate volatility. In contrast, Hong Kong, China and Singapore are characterized as having higher reliance on international wholesale funding, moderate asset growth, and relatively high banking penetration. Cross-country comparisons by the BIS (2014) show Malaysia and Indonesia as having relatively high shares (20 percent or more) of banking deposits accounted for by nonfinancial corporations.

The third road to higher bank capital requirements is through benefit-cost evaluations of alternative capital levels. The benefits are taken to be a lower incidence of systemic banking crises, with attendant lower output, employment, and fiscal losses. The costs are assumed to be higher spreads or reduced availability of bank loans, with negative effects on economic growth. Not surprisingly, the banking industry's evaluation of this benefit-cost calculus is much less favorable than that of both the official sector and, by now, most finance academics.[68]

In making the case that the social costs of higher bank capital are low, Anat Admati and Martin Hellwig (2013) and other proponents stress the following arguments: Bank capital, unlike reserve requirements, is not something that banks must hold in a strongbox at the expense of higher lending; instead, capital requirements are about how banks are permitted to fund themselves. True, the Modigliani-Miller theorem about the total cost of financing being

---

68. The gulf is wide. For example, the IIF (2010) estimated that full implementation of banking reform (of which higher capital standards in Basel III was the most important element) would drive down annual G-3 (United States, European Union, and Japan) real GDP growth by 0.6 percentage points. In contrast the Macroeconomic Assessment Group put together by the BCBS and FSB (2010) concluded that the negative growth effect would be only 0.5 percentage points per year for five years—one-twelfth the IIF's estimate. In 2010, the FSB and the BCBS reviewed the studies on the benefits and costs of Basel III and came to the conclusion that the *net* benefits would be on the order of 30 percent of GDP for G-20 economies (BCBS and FSB 2010).

invariant to the mix of debt and equity does not hold strictly in the real world. Still, its fundamental insight—that higher equity reduces the riskiness of both equity and debt and therefore lowers the required rate of return, blunting any sizeable increase in overall financing costs—is a much better approximation than the doomsday claims of the banking industry.

There is no reason why higher capital requirements must reduce bank lending. If higher capital requirements are expressed in terms of absolute amounts of capital and if higher capital is obtained by a combination of new equity issuance, retained earnings, and a temporary suspension of dividend payments, the effects on the economy are likely to be benign. Any adverse selection and signaling effects of new equity issuance can be minimized by increasing capital requirements across the board.

Time-series evidence for more than 100 years of US and UK data yields no statistically significant link between higher bank equity on the one hand, and interest rate spread on bank loans, loan growth, and economic growth on the other (Hoenig 2012; Miles, Yang, and Marcheggiano 2011). The world's ten largest nonfinancial corporations finance themselves with an equity share of about 50 percent (Ingves 2014a), yet these companies have no problem in expanding their investments. Bank credit crunches typically happen when banks have very low levels of equity, not high ones. Yes, there are a handful of studies that find that higher capital requirements reduce lending. Their conclusions, however, hold only under quite restrictive conditions, unlike those prevailing under, say, a Basel III–type increase in minimum capital standards (e.g., Bridges et al. 2014 and references therein).

The existence of a sizable shadow banking system is not a good reason to avoid raising significantly bank equity standards. Rather, all financial institutions whose failure would have systemic consequences should be required to have enough equity.

Using a sample of 94 large banks from advanced and emerging economies, Benjamin Cohen and Michela Scatigna (2014) study the increase in capital ratios between end-2009 and end-2012. One of their main conclusions is worth repeating: "Bank capital ratios have increased steadily since the financial crisis. . . . On average, banks continued to expand their lending, though lending growth was relatively slower among European banks. . . . Banks that came out of the financial crisis with higher capital ratios and stronger profitability were able to expand lending more" (Cohen and Scatigna 2014, 2).

Of particular interest for emerging Asian economies, Robert McCauley (2014) has examined the results for emerging-market banks from the Cohen and Scatigna (2014) study and reports that emerging-market banks raised their capital ratios over the 2009–12 period by 1.1 percentage points. Their return on assets widened, but not from a raising of the net interest margin (it came instead from lower operating costs and other factors). Emerging-market banks did *not* shrink their loan books[69]; indeed, loan growth was boosted

---

69. Chouinard and Paulin (2014) likewise report that in Canada total credit continued to expand in the postcrisis period, even as banks built up their capital levels.

almost by half over this period. McCauley's (2014, 3) conclusion is worth highlighting: "To sum up, the evidence to date from Asia and the Pacific is that banks have managed to raise their capital ratios without raising the cost of credit in aggregate or by seriously restricting its availability."

While these arguments don't lead to a specific figure for minimum capital requirements, some analysts have interpreted them as pointing to minimum leverage requirements in the neighborhood of 15 to 20 percent. In a November 2010 letter to the *Financial Times*, 20 distinguished professors of finance (including two Nobel laureates) reached the following conclusion: "Basel III is far from sufficient to protect the system from recurring crises. If a much larger fraction, at least 15 percent of banks' total, non-risk-weighted assets, were funded by equity, the social benefits would be substantial. And the social cost would be minimal, if any."[70]

This does not mean that bank stress tests should immediately set hurdle rates at 15 or 20 percent, but it does suggest that over time supervisory authorities should progressively raise the bar to get closer to the optimum.[71] After all, Basel III will be fully phased in by 2019. As Yogi Berra, the NY Yankees Hall of Fame catcher, put it succinctly, "If you don't know where you're going, you may not get there."

Moody's Investors Service (2014) has been tracking the implementation of the Basel III risk-weighted capital standards. Table 8.5 shows its tally for Asia-Pacific and for other regions. With the exception of the Middle East and Africa, no region has exceeded the timetable or minimum CET1 ratio more consistently than Asian emerging economies, with Taipei,China (7 percent), Singapore (6.5 percent), the Philippines (6.0 percent), India (5.5 percent), and the PRC (5.0 percent) opting to go for more than the BCBS 4.5 percent minimum. In addition, the PRC, Indonesia, Thailand, and the Philippines chose to implement ahead of the January 2015 BCBS deadline; only the Republic of Korea and Taipei,China are planning a delayed implementation.[72]

As for the existing level of common equity relative to risk-weighted assets for the region, Moody's (2014) shows the ratio of tangible equity to risk-weighted assets, as of year-end 2013, to be slightly above 10 percent for the Asia-Pacific—clearly above the 7 percent Basel III minimum. The IMF (2014b), in its latest *Regional Economic Outlook*, provides a country-by-country breakdown, but only for the ratio of T1 capital to RWA. In its tabulation, Singapore, Indonesia, Philippines, and Hong Kong, China have the highest T1 ratios (13

---

70. "Healthy Banking System Is the Goal, not Profitable Banks," *Financial Times*, November 9, 2010. Sitting FDIC Vice Chairman Hoenig (2013) has supported a 10 percent minimum for the tangible leverage ratio.

71. In Goldstein (2015), I offer a proposal for how to use the flexibility inherent in stress tests to raise gradually the tangible leverage ratio to roughly 15 percent over a 10-year period.

72. Peter Morgan and Victor Pontines (2013) argue that the more restrictive definition of capital in Basel III (that is, emphasizing T1C) should not be a problem for Asian emerging economies because it will not represent much of a change. They maintain that in these economies there are few alternatives to equity and that the major component of capital has always been common equity.

Table 8.5 Basel III minimum risk-weighted capital requirements by region, CET1, Tier 1, and total capital adequacy ratio

Americas

	BCBS	US (advanced)	US (non-advanced)	Bermuda	Canada[a] ✓	Mexico ✓	Brazil ✓
Minimum CET1	4.5%	4.5%	4.5%	4.5%	4.5%	4.5%	4.5%
Minimum T1	6.0%	6.0%	6.0%	6.0%	6.0%	6.0%	6.0%
Minimum CAR	8.0%	8.0%	8.0%	8.0%	8.0%	8.0%	8.0%[b]
Compliant by	January 2015	January 2015	January 2015	January 2015	January 2015	January 2013	October 2013

Asia Pacific

	BCBS	People's Republic of China ✓	Hong Kong, China	Taipei, China ✓	Australia ✓	Singapore ✓	Indonesia	Malaysia	Thailand ✓	Philippines ✓	India ✓	Republic of Korea	Japan ✓	New Zealand ✓
Minimum CET1	4.5%	5.0%	4.5%	7.0%	4.5%	6.5%	4.5%	4.5%	4.5%	6.0%	5.5%	4.5%	4.5%	4.5%
Minimum T1	6.0%	6.0%	6.0%	8.5%	6.0%	8.0%	6.0%	6.0%	6.0%	7.5%	7.0%	6.0%	6.0%	6.0%
Minimum CAR	8.0%	8.0%	8.0%	10.5%	8.0%	10.0%	8.0%	8.0%	8.5%	10.0%	9.0%	10.5%	8.0%	8.0%
Compliant by	January 2015	January 2013	January 2015	January 2019 ✗	January 2013	January 2015	January 2014	January 2015	January 2014	January 2014	March 2015	January 2019 ✗	January 2015	January 2013

Europe

	BCBS	UK[c]	France	Germany	Austria	Spain ✓	Portugal ✓	Netherlands ✓	Swiss Institute of Bioinformatics ✓	Swiss category 2	Russian Federation ✓	Denmark	Norway ✓	Sweden ✓
Minimum CET1	4.5%	4.5%	4.5%	4.5%	4.5%	4.5%	4.5%	4.5%	10.0%[d]	9.2%	5.0%	4.5%	4.5%	4.5%
Minimum T1	6.0%	6.0%	6.0%	6.0%	6.0%	6.0%	7.0%	6.0%	13.0%[d]	11.4%	6.0%	6.0%	6.0%	6.0%
Minimum CAR	8.0%	8.0%	8.0%	8.0%	8.0%	8.0%	8.0%	8.0%	19.0%[d]	14.4%	10.0%	8.0%	8.0%	8.0%
Compliant by	January 2015	January 2015	January 2015	January 2015	January 2015	January 2014	January 2014	January 2014	January 2019 ✗	January 2017 ✗	January 2015	January 2015	January 2013	January 2014

(continued on next page)

Table 8.5 Basel III minimum risk-weighted capital requirements by region, CET1, Tier 1, and total capital adequacy ratio (continued)

Middle East and Africa	BCBS	South Africa ✓	Israel ✓	Pakistan ✓	Saudi Arabia ✓	Kuwait ✓	Morocco ✓	Oman ✓	Qatar ✓
Minimum CET1	4.5%	5.0%	9.0%	6.0%	4.5%	7.0%	5.5%	7.0%	6.0%
Minimum T1	6.0%	8.25%	9.0%	7.5%	6.0%	8.5%	6.5%	9.0%	8.0%
Minimum CAR	8.0%	9.0%	12.5%e	10.0%	12.0%	10.5%	9.5%	12.0%	10.0%
Compliant by	January 2015	January 2019 ✗	January 2015	January 2015	January 2015	January 2016 ✗	January 2014	January 2014	January 2014

BCBS = Basel Committee on Banking Supervision; CET1 = common equity tier 1; T1 = tier 1; CAR = capital adequacy ratio; CCB = capital conservation buffer; D-SIBs = domestic systemically important banks

✗ = compliant date is less strict than BCBS; ✓ = more strict than BCBS

a. Canadian financial system is dominated by six banks classified as D-SIBs, which hold around 93% of Canada's total banking assets. The D-SIBs are required to meet "all-in" capital targets (including the 2.5% CCB) of 7% for the CET1 ratio by the first quarter of 2013, and 8.5% for the T1 ratio and 10.5% for the total CAR by the first quarter of 2014. Beginning on January 1, 2016, the "all-in" capital target for CET1 ratio for D-SIBs will be 8%, including a D-SIB buffer of 1%.

b. Brazil currently has an 11% total capital ratio requirement under local Banco Central do Brasil rules; the requirement will decrease from 11% in 2013 to 8% in 2019, at the same time as other Basel II rules (such as buffers and capital deductions) are phased in, thus overall capital levels (including buffers) and quality will remain strong.

c. A UK requirement of 7% CET1 by January 2014 (includes CCB) only applies to the largest 8 banks. Others are subject to the 4.5/6/8 phase-in arrangements.

d. For SIBs, minimum CET1 includes 4.5% minimum plus a 5% CET1 buffer component (part of an 8.5% permanent buffer requirement, of which 5.5% must be met through CET1 and up to 3% can be met through high-trigger contingent capital instruments or CoCos). Tier 1 minimum includes 4.5% CET1 plus the 8.5% buffer. The minimum total capital includes a progressive component of up to 6% composed of low-trigger CoCos. The progressive component is revised each year by Swiss regulator FINMA according to the size and resolvability of the institution.

e. CET1 and CAR will increase to 10% and 1.5% respectively for banks with more than 20% market share.

Source: Moody's Investors Service (2014).

to 15 percent), while Taipei,China; the PRC; and India have the lowest (8 to 10 percent); the Republic of Korea and Thailand are in the middle (with 11 to 12 percent).[73]

Lessons for Emerging Asia[74]

This chapter has reviewed the experience of US- and EU-wide supervisors with bank stress tests, with an eye toward identifying lessons for Asian emerging economies considering whether and how to alter their own stress tests. Six lessons stand out.

1. Bank stress tests are likely to become an increasingly important part of bank supervision because they respond to a demand that other parts of the supervisory toolkit cannot easily accommodate, and because they offer more flexibility than the Basel international regulatory regime. There is a strong case for having emerging Asian economies invest in upgrading their stress-testing systems to increase their credibility.[75] The global economic and financial crisis of 2007–09 demonstrated anew how costly systemic banking crises can be. During such crises, the opacity of bank financial statements, combined with elevated uncertainty about macroeconomic and market risks, make it difficult to get an accurate picture of the solvency of individual banks and the banking system as a whole. Bank capital ratios are static and backward-looking and don't address tail risk within a forward-looking set of severe but plausible scenarios. Similarly, analyses of one bank at a time

---

73. Other things equal, countries with TBTF banks need to ensure that these banks have enough self-insurance, that is, capital. One index of TBTF, suggested by William Cline in chapter 3, is the average assets of the country's five largest banks relative to GDP. On this measure some emerging Asian economies have a TBTF problem, but not one in the same league as some EU economies. The average size of the five largest banks in Malaysia is about 30 percent of its GDP; the corresponding figures for the PRC, the Republic of Korea, and Thailand are 25, 20, and 18 percent, respectively. This is considerably worse than in the United States (11 percent), but in the same ballpark as that of Japan and Germany (slightly above 25 percent). But even in Malaysia, the TBTF score is low relative to those of the United Kingdom and the Netherlands (both over 90 percent) and of France (nearly 70 percent).

74. Although this chapter has concentrated on the lessons that emerging Asia might take away from the bank stress testing experiences of the United States and the European Union, the lessons of international experience go in both directions. As but one salient example, macroprudential instruments have been used more extensively in Asia than in any other region (IMF 2014b and McCauley 2014). Fed Chair Janet Yellen (2014) has recently made the case that for the US economy the proper policy instrument assignment is to use macroprudential policies to deal with financial stability risks, thereby leaving monetary policy to concentrate on price stability and full employment. In implementing such a policy assignment, one would think that there would be a lot to learn from emerging Asia's experience with macroprudential policies, especially those related to cooling down overheated property markets.

75. Fischer (2014a, 4) has argued that bank stress tests are likely to add significantly to the quality and effectiveness of financial sector supervision and are an innovation that should "spread internationally as best practice."

fail to provide the horizontal comparison of banks available in a stress test. Stress tests also provide a simple and understandable metric with which to evaluate the capital adequacy of banks, namely, a comparison of the capital ratio under adverse conditions with the capital hurdle rate. And where stress tests are paired with remedial actions to eliminate undercapitalization, they provide an integrated solution to the banking problem at hand.

Forging agreement on an international bank regulatory regime requires painstaking negotiation with a large group of countries. Moving from Basel I (1988) to Basel II (2004) took over a decade, and securing agreement on Basel III took an additional six years. But countries are able to set the design of their own stress tests unilaterally and, where they feel it is necessary, to adopt metrics for bank capital that go beyond the Basel regulatory minimums. They can also customize the scenarios in stress tests to reflect their own structural characteristics and vulnerabilities. Thus, emerging Asian economies may be interested in stress scenarios different from those in US and EU-wide stress tests, including credit and housing booms, a further simultaneous growth slowdown in the PRC and the euro area, the capital flow implications of US monetary policy tightening, and the possibility of reserve-currency liquidity shortages (for the dollar and the euro), like those that occurred in 2007–08. Similarly, if they wish to run a liquidity stress test assuming a more rapid phase-in of liquidity coverage ratio than is envisaged under Basel III, they are free to do so. That flexibility is attractive.

2. Despite the potential of stress tests to contribute to financial stability, their effectiveness in practice depends on the institutional framework and the design. Asian emerging economies should accordingly evaluate their stress test design and framework in light of best practice.[76]

In terms of coverage, the participating financial institutions should account for a substantial part of the system's assets. If the country has a financial system not dominated by banks, it should assess how fragilities in the nonbank sector and in systemically important nonbanks could affect the banking system. The supervisor coordinating the tests should have the authority to obtain the necessary private data inputs from the banks and the capacity to evaluate independently the quality of those inputs and the impact of the shocks assumed in the scenarios on bank capital. Over time, supervisors should develop their own suite of models to guard

---

76. A worthwhile project for the future would be to create a regional stress test "scorecard" for emerging Asian economies, where each economy's stress testing framework could be evaluated against the best practice guidelines outlined in this chapter. After looking through the latest financial stability reports published by emerging Asian central banks and the IMF FSAPs published for these economies over the 2011–14 period, I do not believe that such a scorecard could be constructed from the published materials currently available. However, the IMF, perhaps working in collaboration with the ADB, the Chiang Mai Initiative Multilateralization (CMIM) secretariat, the BIS's Hong Kong, China office, and national authorities, could obtain the necessary inputs and publish the results.

against model risk from a particular model or two and to validate the reasonableness of models used by the banks in any bank-run tests. The test coordinators must also have the political independence to call the results of the tests as they see them. If markets perceive that the tests are "rigged" to produce overly optimistic or politically convenient outcomes, publication is not likely to bolster confidence. The scenarios should address the major risks facing the economy and the banking system. It is not helpful to rule out certain scenarios just because they are counter to current policy objectives. Likewise, scenarios that cover only a minor part of the relevant risk exposures will lack credibility. In short, stress tests are not likely to be reassuring if they don't contain much stress. Linking the results of the stress test with remedial actions to correct undercapitalization is crucial. The innovation of the US CCAR exercises—to embed the stress tests within the wider capital planning process of banks—is a good one that merits serious consideration in other jurisdictions.

There is considerable diversity across emerging and developing Asia in the quality of banking supervision. A major challenge for the region will be to ensure that stress tests run by national bank supervisors are independent and transparent. The challenge is reflected in a 2011 FSB/IMF/World Bank study (FSB et al. 2011)—prepared for G-20 ministers and governors—that reported that emerging and developing Asia ranked lowest among all developing-country regions in compliance with the independence, accountability, and transparency provisions of the Basel Core Principles for Banking Supervision.[77]

3. Bank stress tests are important for crisis prevention. Much of the 2009–14 stress test experience in the United States and the European Union has, in contrast, been for crisis management. Stress tests performed poorly in the run-up to the worst economic and financial crisis since the Great Depression, failing to provide early warning of the banking system's vulnerability not just in the United States but in practically all the economies that subsequently underwent systemic banking crises in 2007–09. Two corrective measures are called for:

First, supervisors should draw more heavily on the empirical literature on early warning models of banking crises and integrate that analysis into the stress testing exercise. These are top-down, dual-threshold models that find that banking system vulnerability is greatest when there is an abnormally rapid rate of growth in credit to the nonfinancial private sector and an abnormally rapid rise in real property prices. These models performed well in forecasting most of the major systemic banking crises of recent decades, including the 2007–09 episodes. Fortunately, this is an easy fix. These are parsimonious models that can be estimated and evaluated in any

---

77. Another challenge for some countries in the region is to deal with the legal liability of bank supervisors, which can deter them from doing their job; see chapter 3 by William Cline in this volume.

economy with a decent time series on credit aggregates and on property prices. Given the BIS's (2014) recent warning that red lights are currently flashing a danger signal for the PRC plus a group of five Asian emerging economies, it would seem prudent to see that this issue is carefully evaluated in current and future stress tests.

The second fix is not so easy. It involves getting enough feedback, contagion, and amplification effects into the modeling of the financial sector during a crisis so that a seemingly moderate shock to the banking system can produce the kind of real economy and bank capital effects that are observed in an actual severe crisis. Even though they are hard to model, runs by nonbank creditors, rapid changes in haircuts on collateral, marked shifts in expectations after credit events that are viewed either as changing the "rules of the game" (like the failure of Lehman Brothers) or as uncovering a heretofore unappreciated vulnerability among a wider set of financial institutions, surges in short selling, and watershed changes in government guarantees and interventions are part and parcel of the dynamics of severe crises. Note that (a) when Fed Chairman Bernanke (2007) testified to Congress in 2007 about the subprime crisis, he estimated that it would generate total losses in the neighborhood of $50 to $100 billion; but (b) when he recently gave testimony in an AIG court case,[78] his appraisal was different: "September and October of 2008 was the worst financial crisis in global history . . . of the 13 most important financial institutions in the United States, 12 were at risk of failure within a period of a week or two." The question for stress test architects and model makers is how to make their models generate a transition from (a) to (b) in the course of, say, a year or two. This is not a technical sideshow. In stress modeling, it is the main event.

4. When banking supervisors make the determination that banks need to reach a higher capital ratio, it is important for economic growth that they translate that higher capital target into an absolute amount of capital. Put simply, the target must be expressed in terms of the numerator of the capital ratio. If, instead, the supervisors allow banks to choose how they will achieve the higher capital ratio, there is a good chance that they will opt to make much of the adjustment by cutting back on loans, by engaging in fire sales of assets, and by manipulating risk weights. These methods of lowering the denominator of the capital ratio—even if they seem to be the lowest-cost option to banks themselves—will not be the lowest-cost option for the macroeconomy. They will be contractionary.

5. Regarding the bank capital metric that would convey the most useful diagnostic information in stress tests, Basel III rightfully put a lot of focus

78. Pedro Nicolaci da Costa, "Bernanke: 2008 Meltdown Was Worse than the Great Depression," *Wall Street Journal, Real Time Economics*, August 26, 2014, http://blogs.wsj.com/economics/2014/08/26/2008-meltdown-was-worse-than-great-depression-bernanke-says/ (accessed on January 26, 2015).

on the numerator in bank capital ratios and helped to move the system in the direction of higher-quality capital. Unfortunately, Basel III did not do enough for the denominator.

The evidence is by now strong that leverage ratios are a better indicator of bank solvency and of bank fragility among large banks than the risk-weighted measures. With hindsight, it should have been obvious early in the global economic and financial crisis that measures of bank capital based on risk-weighted assets just did not smell right. Practically all the largest US financial institutions that ran into trouble during the crisis had risk-weighted capital measures that allowed them to be classified as "well capitalized" on their last reports, whereas low leverage ratios were simultaneously pointing to very thin capital cushions (Hoenig 2012). In Europe, the story was similar. The bank with the highest CT1 capital ratio (over 20 percent) in the 2011 EU-wide stress test, Irish Life and Permanent, had to be placed in a government restructuring plan in 2012 (Verstergaard and Retana 2013). Dexia likewise passed the 2011 test with flying colors, only to fail several months later. Moreover, subsequent analysis by Verstergaard and Retana (2013) demonstrated that the early warning properties of CT1 capital in identifying subsequent bank failures (after the 2011 EU-wide stress test) were inferior to a leverage ratio. Econometric analysis on a wider sample of large international banks has reached the same qualitative conclusion (Blundell-Wignall and Roulet 2012). Moreover, the risk-based measures of bank capital create an uneven playing field internationally and domestically (between large and small banks), and they correlate less well (than do leverage ratios) with market-based measures of bank health.

If Basel III were to be redesigned from scratch, it would make much more sense to make the leverage ratio the dominant bank capital metric. But it is not necessary to recall Basel III (before it is even phased in fully) or to seek to negotiate a Basel III.5 to do so. This is where the flexibility of national and regionwide stress tests comes in handy. Because bank stress tests are becoming the binding constraint on banks' capital plans in many jurisdictions, the same result can be reached by making leverage ratio(s) the key metric in these tests. That flexibility in stress tests would also allow one to move away from sole reliance on a T1 measure of leverage toward two leverage metrics, where the second one would be a "tangible" leverage ratio (Hoenig 2012).

Asian emerging economies could be part of the leading edge of a reform to begin relying on more meaningful measures of bank capital adequacy. Asian emerging economies are either on track or even ahead of schedule in meeting Basel III leverage requirements. Greater reliance on a leverage requirement would also lessen the implicit penalty that the region faces because its ratio of RWA/TA is higher than that of European banks. Going farther, the Asian region is also well placed to lead the charge on downplaying T1 leverage in favor of a tangible leverage ratio. In this connection, a recent IMF *Global Financial Stability Report* (IMF 2014a) compares tangible leverage ratios—corrected for international accounting differences (IFRS vs. US GAAP)—in large banks across regions. That comparison reveals that emerging Asia and advanced Asia had average tangible leverage ratios of 5.8 percent and 6.0 percent, respectively, which are higher than the averages for North America (4.5 percent) and the euro area (3.6 percent). Less ambitiously, emerging Asia could still contribute to reform bank capital metrics by agreeing to include at least one leverage ratio in all future supervisor-led stress tests conducted in the region.

6. Finally, when designing bank stress tests, considerable thought should be given not only to how to define the capital ratio but also to how high to set the capital hurdle rate and to how that hurdle rate should relate to longer-term plans to set appropriate capital standards. Three different approaches to answering the question of how high to set minimum regulatory requirements for bank capital have been reviewed in this chapter. The review demonstrated that the optimal level of the capital ratio is likely to be far above the minimum ratios set out under Basel III and the actual capital ratios currently prevailing around the world. Without pretending to much precision, the review of the available evidence suggests that bank regulators and supervisors ought to pursue a goal of increasing the minimum (tangible) leverage ratio to roughly 15 percent, or about five times higher than the Basel III standard and more than three times as high as the level currently prevailing in the United States and the European Union.

Although this chapter has argued against relying on risk-based measures of capital, the gap between optimal ratios and where we are today with risk-based capital would be almost as wide. That is, the optimal level for CET1 ratios is probably in the 20 to 25 percent plus ballpark, versus a Basel III minimum (inclusive of the capital conservation buffer and the surcharges for systemically important banks) of, say, 11 percent and actual ratios of roughly 12 percent or so as well.

References*

Acharya, Viral, Dirk Schoenmaker, and Sascha Steffen. 2011. How Much Capital Do European Banks Need: Some Estimates. VoxEU (November 22).

Acharya, Viral, and Sascha Steffen. 2014. Falling Short of Expectations? Stress Testing the European Banking System. VoxEU (January 17).

Admati, Anat, and Martin Hellwig. 2013. The Bankers' New Clothes: What's Wrong With Banking and What to Do About It. Princeton, NJ: Princeton University Press.

Ahluwalia, Pavan. 2000. Discriminating Contagion: An Alternative Explanation for Contagious Currency Crises. IMF Working Paper 00/14. Washington: International Monetary Fund.

Ahmed, Enam, Andrea Appeddu, Melanie Bowler, Tomas Holinka, Juan Manuel Licari, Olga Loiseau-Aslanidi, and Zach Witton. 2011. Europe Misses Again on Bank Stress Test. Moody's Analytics. Regional Financial Review (July).

---

*The Asian Development Bank recognizes "China" by the name the People's Republic of China.

Alvarez, Alberto, Nidhi Bhardwaj, Frank Guse, Andreas Kremer, Alok Kshirsagar, Erik Lüders, Uwe Stegemann, and Naveen Tahilyani. 2013. *Between Deluge and Drought: Liquidity and Funding for Asian Banks*. McKinsey Working Papers on Risk 45 (April). New York: McKinsey and Company. Available at www.mckinsey.com.

Anand, Kartik, Guillaume Bédard-Pagé, and Virginie Traclet. 2014. Stress Testing The Canadian Banking System. *Financial Stability Review* (June).

Atkinson, Tyler, David Luttrell, and Harvey Rosenblum. 2013. *How Bad Was It? The Costs and Consequences of the 2007–09 Financial Crisis*. Dallas Fed Staff Paper 20 (July). Dallas: Federal Reserve Bank of Dallas.

Bank of England. 2013. *A Framework for Stress Testing the UK Banking System: A Discussion Paper*. London.

BCBS (Basel Committee on Banking Supervision). 2010. *Basel III: A Global Framework for More Resilient Banks and Banking Systems* (December; revised June 2011). Basel.

BCBS (Basel Committee on Banking Supervision). 2013. *Revised Basel III leverage ratio framework and disclosure requirements* (September). Basel.

BCBS (Basel Committee on Banking Supervision) and FSB (Financial Stability Board). 2010. *Assessing the Macroeconomic Impact of the Transition to Stronger Capital and Liquidity Requirements*. Basel. Available at www.bis.org/publ/othp10.pdf (accessed on January 26, 2015).

Bernanke, Ben. 2013. Stress Testing Banks: What Have We Learned? Paper presented at the Financial Markets Conference, sponsored by the Federal Reserve Bank of Atlanta, April 8. Available at www.federalreserve.gov.

BIS (Bank for International Settlements). 2014. *84th BIS Annual Report, 2013/2014* (June). Basel. Available at www.bis.org.

Blundell-Wignall, Adrian, and Caroline Roulet. 2012. Business Models of Banks, Leverage and the Distance to Default. *Financial Market Trends: 2012.2*. Paris: Organization for Economic Cooperation and Development.

Blundell-Wignall, Adrian, and Patrick Slovik. 2010. *The EU Stress Test and Sovereign Debt Exposures*. OECD Working Papers on Finance 4. Paris: Organization for Economic Cooperation and Development.

Board of Governors of the Federal Reserve System. 2009a. *The Supervisory Capital Assessment Program: Overview of Results* (May). Washington: Federal Reserve System.

Board of Governors of the Federal Reserve System. 2009b. *The Supervisory Capital Assessment Program: Design and Implementation* (April). Washington: Federal Reserve System.

Board of Governors of the Federal Reserve System. 2011. *Comprehensive Capital Analysis and Review: Objectives and Overview* (March). Washington.

Board of Governors of the Federal Reserve System. 2012. *Comprehensive Capital Analysis and Review 2012: Methodology and Results for Stress Scenario Projections* (March). Washington.

Board of Governors of the Federal Reserve System. 2013. *Comprehensive Capital Analysis and Review: Assessment Framework and Results* (March). Washington.

Board of Governors of the Federal Reserve System. 2014. *Comprehensive Capital Analysis and Review 2014: Assessment Framework and Results* (March). Washington.

Borio, Claudio. 2012. *The Financial Cycle and Macroeconomics: What Have We Learnt?* BIS Working Paper 395. Basel: Bank for International Settlements.

Borio, Claudio, and Mathias Drehmann. 2009. Assessing the Risk of Banking Crises Revisited. *BIS Quarterly Review* (March): 29–46.

Borio, Claudio, Mathias Drehmann, and Kostas Tsatsaronis. 2012. *Stress Testing Macro Stress Tests: Does It Live Up to Expectations?* BIS Working Paper 369. Basel: Bank for International Settlements.

Bridges, Jonathan, David Gregory, Mette Nielsen, Silvia Pezzini, Amar Radia, and Marco Spaltro. 2014. *The Impact of Capital Requirements on Bank Lending.* Bank of England Working Paper 486. London: Bank of England.

CEBS (Committee of European Banking Supervisors). 2010 (July). *Aggregate Outcome of the 2010 EU-Wide Stress Test Exercise Coordinated by the CEBS in Cooperation with the ECB.* Brussels.

CEBS (Committee of European Banking Supervisors). 2009 (October). *CEBS's Press Release on the Results of the EU-Wide Stress Testing Exercise.* Brussels.

Chouinard, Éric, and Graydon Paulin. 2014. Making Banks Safer: Implementing Basel III. *Financial Stability Review* (June). Ottawa: Bank of Canada.

Cohen, Benjamin, and Michela Scatigna. 2014. *Banks and Capital Requirements: Channels of Adjustment.* BIS Working Paper 443. Basel: Bank for International Settlements.

Davis Polk. 2014. *Supplementary Leverage Ratio.* Visual Memorandum (September). New York: David, Polk & Wardwell LLP.

EBA (European Banking Authority). 2014a. *Results of 2014 EU-Wide Stress Test* (October 26). London.

EBA (European Banking Authority). 2014b. *Methodological Note: EU-Wide Stress Test 2014, Version 2.0* (April 29). London.

EBA (European Banking Authority). 2013. *EU-Wide Transparency Exercise 2013: Summary Report.* London.

EBA (European Banking Authority). 2012. *Results of the Basel III Monitoring Exercise, Based on Data as of 31 December 2011.* London.

EBA (European Banking Authority). 2011. *2011 EU-Wide Stress Test: Aggregate Report* (July 15). London.

EBA (European Banking Authority). 2010. *Aggregate Outcome of the 2010 EU-Wide Stress Test Exercise Coordinated by CEBS in Cooperation with the ECB* (July 23). London.

ECB (European Central Bank). 2014. *Financial Stability Review* (May). Frankfurt.

Elliott, Douglas. 2010. *A Primer on Bank Capital* (January). Washington: Brookings Institution.

Engle, Robert. 2009. The Risk that Risk Will Change. *Journal of Investment Management* 7, no. 4: 24–28.

Fischer, Stanley. 2014a. *The Great Recession—Moving Ahead.* Paper presented at a conference sponsored by the Swedish Ministry of Finance, Stockholm, August 11.

Fischer, Stanley. 2014b. *Financial Sector Reform: How Far Are We?* (July 10). Cambridge, MA: National Bureau of Economic Research.

FSB (Financial Stability Board), IMF (International Monetary Fund), and World Bank. 2011. *Financial Stability Issues in Emerging and Developing Economies.* Report to G-20 Finance Ministers and Central Bank Governors.

Geithner, Timothy. 2014. *Stress Tests: Reflections on Financial Crises.* New York: Crown Publishers.

Goldstein, Morris. 2015. Banking's Final Exam: Lessons from the US and EU-Wide Stress Tests. Unpublished manuscript. Washington: Peterson Institute for International Economics, forthcoming.

Goldstein, Morris. 2014. The 2014 EU-wide Bank Stress Test Lacks Credibility. *RealTime Economic Issues Watch* (November 5). Washington: Peterson Institute for International Economics. (Also published on VoxEU, November 18, 2014.)

Goldstein, Morris. 2012. The EU's Implementation of Basel III: A Deeply Flawed Compromise. VoxEU (May 27).

Goldstein, Morris. 1998. *The Asian Financial Crisis: Causes, Cures, and Systemic Implications*. Washington: Institute for International Economics.

Goldstein, Morris, and Nicolas Véron. 2011. *Too Big to Fail: The Transatlantic Debate*. PIIE Working Paper 11-2 (January). Washington: Peterson Institute for International Economics.

Goldstein, Morris, and Daniel Xie. 2009. The Impact of the Financial Crisis on Emerging Asia. In *Asia and the Global Financial Crisis*, ed. Reuven Glick and Mark Spiegel. San Francisco: Federal Reserve Bank of San Francisco.

Gorton, Gary, and Andrew Metrick. 2010. *Securitized Banking and the Run on Repo*. NBER Working Paper 15223 (August). Cambridge, MA: National Bureau of Economic Research.

Greenlaw, David, Anil Kashyap, Kermit Schoenholtz, and Hyun Song Shin. 2012. *Stressed Out: Macroprudential Principles for Stress Testing*. Chicago Booth Working Paper 12-08. Chicago: Booth School of Business, University of Chicago.

Haldane, Andrew. 2013. Constraining Discretion in Bank Regulation. Presented at Federal Reserve Bank of Atlanta Conference on Maintaining Financial Stability. Atlanta, April 9. Available at www.bankofengland.co.uk.

Haldane, Andrew. 2012. The Dog and the Frisbee. Paper presented at Federal Reserve Bank of Kansas City Economic Symposium, Jackson Hole, WY, August. Available at www.bankofengland.co.uk/publications.

Hanson, Samuel, Anil Kashyap, and Jeremy Stein. 2010. A Macro-prudential Approach to Financial Regulation. *Journal of Economic Perspectives* 25, no. 1: 3–28.

Heim, Philippe. 2014. Alternative Stress Tests Cannot Compare to Those of the ECB. Letter to the *Financial Times* (October 31).

Hoenig, Thomas. 2013. Basel III Capital: A Well-Intended Illusion. Presented at International Association of Deposit Insurers 2013 research conference, Basel. Available at www.fdic.gov.

Hoenig, Thomas. 2012. Back to Basics: A Better Alternative to Basel Capital Rules. Presented at American Banker Regulatory Symposium, Washington, September 14. Available at www.fdic.gov.

Hoenig, Thomas. 2015. *Release of Fourth Quarter 2014 Global Capital Index* (April 2). Washington: Federal Deposit Insurance Corporation.

Ingves, Stefan. 2014a. Banking on Leverage. Presented at 10th Asia-Pacific High Level Meeting on Banking Supervision. Auckland, February 25–27. Available at www.riksbank.se/en/.

Ingves, Stefan. 2014b. Restoring Confidence in Banks. Presented at 15th Annual Convention of the Global Association of Risk Professionals, New York, March 4. Available at www.riksbank.se/en.

IIF (Institute of International Finance). 2010. *Interim Report on the Cumulative Impact on the Global Economy of Proposed Changes in the Banking Regulatory Framework* (June). Washington.

IMF (International Monetary Fund). 2014a. *Global Financial Stability Report: Moving from Liquidity to Growth-Driven Markets* (April). Washington.

IMF (International Monetary Fund). 2014b. *Regional Economic Outlook, Asia and Pacific: Sustaining the Momentum: Vigilance and Reforms* (April). Washington.

IMF (International Monetary Fund). 2011a. *Global Financial Stability Report: Grappling with Crisis Legacies* (September). Washington.

IMF (International Monetary Fund). 2011b. *Global Financial Stability Report: Getting There from Here* (April). Washington.

IMF (International Monetary Fund), Independent Evaluation Office. 2011c. *IMF Performance in the Run-Up to the Financial and Economic Crisis: IMF Surveillance in 2004–07*. Washington.

IMF (International Monetary Fund). 2010. Systemic Liquidity Risk: Improving the Resilience of Institutions and Markets. *Global Financial Stability Report* (October). Washington.

IMF (International Monetary Fund). 2006. *Denmark: Financial System Stability Assessment* (September). Washington.

Laeven, Luc, and Fabian Valencia. 2013. Systemic Crises Data Base. *IMF Economic Review.*

Lagarde, Christine. 2011. Global Risks Are Rising, But There is a Path to Recovery. Remarks at Federal Reserve Bank of Kansas City Symposium, Jackson Hole, WY, August 27.

Lardy, Nicholas R. 2014. Financial Instability in China? Paper presented at Global Economic Prospects meeting, hosted by the Peterson Institute for International Economics, Washington, April.

Le Leslé, Vanessa, and Sofiya Avramova. 2012. *Revisiting Risk-Weighted Assets.* IMF Working Paper 12/90 (March). Washington: International Monetary Fund.

McCauley, Robert. 2014. *Is Basel III Enough for Macroprudential Policy in Asia and the Pacific?* Pacific Trade and Development Working Paper Series 36-02. Canberra: Australian National University.

Moody's Investors Service. 2014. *Basel III Implementation in Full Swing: Global Overview and Credit Implications* (August 4). New York and London.

Morgan, Peter, and Victor Pontines. 2013. *An Asian Perspective on Global Financial Reforms.* ADBI Working Paper Series. Manila: Asian Development Bank.

OECD (Organization for Economic Cooperation and Development). 2013. *Economic Outlook: Focus: Strengthening Euro-Area Banks* (October). Paris.

Pagano, Mark, Sam Langfield, Viral Acharya, Amoud Boot, Markus Brunnermeir, Claudia Buch, Martin Hellwig, Ándre Sapir, and Leke van dan Burg. 2014. *Is Europe Overbanked?* Report of the Advisory Scientific Committee (June). European Systemic Risk Board.

Posen, Adam, and Nicolas Véron. 2014. Europe's Half a Banking Union. *Europe's World* (June 15).

Reinhart, Carmen, and Kenneth Rogoff. 2009. *This Time Is Different: Eight Centuries of Financial Folly.* Princeton, NJ: Princeton University Press.

Rosengren, Eric. 2014. Broker-Dealer Finance and Financial Stability. Paper presented at a conference on the Risks of Wholesale Funding, sponsored by the Federal Reserve Banks of Boston and New York, New York, August 13.

Sheng, Andrew. 2013. *Basel III and Asia.* Finance Working Paper (May). Available at www.fung globalinstitute.org/en/wp-content/uploads/WP%20Basel%20III_Jan%2029_ONLINE.pdf (accessed on January 29, 2015). Hong Kong: Fung Global Institute.

Steil, Benn, and Dinah Walker. 2014. *Bank Valuations Tank as ECB Flubs Its Stress Test.* Geo-Graphics (November 20). New York: Council on Foreign Relations.

Tarullo, Daniel. 2014a. Dodd-Frank Implementation. Testimony before the Committee on Banking, Housing, and Urban Affairs, US Senate. September 9, 2014. Available at www.bis.org.

Tarullo, Daniel. 2014b. Stress Testing After Five Years. Presented at Federal Reserve Third Annual Stress Test Modeling Symposium, Boston, June 25.

Turner, Philip. 2014. *The Global Long-Term Interest Rate, Financial Risks, and Policy Choices in Emerging Market Economies.* BIS Working Paper 441 (February). Basel: Bank for International Settlements.

Véron, Nicolas. 2014. European Banking Union/Asset Quality Review: Not Yet Out of the Woods. Presentation at Global Economic Prospects meeting, Peterson Institute for International Economics, Washington, April 9.

Vestergaard, Jakob, and María Retana. 2013. *Behind Smoke and Mirrors: On the Alleged Capitalisation of Europe's Banks.* Copenhagen: Danish Institute of International Affairs.

Yellen, Janet. 2014. Monetary Policy and Financial Stability. 2014. Michel Camdessus Lecture, International Monetary Fund, Washington, July 2. Available at www.federalreserve.gov.

9

The People's Republic
of China:
Maintaining Financial Stability
amidst Financial Liberalization

NICHOLAS BORST and NICHOLAS R. LARDY

After a period of rapid growth and development, the financial system of the People's Republic of China (PRC) has taken on global importance. The country's banking system is now the largest in the world, and its capital markets are rapidly approaching the size of those in the advanced economies. During this period of growth, the underlying structure of the financial system has evolved significantly. Previously characterized by a traditional banking model, the Chinese financial system has become much more complex over the past decade. A large and dynamic shadow banking system now plays an important role in the allocation of credit. These new developments have helped create a more market-based financial system, but they have also brought along new risks.

Over the past decade and a half, the Chinese financial system has progressed through many stages. The late 1990s and early 2000s were a period of important structural reforms following the nonperforming loan crisis. With the onset of the global financial crisis, financial reforms slowed and the government encouraged rapid credit growth to stimulate the economy. As a result, significant risks have accumulated within the financial system, which have the potential to threaten the entire economy. Aware of these growing risks, the new Chinese leadership has renewed its commitment to financial reform.

Nicholas Borst is an analyst in the Country Analysis Unit within the Division of Banking Supervision and Regulation at the Federal Reserve Bank of San Francisco. He was a research associate and the China program manager at the Peterson Institute for International Economics. Nicholas R. Lardy is the Anthony M. Solomon Senior Fellow at the Peterson Institute for International Economics. The opinions expressed here by the authors are their own and do not necessarily represent those of the Federal Reserve System.

A wide range of reforms, many of which have been policy goals for more than a decade, are now being implemented with a renewed sense of urgency.

Many of the existing problems in the financial system stem from the inconsistent policy priorities of financial regulators. Government intervention is excessive in some areas of the financial system and wholly insufficient in other areas. For example, while much of the rest of the economy has been opened to competition from private and foreign enterprises, the financial sector is still dominated by large state-owned institutions. Similarly, market-determined prices are the norm in most sectors, except in the financial sector, where the government carefully controls the cost and quantity of capital. At the same time, a shadow banking system has emerged over the past several years, bringing with it many risks, primarily due to insufficient regulation.

The path toward resolving these risks involves implementation of the financial liberalization agenda outlined in the Third Plenum of the 18th Chinese Communist Party Congress in November 2013. The reforms include establishing private financial institutions, expanding the capital markets, allowing market-determined interest rates, further opening the capital account, creating a deposit insurance system, allowing the market-based exit of failing financial institutions, and experimenting with mixed ownership reforms. However, without careful sequencing these same reforms could trigger many of the risks policymakers are seeking to avoid. For example, opening the capital account without addressing many of the underlying imbalances in the domestic financial system could increase the probability of a financial crisis. Financial reform must strike a balance between implementation of reform and allowing incumbents sufficient time to adapt to the new system.

Though the PRC's financial system is unique in size and structure, many of the challenges it faces are common in other Asian economies. State-owned financial institutions remain an important part of many Asian financial systems. The PRC's experience with restructuring and reforming its state-owned banks offers valuable insights for countries seeking to reform their own state banks. Additionally, lessons can be drawn from the PRC on the difficulty in rooting out moral hazard and addressing regulatory arbitrage occurring via the shadow banking system. These lessons may help other Asian policymakers avoid the pitfalls of financial reform.

Reforms in the 1990s and 2000s

At the end of the 1990s, the Chinese financial system faced both international and domestic economic crises. Internationally, the Asian financial crisis was wreaking havoc on many of the PRC's economic partners, countries whose economic models PRC policymakers had consciously emulated. The Republic of Korea, Thailand, Malaysia, and others faced attacks on their currencies and capital flight. The PRC's leaders recognized that absent structural reforms and improved regulation, the PRC would also be vulnerable to this type of international volatility (Zhou 2013). Domestically, the Chinese financial system experienced a massive increase in the amount of nonperforming loans, primarily originating in inefficient state-owned borrowers. Dai Xianglong, who served as governor of the central bank during this period, declared in 1998 that 25 percent of total loans were nonperforming (Lardy 1998). By the late 1990s, most of the major banks in the PRC were effectively bankrupt (Huang 1998). Internal and external pressures had put the Chinese financial system in an extremely vulnerable position.

The response of Chinese policymakers to the accumulating risks in the financial system was dramatic. In December 1997, the State Council released the *Notice Concerning Deepening Financial Reform, Rectifying Financial Order and Preventing Financial Risk,* which outlined the risks facing the financial system and set forth a plan for reform (Chinese Communist Party News and Documents 1997). In a speech at a national financial work conference held shortly afterward, Premier Zhu Rongji identified excessive government interference in bank lending decisions, overheating in the real estate market, heavily indebted state-owned enterprises, unnecessary government investment projects, and misappropriation of bank funds as sources of the problems in the financial system (Zhu 2013). Over the next several years, the premier would spearhead an ambitious financial restructuring program, which spanned a decade and required more than RMB4 trillion in financial commitments, an amount equivalent to half of the GDP at the beginning of the process in 1998.

The first phase of the reform was designed to fix the balance sheets of banks and improve their efficiency. In 1998, the Ministry of Finance issued a RMB270 billion bond, which was sold to the four big state-owned commercial banks. The funds raised from the bond issuance were then used to significantly increase the capital base of the banks. At the same time, large state-owned banks initiated a restructuring campaign designed to increase efficiency and cut costs. Between 1998 and 2002, the banks laid off 556,000 employees and closed more than 40,000 branches (China Finance Society 1999, 2003). In 1999, the government established four asset management companies to dispose of the nonperforming loans held by the large state-owned banks. The first round of bad asset disposal involved transferring RMB1.4 trillion in nonperforming loans, or 20 percent of the total loan balance. The nonperforming loans were transferred from the books of the banks to the newly created asset management companies at par value. As with the capital injections by the Ministry of Finance, the asset management companies were largely financed by selling bonds to the banks and then using those proceeds to purchase the bad loans. As a result of capital infusions, cost-cutting measures, and disposal of bad assets, the financial situation of the banks improved rapidly.

The next phase of reform included a series of changes to the financial regulatory structure. In 2003, the State Council moved banking regulatory responsibility away from the People's Bank of China to the newly established China Banking Regulatory Commission (CBRC). The commission was tasked with monitoring and assessing risks in the banking system, protecting depositors, and formulating new supervisory rules and regulations. The government believed the creation of an independent banking regulator would be an improvement over delegating that responsibility to the central bank, which has numerous, and often conflicting, mandates set for it by the State Council. The government also reformed the ownership structure of the banks in 2003. Central Huijin, a government-owned holding company, was established to exercise the government's shareholder rights in the large state-owned commercial banks. Creating a consolidated owner was designed to remove conflicts of interest between the ownership and operation of the banks. That year Huijin made a capital investment of $45 billion in China Construction Bank and Bank of China, acquiring almost all of their equity (Walter and Howie 2011). A similar transaction was made in 2005 with Industrial and Commercial Bank of China for $15 billion and half of the bank's equity.

The final phase of the restructuring of banks was the corporatization and public listing of the major national banks. Between 2002 and 2006, foreign financial institutions were encouraged to make strategic investments in Chinese banks. These strategic partners helped establish modern corporate governance structures and implement international best practices for operations. They also contributed $17 billion in new capital in return for equity stakes in the banks (Leigh and Podoiera 2006). After these internal reorganizations, the large state-owned commercial banks were listed on the stock exchanges in Hong Kong, China and Shanghai, raising $74 billion (Turner, Tan, and Sadeghian 2012). In addition to raising new funds, an important benefit from the public listing was imposing greater disclosure and transparency on the banks as required by the exchanges and shareholders.

Response to the Global Financial Crisis

The onset of the global financial crisis precipitated a transformation in the PRC's financial development. In the fall of 2008, the Chinese government approved a large stimulus to support the economy. Most of the stimulus was transmitted through the financial system through a large increase in the stock of credit.[1] Between 2008 and 2009, the flow of new social financing almost doubled, from RMB6.98 trillion to RMB13.91 trillion.[2] Most of this increase in credit was in the form of bank loans, since commercial banks were encouraged to lend freely to stimulate investment. Another RMB2.5 trillion of credit was extended outside of traditional bank loans through products

---

1. For this analysis, credit is defined as borrowing by households and nonfinancial corporations, including local government financial vehicles and state-owned enterprises. Borrowing by the central government and financial institutions is not included.

2. Total social financing is a monthly time series produced by the People's Bank of China that measures the flow of new credit to the nonfinancial sector. The subcategories of social financing include renminbi loans, foreign currency loans, entrusted loans, trust loans, corporate bonds, and banker's acceptances. New issuances of equity by nonfinancial corporations, a noncredit measure of financing, are also included in social finance. However, equity issuances account for a small share of total social financing.

Figure 9.1   Retained earnings share of gross capital formation, 2000–11

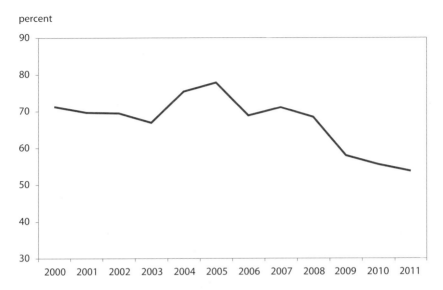

Sources: National Bureau of Statistics of China; authors' calculations.

like entrusted loans, trust loans, banker's acceptances, and corporate bonds. The stimulus was quite successful in offsetting shortfalls in external demand. Fueled by cheap credit, the investment share of GDP increased from 42 percent in 2007 to 48 percent by 2010. As a result, while much of the world fell into recession, the Chinese economy continued to grow rapidly, dipping to 9.2 percent in 2009 before accelerating to 10.4 percent in 2010. However, the financing of this investment became increasingly dependent on new credit. Figure 9.1 shows the sharp decline in the share of investment of nonfinancial corporations financed by the retained earnings. As a result of this shift, Chinese economic growth has become significantly more credit intensive.

After 2009, credit continued to grow rapidly, but the composition of the growth changed significantly in at least two dimensions. First, the share of bank loans made to private enterprises rose substantially. In 2009, state firms accounted for 56 percent of all bank loans outstanding to enterprises while the share of private firms was only 26 percent.[3] But in the ensuing three years, on average 52 percent of all new loans to enterprises went to private firms while

---

3. These data on lending by ownership are classified based on the concept of control. That means lending to state firms includes not only lending to traditional state-owned companies but also to limited liability companies and shareholding limited companies in which the state is the sole, majority, or dominant owner. Similarly, lending to private companies includes loans to registered private companies and to limited liability companies and shareholding limited companies in which the sole, majority, or dominant owner is private.

the share of state firms was only 32 percent. As a result, by the end of 2012 the share of loans outstanding to private firms had increased to 36 percent (Lardy 2014, 104–108). This shift in the ownership profile of bank borrowers reflects the increasingly commercial orientation of PRC banks. The return on assets of state industrial companies has declined substantially since 2006, and on average they earn less than the cost of capital. In contrast, private firms' returns continued to rise, with the result that by 2012 their return on assets was more than twice that of state companies. As a result the interest coverage ratio of private industrial firms, an important indicator of creditworthiness, by 2012 was more than twice that of state firms (Lardy 2014, 110).

The second change in the composition of credit after 2009 was that the growth rate of bank loans moderated while other financial products, such as entrusted loans,[4] trust loans, bankers' acceptances, and corporate bonds, expanded rapidly. By 2013, new renminbi bank loans accounted for only 51 percent of new social financing, a sharp divergence from 2002, when renminbi bank loans accounted for 92 percent. The growth of financial products other than traditional bank loans did not signal a decline in the role of banks in the financial system. Instead, faced with binding constraints in the form of a loan-to-deposit ratio, required reserve ratio, capital requirements, and the less formal but equally important window guidance on loan quantities from the central bank, banks turned to these new methods of financing as a way to continue to extend credit (IMF 2014).

Motivated by regulatory arbitrage, the growth of these alternative financial products has created new risks in the financial system. While regulators have done much to tighten supervision of traditional banking activities, these fast-growing products are often off–balance sheet and are less well supervised. The degree of risk varies by type of product. Corporate bonds appear to be relatively safe given their higher levels of disclosure and issuance by established state-owned enterprises or local government-affiliated financing companies. Entrusted loans are typically made within corporate groups, with a bank acting as middleman, but a portion is made to unrelated third parties.[5] Bankers' acceptances are short-term debt instruments that are ultimately settled by funds from a corporate depositor and are guaranteed by the issuing bank. Trust loans are made by Chinese-style shadow banks called trust companies, which collect funds from individuals and financial institutions.

On the liability side, the composition of financial activities has changed as well. Wealth management products, a type of deposit-like financial product, started growing quickly in 2008. Offered by banks or third-party com-

---

4. Entrusted loans are corporate-to-corporate loans in which banks act as an intermediary, often providing guarantees and other credit enhancements to these loans.

5. Two studies reviewed by reporters at the *Wall Street Journal* found that around 20 percent of entrusted loans were made to unrelated third parties. Dinny McMahon and Lingling Wei, "A Partial Primer to China's Biggest Shadow: Entrusted Loans," *Wall Street Journal*, May 2, 2014, http://blogs.wsj.com (accessed on May 2, 2014).

panies, wealth management products are short-term and offer a return that is frequently several hundred basis points higher than the retail deposit rate set by the central bank. These products are largely unguaranteed, but many investors assume they have an implicit guarantee given that they are sold by banks or in banks. Regulators have taken steps to address some of the more acute risks posed by wealth management products, such as asset pooling and investing funds in illiquid financial products. However, the larger problem of implicit guarantees remains unsolved. By the end of May 2014, the outstanding amount of wealth management products had reached RMB12.8 trillion, compared with half a trillion at the end of 2007.[6] This amount is equivalent to 25 percent of total household deposits in the banking system.

The other component of banking liabilities that is growing quickly is interbank borrowing. After the global financial crisis, small and medium-sized banks in the PRC expanded rapidly. The growth rate of urban commercial bank assets in the PRC, for example, was twice that of the large national banks, made possible by smaller banks borrowing through the interbank market. Large banks, endowed with national deposit networks, are large net lenders via the interbank market. This created a new vulnerability in the financial system through the reliance of smaller banks on potentially unstable wholesale funding markets. The interbank credit crunch of June 2013 illustrated the volatility of short-term funding markets in the PRC when overnight rates shot up by as much as 1,000 basis points. Borrowers in the interbank market were unable to find sufficient funding or funding at a reasonable price. The crisis abated only when the central bank stepped in to provide funding and put pressure on the large banks to begin lending again.

The overall impact of the global financial crisis on the PRC's financial system is remarkable. Not only did the structure of assets and liabilities transform significantly but also the overall size of the financial system increased by an enormous margin. Between the fourth quarter of 2008 and the fourth quarter of 2013, the credit-to-GDP ratio, measured by the stock of credit to households and nonfinancial corporations, increased by 69 percentage points. Starting from an already high level of credit relative to GDP, the PRC now has an almost unprecedented level of indebtedness given its level of economic development. Periods of rapid credit growth, especially relative to the size of GDP, are a reliable early warning indicator of subsequent financial distress. Looking at a sample of 43 countries over 50 years, economists at the International Monetary Fund (IMF 2014) found only four episodes of credit growth similar in scale to the PRC's current boom. Each of those four countries experienced a banking crisis within three years of the boom period. The growth and evolution of the Chinese financial system after the global financial crisis

---

6. Zhang Chen, "The Value of Wealth Management Products Reaches RMB12.8 trillion," *People's Daily*, June 23, 2014, http://finance.people.com.cn/money/n/2014/0623/c218900-25184608. html (accessed on December 2, 2014).

has in many ways set back much of the reform achieved during the 2000s and created significant new risks.

The Current Financial Reform Agenda

Chinese policymakers have not been complacent in addressing the accumulating risks in the financial system. In November of 2013, the Central Committee of the Chinese Communist Party convened to set the agenda for the country's next wave of economic and political reform. During the Third Plenum, the party issued a document entitled *A Decision on Major Issues Concerning Comprehensive and Far-Reaching Reform*, which included a clear outline for financial reform.[7] The main reforms set forth in the document include:

Establish Private Financial Institutions. The creation of private financial institutions is a new addition to the PRC's financial reform plans. Currently, financial institutions in the PRC are predominately state-owned. Figure 9.2 shows that the large national commercial banks are majority-owned by Central Huijin, the holding company for state-owned banks established in 2003, and the Ministry of Finance (MoF).[8] The average share held by the central government in these institutions was 69 percent at the end of 2013.[9] For smaller financial institutions, the share of private capital is higher. At the end of 2011, private shareholders held 42 percent of joint-stock bank capital. The figure for urban commercial banks was 54 percent. For small and medium-sized rural financial institutions, private capital accounted for 92 percent of the total (CBRC 2012). The central government directly owns the PRC's national policy banks, China Development Bank, Agricultural Development Bank of China, and the Export-Import Bank of China.

In March 2014, the CBRC accepted applications from five investor groups to establish private banks. The applications were accepted in two groups in July and September with the expectation that operations would begin in 2015. The scope of operations for these new banks will be more limited than that of traditional banks. Each bank will select a relatively narrow focus for its lending operations and will initially be confined to one preapproved test city. The primary motivation behind allowing the creation of fully private financial institutions is that they will be completely free from implicit guarantees by the government. With no government shareholders, these banks will be forced to

---

7. Xinhua News, "Authorized Release: A Decision on Major Issues Concerning Comprehensive and Far-Reaching Reform," November 15, 2013, http://news.xinhuanet.com/politics/2013-11/15/c_118164235.htm (accessed on August 25, 2014).

8. The MoF exercises considerable indirect influence over Central Huijin and its parent company, China Investment Corporation.

9. The next largest shareholder in these institutions is Hong Kong Exchanges and Clearing Limited, which is the clearinghouse representing the shares floated in Hong Kong, China. These shares are owned by a mix of private and state-owned investors.

Figure 9.2   Shares held by Huijin and Ministry of Finance, 2013

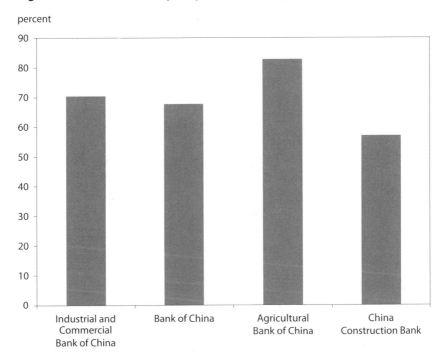

percent

Source: Bank Annual Reports.

bear full responsibility for any risks they take. Firms that fail will be forced to exit the market, currently a rare occurrence for financial firms. Policymakers believe applying this rule to these newly created banks, rather than the much larger existing banks, will provide a buffer against possible financial contagion from failing institutions.

Develop the Capital Markets. The expansion and development of capital markets are a major component of the Third Plenum financial reforms. The new reforms aim at improving access to financing for small and medium-sized firms, establishing a registration-based stock issuing system, and increasing the proportion of direct financing. Direct financing refers to financial transactions that occur through capital markets, such as stocks and bonds, rather than intermediated via banks. As figure 9.3 shows, the PRC's share of direct financing is well below that of advanced economies. Historically, this is quite natural since the share of direct finance typically increases as countries develop economically. However, the Chinese share of direct finance is even lower than that of other emerging markets, such as India and Indonesia. The Chinese government has sought to increase the country's proportion of direct finance for more than a decade.

Figure 9.3   Proportion of direct financing in the financial system, 2012

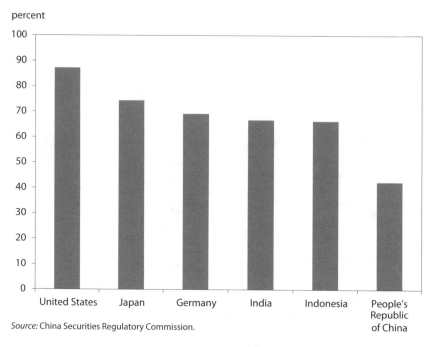

percent

Source: China Securities Regulatory Commission.

The PRC's capital markets are not especially small, even when compared with its enormous economy. Measured by value of bonds outstanding, the Chinese bond market is now the world's third largest, and its corporate bond market is the largest in Asia. It accounts for 62 percent of the entire East Asian ex-Japan bond market (ADB 2014). The Shanghai stock exchange is currently the seventh largest in the world in terms of market capitalization and the fourth largest in terms of trading volume. Looking at combined market capitalization of all national exchanges, the PRC's equity markets are the second largest in the world, after those in the United States.[10]

However, the share of financing that the PRC's corporations obtain from the capital markets is relatively insignificant. Issuances of new equity by nonfinancial corporations accounted for only 1.3 percent of total social financing in 2013, down from 7.3 percent in 2007. The share of corporate bonds in new financing was 10.4 percent in 2013, down from 14.3 percent the previous year. The distribution of total financial assets also makes the dominance of the banking system clear. The stock of corporate bonds was slightly over RMB10 trillion at the end of 2013. In contrast, bank loans to enterprises and other

10. For the PRC, this includes both the Shanghai and Shenzhen stock exchanges. See "China overtakes Japan in stock market cap," *Financial Times*, November 27, 2014, www.ft.com/intl/fastft/242222/china-overtakes-japan-stock-market-cap (accessed on January 25, 2015).

institutions[11] were around RMB55 trillion. Overall, nonbank financial institutions accounted for only 2.6 percent of total financial assets at the end of 2013.

A larger problem is that the capital markets allocate capital in a suboptimal manner, biased in favor of state-owned enterprises. The Chinese private sector accounts for two-thirds to three-quarters of all economic output. Yet private sector firms receive a disproportionately small share of capital market funding. In the corporate bond market, private enterprises account for only 10 percent of the total amount outstanding. The situation is only marginally better in the equity markets, where state-owned enterprises account for 70 percent of the market capitalization of listed A-share firms. Access to capital markets for private firms has been improving in recent years, but their share of financing is still well below their contribution to the overall economy.

Accelerate Interest Rate Liberalization. The Third Plenum reaffirmed the commitment of Chinese policymakers to liberalize interest rates. The process began almost two decades ago with the interbank rate (Li 2014). Soon afterward, bond repurchase rates were liberalized and government bonds were offered via a bidding process. In the late 1990s, banks were allowed to make loans to certain classes of enterprises at multiples of the benchmark interest rate. Deposit rates remained subject to a ceiling imposed by the central bank. In the mid-2000s, the upper limit on the lending rate was removed. In 2012, some flexibility was granted for deposit rates, allowing banks to pay a rate of interest that was 1.1 times the benchmark rate. In 2013, the lending rate was fully liberalized, removing any downward rate restrictions. Also in 2013, banks were permitted to issue large-scale negotiable certificates of deposit in the interbank market. In 2014, the flexibility around the benchmark deposit rate was increased from 1.1 times to 1.2 times. Deposit rates were further liberalized in 2015, when flexibility around the benchmark was increased again to 1.5 times.

The PRC has made substantial progress on interest rate liberalization over the past two decades. However, financial repression remains a significant problem. Figure 9.4 shows that throughout most of the last decade, Chinese real deposit rates have been at or near zero. The low rate on deposits filters through to low lending rates, which have been strikingly low in the PRC compared with other Asian nations. Figure 9.5 shows that between 2007 and 2013, the average real lending rate in the PRC was 1.8 percent, around half the average real lending rate for Thailand, the Republic of Korea, Japan, Indonesia, and India during the same period. The low lending rate in the PRC is one of the driving factors behind the credit and investment boom and the regulatory arbitrage that occurs via the shadow banking system.

Move towards a Market-Based Exchange Rate. Mirroring the progress on interest rate liberalization, the renminbi exchange rate has been on a long and uneven path toward liberalization. In 1994, the PRC merged its dual-track

---

11. Other institutions include organizations that are not classified as corporations, such as hospitals and schools. The amount of strictly enterprise loans was 45 trillion renminbi.

Figure 9.4　Real interest rate on one-year deposits, 2004–14

percent

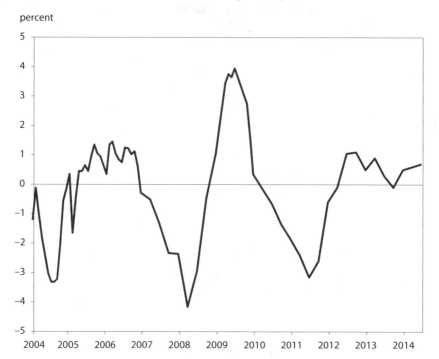

Sources: National Bureau of Statistics of China; People's Bank of China.

exchange rate system to a unified regime and implemented a tightly managed float versus the dollar (Yi 2013). Beginning in the mid-2000s, the intervention required to keep the exchange rate from appreciating more rapidly led to the massive accumulation of foreign exchange reserves. Figure 9.6 shows the increase in the stock of foreign exchange reserves held by the central bank during the past 15 years. In 2005, the renminbi was unpegged from the dollar and instead tracked a basket of currencies. This new approach resulted in a modest appreciation of the currency. Appreciation was suspended during the global financial crisis, not resuming until mid-2010. Since then, the renminbi has gradually become less undervalued as reflected by declines in the PRC's large external current account surpluses. The central bank has taken steps to increase the flexibility of the day-to-day rate by expanding the daily trading band to 1 percent in 2012 and 2 percent in 2014.

Although the renminbi is less undervalued now than during the 2000s, it remains subject to occasional heavy government interference. The accumulation of new reserves on an annual basis peaked at 13 percent of GDP before declining to 2 percent of GDP in 2012. However, in 2013 the accumulation of reserves climbed back up to 5 percent of GDP despite statements by top offi-

Figure 9.5 Average annual real lending rate, 2007–13

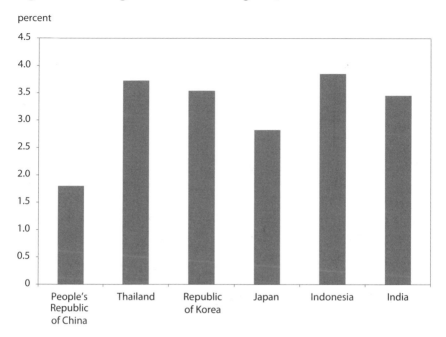

percent

Source: World Bank, *World Development Indicators.*

cials that acquiring additional reserves is detrimental.[12] Establishing a market-based exchange rate is important for reducing internal imbalances within the Chinese economy. Previously, the undervalued exchange rate favored the development of export- and import-competing industries at the expense of the nontradable part of the economy. This harmed the growth of the service sector and led to a more capital-intensive model of growth throughout the 2000s. A market-determined exchange rate is also important for the conduct of monetary policy. Intervention in the foreign exchange markets requires offsetting sterilization measures in the banking system to prevent inflation. Reducing the degree of currency intervention will give the central bank greater flexibility by eliminating the need to impose strict sterilization requirements on banks. This will make it easier for the central bank to focus its policy tools on achieving economic and financial stability.

Promote Capital Account Convertibility. Chinese authorities have pursued the goal of achieving full convertibility of the renminbi since 1993 (Lardy

12. "PBOC Says No Longer in China's Interest to Increase Reserves," Bloomberg News, November 20, 2013, www.bloomberg.com/news/2013-11-20/pboc-says-no-longer-in-china-s-favor-to-boost-record-reserves.html (accessed on January 24, 2015).

Figure 9.6 Foreign exchange reserves, 2000–14

billions of US dollars

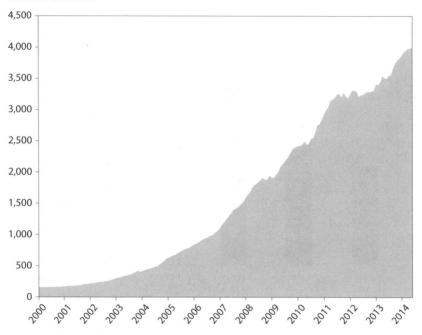

Source: People's Bank of China.

2011). Despite this long-standing policy goal, parts of the PRC's capital account remain closed. Foreign direct investment (FDI) is relatively open, apart from a few restricted sectors, but portfolio inflows and outflows are highly constrained. The PRC's capital account controls are judged significantly more restrictive than those of the advanced economies and even more restrictive than those present in India (Hooley 2013). Notwithstanding, the closed nature of the capital account, regulators have taken steps to increase cross-border flows in certain areas. Institutional investors are permitted to make cross-border investments in securities through the Qualified Foreign Institutional Investors (QFII), Renminbi Qualified Foreign Institutional Investors (RQFII), and Qualified Domestic Institutional Investors (QDII) programs. Authorities have taken steps recently to reduce and simplify the process for approving new FDI and obtaining foreign currency. Additionally, new reforms in the China (Shanghai) Pilot Free Trade Zone will relax restrictions on foreign borrowing. In 2014, the Chinese government approved the Shanghai–Hong Kong Connect program, which allows investors in Hong Kong, China and the PRC to purchase eligible listed securities in both markets, subject to a quota.

Even with these measures, the share of Chinese financial assets available for purchase by foreigners is extremely small. At the end of 2013 the total amount of offshore renminbi liquidity was $300 billion to $400 billion

(Anderson 2014). The total amount of QFII and RQFII assets was equivalent to $82 billion during the same period. In its initial phase, the Shanghai–Hong Kong Connect program has an aggregate quota of RMB300 billion ($49 billion) once it is fully utilized. Combined, these amounts are well below 10 percent of 2013 GDP. For comparison, foreign ownership of US financial assets is in excess of 100 percent of GDP.

Establish a Deposit Insurance Scheme. As with many of the reform priorities outlined in the Third Plenum, the establishment of a deposit insurance scheme in the PRC has been on the policy agenda for more than a decade (World Bank 2013). Although it has the largest banking system in the world, the PRC has lacked this basic safety net for depositors, which all other major financial systems have established. In place of a formal deposit insurance scheme, the government has provided an implicit guarantee to deposit-taking financial institutions of all sizes. Many factors have delayed the implementation of a deposit insurance scheme. Various potential regulators have disagreed over who will be granted authority over funds collected and leadership over resolution of failing banks. Moreover, banks have been reluctant to pay additional insurance premiums, and smaller banks have objected to paying higher rates based on risk. These obstacles have finally been surmounted, and the State Council released a draft proposal for the system at the end of 2014. The new scheme will include a new deposit insurance agency and will cover deposits up to RMB500,000 per account. The new deposit insurance fund began operation in May of 2015 and will operate under the management of the PBoC until an independent agency is established.

Create a Market-Based Exit Mechanism. The Third Plenum financial reform agenda calls for the creation of a market-based exit mechanism for financial institutions. At present, the failure of financial institutions, especially banks, is exceedingly rare in the PRC. Financial institutions with shares owned by the government, that is, the majority of financial institutions in the PRC, are widely believed to have implicit guarantees from the government. These widespread implicit guarantees have contributed to misallocation of credit and overinvestment (IMF 2014). The new reform would aim to create procedures for the orderly resolution of failing financial institutions, similar to the "living will" reforms embodied in the Dodd-Frank Act in the United States. The details on how and when these new policies will be implemented have not yet been released.

Experiment with Mixed Ownership Reform. The Third Plenum included a call for vigorously developing a mixed ownership economy, allowing state-owned enterprises to attract capital from private sources. At present, this reform has mainly been implemented by nonfinancial companies. Sinopec, for example, has sold a 30 percent stake in its distribution business to a consortium of private businesses. Sinopharm Group and China National Building Material Group are also considering partial privatization. At the local level,

Shanghai, Guangdong, and Shandong have taken the lead on implementing the mixed ownership reform. All three local governments have recently experimented with altering the ownership structures of local state-owned enterprises in an effort to attract outside investment and increase efficiency. Guangdong has a stated target of putting 80 percent of its local state-owned enterprises into mixed ownership reform by 2020. The first major financial institution to explore the mixed ownership reform is the Bank of Communications (BoCom). In July 2014, BoCom announced that it was studying the feasibility of deepening its existing mixed ownership structure and improving its corporate governance system. In June of 2015, the bank received approval from the PBoC to proceed with mixed-ownership reform, which consist of offering a greater number of shares to private investors and employees. This will result in a reduction in the number of shares held by the Ministry of Finance, which currently stands at 26 percent of total shares. If BoCom's experiment with mixed ownership advances, many other banks will likely follow suit.

Sequencing and Risk Management

Financial reform is a risky process that often exacerbates the very problems it is seeking to address. There is a strong tendency for banking and currency crises to follow financial liberalization (Kaminsky and Reinhart 1999). Yet, there are also dangers from inaction. Delaying financial reforms can allow the buildup of imbalances and the misallocation of capital, both of which can significantly impede growth and create financial crises. Successful implementation of the financial reforms outlined in the Third Plenum will therefore require careful sequencing to minimize the potential risks.

International experience shows that it is critical to address domestic financial weaknesses and imbalances before opening up the financial system to foreign capital inflows and outflows (Chalk and Syed 2013). International capital flows tend to be volatile, and policymakers lose much of their ability to influence these flows once capital controls are abandoned. Without effective regulation, domestic banks often borrow heavily from foreign lenders. Negative shocks to the economy can spark capital flight and lead to a disorderly deleveraging of the financial system. This was one of the key triggers of the Asian financial crisis. In the PRC, external debt levels, both official and private, are currently relatively low. Yet if barriers are lowered, existing distortions in the domestic financial system could encourage disruptive capital flows in both directions. An undervalued exchange rate will encourage hot money to flow into the country and exacerbate existing asset price bubbles. If deposit interest rates remain artificially low, savings may flee the domestic banking system in search of higher returns. Smaller banks, which generally have weaker deposit bases, would be hit especially hard. These potentially volatile inflows and outflows could destabilize the entire financial system. Thus it is incumbent on policymakers to address these underlying domestic distortions before opening the capital account.

There are three main priorities for reforming the domestic financial system. The first priority is ending the systematic underpricing of capital. Resolving this distortion and moving towards a more market-determined interest rate requires eliminating the deposit ceiling. After liberalization, large deposits, money market rates, short-term bond rates, and small deposit rates are all likely to increase (He, Wang, and Yu 2014). This increase in the cost of funding will, in turn, lead to higher borrowing rates. Faced with higher funding costs, many borrowers and projects will be less creditworthy. Banks, which have become increasingly profit-oriented following the restructuring of the 2000s, are likely to allocate an increasing share of their lending to more efficient borrowers. This will improve the allocation of capital while offsetting some of the negative impact of a slowdown in credit growth (Borst 2014).

The People's Bank of China has outlined a sensible framework for deposit interest rate liberalization based on three principles. First, interest rates on foreign currency deposits will be liberalized before renminbi deposits. Second, long-term deposits will be liberalized before short-term deposits. Third, large-scale deposits will be liberalized before small-scale deposits.[13] The logic behind this sequence is that the more stable and secure types of deposits will be liberalized first. This gives banks adequate time to adapt to a change in their business environment and gain experience with more volatile interest rates. However, despite having this framework for a decade, implementation has been slow. Only rates on large-scale foreign currency deposits have been fully liberalized.[14] Financial institutions are permitted to issue large-scale domestic currency negotiable certificates of deposits in the interbank market, but that right is only slowly being extended to corporates. The vast majority of bank deposits remain subject to the same controls that existed a decade ago.

The reason deposit interest rate liberalization has progressed so slowly is the fear that fully liberalized rates could lead to unhealthy competition for deposits among banks. Competition for deposits is frequently a trigger for financial distress because banks promise unsustainably high rates to hold onto funds. In an attempt to generate the income to pay these higher deposit rates, banks often lend to riskier borrowers at high yields. Inevitably many of these loans go bad and force some banks into failure, ultimately imposing losses on depositors. If this type of deposit competition took hold, especially among the smaller and regional banks, the Chinese government would face large contingent liabilities given its implicit guarantee for all deposits in the banking system. To prevent this, regulators seek to implement a formal deposit insurance scheme that would remove the implicit guarantee in favor of a formal system with measures to discipline riskier banks. The establishment of a deposit insurance system is therefore seen as a prerequisite for moving forward more aggressively with deposit rate liberalization. The delay in the creation of the

---

13. For an explanation of the central bank's interest rate liberalization strategy, see www.pbc.gov.cn/history_file/files/att_12766_1.pdf.

14. Interest rates on small-scale deposits have recently been liberalized in the Shanghai area.

deposit insurance system has thus stymied the larger project of interest rate liberalization. With the draft proposal for a new deposit insurance system now released, this obstacle may be removed.

The second priority for domestic reform is capital market development. Expanding the PRC's capital markets is an important step in the sequencing of financial liberalization for two principal reasons. First, capital markets can help reduce the degree of moral hazard in the currently bank-dominated financial system. The bank restructuring in the late 1990s and 2000s confirmed the government's willingness to offer substantial aid to failing banks, both small and large. As long as most banks remain predominantly state-owned, which is likely for the foreseeable future, some level of implicit government support will be assumed. This leads to the problem of moral hazard for both the management and nonstate shareholders of these banks. Banks that are too big to fail have incentives to take on additional risks because they know that the government will save them. Strong regulation can help control these risks but it cannot alter the underlying incentives at play. Increasing the share of credit allocated through the capital markets will reduce the role of the banks in the financial system. However, moral hazard will decline only if regulators reduce state involvement in the capital markets. Intervention to prevent bond defaults and heavy restrictions placed on companies seeking initial public offerings have impaired market discipline in the capital markets.

The second benefit from developing the PRC's capital markets is their potential to improve the allocation of capital. As mentioned above, in their current form the PRC's capital markets do not appear to be better at allocating financial resources than banks. State-owned enterprises continue to occupy an outsized position as borrowers in the capital markets, which is completely disproportionate to their share of economic output and inconsistent with their very low returns compared with private firms.[15] Part of this is the result of the current structure of the economy. In general, state-owned enterprises tend to be larger and better established than private enterprises in the PRC. Therefore, it is easier for these firms to undertake the costs and regulatory requirements of issuing securities. However, much of the bias toward state-owned enterprises is also explained by government policy. Until 2000, the PRC had a quota system for stock listings (Lardy 2014). Under the quota system, the State Planning Commission, government ministries, and local governments mostly selected state-owned enterprises for listing. These trends have improved in recent years, but this historical bias continues to distort the makeup of the equity markets.

Similar problems exist in the corporate bond market. State-owned enterprises dominate all three types of corporate bonds in the PRC—enterprise bonds, exchange-traded corporate bonds, and medium-term notes. Enterprise

---

15. In the industrial sector, the gap between the returns of private and state firms is close to 3:1. The return on assets of private firms was almost 15 percent versus less than 5 percent for state firms. The ratio for the service sector is 2:1 (Lardy 2014, 97–99).

bonds are issued by nonlisted firms and are approved by the National Development and Reform Commission (NDRC). Exchange-traded corporate bonds, regulated by the China Securities Regulatory Commission, are issued by listed companies and thus distorted by the same historical bias as the stock market. Medium-term notes are approved by the People's Bank of China and trade over the counter in the interbank market. Despite what appear to be easier requirements for issuance, private firms have struggled to make inroads into this market thus far.[16]

The third major component of the sequencing of domestic financial reform involves establishing a market-based exchange rate and creating a more effective framework for monetary policy. Ending routine intervention in the foreign exchange market is necessary for the establishment of a market-determined exchange rate.[17] A market-determined exchange rate, in turn, will help improve the conduct of monetary policy. Zhou Xiaochuan, the governor of the People's Bank of China, publicly declared in November 2013 that the central bank would begin to phase out routine intervention. Despite this statement, the PRC accumulated another $292 billion in foreign reserves in the fourth quarter of 2013 and the first half of 2014.

Once the degree of intervention is reduced and the exchange rate becomes more flexible, monetary policy can be handled more effectively (Roache and Maziad 2013). Many core tools of monetary policy in the PRC currently are primarily used to offset the effects of the PRC's currency policy. To maintain an undervalued currency and provide stability, the PRC must sterilize its intervention in foreign exchange markets using tools such as the required reserve ratio and open market operations. Figure 9.7 shows the amount of foreign reserves relative to the economies of several Asian nations. Asia as a whole has very large reserves relative to the world average, and the PRC is among the top reserve holders in the region. Although on a flow basis the amount of sterilization in relative terms has declined in recent years, an immense stock of sterilization liabilities remains to be unwound.[18] Once this is accomplished and the currency becomes market-determined, many of the tools available to the central banks will be freed up for the normal management of monetary policy instead of sterilization operations (Chalk and Syed 2013). The central bank will then have greater leeway in dealing with the potential volatility created by financial reform.

---

16. An estimate by Barclays put the private share of the medium-term note market in 2013 at around 8 percent. Barclays, *Financial disintermediation: acceleration of corporate bonds—good or bad?* China Banks: Cross Asset Report, November 28, 2012.

17. This does not preclude all intervention. Monetary authorities around the world reserve the right to intervene during exceptional circumstances.

18. The PRC's required reserve ratio is extraordinarily high. The ratio is 20 percent for large banks and 18 percent for small and medium-sized banks. In 2014 authorities made a small cut in the ratio, 0.5 percent, for banks that had met a certain threshold for loans to small and rural borrowers.

Figure 9.7   Foreign reserves relative to GDP

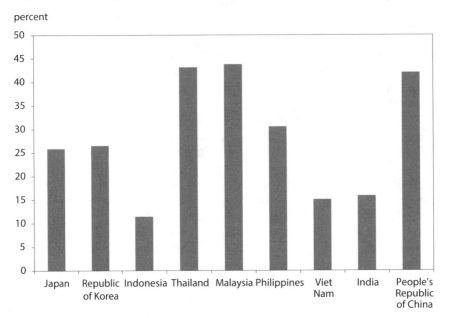

percent

Sources: World Bank; authors' calculations.

If the reforms mentioned above are put in place and macroeconomic conditions are stable, policymakers can move forward with capital account opening. The three main categories of financial flows to liberalize are FDI, portfolio investment, and bank cross-border transactions. The PRC's international liabilities are dominated by FDI. At the end of 2013, FDI accounted for nearly 60 percent of total international liabilities (Hanemann 2014). This is a source of strength because FDI tends to be stable and long-term. During the Asian and global financial crises, FDI flows were less volatile than portfolio investment and bank cross-border transactions in Indonesia, Malaysia, the Republic of Korea, the Philippines, and Thailand (Jeanne 2014). In an open capital account environment, this pattern is likely to hold true for the PRC as well.

In general, FDI is the most open component of the capital account in the PRC. Over the past several decades, authorities have gradually opened up much of the economy to foreign investment, particularly in the manufacturing sector. More recently Chinese enterprises have been encouraged to invest abroad as part of the Going Out Policy. Project approvals, a requirement for new investments to be approved by the NDRC, were significantly relaxed following the Third Plenum.[19] In 2014, the State Council eased barriers to estab-

---

19. FDI into sectors labeled "encouraged" or "permitted" in the investment catalogue no longer require approval from the central or local NDRC if the amount is less than $300 million. For outward investments, this threshold is set at $1 billion.

lishing foreign-invested enterprises by removing the registered capital requirement in most circumstances. However, despite these improvements many barriers to inbound direct investment remain. Many foreign investments are still subject to a complex web of approval requirements from local and central authorities. Moreover, much of the service sector and some strategic areas of the industrial sector remain off-limits to foreign investment. The new Chinese leadership appears to be committed to addressing these issues. It recently agreed to negotiate a bilateral investment treaty with the United States on the basis of a negative list approach to investment approval.[20] This will potentially remove many of the remaining restrictions on investment. Continuation of these trends toward full liberalization of inward and outward direct investment is unlikely to cause financial instability.

Relaxing rules on portfolio investment and cross-border borrowing is more complicated. With respect to portfolio investment, institutional investors tend to have a longer-term perspective and therefore play a stabilizing role in financial markets. Portfolio investment for institutional investors is already partially liberalized, but the overall amounts of portfolio investment are strictly controlled via the QFII, RQFII, and QDII programs. These quotas have increased rapidly over the past several years, with the QFII quota now almost six times larger than it was at the beginning of 2008. However, the quotas' overall size relative to the total financial market is insignificant. Encouraging growth of portfolio inflows and outflows will require expanding the quota amounts, continuing to ease the process of qualification for a quota, and removing restrictions on the type of securities that can be held. Once foreign institutional investors have a greater presence in the PRC's securities markets, policymakers should increase investment opportunities for retail investors. Full and unrestricted portfolio investment by foreign retail investors should be considered only as a final step.

The cross-border activities of Chinese banks have grown steadily, but overall the financial system remains domestically focused. Between January 2011 and June 2014, the stock of foreign assets held by Chinese banks increased by 73 percent. However, because of rapid growth of the financial system during this period, the share of foreign assets remained virtually unchanged at 2.1 percent of total assets. Foreign liabilities are also minimal, equaling 1.5 percent of total banking liabilities during the same period. Figure 9.8 shows the share of the "other investments" component of the PRC's international investment position, which includes cross-border lending, trade credits, foreign currency, and deposits, relative to GDP. The figure reveals a significant decline in cross-border activity during the global financial crisis followed by a recovery in recent years although in comparison to many developed economies, these numbers remain quite low. For example, at the end of 2013, other investment

---

20. A negative list approach means that areas not specifically prohibited to investment will be open. In contrast, a positive list approach requires approvals for areas not specifically listed.

Figure 9.8   Other investments relative to GDP, 2004–13

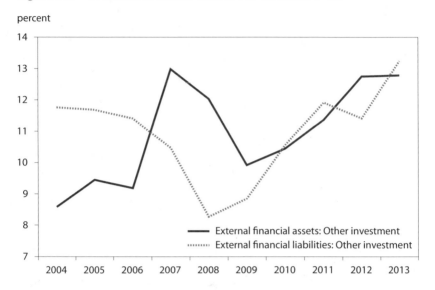

percent

Note: Other investments include cross-border lending, trade credits, foreign currency, and deposits.
Sources: National Bureau of Statistics of China; People's Bank of China.

assets and liabilities relative to GDP for Japan were equal to 37 and 40 percent, respectively.

As the capital account opens, it is likely that Chinese banks will further increase their cross-border activities. Greater openness will increase competition within the domestic banking system, forcing Chinese banks to become more efficient or lose market share to foreign competitors. Loosening restrictions on cross-border lending can also help Chinese banks diversify their range of borrowers and transform themselves into true multinational banks. However, increasing banking openness is not without risks. Reliance on foreign funding, particularly short-term wholesale funding markets, can turn into an acute financial risk during periods of financial distress (Jeanne 2014). Currently, the overwhelming domestic focus of Chinese banks means that this type of dependence is unlikely to occur in the near term, even if restrictions are eased. If Chinese regulators maintain strong prudential standards, this risk can be avoided, and increasing the share of cross-border banking activity can be a net positive for the financial system.

Overall, the priorities for the sequencing of financial reform are clear. Policymakers should first strengthen the domestic financial system by simultaneously implementing three broad reforms. First, distortions to interest rates, primarily in the form of the ceiling on deposit rates, should be eliminated. Second, financial deepening should be promoted by expanding the PRC's capital markets. Third, the exchange rate should become market-

Figure 9.9 Credit to GDP and per capita GDP, 2013

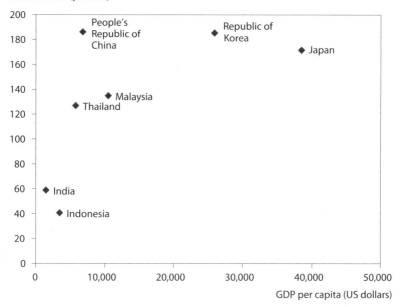

credit to GDP (percent)

Sources: Bank for International Settlements; World Bank.

determined, freeing up the PRC's central bank to concentrate on domestic economic management. Once these prerequisites are in place, policymakers can move forward with opening the capital account, gradually removing restrictions on portfolio investing and overseas borrowing and lending.

Lessons for Other Asian Countries

Drawing lessons for the rest of Asia from the PRC's experience is difficult given the unique characteristics of the country's financial system. The Chinese financial system is set apart by having grown to a very large size, relative to GDP, at an early stage in economic development. Figure 9.9 plots out the stock of credit, measured as borrowing by households and nonfinancial enterprises, relative to GDP and per capita GDP, a proxy for level of economic development. The PRC stands out in terms of having a stock of credit relative to GDP that is comparable to that of the Republic of Korea and Japan, yet having a much lower level of per capita income. In general, as countries grow richer they undergo financial deepening, that is, the size and complexity of the financial system increase. East Asian economies tend to have particularly large financial systems at an earlier stage of development.[21] However, the PRC is an outlier

---

21. Much of this can be attributed to extremely high saving and investment rates in East Asia.

even in this group with a stock of credit much larger than that of Malaysia and Thailand, two countries at similar levels of economic development.

The large size of the Chinese financial system is not a recent phenomenon. In fact, the PRC may have been even more of an outlier in the past. In the early 1990s, the PRC's credit-to-GDP ratio was already near 100 percent at a time when per capita income levels were much lower. The roots of this can be traced back to the old model of the financial system in which the State Planning Commission and the central bank set lending targets and priorities for each of the banks. Facing soft budget constraints and easy access to credit, state-owned enterprises borrowed heavily during the 1980s and 1990s, inflating the size of the PRC's financial system. The other unique factor contributing to the size of the Chinese financial system is the financing of fiscal expenses through the banking system. Originally, state-owned enterprises borrowed from banks to provide education, housing, and health care to workers and their families. More recently, the banking system has financed a spree of infrastructure projects through lending to local government-linked platform companies. If the government had financed these projects through more traditional borrowing methods, such as issuing bonds, explicit government debt levels would have been larger and the amount of corporate debt smaller.

In addition to size, the other distinguishing feature of the Chinese financial system is its bias toward serving corporate rather than household borrowers. Figure 9.10 shows the credit outstanding, relative to GDP, to both the corporate and household sectors. The skew in the direction of lending to companies is related to the relatively recent emergence of a private housing market in the PRC. Household borrowing is dominated by mortgage loans, with consumption and auto loans still accounting for a very small percentage of borrowing. In recent years, however, households are increasingly gaining access to financing. The share of new lending going to households increased to 42 percent in 2013, up from 14 percent in 2006. Regardless, even if these trends persist the Chinese financial system will be unusually dominated by corporate borrowing for many years to come.

Despite these differences, Asian economies implementing financial reform can draw several useful lessons from the Chinese experience. The first lesson is that it is possible to rapidly improve the efficiency of state-owned banks. The PRC's banks went from being technically bankrupt in the late 1990s to earning large profits less than a decade later. The turnaround initially required a large injection of capital from the central government and indirect support to offload bad loans to asset management companies. However, the reforms went farther than a simple bailout. State-owned banks dramatically reduced their employee and branch numbers to boost efficiency. An independent banking regulator was established and a separate body was created to manage the state's ownership interests. Chinese banks also brought in foreign strategic investors and listed on international exchanges to reinforce corporate governance improvements. These reforms dramatically increased the

Figure 9.10   Corporate and household credit to GDP, 2013

percent

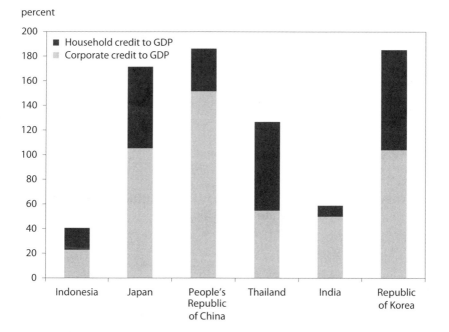

Sources: Bank for International Settlements; World Bank.

operational efficiency and profitability of the PRC's commercial banks, in part due to increased lending to private firms, which generate higher returns, and reduced lending to state-owned firms, which on average earn substantially less on their assets (Lardy 2014).[22] Table 9.1 shows that dramatic improvement in the performance of Chinese banks since the banking cleanup in the late 1990s. The table also shows that Chinese banks meet or exceed the performance of their G-20 counterparts on a variety of performance metrics.

State-owned banks are prevalent across many Asian countries. Figure 9.11 shows that in many financial systems state-owned banks account for more than 20 percent of total banking assets. These banks are often inefficient and in need of reform. In the process of cleaning up their banks, Chinese regulators undertook unusually large and dramatic interventions. Though other banking regulators may not have the need or desire to make such herculean efforts, the basic principles of the PRC's banking cleanup are transferable across borders. These lessons include reducing waste and inefficiency, estab-

---

22. It should be noted, however, that significant concerns exist with respect to the off–balance sheet activities of Chinese banks. Investors' calculation that these activities may ultimately lead to losses for the banks mean that Chinese bank stocks often trade below their book value.

Table 9.1 Performance of Chinese banks versus G-20 average
(percent)

Year	Return on assets	Net interest margin	Return on equity	Cost-to-income ratio
The People's Republic of China, 1999	0.7	1.9	9.8	65.5
The People's Republic of China, 2011	1.1	2.9	18.3	38.3
G-20 2011 average	1.2	3.0	13.5	59.3

Source: World Bank, *Global Financial Development* Database.

Figure 9.11 Share of banking assets held by entities with more than 50 percent state ownership, 2010

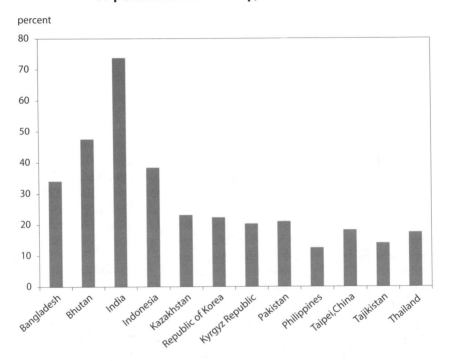

Source: World Bank, Banking Regulation and Supervision Survey.

lishing a banking regulator with a clear mandate, separating ownership and regulation, and bringing in international experience and scrutiny. Of course, there are inherent problems associated with maintaining a large role for state-owned banks in the financial system. Therefore, reforming state-owned banks as the PRC has done may be only a second-best solution to overall financial sector reform.

The second lesson to be drawn from the Chinese financial reform experience is that incrementalism can lead to unintended consequences. The big bang approach to financial reforms advocated to many developing countries in the 1990s was soundly rejected by Chinese authorities. In the wake of the economic collapse of many post-Soviet countries and the turmoil in Asia during the Asian financial crisis, the Chinese approach of slow and incremental financial reform seemed vindicated. However, the slow progress of many financial reforms, most notably liberalization of interest rates on deposits and exchange rate reform, has created adverse side effects. The glacial pace of interest rate liberalization has increased credit to unsustainable levels and created a large shadow banking system. On the deposit side, wealth management and trust products have proliferated as savers seek alternatives to artificially low bank deposit rates. On the lending side, low interest rates have led to excessive investment and regulatory arbitrage by banks to extend credit to borrowers. This created a boom in finance products like entrusted loans, trust loans, and bankers' acceptances. With respect to the exchange rate, policymakers' desire to maintain an undervalued exchange rate required the central bank to intervene on an unprecedented scale. As a result, drastic measures were imposed on the domestic banking system to prevent inflation. Measured and incremental financial reform may be preferable to overnight liberalization. However, lack of reform can also create risks within the financial system.

The final lesson from the experience of the PRC is the difficulty of rooting out implicit guarantees and moral hazard in a financial system dominated by state-owned actors. The PRC has the largest banking system in the world and its newly created deposit insurance fund faces the monumental task of protecting more than RMB100 trillion in deposits, almost twice the PRC's GDP. Even worse, depositors assume that banks will make them whole for a variety of other financial products, such as trust and wealth management products, irrespective of whether the issuing bank has a legal responsibility to do so. The central government remains the ultimate guarantor of a large and increasingly complex banking system. In the capital markets, regulators have been reluctant to let market forces play out. Regulators manipulate stock prices by instructing state-owned enterprises to buy stocks on market dips and by restricting new offerings, primarily to bolster existing prices. Corporate bonds, dominated by state-owned enterprises, rarely go into default due to extensive work by the government behind the scenes to provide support to failing firms. These government actions distort the financial system by short-circuiting the price discovery mechanism and encouraging excessive risk taking. Without a paradigm change in the approach of regulators and the introduction of private financial institutions capable of failing, these problems seem destined to persist.

References*

ADB (Asian Development Bank). 2014. *Asia Bond Monitor June 2014*. Manila. Available at http://asianbondsonline.adb.org/documents/abm_jun_2014.pdf (accessed on July 31, 2014).

Anderson, Jonathan. 2014. How to Think About China—Back to Obscurity for the Renminbi. Emerging Advisors Group (March 11).

Borst, Nicholas. 2014. Growing Out of Debt: Lowering the Credit-Intensity of Chinese Economic Growth. In *The US-China-Europe Economic Reform Agenda*. Papers presented at a symposium in Beijing, May 1. Washington: Peterson Institute for International Economics. Available at www.piie.com/publications/papers/201405piie-cf40conference.pdf (accessed on August 8, 2014).

CBRC (China Banking Regulatory Commission). 2012. *Annual Report 2011*. Beijing. Available at www.cbrc.gov.cn/chinese/files/2013/8FC77357E36D44D2BD8B3C4BE97F965F.pdf (accessed on July 31, 2014).

Chalk, Nigel, and Murtaza Syed. 2013. Financial Reform: An Essential Ingredient in Transforming China's Economic Model. In *China's Road to Greater Financial Stability: Some Policy Perspectives*, ed. Udaibir S. Das, Jonathan Fiechter, and Tao Sun. Washington: International Monetary Fund.

China Finance Society. 1999. *Almanac of China's Finance and Banking*. Beijing.

China Finance Society. 2003. *Almanac of China's Finance and Banking*. Beijing.

Chinese Communist Party News and Documents. 1997. *Notice Concerning Deepening Financial Reform, Rectifying Financial Order and Preventing Financial Risk* (December 1). Available at http://cpc.people.com.cn/GB/64184/64186/66688/4494459.html (accessed on August 25, 2014).

Hanemann, Thilo. 2014. China's International Investment Position: 2014 Update. New York: Rhodium Group (April 1). Available at http://rhg.com/notes/chinas-international-investment-position-2014-update (accessed on August 21, 2014).

He, Dong, Honglin Wang, and Xiangrong Yu. 2014. *Interest Rate Determination in China: Past, Present, and Future*. HKIMR Working Paper 04/2014 (February 20). Hong Kong, China: Hong Kong Institute for Monetary Research. Available at http://ssrn.com/abstract=2398801 (accessed on January 24, 2015).

Hooley, John. 2013. Bringing down the Great Wall? Global Implications of Capital Account Liberalisation in China. *Bank of England Quarterly Bulletin* 53, no. 4: 304–15. Available at http://EconPapers.repec.org/RePEc:boe:qbullt:0118.

Huang, Yiping. 1998. Challenges for China's Financial Reform. *China Update: Conference Papers*. Available at https://digitalcollections.anu.edu.au/bitstream/1885/40417/1/cu98-1.pdf (accessed on July 31, 2014).

IMF (International Monetary Fund). 2014. *2014 Article IV Consultation*. Washington. Available at www.imf.org/external/pubs/ft/scr/2014/cr14235.pdf (accessed on August 1, 2014).

Jeanne, Olivier. 2014. Capital Flow Management and Macroprudential Policies in Asia. In *Asian Capital Market Integration: Challenges and Opportunities*, 91–132. New Delhi: Oxford University Press.

Kaminsky, Graciela L., and Carmen M. Reinhart. 1999. The Twin Crises: The Causes of Banking and Balance-of-Payments Problems. *American Economic Review* 89, no. 3: 473–500.

Lardy, Nicholas R. 1998. *China's Unfinished Economic Revolution*. Washington: Brookings Institution.

Lardy, Nicholas R. 2014. *Markets over Mao: The Rise of Private Business in China*. Washington: Peterson Institute for International Economics.

---

*The Asian Development Bank recognizes "China" by the name the People's Republic of China.

Leigh, Lamin, and Richard Podoiera. 2006. *The Rise of Foreign Investment in China's Banks: Taking Stock.* IMF Working Paper 292. Washington: International Monetary Fund. Available at www.imf.org/external/pubs/ft/wp/2006/wp06292.pdf (accessed on September 11, 2013).

Li, Cindy. 2014. China's Interest Rate Liberalization Reform. *Asia Focus.* San Francisco: Federal Reserve Bank of San Francisco, Country Analysis Unit. Available at www.frbsf.org/banking-supervision/publications/asia-focus/2014/may/china-interest-rate-liberalization-reform/Asia-Focus-China-Interest-Rate-Liberalization.pdf (accessed on July 31, 2014).

Roache, Shaun K., and Samar Maziad. 2013. Structure of the Banking Sector and Implications for Financial Stability. In *China's Road to Greater Financial Stability: Some Policy Perspectives,* ed. Udaibir S. Das, Jonathan Fiechter, and Tao Sun. Washington: International Monetary Fund.

Turner, Grant, Nicholas Tan, and Dena Sadeghian. 2012. *Bulletin: The Chinese Banking System.* Sydney. Reserve Bank of Australia. Available at www.rba.gov.au/publications/bulletin/2012/sep/pdf/bu-0912-7.pdf (accessed on September 9, 2013).

Walter, Carl E., and Fraser J. T. Howie. 2011. *Red Capitalism: The Fragile Foundation of China's Extraordinary Rise.* Singapore: John Wiley & Sons (Asia).

World Bank. 2013. *China 2030: Building a Modern, Harmonious, and Creative Society.* Washington. Available at www.worldbank.org/content/dam/Worldbank/document/China-2030-complete.pdf (accessed on July 31, 2014).

Yi, Gang. 2013. *Exchange Rate Arrangement: Flexible and Fixed Exchange Rate Revisited.* Paper presented at the Rethinking Macro Policy II: First Steps and Early Lessons Conference, sponsored by the International Monetary Fund, Washington, April 16–17. Available at www.imf.org/external/np/seminars/eng/2013/macro2/pdf/gy.pdf (accessed on July 31, 2014).

Zhou, Xiaochuan. 2013. Afterword: China's Road to Greater Financial Stability: Some Policy Perspectives. In *China's Road to Greater Financial Stability: Some Policy Perspectives,* ed. Udaibir S. Das, Jonathan Fiechter, and Tao Sun. Washington: International Monetary Fund.

Zhu, Rongji. 2013. *Zhu Rongji on the Record—The Road to Reform: 1998–2003.* Washington: Brookings Institution Press.

10

Bond Market Development in Developing Asia

JOHN D. BURGER, FRANCIS E. WARNOCK, and
VERONICA CACDAC WARNOCK

A decade ago emerging-market-economy (EME) local-currency markets were small—and some might say irrelevant. Many doubted that local bond markets in EMEs would ever develop. One aspect of this thinking was the "original sin" hypothesis, which, in its strongest form, suggests that EMEs would forever have small, inconsequential bond markets.[1] The proposition is that small countries have an innate condition that precludes the development of a local bond market no matter how hard they try, whatever policies they put in place or institutions they develop.

The past decade saw a strong rejection of this hypothesis. A wide range of EMEs have indeed been able to grow their local-currency bond markets, both in raw size and relative to GDP. This chapter describes the structure of financial systems (banking systems and stock and bond markets) in Asia and, to provide a point of comparison, in other regions. It examines the development of bond markets using two global databases (one from the Bank for International Settlements [BIS] and one from the World Bank) and one database on developing Asia (from the Asian Development Bank [ADB]). The chapter draws on knowledge acquired from past analyses of bond market development to suggest ways smaller developing Asian economies can develop their markets.

John D. Burger is professor of economics in the Sellinger School of Business at Loyola University Maryland. Francis E. Warnock holds the James C. Wheat, Jr. Chair at the University of Virginia's Darden Business School. Veronica Cacdac Warnock is senior lecturer and Batten Institute Fellow at the University of Virginia's Darden Business School. The authors thank the Asian Development Bank for support during this project and Burger acknowledges a research grant from Loyola University Maryland.

1. On the original sin hypothesis, see Eichengreen and Hausmann (1999, 2005), among others. The view has since evolved to a much narrower form: the unlikelihood of any small country currency ever becoming truly international.

Bond markets have positive externalities with respect to economic growth, financial inclusion, and financial stability. They represent an important component of a diversified financial sector. On a macro level, financial development has been linked to economic growth and poverty reduction (Levine 2005, 2008). On financial inclusion, the core factors that enable bond market development are the same factors that enable borrowing and lending within an economy (Burger and Warnock 2006). In a region in which 70 percent of households in one of the largest developing countries (the Philippines) do not have formal bank accounts, anything that improves financial inclusion should be a priority. Finally, and perhaps most directly, the growth in EME bond markets that this chapter documents has likely improved financial stability, as EMEs are now much less reliant on foreign currency–denominated bonds, which can result in currency mismatches and are susceptible to depreciation-related crises. The development of local-currency bond markets and the concomitant reduction in reliance on foreign-currency borrowing is a fundamental—and positive—change in the structure of EME financial systems. EME financial systems are more resilient now that the currency mismatches of the past have been greatly reduced, and this improved financial stability extends to the global economy, as the lack of reliable financial instruments in EMEs drove flows to developed markets and helped spark the global financial crisis, as Ricardo Caballero, Emmanuel Fahri, and Pierre-Olivier Gourinchas (2008) note. The development of local-currency bond markets should thus improve financial stability in individual economies and perhaps increase global financial stability.

Financial Systems in Developing Asia

We first place developing Asia's bond markets in the context of their overall financial systems and compare those systems with systems in other regions, using 2011 data from the World Bank's financial structure database (Beck, Demirgüç-Kunt, and Levine 2000, 2009; Čihák et al. 2012). For developing Asia as a whole, the banking system has deposits equivalent to 60 percent of GDP, stock market capitalization is 71 percent of GDP, total public bonds are worth 26 percent of GDP, and total private bonds are worth 20 percent of GDP (table 10.1). Variation within the region is large, with much lower figures in Central Asia and the Pacific.

Developing Asia's banking systems and stock and bond markets are on average larger than those of other developing regions and high-income countries that are not members of the Organisation for Economic Co-operation and Development (OECD). Compared with OECD members, developing Asia's banking system and especially its bond markets are small.

Central Asia and the Pacific have underdeveloped financial systems (table 10.2). No country in either region has a bond market, and many countries in both regions have no stock markets. Funding in Central Asia and the Pacific comes largely through the banking system.

Table 10.1   Financial structure around the world, 2011 (percent of GDP)

Economy	Size of banking system (measured as amount of deposits)	Stock market capitalization	Public bonds outstanding	Private bonds outstanding
Developing Asia	60.0	71.0	25.7	20.4
Central Asia	23.1	25.0	0.0	0.0
East Asia	60.1	73.4	25.9	27.8
South Asia	57.0	60.3	27.0	4.0
Southeast Asia	67.9	77.7	28.3	11.8
The Pacific	44.5	54.1	0.0	0.0
Rest of the world, developing	43.5	41.5	18.4	8.5
Europe and Central Asia	42.7	23.6	17.5	0.8
Latin America and the Caribbean	41.9	45.5	25.2	13.5
Middle East and North Africa	67.4	12.5	1.9	0.0
Sub-Saharan Africa	38.4	72.1	8.7	5.2
High-income	104.3	81.3	78.7	53.0
OECD members	110.2	84.3	85.3	57.6
Non-OECD members	41.2	46.7	2.8	0.0

OECD = Organisation for Economic Co-operation and Development

Note: Regional averages are weighted by GDP.

Source: Authors' calculations using data from Beck, Demirgüç-Kunt, and Levine (2000, 2009) and Čihák et al. (2012).

Kazakhstan has the largest financial system in Central Asia, with bank deposits worth 28 percent of GDP and a stock market worth 29 percent of GDP. The financial systems of other countries in the subregion are much smaller. No country in Central Asia has a public or private bond market of any size, at least according to World Bank data on bond markets.

Papua New Guinea's stock market is large relative to its GDP (80 percent). No other country in the Pacific has a significant stock market, and the banking systems in the subregion are small, with the exception of Vanuatu's (73 percent of GDP).

The financial sectors in the three other subregions in Asia—East Asia, Southeast Asia, and South Asia—are much more developed. The financial sector of East Asia is well developed. Only Mongolia lags, with a financial structure that is much more like that of a Central Asian economy. East Asia dominates developing Asia, with 64 percent of overall regional economic activity. Within East Asia, the People's Republic of China (PRC) accounts for 83 percent of activity. The PRC has a banking system that has deposits worth 50 percent of GDP, a stock market that is worth 59 percent of GDP, and public and private bond markets that are worth 22 and 23 percent of GDP, respectively. Hong Kong, China has a very large banking system (302 percent of GDP) and stock market (397 percent of GDP). The Republic of Korea has the most developed and balanced financial sector, with a substantial banking system (72 percent of GDP) and stock market (96 percent of GDP). Its sover-

Table 10.2   Financial structure in developing Asia (ADB classification), 2011 (percent of GDP)

Economy	Size of banking system (measured as amount of deposits)	Stock market capitalization	Public bonds outstanding	Private bonds outstanding
Developing Asia	**60.0**	**71.0**	**25.7**	**20.4**
Central Asia	**23.1**	**25.0**	**0.0**	**0.0**
Armenia	18.1	0.3	0.0	0.0
Azerbaijan	11.7	n.a.	0.0	0.0
Georgia	21.9	6.8	0.0	0.0
Kazakhstan	27.5	28.5	0.0	0.0
Kyrgyz Republic	n.a.	2.1	0.0	0.0
Tajikistan	n.a.	n.a.	0.0	0.0
Turkmenistan	n.a.	n.a.	0.0	0.0
Uzbekistan	n.a.	n.a.	0.0	0.0
East Asia	**60.1**	**73.4**	**25.9**	**27.8**
People's Republic of China	49.9	58.8	22.4	23.1
Hong Kong, China	301.6	396.8	36.0	15.3
Republic of Korea	72.1	96.2	44.8	59.3
Mongolia	46.5	15.9	0.0	0.0
South Asia	**57.0**	**60.3**	**27.0**	**4.0**
Afghanistan	15.7	0.0	0.0	0.0
Bangladesh	49.5	17.3	0.0	0.0
Bhutan	60.1	0.0	0.0	0.0
India	62.0	69.7	29.6	4.9
Maldives	79.3	0.0	0.0	0.0
Nepal	58.7	25.3	0.0	0.0
Pakistan	27.5	16.9	30.7	0.0
Sri Lanka	31.6	33.8	0.0	0.0
Southeast Asia	**67.9**	**77.7**	**28.3**	**11.8**
Brunei Darussalam	60.4	0.0	0.0	0.0
Cambodia	32.0	0.0	0.0	0.0
Indonesia	32.0	45.1	10.8	1.4
Lao People's Democratic Republic	n.a.	0.0	0.0	0.0
Malaysia	120.9	144.1	54.0	58.1
Myanmar	n.a.	0.0	0.0	0.0
Philippines	51.3	73.9	29.1	1.0
Singapore	125.8	148.1	45.4	10.0
Thailand	99.7	81.7	49.8	12.7
Viet Nam	12.2	15.4	0.0	0.0
The Pacific	**44.5**	**54.1**	**0.0**	**0.0**
Fiji	51.8	38.4	0.0	0.0
Kiribati	n.a.	0.0	0.0	0.0
Marshall Islands	n.a.	0.0	0.0	0.0
Federated States of Micronesia	n.a.	0.0	0.0	0.0
Palau	n.a.	0.0	0.0	0.0

(continued on next page)

Table 10.2   Financial structure in developing Asia (ADB classification), 2011 (percent of GDP) *(continued)*

Economy	Size of banking system (measured as amount of deposits)	Stock market capitalization	Public bonds outstanding	Private bonds outstanding
Papua New Guinea	43.1	79.7	0.0	0.0
Samoa	44.7	0.0	0.0	0.0
Solomon Islands	30.2	0.0	0.0	0.0
Timor-Leste	29.1	0.0	0.0	0.0
Tonga	38.1	0.0	0.0	0.0
Tuvalu	n.a.	0.0	0.0	0.0
Vanuatu	73.1	0.0	0.0	0.0

n.a. = data not available; ADB = Asian Development Bank

Notes: Regional averages are weighted by GDP. Due to lack of data three developing Asian economies are not included: Cook Islands; Nauru, and Taipei,China.

Source: Authors' calculations using data from Beck, Demirgüç-Kunt, and Levine (2000, 2009) and Čihák et al. (2012).

eign bond market, worth 45 percent of GDP, is the largest in the subregion (and the third-largest in developing Asia, after Malaysia and Thailand), and its corporate bond market, worth 59 percent of GDP, is the largest in all of developing Asia.

In Southeast Asia, Malaysia has the most developed financial system, with a sizable banking sector (121 percent) and stock market (144 percent). Its public bond market (54 percent of GDP) is developing Asia's largest, and its private bond market (58 percent) the second largest, after the Republic of Korea.

India dominates South Asia, with a banking system, stock market, and public bond market that are on a par with the averages in developing East Asia. In contrast, India's corporate bond market is small (5 percent of GDP). Other countries in South Asia are less developed financially. Other than India, Pakistan is the subregion's only country with a bond market.

In sum, in many of the larger economies in the region, banking systems and stock markets are well developed, albeit not at OECD levels, whereas public and private bond markets are underdeveloped. In contrast, the median economy in developing Asia has a banking system whose deposits represent 47 percent of GDP, a stock market whose capitalization is just 4 percent of GDP, and no sovereign or corporate bond market.

Structure of Bond Markets around the World

Because of data limitations, this section includes data on only 46 economies, including just a small subset of developing Asia's larger economies (PRC, India, Indonesia, Malaysia, Pakistan, the Philippines, and Thailand). Although it covers fewer countries, the analysis is useful because it helps place some of Asia's larger EME bond markets in the context of bond markets around the world.

Table 10.3 presents information on the size and composition of global bond markets as of 2011. Table 10.4 presents selected data on individual economies.[2]

The BIS data are compiled from multiple sources and are built from two complementary databases on the value of outstanding local and foreign-currency bonds. Given that the BIS changed its methodology in 2012 (see Gruić and Wooldridge 2012) and more recent data may not be consistent with the historical data, the data in tables 10.3 and 10.4 end in 2011. The following description refers to the pre-2012 BIS methodology.

One BIS dataset is on domestic debt, which the BIS defines as local-currency bonds issued by local firms in the local market. These data appear in table 16A (Domestic Debt Securities) of the BIS Quarterly Review, but that table includes debt securities of all maturities, including very short-maturity "bills" and commercial paper. Because the focus here is on bonds (defined as debt securities with original maturity of at least one year), we obtained the data underlying table 16A to separate short-term bills and commercial paper from long-term debt securities.

The other BIS dataset is on international bonds—bonds issued in either a different currency or a different market. We obtained the underlying security-level data from table 14B (International Bonds and Notes by Country of Residence) of the BIS Quarterly Review (which does not present issuance by currency by country) in order to calculate our own aggregates.

With these two sources (and our calculations), local currency–denominated debt is the sum of the long-term debt component of domestic debt and the local currency/local issuer portion of international bonds. US dollar–denominated debt is the dollar portion of international bonds. Our measures include all bonds issued by all types of issuers (government and private).

Some features of tables 10.3 and 10.4 are worth noting:

- The past decade witnessed extraordinary growth in the size of global bond markets. At the end of 2011, the global bond market was worth $82.5 trillion, almost three times its value in 2001 ($30 trillion).

- Most bonds are denominated in local currency. For the 46 economies in tables 10.3 and 10.4, most bonds—91 percent of advanced-economy bonds and 87 percent of EME bonds—are denominated in local currency.

---

2. Unlike tables 10.1 and 10.2, which come from the World Bank's financial structure database, tables 10.3 and 10.4 are built from Bank for International Settlements (BIS) databases on domestic and international bonds. One would hope that both databases would provide identical information on bond markets, but bond market data are not as readily available as stock market data, and some discrepancies are likely.

Table 10.3   Bond market characteristics, by region, end of 2011

Economy	Total (billions of US dollars)	Local currency denominated				US dollar denominated		
		Billions of US dollars	Percent of GDP	Percent of total	Percent government	Billions of US dollars	Percent of total	Percent government
Advanced economies								
Total	74,371	67,912	164	91	49	31,403	42	37
Euro area	22,106	20,147	157	91	39	1,071	5	7
Other	22,857	19,134	140	84	72	1,702	7	6
United States	29,409	28,630	191	97	40	28,630	97	40
Emerging-market economies								
Total	8,119	7,070	32	87	59	770	9	37
Europe	699	500	24	72	89	68	10	88
Latin America	1,406	1,053	22	75	80	302	21	44
Asia	5,667	5,260	41	93	50	326	6	18
Other	347	255	11	74	75	75	22	49

Note: Local-currency-denominated debt is the sum of the local currency portion of BIS table 14B and the long-term debt component from table 16A. The amount of US dollar denominated debt is calculated from BIS table 14B. Country groupings follow International Monetary Fund classifications of "advanced economies" and "other emerging-market and developing economies" with the exceptions of Hong Kong, China; the Republic of Korea; and Singapore, which are grouped under emerging-market economies (i.e., developing Asia following ADB classification). See table 10.4 for economies included in the aggregates.

Source: Authors' calculations using Bank for International Settlements (BIS), BIS Quarterly Review, tables 14B and 16A, www.bis.org/search/?q=Table+14B and www.bis.org/search/?q=Table+16A; and IMF (2013).

Table 10.4 Bond market development according to Bank for International Settlements data

Economy	Total (billions of US dollars)	Local currency denominated						
		2011			2006		2001	
		Billions of US dollars	Percent of GDP	Percent of total	Percent of GDP	Percent of total	Percent of GDP	Percent of total
Advanced economies (AEs)	**74,371**	**67,912**	**164**	**91**	**134**	**91**	**107**	**93**
Euro area	**22,106**	**20,147**	**157**	**91**	**133**	**91**	**94**	**89**
Austria	672	588	141	88	132	82	90	74
Belgium	765	747	145	98	104	97	118	96
Finland	193	149	57	77	53	85	41	72
France	4,397	4,012	145	91	112	92	82	91
Germany	4,269	3,792	105	89	119	91	96	92
Greece	556	550	190	99	107	97	74	89
Ireland	1,259	1,020	470	81	285	78	46	65
Italy	4,021	3,953	180	98	147	97	114	96
Netherlands	2,817	2,265	271	80	241	81	165	74
Portugal	400	396	167	99	88	98	57	89
Spain	2,756	2,676	181	97	135	97	53	92
Other AEs	**22,857**	**19,134**	**140**	**84**	**104**	**81**	**84**	**87**
Australia	1,216	777	56	64	41	51	30	55
Canada	1,957	1,527	88	78	65	77	69	72
Denmark	840	704	211	84	194	86	160	90
Iceland	41	19	132	45	358	58	78	63
Japan	12,331	12,253	209	99	158	99	108	99
New Zealand	64	46	29	72	17	57	22	64
Norway	430	220	45	51	33	52	27	54
Sweden	745	449	83	60	72	65	57	63
Switzerland	327	312	47	95	55	95	58	97
United Kingdom	4,907	2,827	115	58	65	52	46	62
United States	**29,409**	**28,630**	**191**	**97**	**158**	**96**	**131**	**98**

Emerging-market economies (EMEs)							
8,119	**7,070**	**32**	**87**	**31**	**83**	**26**	**75**
Europe							
699	**500**	**24**	**72**	**30**	**77**	**25**	**76**
Croatia 18	10	15	52	13	49	9	33
Czech Republic 97	74	34	76	29	88	14	85
Hungary 75	39	28	52	46	66	28	60
Poland 223	161	31	72	34	77	20	86
Slovakia 36	22	23	61	23	81	18	68
Turkey 249	195	25	78	27	80	36	78
Latin America 1,406	**1,053**	**22**	**75**	**20**	**70**	**19**	**54**
Argentina 93	38	8	40	30	50	14	29
Brazil 582	456	18	78	15	69	20	59
Chile 105	79	32	75	24	72	42	77
Colombia 107	86	26	80	28	76	19	61
Mexico 477	370	32	78	24	78	17	59
Peru 41	24	14	59	12	54	12	60
Asia 5,667	**5,260**	**41**	**93**	**39**	**90**	**33**	**88**
People's Republic of China 2,956	2,938	40	99	27	98	18	95
Hong Kong, China 116	45	18	39	19	53	15	54
India 515	489	26	95	30	95	25	97
Indonesia 113	84	10	74	15	87	27	96
Republic of Korea 1,265	1,117	100	88	94	91	85	91
Malaysia 260	233	81	90	59	79	57	77
Pakistan 34	32	15	94	15	90	22	96
Philippines 101	63	28	62	26	50	21	48
Singapore 130	90	37	69	40	60	35	69
Thailand 175	170	49	97	37	89	28	80
Other EMEs 347	**255**	**11**	**74**	**11**	**69**	**10**	**50**
Russian Federation 156	91	5	59	3	41	2	13
South Africa 191	164	40	86	39	90	32	87

Note: The amount of US dollar–denominated debt is calculated from BIS table 14B. Country groupings follow International Monetary Fund classifications of "advanced economies" and "other emerging market and developing economies" with the exceptions of Hong Kong, China; the Republic of Korea; and Singapore, which are grouped under EMEs (i.e., developing Asia following ADB classification).

Source: Authors' calculations using Bank for International Settlements (BIS), *BIS Quarterly Review*, tables 14B and 16A, www.bis.org/search/?q=Table+14B and www.bis.org/search/?q=Table+16A; and IMF (2013).

- Bond markets are much larger in advanced economies (164 percent of GDP) than in EMEs (32 percent of GDP), but they grew substantially in both. In advanced economies the size of local bond markets increased from being roughly equal to GDP in 2001 to being equivalent to 1.6 times GDP in 2011. Over the same period, the size of local bond markets in EMEs increased from 26 to 32 percent of GDP.

- The value of local-currency bonds in EMEs nearly doubled as a share of the total global bond market, rising from 5.1 percent in 2001 to 8.6 percent in 2011.

- The share of EME bonds denominated in foreign currency fell from 25 percent in 2001 to 13 percent in 2011—an unambiguously positive development, in our view.

- The share of foreign currency–denominated bonds in developing Asia was only 7 percent in 2011. Economies that still had a high proportion of foreign-currency bonds included the Philippines (38 percent) and Indonesia (26 percent). In contrast, in the PRC, India, Malaysia, Pakistan, and Thailand, local currency–denominated bonds represented more than 90 percent of all bonds.

- The development of local-currency bond markets was particularly striking in Latin America. In 2001 nearly half of Latin American bonds were denominated in a foreign currency; by 2011 local-currency bond markets had grown to the point where only a quarter of bonds in the region were issued in a foreign currency.

The evolution of global bond markets is evident in figure 10.1. As a share of GDP, local-currency bond markets are largest in advanced economies. EME bond markets are, on average, small (panel a). The structure of many EME bond markets improved dramatically over the past decade, however, with many reducing their reliance on foreign currency–denominated bonds (panel c). In sum, recent growth has been accompanied by a move toward an improved structure, but EME bond markets have room to grow.

In advanced economies (panel b of figure 10.1), most bonds are denominated in local currency. In EMEs (panel d), most bonds are sovereign and denominated in local currency, although the value of private local currency–denominated bonds increased sharply between 2007 and 2011.

Factors Affecting the Size of Bond Markets in Emerging-Market Economies

Why do some EMEs have larger local-currency bond markets than others? According to the "original sin" hypothesis, some economies are just naturally larger than others. Nothing other than sheer size distinguishes one economy from another, and the bond markets of smaller economies will forever be inconsequential.

Figure 10.1 Structure of global bond markets

a. Local-currency bonds as percent of GDP, 2000–11

percent of GDP

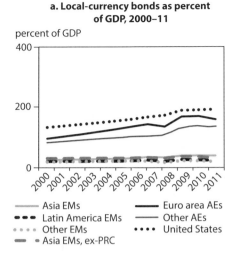

- Asia EMs
- Latin America EMs
- Other EMs
- Asia EMs, ex-PRC
- Euro area AEs
- Other AEs
- United States

b. Bonds in advanced economies: Local currency and US dollar, 2006–11

billions of US dollars

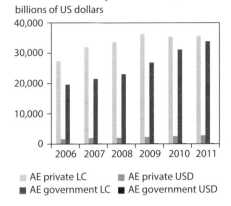

- AE private LC
- AE government LC
- AE private USD
- AE government USD

c. Local-currency bonds as percent of total bonds issued, 2001–11

percent of GDP

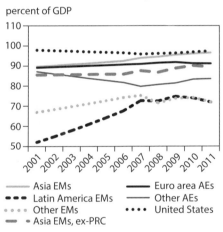

- Asia EMs
- Latin America EMs
- Other EMs
- Asia EMs, ex-PRC
- Euro area AEs
- Other AEs
- United States

d. Emerging-market bonds: Local currency and US dollar, 2006–11

billions of US dollars

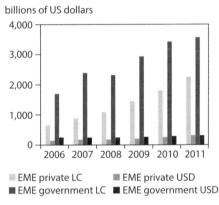

- EME private LC
- EME government LC
- EME private USD
- EME government USD

AE = advanced economy; EM = emerging market; EME = emerging-market economy; LC = local currency; ex-PRC = excluding the People's Republic of China; USD = US dollars

Source: Authors' calculations using Bank for International Settlements (BIS), *BIS Quarterly Review,* tables 14B and 16A, www.bis.org/search/?q=Table+14B and www.bis.org/search/?q=Table+16A; and IMF (2013).

The evidence is not consistent with this hypothesis. Economies can (and have) put in place institutions and policies that foster the development of debt markets (Burger and Warnock 2006). Economies with better inflation performance (an outcome of creditor-friendly policies) have more developed local bond markets, both private and government, and rely less on foreign currency–denominated bonds. Creditor-friendly laws matter. Stronger rule of

Figure 10.2 Two fundamental determinants of local bond market development

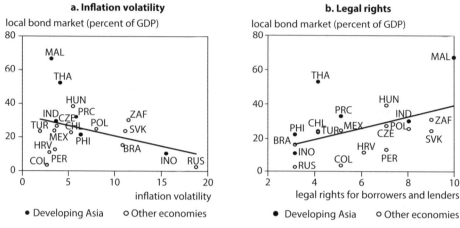

a. Inflation volatility
local bond market (percent of GDP)

b. Legal rights
local bond market (percent of GDP)

• Developing Asia   ○ Other economies   • Developing Asia   ○ Other economies

ARG = Argentina, BRA = Brazil, CHL = Chile, COL = Colombia, CZE = Czech Republic, HRV = Croatia, HUN = Hungary, INO = Indonesia, IND = India, MAL = Malaysia, MEX = Mexico, PAK = Pakistan, PER = Peru, PHI = Philippines, POL = Poland, PRC = People's Republic of China, RUS = Russian Federation, SVK = Slovakia, THA = Thailand, TUR = Turkey, VEN = Venezuela, ZAF = South Africa

Note: Inflation volatility is shown as the volatility of 10 years of quarterly year-over-year inflation.

Source: Authors' calculations using Čihák et al. (2012) and World Bank (2014).

law is associated with deeper local bond markets, and countries with stronger creditor rights are able to issue a larger share of bonds in their local currencies.

Many studies corroborate these results; they include La Porta et al. (1997); Claessens, Klingebiel, and Schmukler (2007); Jeanne and Guscina (2006); Eichengreen and Luengnaruemitchai (2006); and Mehl and Reynaud (2005). Stijn Claessens, Daniela Klingebiel, and Sergio Schmukler (2007) find that government bond markets are larger in large economies with deeper domestic financial systems, lower inflation, larger fiscal deficits, stronger legal origins, and greater capital account openness. Barry Eichengreen and Pipat Luengnaruemitchai (2006) find that larger size, stronger institutions, less volatile exchange rates, and more competitive banking sectors tend to be positively associated with bond market capitalization.

There are at least two caveats for the list of possible determinants of bond market development. In Burger and Warnock (2006) we show the fiscal balance result applies to government bond markets (everything else equal, larger fiscal deficits imply more government borrowing and hence larger government bond markets) but not to private bond markets, and bond markets and banking systems share some fundamental factors.

In Burger, Warnock, and Warnock (2012) we assess the size of local-currency bond markets in 2008. As in previous studies, we find that EMEs with lower inflation volatility and stronger legal rights have more developed local bond markets (figure 10.2). Macroeconomic stability (low inflation volatility) and strong creditor rights enable many positive developments in EMEs, including the development of their bond markets. Over the past decade, some countries with historically high and volatile inflation (such as Brazil and Mexico) made the macroeconomic policy adjustments necessary to bring inflation under control. In general, the local currency bond markets in these countries grew and reliance on foreign-currency debt declined. Other EMEs, including Argentina, Pakistan, and the Russian Federation, had less success bringing inflation under control. They continue to have less developed and less attractive local-currency bond markets.

What Determines the Development of Local-Currency Bond Markets?

It is instructive to examine the regression results from Burger and Warnock (2006) on the factors behind local-currency bond market development. This work analyzes two measures of local bond market development: the ratio of the size of the local bond market to GDP (local bond market development) and the share of the country's outstanding bonds denominated in the local currency (local-currency share). Explanatory variables include the rule of law, creditor rights, fiscal balance, country size, growth rate, and inflation volatility. Creditor rights measure whether the laws of the country are creditor friendly; inflation volatility measures whether policies have been creditor friendly.

The evidence indicates that countries with better inflation performance (the result perhaps of more stable monetary and fiscal policies) have larger local-currency bond markets and rely less on foreign-currency bonds. It also suggests that countries with stronger institutions have broader local-currency bond markets and that economies with stronger creditor rights rely less on foreign-currency bonds. The determinants of the size of government and private bond markets are similar. The main difference is the influence of fiscal policy. A tendency to run fiscal deficits is associated with larger government bond markets (larger deficits require more government borrowing) but not larger private bond markets.

One concern about the baseline results is that virtuous interactions between the development of the bond market and future inflation performance suggest that inflation could plausibly be considered endogenous in bond market development regressions. At one level, inflation is endogenous: when a country has a well-developed bond market that many of its citizens use as a means to save, the government has an implicit promise to keep inflation under control (else savings be reduced in real terms). Concerns about the potential endogeneity of inflation are alleviated to some extent because inflation volatility is already a lagged measure and could be lagged even more without affecting the basic results. More formally, an instrumental variable approach could be used to address the potential endogeneity of inflation.

We instrumented for the mean of inflation (finding instruments for the variance proved difficult) using a measure of central bank independence and the fiscal balance. The fiscal balance would be endogenous to the development of government bond markets—larger deficits directly result in more government bonds outstanding—but should affect private bond market development only to the extent that it affects inflation. Similarly, the degree to which a central bank is independent should not directly affect private bond market development, but it may well do so through its impact on past and prospective inflation. The message is clear: even when instrumenting for inflation, countries with worse inflation performance have smaller local-currency bond markets.

It is also important to consider the relationship between bond market and banking sector development. The conditions necessary for bond market development, such as creditor-friendly policies and laws, are similar to the conditions that foster the development of the banking system. Countries in which people are not willing to become creditors—at one extreme because they are unwilling to deposit money in banks—have undeveloped banking systems and underdeveloped bond markets. Countries with larger bond markets tend to have larger banking systems (but not larger stock markets). There is not a tradeoff between bond market development and banking system development; the factors that foster both are similar.

Going forward, one would expect to see bond market development in countries with macroeconomic stability and strong creditor rights. Figure 10.2 provides some guidance for the future. The fact that Colombia, Croatia, and Peru score far better on both macroeconomic stability and legal rights than the size of their bond markets suggests may mean that their bond markets are poised for growth. In contrast, Brazil's bond market is close to its predicted size, suggesting that macroeconomic stability and creditor rights should improve before the market grows much more. Our estimates suggest that if Brazil were able to strengthen creditor rights to be the level of the Czech Republic (an increase in its legal rights index from 3 to 7), it could double the size of its local-currency bond market. Significant growth in Brazil's market that is not accompanied by improvements in creditor rights and macroeconomic stability should be viewed with caution.

Caveats on Developing Bond Markets

Bond markets are not immune to instability. In the past, one source of instability was currency mismatches. That risk has diminished as a result of reduced reliance on foreign-currency borrowing.

Not all developments in bond markets have been benign, however. Some bond markets, especially in advanced economies, grew too rapidly. For example, Ireland's euro-denominated bond market grew by a factor of 10 in just 7 years, rising from 46 percent of GDP in 2001 to 336 percent in 2008. This increase proved unsustainable; Ireland is still paying for its unbridled bond market growth. The size of Iceland's local-currency bond market soared from 91 percent of GDP in 2001 to 396 percent by 2006. Over this period, 40 percent of its bonds were denominated in foreign currency. As a result of the

2008 depreciation, crisis, and defaults, its bond market shrunk to 104 percent of GDP (although the currency mismatch did not immediately improve). Although EME bond markets fared better in the past decade, countries must remain wary of unsustainable growth and of developing currency mismatches.

Another concern is that alleviating one mismatch (currency) may exacerbate another (maturity). This concern may be unwarranted: In Burger, Warnock, and Warnock (2012) we show that reduced reliance on foreign-currency borrowing was not replaced by greater reliance on short-term borrowing. Average local-currency bond maturities generally increased over the past decade, with impressive lengthening in Latin America.

The work of developing bond markets is never over. High and volatile inflation smothers bond markets (and borrowing and lending in general). Any surge in inflation therefore merits close attention. If an increase is contained and proves short lived, local-currency bond markets will not be adversely affected. If, however, a spike turns into persistently high and volatile inflation, progress could quickly reverse.

Insights into Developing Asia's Bond Markets

Data for the larger Asian economies are available from the ADB's Asian Bonds Online along two dimensions: the size of the local-currency bond market as a percent of GDP and the share of foreign-currency bonds in total bonds. These data indicate that the PRC's local-currency bond market grew from about 5 percent of GDP in 1997 to 50 percent of GDP by the end of 2013 and that its share of foreign-currency bonds has been low, at about 5 percent (figure 10.3). Local-currency bond markets were largest in the Republic of Korea (120 percent of GDP) and Malaysia (110 percent). Most economies did not display currency mismatches, with most foreign-currency shares below 10 percent. One exception was Hong Kong, China. Its 40 percent foreign-currency share would be considered very high were it not for its peg to the US dollar and its significant US dollar export revenues.

As an illustrative example of financial stability issues related to bond market development, consider the Philippines and Viet Nam, two economies in which reliance on foreign-currency bonds declined significantly in recent years. The foreign-currency share of the bond market fell from 45 percent to 30 percent in the Philippines and from 100 percent to just 10 percent in Viet Nam. Reduced foreign-currency borrowing should improve financial stability by reducing vulnerability to exchange rate shocks, but it raises the question of whether the currency mismatch is being replaced by a maturity mismatch.

Figure 10.4 shows the share of sovereign local-currency bonds with maturities greater than 10 years as a proxy for the evolving maturity structure in the Philippines and Viet Nam. It reveals a striking contrast: The Philippines reduced foreign-currency borrowing and expanded the share of long-term bonds, whereas Viet Nam's increased local-currency issuance was coupled with a reduction in the share of long-term bonds. About two-thirds of its local-

Figure 10.3 Emerging Asian bond markets, 1995–2013

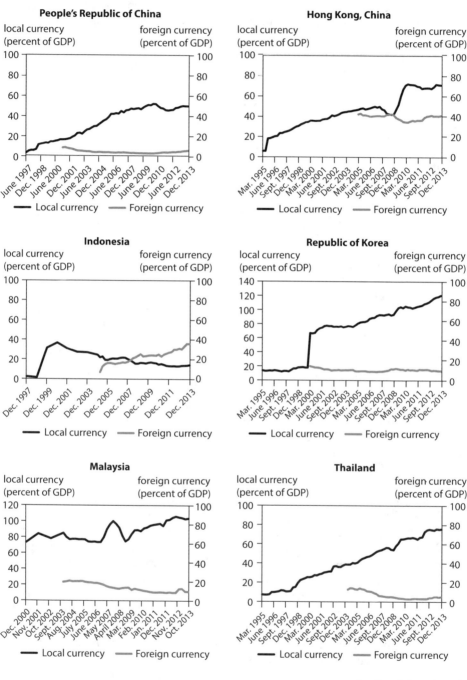

(continued on next page)

Figure 10.3   Emerging Asian bond markets, 1995–2013 *(continued)*

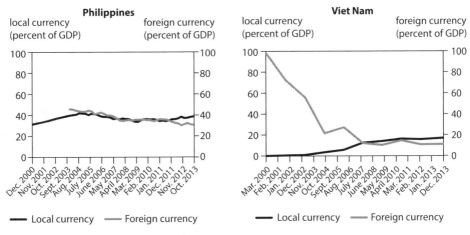

Source: Authors' calculations using Asian Development Bank's *Asian Bonds Online,* http://asianbondsonline.adb.org.

Figure 10.4   Maturity structure of sovereign local currency bonds: Philippines and Viet Nam, 2007–13

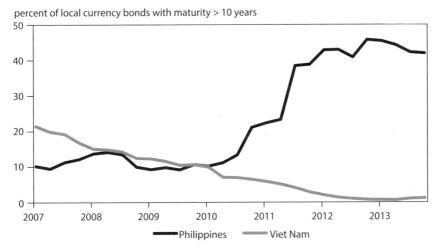

Source: Authors' calculations using Asian Development Bank's *Asian Bonds Online,* http://asianbondsonline. adb.org.

currency bonds have maturities of one to three years, suggesting that Viet Nam may have replaced its currency mismatch with a maturity mismatch, leaving it vulnerable to changes in financing conditions.

The Asian Bonds Online data are useful, but like the BIS data, they are available only for the larger developing Asian economies. The financial structure of the smaller developing economies is quite different: the median bond market size in the 42 economies is zero.

To assess factors that could enable bond market development in the smaller economies, we merge what we have learned from the statistical analyses in our previous papers with World Bank data on bond market size as well as two fundamental factors in bond market development. Alongside data on the size of public and private bonds outstanding, (both expressed as a percentage of GDP) from the World Bank's Financial Structure database, table 10.5 shows data on two fundamental factors of local-currency bond market development: inflation volatility and the legal rights of borrowers and lenders (World Bank 2014). In advanced economies and larger EMEs, stronger legal rights for borrowers and lenders and lower inflation volatility are associated with larger local-currency bond markets (see figure 10.2). Formal analysis of the 42 developing economies in Asia is limited by the fact that the vast majority lack a bond market of any size. Nonetheless, descriptive analysis suggests that inflation volatility plays an important role in explaining the cross-sectional variation in bond market development. For example, historical inflation volatility is on average twice as high in the developing Asian economies that lack bond markets than in the developing Asian economies that have them.

Figure 10.5 presents a scatterplot of a negative and statistically significant relationship between inflation volatility and bond market development. The data suggest a concrete policy prescription: countries with high inflation volatility could spur bond market development by reducing that volatility. Such countries include Afghanistan, Cambodia, the Kyrgyz Republic, Mongolia, and Myanmar.

Our empirical work did not find a statistically significant relationship between bond market development and legal rights in developing Asia. Earlier studies do find an important role for creditor rights, however (Burger and Warnock 2006). Countries that score low on legal rights for borrowers and lenders (perhaps below 6) could strengthen those rights to enable bond market development. Such countries include Azerbaijan, the Maldives, Myanmar, Pakistan, Papua New Guinea, the Philippines, Tajikistan, Thailand, and Uzbekistan.

Conclusion

This chapter provides a descriptive analysis of the structure of financial systems (banking systems and stock and bond markets) in emerging Asia and (for comparison) other regions. It brings together bond market data from the BIS, the World Bank, and the ADB. Most analyses of bond markets use only data on advanced economies and the largest developing economies. This analysis includes data on 42 smaller Asian economies, where the median size of the bond market is zero.

The lessons of our past analyses of bond market development are applicable to developing Asia. They suggest that historically high inflation volatility presents a serious obstacle to bond market development. Smaller developing

Table 10.5   Bond markets in developing Asia and fundamental factors

Economy	Weights	Public bonds outstanding (percent of GDP)	Private bonds outstanding (percent of GDP)	Inflation volatility	Legal rights
Developing Asia	**0.01**	**25.7**	**20.4**	**n.a.**	**n.a.**
Central Asia	**0.06**	0.0	0.0	n.a.	n.a.
Armenia	0.00	0.0	0.0	3.3	5
Azerbaijan	0.07	0.0	0.0	6.4	2
Georgia	0.84	0.0	0.0	4.6	9
Kazakhstan	0.00	0.0	0.0	3.7	3
Kyrgyz Republic	0.03	0.0	0.0	7.8	8
Tajikistan	0.00	0.0	0.0	0.6	1
Turkmenistan	0.00	0.0	0.0	n.a.	n.a.
Uzbekistan	0.00	0.0	0.0	n.a.	1
East Asia	**0.64**	**25.9**	**27.8**	**n.a.**	**n.a.**
People's Republic of China	0.83	22.4	23.1	2.2	4
Hong Kong, China	0.03	36.0	15.3	2.0	7
Republic of Korea	0.14	44.8	59.3	1.0	5
Mongolia	0.00	0.0	0.0	6.6	5
South Asia	**0.18**	**27.0**	**4.0**	**n.a.**	**n.a.**
Afghanistan	0.01	0.0	0.0	10.1	9
Bangladesh	0.05	0.0	0.0	1.9	6
Bhutan	0.00	0.0	0.0	2.5	4
India	0.83	29.6	4.9	3.0	6
Maldives	0.00	0.0	0.0	5.8	2
Nepal	0.01	0.0	0.0	2.8	7
Pakistan	0.08	30.7	0.0	4.6	3
Sri Lanka	0.02	0.0	0.0	5.9	3

(continued on next page)

Table 10.5 Bond markets in developing Asia and fundamental factors (*continued*)

Economy	Weights	Public bonds outstanding (percent of GDP)	Private bonds outstanding (percent of GDP)	Inflation volatility	Legal rights
Southeast Asia	**0.16**	**28.3**	**11.8**	**n.a.**	**n.a.**
Brunei Darussalam	0.01	0.0	0.0	0.7	4
Cambodia	0.01	0.0	0.0	7.3	11
Indonesia	0.39	10.8	1.4	3.7	4
Lao People's Democratic Republic	0.00	0.0	0.0	3.0	7
Malaysia	0.13	54.0	58.1	1.7	7
Myanmar	0.00	0.0	0.0	11.7	2
Philippines	0.11	29.1	1.0	1.9	3
Singapore	0.12	45.4	10.0	2.2	8
Thailand	0.17	49.8	12.7	2.0	3
Viet Nam	0.06	0.0	0.0	6.1	7
The Pacific	**0.00**	**0.0**	**0.0**	**n.a.**	**n.a.**
Fiji Islands	0.20	0.0	0.0	2.5	5
Kiribati	0.00	0.0	0.0	n.a.	4
Marshall Islands	0.00	0.0	0.0	n.a.	10
Federated States of Micronesia	0.00	0.0	0.0	n.a.	11
Palau	0.00	0.0	0.0	n.a.	10
Papua New Guinea	0.60	0.0	0.0	3.2	3
Samoa	0.04	0.0	0.0	5.9	5
Solomon Islands	0.04	0.0	0.0	5.1	10
Timor-Leste	0.05	0.0	0.0	n.a.	0
Tonga	0.02	0.0	0.0	3.8	10
Tuvalu	0.00	0.0	0.0	n.a.	n.a.
Vanuatu	0.04	0.0	0.0	1.5	10

n.a. = not available

Note: Inflation volatility is the standard deviation of quarterly year-over-year inflation computed from 2004 to 2013. The legal rights measure for borrowers and lenders is scored from 0 (poor) to 12 (best).

Source: Authors' calculations using using data from Beck, Demirgüç-Kunt, and Levine (2000, 2009), Čihák et al. (2012), and World Bank (2014).

Figure 10.5   Inflation volatility versus bond market development in Asia (ADB classification)

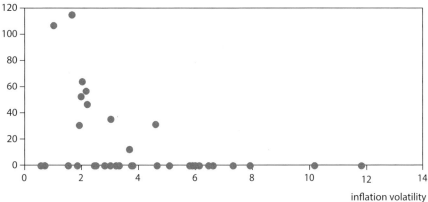

total bonds as percent of GDP

inflation volatility

Note: Inflation volatility is the standard deviation of quarterly year-over-year inflation computed from 2004 to 2013.

Source: Authors' calculations using Čihák et al. (2012) and World Bank (2014).

Asian economies could enable bond market development by pursuing creditor-friendly policies (for example, stabilizing inflation) and strengthening the legal rights of borrowers.

The larger EMEs in Asia have experienced impressive development of their local-currency bond markets, which should contribute to continued growth and financial stability. They have reduced their reliance on foreign-currency borrowing, thereby making their financial systems more resilient. Maturity mismatches have not replaced currency mismatches in most cases; most major Asian EMEs have demonstrated their ability to borrow long term in local currency. Viet Nam provides a notable exception and perhaps a cautionary tale. It recently developed a local-currency bond market and has greatly reduced its reliance on foreign-currency bonds, but the vast majority of its local-currency bonds have maturities of one to three years. Further progress on creditor-friendly policies and institutions will likely be necessary before Viet Nam is able to borrow long term in its own currency.

References

Beck, T., A. Demirgüç-Kunt, and R. Levine. 2000. A New Database on Financial Development and Structure. *World Bank Economic Review* 14: 597–605.

Beck, T., A. Demirgüç-Kunt, and R. Levine. 2009. *Financial Institutions and Markets across Countries and over Time: Data and Analysis.* World Bank Policy Research Working Paper 4943. Washington: World Bank.

Burger, J. D., and F. E. Warnock. 2006. *Local Currency Bond Markets.* IMF Staff Paper 53 (Special Issue): 133–46.

Burger, J. D., F. Warnock, and V. Warnock. 2012. Emerging Local Currency Bond Markets. *Financial Analysts Journal* 68, no. 4: 73–93.

Caballero, R., E. Farhi, and P.-O. Gourinchas. 2008. An Equilibrium Model of Global Imbalances and Low Interest Rates. *American Economic Review* 98, no. 1: 358–93.

Čihák, M., A. Demirgüç-Kunt, E. Feyen, and R. Levine. 2012. *Benchmarking Financial Development around the World*. World Bank Policy Research Working Paper 6175. Washington: World Bank.

Claessens, S., D. Klingebiel, and S. L. Schmukler. 2007. Government Bonds in Domestic and Foreign Currency: The Role of Institutional and Macroeconomic Factors. *Review of International Economics* 15, no. 2: 370–413.

Eichengreen, B., and P. Luengnaruemitchai. 2006. *Why Doesn't Asia Have Bigger Bond Markets?* BIS Paper 30. Basel: Bank for International Settlements.

Eichengreen, B., and R. Hausmann. 1999. Exchange Rates and Financial Fragility. In *New Challenges for Monetary Policy*. Kansas City, MO: Federal Reserve Bank of Kansas City.

Eichengreen, B., and R. Hausmann. 2005. *Other People's Money: Debt Denomination and Financial Instability in Emerging Market Economies*. Chicago: University of Chicago Press.

Gruić, B., and P. Wooldridge. 2012. Enhancements to the BIS Debt Securities Statistics. *BIS Quarterly Review* (December): 63–76.

IMF (International Monetary Fund). 2013. *World Economic Outlook Statistical Appendix* (April). Available at www.imf.org/external/pubs/ft/weo/2013/01/pdf/statappx.pdf.

Jeanne, O., and A. Guscina. 2006. *Government Debt in Emerging Market Countries: A New Data Set*. IMF Working Paper 06/98 (April). Washington: International Monetary Fund.

La Porta, R., F. L.-de-Silanes, A. Shleifer, and R. W. Vishny. 1997. Legal Determinants of External Finance. *Journal of Finance* 52, no. 3: 1131–50.

Levine, R. 2005. Finance and Growth: Theory and Evidence. In *Handbook of Economic Growth*, ed. Philippe Aghion and Steven N. Durlauf. Amsterdam: Elsevier.

Levine, R. 2008. Finance and the Poor. *The Manchester School* 76, no. 1: 1–13.

Mehl, A., and J. Reynaud. 2005. *The Determinants of Domestic Original Sin in Emerging Market Economies*. ECB Working Paper 560 (December). Frankfurt: European Central Bank.

World Bank. 2014. *Doing Business 2015: Going Beyond Efficiency*. Washington.

About the Contributors

Joshua Aizenman joined the faculty at University of Southern California in 2013, where he serves as the Dockson Chair in Economics and International Relations. He is also research associate at the National Bureau of Economic Research and coeditor of the *Journal of International Money and Finance.* Other affiliations have included teaching and research positions at University of California Santa Cruz (served as Presidential Chair of Economics), Dartmouth (served as the Champion Professor of International Economics), Hebrew University of Jerusalem, University of Chicago GSB, and University of Pennsylvania. Consulting relationships include the International Monetary Fund, the World Bank, the Inter-American Development Bank, the Asian Development Bank, and the Federal Reserve Bank of San Francisco.

Nicholas Borst is an analyst in the Country Analysis Unit within the Division of Banking Supervision and Regulation at the Federal Reserve Bank of San Francisco. In that capacity, he conducts research into Asian financial and economic issues and produces analyses of Asian foreign banking organizations. He monitors financial, regulatory, and economic developments in Asia with a focus on Greater China and South Asia. Before joining the Federal Reserve, Borst was a research associate and the China program manager at the Peterson Institute for International Economics. He has also worked as an analyst at the World Bank.

John D. Burger is professor of economics in the Sellinger School of Business at Loyola University Maryland. He has published research in a number of areas including international finance, monetary policy, and sports economics. Burger has served as a consultant to the Asian Development Bank, World Bank, and Inter-American Development Bank. Over the course of his career, Burger has been invited to present his research at the Federal Reserve Board, International Monetary Fund, World Bank, Banco de España, Central Bank of Peru, and the Federal Reserve Bank of San Francisco. Burger received his BS degree from Wake Forest University and PhD from the University of North Carolina at Chapel Hill.

Ajai Chopra is a visiting fellow at the Peterson Institute for International Economics. Before joining the Institute, Chopra worked for three decades at the International Monetary Fund (IMF), where his career focused on country surveillance and IMF lending programs primarily in Europe and Asia. As deputy director of the IMF's European Department, his last position at the IMF, he was part of the department's senior management team. Chopra has authored numerous country reports for IMF Article IV consultations and IMF lending programs and has published papers in the IMF's *Working Paper* and *Occasional Paper* series and also *IMF Staff Papers*.

William R. Cline has been senior fellow at the Peterson Institute for International Economics since its inception in 1981. During 1996–2001 while on leave from the Institute, Dr. Cline was deputy managing director and chief economist of the Institute of International Finance (IIF) in Washington, DC. From 2002 through 2011 he held a joint appointment with the Peterson Institute and the Center for Global Development, where he is currently senior fellow emeritus. His numerous publications include *Managing the Euro Area Debt Crisis* (2014), *Financial Globalization, Economic Growth, and the Crisis of 2007–09* (2010), and *The United States as a Debtor Nation* (2005).

Gemma B. Estrada is senior economics officer in the Macroeconomics Research Division of the Economic Research and Regional Cooperation Department at the Asian Development Bank (ADB). Her recent research has been on financial development, structural change, and fiscal policy. She is also involved with the *Asian Development Outlook*, an annual flagship publication of the ADB.

Morris Goldstein, nonresident senior fellow at the Peterson Institute for International Economics, has held several senior staff positions at the International Monetary Fund (1970–94), including deputy director of its Research Department (1987–94). From 1994 to 2010, he held the Dennis Weatherstone Senior Fellow position at the Peterson Institute. He has written extensively on international economic policy and on international capital markets. His numerous publications include *The Future of China's Exchange Rate Policy* (2009), *Debating China's Exchange Rate Policy* (2008), *Assessing Financial Vulnerability: An Early Warning System for Emerging Markets* (2000), and *The Asian Financial Crisis: Causes, Cures, and Systemic Implications* (1998).

Yothin Jinjarak is associate professor in the School of Economics and Finance at Victoria University of Wellington, New Zealand. His areas of research include international development, trade, finance, and macroeconomics.

Nicholas R. Lardy, an expert on the Chinese economy, is the Anthony M. Solomon Senior Fellow at the Peterson Institute for International Economics. He previously served at the Brookings Institution, the University of Washington, and at Yale University. Lardy's most recent books are *Markets over Mao: The Rise of Private Business in China* (2014) and *Sustaining China's Economic Growth after the Global Financial Crisis* (2012). He is a member of the Council on Foreign Relations and is a member of the editorial boards of *Asia Policy* and the *China Review*.

Minsoo Lee is senior economist in the Macroeconomics Research Division of the Economic Research and Regional Cooperation Department at the Asian Development Bank (ADB). Prior to joining ADB, he was an associate dean and a tenured full professor at Peking University, HSBC Business School in the People's Republic of China. His main research fields are international finance, open macroeconomics, applied econometrics and energy economics.

Marcus Noland, executive vice president and director of studies, has been associated with the Peterson Institute for International Economics since 1985. From 2009 through 2012, he served as the Institute's deputy director. He is also senior fellow at the East-West Center. He was previously a senior economist at the Council of Economic Advisers in the Executive Office of the President of the United States. His numerous publications include *Confronting the Curse: The Economics and Geopolitics of Natural Resource Governance* (2014), *Korea after Kim Jong-il* (2004), and *Avoiding the Apocalypse: The Future of the Two Koreas* (2000), for which he won the 2000–01 Ohira Memorial Award.

Donghyun Park is principal economist at the Economic Research and Regional Cooperation Department (ERCD) of the Asian Development Bank (ADB), which he joined in April 2007. Prior to joining ADB, he was a tenured associate professor of economics at Nanyang Technological University in Singapore. His main research fields are international finance, international trade, and development economics. His research, which has been published extensively in journals and books, revolves around policy-oriented topics relevant for Asia's long-term development, including the middle-income trap, Asia's service sector development, and Asia's financial development. Park plays a leading role in the production of *Asian Development Outlook,* ADB's flagship annual economic publication.

Adam S. Posen is president of the Peterson Institute for International Economics. His has received numerous major research grants and fellowships for his research on macroeconomic policy, resolution of financial crises, the economies of Europe, Japan, and the United States, and central banking issues. He is editor or coeditor of four books, including *Responding to Financial Crisis: Lessons from Asia Then, the United States and Europe Now* (2013), author of *Restoring Japan's Economic Growth* (1998), and coauthor of *Inflation Targeting* (1999). From September 2009, by appointment of the UK Chancellor of the Exchequer, he served for three years as an external member of the Bank of England's rate-setting Monetary Policy Committee during the Global Financial Crisis. Posen was made an Honorary Commander of the Most Excellent Order of the British Empire (CBE) by Her Majesty Queen Elizabeth II for his service to the United Kingdom during this period. He has been an economic advisor to the US Congressional Budget Office since 2007, and a consultant to several departments of the US government and of the International Monetary Fund, as well as a visiting scholar at central banks throughout East Asia, Europe, and North America.

Arief Ramayandi is senior economist at the Economic Research and Regional Cooperation Department of the Asian Development Bank (ADB). Prior to joining ADB, he was the director for the Center of Economics and Development Studies at Padjadjaran University in Bandung, Indonesia. He holds a PhD in economics from the Australian National University.

Nicolas Véron, visiting fellow at the Peterson Institute for International Economics since October 2009, is also a senior fellow at Bruegel, a Brussels-based economic policy think tank he helped cofound in 2002–04. He has held various positions in the public and private sectors, including as corporate adviser to France's labor minister (1997–2000), as chief financial officer of Multi-Mania/Lycos France (2000–2002), and as an independent financial services consultant. Since 2008 he has been a member of the CFA Institute's Corporate Disclosure Policy Council, and since July 2013 a board member of the derivatives arm of the Depository Trust and Clearing Corporation. He is coeditor of *Transatlantic Economic Challenges in an Era of Growing Multipolarity* (2012) and coauthor of *Smoke and Mirrors, Inc.: Accounting for Capitalism* (2006).

Francis E. Warnock holds the James C. Wheat, Jr. Chair at the University of Virginia's Darden Business School. He is also research associate at the National Bureau of Economic Research (NBER); senior fellow at the Federal Reserve Bank of Dallas' Globalization and Monetary Policy Institute; and research associate at the Institute for International Integration Studies (IIIS) at Trinity College Dublin. Prior to joining Darden, Warnock was senior economist at the Federal Reserve Board. His research areas include international capital flows, international portfolio allocation, and financial sector development (with particular focus on local bond markets and housing finance systems around the world). He has also worked closely with housing microlenders in South Africa and mobile banking initiatives in Bangladesh. Warnock received his bachelor's degree from Johns Hopkins University and his doctorate from the University of North Carolina at Chapel Hill.

Veronica Cacdac Warnock is senior lecturer and Batten Institute Fellow at the University of Virginia's Darden Business School. Her research focuses on bond market development, housing finance, and inclusive finance. She has served as economic consultant for international organizations such as the World Bank, Bank for International Settlements, Asian Development Bank, Inter-American Development Bank, National Association of Realtors, and other nonprofit organizations. She has held visiting positions at the Asian Institute of Management, Hong Kong Institute for Monetary Research, and IIIS at Trinity College Dublin. Previously, she was director/senior economist at the Mortgage Bankers Association (of America) and research associate at Haver Analytics. Warnock received her PhD in economics from Fordham University and her AB in economics from Ateneo de Manila University.

Michael J. Zamorski is an adviser on financial stability and supervision to the South East Asian Central Banks (SEACEN) Research and Training Centre. He has 33 years of experience in financial institution supervision and was a bank chief risk officer. As director of bank supervision for the US Federal Deposit Insurance Corporation, he oversaw prudential supervision for 5,200 US banks. He was a member of the Basel Committee from 2000 to 2006.

Index

access to financial services
    by income distribution, 18, 19*f*
    innovation funding, 219–22
    regional differences, 140, 142*t*–146*t*,
        147*f*–149*f*
    small and medium enterprises, 18, 140,
        149*f,* 173, 203–205, 208, 222,
        325
    technology-enabled, 237–38, 248
accounting standards, 91, 240, 312
Additional Criteria (BCBS), 255
aging population, 15
AIG, 79*n*
Alipay payment platform, 238
Annual Report on Exchange Rate Arrangements
        and Exchange Restrictions (IMF), 29,
        34, 98, 102
Arellano-Bond generalized method of
        moments, 35, 36
Argentina
    bank assets in, 87*n*
    financial crisis in (2001–02), 78
Article IV reports (IMF), 104, 111–16, 291
ASEAN+3 Bond Market Initiative, 200*n*
Asia. *See also specific country*
    financial sector in (*See* financial sector
        development)
    list of countries in, 9*n*, 59
Asia Bond Monitor (ADB), 198, 200*n*

Asian Bond Fund, 200*n*
Asian Development Bank (ADB)
    Asia Bond Monitor, 198, 200*n*
    growth accounting framework, 179
    Innovative Asia: Advancing the Knowledge-
        Based Economy, 205
    members of, 9*n*
Asian financial crisis (1997–98)
    bank losses during, 300
    causes of, 78, 230, 238
    contagion, 293
    financial sector development since, 10,
        10*f*–13*f*
    impact of, 3, 20–21
    lessons learned, 109
    versus other financial crises, 245
Association of Southeast Asian Nations
        (ASEAN), 200*n,* 244, 251

bail-ins, 236
bailouts, 236–37
Baltic states, 243
Bangladesh, 106, 117–18
banks, 86–92
    assets (*See* bank assets)
    banking conglomerates, 263–66
    banking policy, 231–38
    bond market development and, 360
    capital (*See* bank capital)

banks—*continued*
    credit from (*See* credit)
    crisis management frameworks, 236–37,
        265–68
    depositors with, 140, 148*f*, 172
    effect of financial openness on, 97, 104
    financial stability and, 231–38
    foreign-owned, 88*t*–89*t*, 91–92, 97–99, 243
    indicators for, 87, 88*t*–89*t*
    lending (*See* loans)
    long-term finance flows and, 198–201
    national champion, 247
    offshoring by, 243
    regulation of (*See* bank supervision)
    sectoral reforms, 211–12
    separation of commerce from, 233–35
    shadow (*See* shadow banking)
    state-owned (*See* state-owned banks)
    stress testing (*See* bank stress tests)
bank assets
    concentration of, 87–92, 88*t*–89*t*
    as productivity growth indicator, 188,
        191*f*–192*f*, 196
    ratio of capital to, 88*t*–89*t*, 90–91
bank capital
    levels of
        Basel III rules (*See* Basel III accord)
        benefit-cost evaluations of, 302
        social costs of, 302–303
    measures of, 274*n*, 274–75, 300, 311
        criticisms of, 289–307
    ratio of assets to, 88*t*–89*t*, 90–91
    regulation of, 105, 108, 235–36, 260
    since Asian crisis, 10, 11*f*
    stress testing and, 273, 286–87
Bank for International Settlements (BIS)
    Basel Committee on Banking
        Supervision (*See* Basel
        Committee on Banking
        Supervision)
    bond market dataset, 352, 353*t*–355*t*
    Irving Fisher committee, 242
    role of, 254
    systemic risk report, 253
Banking Integration Framework (ASEAN),
        244, 251
Bank of Communications (BoCom), 332
Bank Recovery and Resolution Directive
        (BRRD), 237
bankruptcy
    recovery rate, 211, 212*f*
    regulation of, 211, 239–40
    resolving insolvency index, 140, 149*f*, 172

bank stress tests
    overview, 270–72
    credibility of, 272, 308–309
    for crisis prevention, 272–73, 290,
        309–10
    criticisms of, 289–307
    design of, 310–12
    in European Union, 276–89, 284*t*–285*t*
    lessons learned, 307–12
    as supervisory tool, 236, 272, 307–308
    in United States, 273–76, 281–89,
        282*t*–283*t*
bank supervision
    overview, 251, 268–69
    Basel Committee on Banking
        Supervision (*See* Basel
        Committee on Banking
        Supervision)
    conglomerates, 263–66
    crisis management, 236–37, 265–68
    Financial Sector Assessment Program,
        104, 111–16, 262–63,
        266, 291
    global crisis and, 252–53, 256–62
    legal protection for, 105, 108
    macroeconomic policy and, 259–61, 301
    material loss reviews, 261–62
    off-site surveillance, 259
    on-site surveillance, 258
    quality of, 236, 309
    self-assessment, 256
    shadow banking, 21, 108
    stress tests in, 236, 272, 307–308
    thematic reviews, 258–59
Basel Committee on Banking Supervision
        (BCBS)
    Asian representation in, 230
    bank capital measures, 274*n*
    on bank crisis management, 265
    Core Principles, 254–56, 265
    global crisis analysis, 257–58
    macroprudential perspective, 259
    Regulatory Consistency Assessment
        Program, 235
    regulatory reform agenda, 253
Basel Core Principles (BCP), 254–56, 265
Basel III accord
    overview, 235–36
    criticisms of, 235
    implementation of, 304–307, 305*t*–306*t*
    infrastructure finance, 202*n*
    as minimum goals, 105, 108, 273
    phase-in arrangements, 287, 298, 299*t*

Ponzi finance, 79
population aging, 15
portfolio equity opening, 97, 336–37
poverty, 2–3, 17–18, 22
principal-agent problems, 208, 213
private credit. *See* credit
productivity growth
    overview, 177–79, 221–22
    external finance and, 97
    importance of, 2, 16–17
    literature review, 181–86
    long-term growth and, 179–81
    policy priorities, 178, 184, 186–205
        bank assets, 188, 191*f*–192*f*, 196
        debt financing, 188, 196*f*, 197
        debt securities, 188, 193*f*, 197
        financial access for SMEs, 203–205
        long-term finance flows, 197–203,
            199*f*
        private credit, 188, 189*f*–190*f*, 196
        stock market capitalization, 188,
            194*f*–195*f*, 197
prompt corrective action (PCA) statutes, 256*n*
property rights, 138
public-private investment funds, 215,
    331–32

Qualified Domestic Institutional Investors
    (QDII) program (People's
    Republic of China), 330, 337
Qualified Foreign Institutional Investors
    (QFII) program (People's Republic
    of China), 330, 337
quantitative easing (QE), 3, 18, 100, 252
quantitative measures of development, 136,
    165
Quinn index, 97, 100

real estate, 79, 105, 241–42
Regional Economic Outlook (IMF), 304
Regulatory Consistency Assessment
    Program (RCAP), 235
regulatory supervision
    banking sector (*See* bank supervision)
    bankruptcy, 211, 239–40
    effect on financial stability, 21–22, 79,
        186, 221, 229–31, 247
    long-term finance flows and, 201
    supranational, 244
Renminbi Qualified Foreign Institutional
    Investors (RQFII) program
    (People's Republic of China), 330,
    337

Republic of Korea
    banking sector, 98–99, 110
    bond market in, 361, 362*f*
    capital flow management in, 101
    financial openness in, 104
    FSAP report, 114
    IMF Article IV report, 114
research and development (R&D), 17, 22,
    213–15. *See also* innovation
resolving insolvency index, 140, 149*f*, 172
resource allocation, 25–26, 51, 136, 177, 184,
    201, 327, 334
risk, systemic, 252–53, 259–61, 267–68
risk premium on lending, 160, 173
risk-sharing schemes, 214–15
risk-weighted assets (RWAs), 91, 274*n*,
    294–96, 304–307
rural labor, 76
Rymer, Jon T., 261–62

saving programs, 201
saving rate, 14
sectoral analysis, 135–76
    overview, 135–37, 165–69
    alternative specifications, 161–65,
        163*t*–164*t*, 166*t*–168*t*
    control variables, 157, 158*f*–159*f*
    data, 139–40, 141*f*, 142*t*–146*t*, 147*f*–149*f*,
        150*t*
    data variables, 171–73
    empirical framework and results,
        146–51, 152*t*–156*t*
    financial service sector flows, 161–65,
        163*t*–164*t*
    literature review, 137–39
    macroeconomic policy, 160, 162*t*
    policy implications, 157–65
    sample countries and regions, 174–75
sectoral output growth per worker, 140,
    141*f*, 171
securities
    debt
        as productivity growth indicator,
            188, 193*f*, 197
        role of, 92–97, 93*t*–94*t*
        for SMEs, 239
        mortgage-backed, 11, 26–27, 79
services, quality of, 135
shadow banking
    in the People's Republic of China,
        238–39, 318
    defined, 258*n*
    equity standards and, 303

Publications from the Peterson Institute for International Economics

Books, Policy Analyses, and Special Reports
http://bookstore.piie.com

Policy Briefs
http://www.piie.com/publications/pubs_year.cfm?ResearchTypeID=2

Working Papers
http://www.piie.com/publications/pubs_year.cfm?ResearchTypeID=1&ResearchYear=2015

PIIE Briefings
http://www.piie.com/publications/briefings/briefings.cfm

International Sales
United Kingdom, Europe (including Russian Federation and Turkey), Africa, and Israel

The Eurospan Group
c/o Turpin Distribution
Pegasus Drive
Stratton Business Park
Biggleswade, Bedfordshire
SG18 8TQ
United Kingdom

Tel: 44 (0) 1767-604972
Fax: 44 (0) 1767-601640

Email: eurospan@turpin-distribution.com
www.eurospangroup.com/bookstore